Positioning	Blocking?	Noncollective operations
Local pointer	blocking	MPI_File_read
		MPI_File_write
	nonblocking	MPI_File_iread
		MPI_File_iwrite
Explicit offset	blocking	MPI_File_read_at
		MPI_File_write_at
	nonblocking	MPI_File_iread_at
		MPI_File_iwrite_at
Shared pointer	blocking	MPI_File_read_shared
		MPI_File_write_shared
	nonblocking	MPI_File_iread_shared
		MPI_File_iwrite_shared

MPI-IO noncollective data access functions. (Adapted from the MPI-2 standard [63], Chapter 9.)

Positioning	Blocking?	Collective operations
Local pointer	blocking	MPI_File_read_all
		MPI_File_write_all
	split	MPI_File_read_all_begin
		MPI_File_read_all_end
		MPI_File_write_all_begin
		MPI_File_write_all_end
Explicit offset	blocking	MPI_File_read_at_all
		MPI_File_write_at_all
	split	MPI_File_read_at_all_begin
		MPI_File_read_at_all_end
		MPI_File_write_at_all_begin
		MPI_File_write_at_all_end
Shared pointer	blocking	MPI_File_read_ordered
		MPI_File_write_ordered
	split	MPI_File_read_ordered_begin
		MPI_File_read_ordered_end
		MPI_File_write_ordered_begin
		MPI_File_write_ordered_end

MPI-IO collective data access functions. (Adapted from the MPI-2 standard [63], Chapter 9.)

Parallel I/O for High Performance Computing

About the Author

John May is the group leader for computer science in the Center for Applied Scientific Computing (CASC) at the Lawrence Livermore National Laboratory. His interests include parallel programming models, performance analysis, parallel I/O, and parallel programming tools. He has served on the MPI-2 Forum, the High Performance Debugger Forum, and the Steering Committee of the Parallel Tools Consortium. Currently, he works on the Parallel Performance Improvement Project, where he is investigating performance analysis techniques for massively parallel computers.

Dr. May joined LLNL in 1994 after receiving his Ph.D. in computer science from the University of California, San Diego. He also holds a B.A. in physics from Dartmouth College. Prior to entering graduate school, he worked at AT&T (now Lucent) Bell Laboratories on optoelectronic device technology.

Parallel I/O for High Performance Computing

John M. May

Lawrence Livermore National Laboratory

MORGAN KAUFMANN PUBLISHERS

AN IMPRINT OF ACADEMIC PRESS

A Harcourt Science and Technology Company

SAN FRANCISCO SAN DIEGO NEW YORK BOSTON

LONDON SYDNEY TOKYO

Senior Editor	Denise E. M. Penrose
Senior Production Editor	Edward Wade
Editorial Coordinator	Emilia Thiuri
Cover Design	Ross Carron Design
Cover Image	© Stone/Kathleen Campbell
Text Design	Rebecca Evans & Associates
Technical Illustration	Dartmouth Publishing, Inc.
Composition	TechBooks
Copyeditor	Ken DellaPenta
Proofreader	Jennifer McClain
Indexer	Ty Koontz
Printer	Courier Corporation

ACADEMIC PRESS
A Harcourt Science and Technology Company
525 B Street, Suite 1900, San Diego, CA 92101-4495, USA
http://www.academicpress.com

Academic Press
Harcourt Place, 32 Jamestown Road, London, NW1 7BY, United Kingdom
http://www.academicpress.com

Morgan Kaufmann Publishers
340 Pine Street, Sixth Floor, San Francisco, CA 94104-3205, USA
http://www.mkp.com

Printed in the United States of America

05 04 03 02 01 5 4 3 2 1

Library of Congress Cataloging-in-Publication Data

May, John M.
Parallel I/O for high performance computing / John M. May.
p. cm.
Includes bibliographical references and index.
ISBN 1-55860-664-5
1. High performance computing. 2. Parallel processing (Electronic computers)
3. Computer input-output equipment. I. Title.

QA76.88.M39 2001
004′.3—dc21 00-043508

This book is printed on acid-free paper.

For Mom and Dad

Foreword

Dan Reed
University of Illinois, Urbana-Champaign

I/O has long been the "poor stepchild" of scientific computing, especially high-performance computing. Indeed, the very fact that we call it computing, rather than data management or manipulation reflects that bias and vocabulary. We speak of central processing units and primary memory, but of peripherals, secondary and even tertiary storage. In scientific computing, we focus on FLOPS (floating point operations/second) and eagerly rate computers in gigaflops, teraflops, and someday soon, petaflops, but all too rarely do we discuss petabytes stored or terabytes/second transferred.

This compute-centric view belies the fact that scientific computing is increasingly about intelligent data management. Faster and more powerful computer systems, along with the emergence of computational science as a true third member of the theory, experiment, and computational simulation triumvirate, mean that extracting meaning from data, both experimental and computer-generated, is central to scientific discovery.

Terascale simulations can produce prodigious amounts of data, and gaining insights from that data via visualization or intelligent data reduction requires I/O hardware and software that can move data rapidly across networks and to and from arrays of storage devices. Equally importantly, and oft overlooked, a new generation of high-resolution scientific instruments is coming online, and these instruments, ranging from large radio telescopes to advanced particle detectors, also produce large volumes of data in real time.

Given the opportunities and challenges posed by new, high-performance computer systems, this book appears at a most propitious time. John May has long been an active and respected researcher in parallel I/O; his technical expertise, and equally importantly, his practical experience with real systems are evident in this book.

Combining just the right mixture of research results and insights from experimental validation, this book begins with an analysis of the physical device characteristics that constrain design of sequential and parallel file systems. With this base, John analyzes the design of research and commercial file systems and their behavior under realistic loads. In turn, this leads to a discussion of scientific libraries and recognition that large-scale scientific data management must move beyond files to encompass data and metadata via data mining.

There is no doubt that this book will become one of the "instant classics"—referenced and read by everyone concerned about high-performance I/O in a data centric world.

Contents

Preface

Parallel programs cannot afford to treat I/O as an afterthought. The speed, memory size, and disk capacity of parallel computers continue to grow rapidly, but the rate at which disk drives can read and write data is improving much more slowly. As a result, the performance of carefully tuned parallel programs can slow dramatically when they read or write files, and the problem is likely to get worse.

Parallel input and output techniques can help solve this problem by creating multiple data paths between memory and disks. However, simply adding disk drives to an I/O system without considering the overall software design will improve performance only minimally. To reap the full benefits of a parallel I/O system (and therefore the full benefits of a parallel computer), application programmers must understand how parallel I/O systems work and where the performance pitfalls lie.

This book is an introduction to parallel I/O hardware and software. It is aimed at application developers, researchers, and students who are familiar with high performance computing but who don't necessarily know the details of storage devices or file systems. Although I expect that readers will be experienced programmers, I don't assume much formal training in computer science.

I consider this book a tour of the field and not a reference manual because it doesn't give equal attention to equally important topics. In presenting this material, I have tried to choose the most significant and interesting landmarks and to organize them in a logical sequence. Like any tour guide, I have my own favorite sites, to which I have given perhaps more attention than they deserve.

The book describes parallel I/O from the bottom up: beginning with the design of storage devices and interconnection networks, it proceeds through file systems, I/O access patterns, and optimization techniques. It then examines a variety of low-level and high-level I/O programming interfaces. The book concludes with a discussion of data management techniques for very large data sets. Of course, most readers will have more experience in some areas than in others. Some readers may be unfamiliar with certain topics and not interested in learning about them. However, I encourage all readers to skim at least the early chapters, since they define many terms and present many ideas that later chapters build upon. In particular, Chapter 2 defines the terminology of storage devices and networks, and it introduces striping and RAID (redundant arrays of independent disks). Chapter 3 describes some important file system concepts such as sequential consistency, concurrency control, and asynchronous I/O. These ideas are important throughout the rest of the book.

One challenge in writing a technical book in a rapidly changing field is to keep it from becoming obsolete even before it is published. I have tried to address this problem by organizing the discussion of most topics in two parts: first a description of the important problems and ideas in the area, and then a discussion of specific research or development projects that address these problems. Research projects and company products come and go, but omitting any mention of them would make the book too abstract. By describing the main ideas separately from the projects that produced or incorporated them, I hope to keep this book from seeming outdated even after many of the projects have ended.

Readers interested in learning more about I/O topics should consult the Further Reading sections at the end of each chapter. Also, many of the bibliographic entries are annotated to help readers decide which references will be most useful to them.

Acknowledgments

It is a pleasure to thank the many friends and colleagues who have helped bring this book to life.

The project began as a two-week class I taught in 1998 at a summer school on parallel computing. It was organized by CEA (the French Atomic Energy Commission), EDF (Electricité de France), and INRIA (the French National Institute for Research in Computer Science and Control). My host, François Robin, and students at the summer school and at later presentations of the course made many useful and thought-provoking comments that have helped improve the presentation of this material.

When I was offered the opportunity to turn the course into a book, Michel McCoy and Steven Ashby, my managers at Lawrence Livermore National Laboratory (LLNL), encouraged me immediately, and they have continued to support the project steadfastly. Meanwhile, John Wooldridge of the LLNL Intellectual Property Law Group helped craft an agreement that my employer, my publisher, and I could all live with.

Many people have helped me with the technical content of the book by reviewing chapters, discussing technical questions with me, or directing me to useful references. In alphabetical order, they are K.C. Claffy, Terence Critchlow, David

Culler, Mike Declerck, Bronis de Supinski, Don Dossa, Barbara Duffy, Allyson Klein, Celeste Matarazzo, Ethan Miller, Kim Minuzzo, Ron Musick, Nils Nieuwejaar, James Porter, Jean-Pierre Prost, Apratim Purakayastha, Evgenia Smirni, Rajeev Thakur, Deborah Walker, Patrick Weidhaas, Dave Wiltzius, Kim Yates, and Mary Zosel. I thank them all for making this book better and sounder than it would have been without their help.

Dr. Alice Koniges of the Lawrence Livermore National Laboratory, Professor Peter Pacheco of the University of San Francisco, and Alan Sussman of the University of Maryland reviewed the entire book and made numerous helpful suggestions.

Denise Penrose, senior editor at Morgan Kaufmann, approached me with the idea of writing this book and guided me through the process of getting it published. I have greatly enjoyed working with her and the capable Morgan Kaufmann staff.

Finally, to Debbie, thanks for your patience, understanding, and love.

Notices

This work was performed under the auspices of the U.S. Department of Energy by University of California Lawrence Livermore National Laboratory under contract number W-7405-Eng-48, UCRL-JC-138216.

This book contains programming examples and descriptions of algorithms that illustrate a variety of I/O techniques. If implemented or used incorrectly, these examples and algorithms could cause a program to terminate unexpectedly, operate incorrectly, or corrupt stored data. Readers must evaluate the suitability of any techniques described here before incorporating them into their programs. Neither the author nor the University of California warrants that the programming examples and algorithms presented here are correct or that they are suitable for any particular application.

Chapter One Introduction

The first commercial disk drive, the IBM RAMAC 350, was introduced in 1956. It stored 5 million seven-bit characters on fifty 24-inch disks [138]. Then, as now, the ability to store data externally to the computer's main memory was essential for large applications. Although magnetic storage had existed for several years in the form of tapes, drums, and core memory, disks offered an unprecedented combination of capacity and speed. The popularity of disk drives continues today for essentially the same reason. Other devices can store more data or access it faster, but no current system does both at a comparable price.

However, this combination of capacity, speed, and price makes disk drives inherently a compromise. In many applications, and especially in high performance computing, users often wish for higher capacity or (more likely) better performance. The solution to both problems is usually to add more disks to the I/O system, increasing both capacity and parallelism.

How can programs use these disks effectively? That question is the focus of this book. It will be helpful along the way to look at several related questions:

- How do disk drives and other storage devices work?
- How does data move between these devices and main memory?
- How do file systems manage files?
- What are the input and output (I/O) patterns of large scientific applications?
- How can I/O requests be made to execute more efficiently?
- What programming interfaces are available to read and write data, and how should they be used?
- How can users manage and analyze large data sets?

It's useful at the outset to define some terms, including those in the title of this book, *Parallel I/O for High Performance Computing*. The term *parallel I/O* as used here means reading and writing data on multiple storage devices (disks, tape drives, etc.) from parallel programs. Other forms of I/O, such as moving data between processing nodes or between separate computers over a network, are discussed only peripherally. A *parallel program* is a program in which multiple tasks (threads or processes) work concurrently on a single problem. Parallel programs usually run on parallel computers—systems with more than one central processing unit (CPU)—but they can also run on sequential (single-CPU) computers for development and testing. Finally, *high performance computing* is running an application that requires the capabilities of a high performance computer to complete in a reasonable length of time. The definition of a *high performance computer* must remain vague because specific performance levels change so rapidly and because there is no clear distinction between high performance computers and "ordinary" ones. Perhaps the most definitive statement possible is that nearly all high performance computers today use some form of parallel processing. Many kinds of applications run on high performance computers, but this book focuses on scientific applications, such as simulating physical phenomena and analyzing scientific data.

1.1 High Performance I/O Requirements

High performance applications have unique needs that "commodity" hardware and software developed for larger markets do not always meet. These needs vary widely between different kinds of applications, so before developing sophisticated I/O techniques, you must first understand the demands of the application.

1.1.1 Scientific Applications vs. Other I/O-Intensive Codes

Three categories of applications that demand good I/O performance are database management systems (DBMSs), multimedia applications, and scientific simulations.

DBMSs manage collections of data records, usually stored on disk. The collections can be quite large, containing millions of records or more, and the DBMS must often search for individual records that meet certain criteria. Depending on the task at hand, the DBMS may examine every record in the database, or it may look at a subset of records scattered across the database. Reading or writing data in small pieces (roughly, less than 1000 bytes) is called *fine-grained* access, and it is less efficient than accessing data in larger pieces (Chapter 2 explains why).

Multimedia applications process sound, still images, and video data. Unlike a DBMS, a multimedia application can often access large blocks of data in a predictable sequence. For example, if the application is presenting a video, it can determine well in advance what data to read, so it can schedule disk accesses in an efficient sequence. The user may search forward and backward through the video or take different branches through an interactive story, but even then the program can usually access data in large blocks. However, unlike many other applications, multimedia programs often require the I/O system to read the data at no less than a specified minimum rate; this rate must be sustained to make the sound and pictures move smoothly.

In scientific applications, the granularity may be coarse or fine, and the access patterns may be predictable or random. Many scientific applications read and write data in well-defined phases: the program will read some data, compute for a while, then write some data. Usually, a program will continue computing in many steps, writing data each time the program has completed a specified number of steps. In a parallel application, the individual tasks within a job will often write their data at the same time. Parallel I/O libraries can take advantage of this synchrony to improve performance, as described in Chapter 4.

An important difference between scientific applications and database or multimedia applications is that the latter two are often designed specifically to do I/O. The application designers recognize that accessing data in external storage is essential to the program's performance. In scientific applications, on the other hand, the central task is usually a numerically intensive computation involving data that is already in memory. Moving the data between memory and external storage is a secondary problem. Therefore, designers of scientific codes may be less interested in I/O issues than in issues of numerical accuracy and computational efficiency. Also, many database and multimedia applications focus on reading data, while many scientific applications focus on writing it.

1.1.2 Estimating I/O Requirements

The two main requirements for most I/O-intensive applications are I/O speed and storage capacity. (Maintaining data integrity and availability are also important for many applications, but they are not the main focus of this book.) "Speed" is actually a combination of *transfer rate* and *access time,* which are defined in Chapter 2. For this discussion, though, assume that "speed" is synonymous with the rate at which a program can read or write data.

A useful measure for evaluating the I/O needs of a scientific application is the number of floating-point operations (FLOPs) executed per byte of data read or written.[1] This ratio can vary over two or three orders of magnitude for different

1 The term "FLOPS," with a capital *S,* often stands for floating-point operations *per second.* For this discussion, however, it is convenient to call a floating-point operation a "FLOP." To avoid confusion, FLOPs per second will be abbreviated FLOP/sec.

applications, but values in the range of 500 FLOPs per byte are not unusual. A lower ratio implies a more I/O-intensive program. This ratio is averaged over the whole execution time of the program; instantaneous I/O and computation rates fluctuate as a program runs.

In 2000, the fastest computers in the world were rated at peak theoretical rates ranging from 1 to 10 teraFLOPs (trillions of operations, TFLOP) per second. However, the actual computation rate that most scientific programs can sustain is much lower, for a variety of reasons. First, the peak rate established for most processors assumes that the program is performing only floating-point multiply-add (FMA) instructions. These instructions compute $x = a \times b + c$ in a single operation. If the floating-point unit of the processor can complete an FMA once per processor clock cycle, then it produces two FLOPs (an addition and a multiplication) per cycle. Although FMA operations are common in many scientific codes, no code uses them exclusively, and any other floating-point instruction produces no more than one FLOP per cycle. Another limit on performance is the rate at which the memory system can supply data to the processor. Most modern computers have multilevel memory hierarchies, in which a small amount of very fast memory is devoted to a primary cache of values that the computer expects to need soon. Successively larger and slower pools of memory contain the rest of a program's data and instructions. In most computers, only the fast memory of the primary (or "level one") cache can supply data fast enough to keep up with the peak FLOP rate of the processor. In well-tuned applications, more than 90% of the data does indeed reside in the primary cache when the program needs it. However, the cost of a "cache miss" (failing to find the needed data in the cache) can range from several cycles to tens of cycles, which is large enough that even a small percentage of cache misses greatly reduces a computer's overall performance. Finally, few programs perform floating-point operations continuously. Other program instructions, such as subroutine calls and evaluating conditional expressions, as well as higher-level activities, such as interprocessor communication, synchronization, and I/O, take time away from raw computation. The result is that modern computers rarely achieve a large percentage of peak performance. This is especially true in large parallel systems built from commodity processors (rather than vector processors). A few specially tuned applications that demand little of a computer's other systems can achieve phenomenal percentages of the theoretical peak: more than 90% for vector systems and more than 70% for commodity CPU systems [168]. However, in day-to-day operation, a system may operate at only a few percent of peak performance [16].

To see the typical I/O needs for a scientific application on a high performance computer, consider a hypothetical parallel computer with a peak performance rating of 1 TFLOP/sec. Assume, optimistically, that applications attain 10% of this peak in daily use. Now, taking a FLOP-to-byte ratio of 500:1, the computer would need to *sustain* 200 megabytes per second (MB/sec) of I/O. This requirement may appear easy to meet, since stand-alone storage systems using RAID technology offer peak read and write performance at about this rate. (See Section 2.6 for a definition of "RAID.") However, storage devices, like processors, require very favorable circumstances to approach peak performance. Later chapters discuss this issue in detail, but the main consideration is that storage devices perform best when they can access data in long, uninterrupted streams. In earlier generations of high performance computers, this was easy to arrange because all the data resided in a single large memory pool. In newer parallel computers with distributed memory, a single data set may be scattered in small pieces over many processing nodes. Even within a processing node (and in shared memory computers), data in memory may be stored in a different order from how it should end up in the file. Likewise, a program that reads data from a single file needs to "scatter" this data to the correct memory locations on a collection of nodes. Both situations reduce I/O performance by splitting file accesses into many operations that move data in small increments. Therefore, an important requirement for a high performance parallel I/O system is the ability to manage distributed data efficiently.

Now consider how much storage capacity a high performance computer needs. Suppose the machine could sustain 200 MB/sec of file output. Running continuously for a week, it would produce about 120 terabytes (TB) of data. This is quite a bit. For example, one RAID storage system available in 2000 that advertised a maximum transfer rate of 250 MB/sec could hold less than 2 TB of data. Clearly, for this example, storage capacity, not I/O speed, is the limiting parameter.

Another way to estimate the storage capacity needs of a system is to look at the ratio of main memory to disk space. The amount of memory in a large computer is often decided based on its FLOP rate. Let F be the computation rate of the computer in FLOP/sec, and let M be the main memory capacity. Typical values of M/F range from 0.5 to 1 byte/(FLOP/sec). Thus, a 1 TFLOP/sec computer would typically have 500 gigabytes (GB) to 1 TB of main memory. The total disk capacity, C_{total}, is often chosen as a ratio of C_{total}/M, with ratios of 10 to 20 being common. That figure has moved closer to 20 in recent years, in part because the cost of disk capacity is dropping faster than the cost of memory. Assuming $M/F = 1$ byte/(FLOP/sec) and $C_{\text{total}}/M = 20$, a 1 TFLOP/sec computer would need

$$F \frac{M}{F} \frac{C_{\text{total}}}{M} = 20 \text{ TB}$$

of disk capacity.

Even a computer generously endowed with disk capacity would quickly fill it up, so users face a choice: generate less data, discard some of the data they generate, or move data off the disks to archival storage. In practice, users do all three. The first solution has the advantage of reducing the need for both capacity and speed, but it partly defeats the purpose of a scientific simulation: to produce data. Of course, data and information are not the same thing. Computer programs produce data, and it is up to a human to glean information from this data. Chapter 8 discusses some methods to help automate the process of extracting information from data. In some situations, it might be possible to reduce the number of bytes stored by analyzing the data while it still resides in main memory. However, most scientists want to store the raw data that forms the basis of the analysis, so preanalysis is not an entirely satisfactory way to reduce data output. The second solution, discarding data, is quite reasonable in some circumstances. Not all data that programs produce turns out to be useful, and much of the data is needed only temporarily. However, even if only a small fraction of the data produced by all programs turns out to have long-term value, large-scale scientific computations will fill up the available disk capacity faster than most computer centers can add more. Therefore, another requirement for a high performance parallel I/O system is a way to move data to long-term archival storage, where the marginal cost of adding capacity (for example, buying more tape cartridges) is much less than the cost of adding disks.

1.2 Trends in I/O Performance

Like other computer components, such as processors, memory, and interconnection networks, external storage devices continue to improve at a phenomenal rate. However, these components are all improving at different rates, which creates an imbalance between the performance of different computer subsystems.

Many computer users are familiar with Moore's law, an observation about the exponential growth over time of the number of electronic components on a chip. In its current form, Moore's law states that the number (not the density) of components on an integrated circuit die doubles every 18 months, which works out to a growth rate of about 60% per year [142]. Although the rates of improvement for many figures of merit in computation are often described as following Moore's law, the true scope of the "law" is relatively narrow. It says nothing directly about the growth rate of processor speeds, interconnect speeds, memory latency, disk capacity, tape capacity, or any other factor that affects the performance of a computer. Some of these parameters are growing at the same 60% per year as the number of components on a die; others are growing slower or faster. Disk capacity is an interesting example. As Chapter 2 will show, the amount of data per unit area that could be stored on a disk platter grew steadily at 25% per year for nearly three decades, from the early 1960s until about 1991. In that year, a development in disk drive technology called magnetoresistive heads pushed the growth rate abruptly upward to 60% per year. In some recent years, the growth rate has been close to 100% annually. Meanwhile, the density of components on chips has grown at a steady rate of 40% per year since the early 1970s [62]. (The rest of the annual growth in the number of components per die comes from increases in the die size.)

These different rates illustrate some important points. Moore's law and related growth "laws" are merely observations about past trends, not immutable laws of nature. Together, they have become a sort of self-fulfilling prophecy. Customers expect the improvement of various parameters to continue at their historical rates, so the electronics and storage industries aim for those rates as they design their products. The abrupt shift upward in the density of data on disks shows that technological breakthroughs can produce growth rates that exceed their historical levels; presumably, technological failures can have the opposite effect.

The other point to be seen in the differing growth rates is the connection between density and the size of a substrate. When component density was growing faster than disk density, disk drives had to remain relatively large to keep up with increases in memory size, or at least the drives could not shrink very fast. Once the growth rate of disk density turned upward, disk manufacturers began to reduce the size of disk drives while continuing to increase total capacity. Smaller drives offer several advantages, including lower power consumption and faster data access.

The growth in the rate at which disks can read and write data has always lagged the growth in capacity. Again, Chapter 2 looks at the reasons for this. At present, the improvement in data transfer rates is only 40% per year. This lower rate will have a major effect on I/O systems. Consider again the hypothetical 1 TFLOP/sec system described earlier. The number of disk drives it needs (not counting extra drives for redundancy, spares, etc.) is $d = C_{\text{total}}/C_{\text{drive}}$, where C_{drive} is the capacity of a single disk drive. For 20 TB of disk space and 20 GB drives, $d = 20\,\text{TB}/20\,\text{GB} = 1000$. (This assumes a gigabyte is exactly 1 billion bytes, but see Chapter 2.) Let R_{disk} be the transfer rate of a single disk drive in bytes per second, and suppose $R_{\text{disk}} =$ 10 MB/sec. The aggregate transfer rate (not likely to be achieved in practice) is then

$$R_{\text{total}} = dR_{\text{disk}} = \frac{C_{\text{total}}}{C_{\text{disk}}} R_{\text{disk}} = 10\,\text{GB/sec}.$$

The ratio F/R_{total} relates compute performance to I/O performance (in FLOP/sec per byte/sec), and for the 1 TFLOP/sec machine in this example, $F/R_{\text{total}} =$ 100.

Holding $(M/F)(C_{\text{total}}/M)$ constant at 20, consider how F/R_{total} will change over time.

$$R_{\text{total}} = \frac{20F}{C_{\text{disk}}} R_{\text{disk}}, \quad \text{so} \quad F/R_{\text{total}} = \frac{C_{\text{disk}}}{20\,R_{\text{disk}}}.$$

Suppose that five years later, a new computer is built with 10 times the FLOP rate and memory capacity, reflecting a 60% annual increase in performance. A corresponding increase in storage capacity would give it 200 TB of disk space. If disk drive capacity doubled every year for those five years (this would assume that the physical disks remained the same size), $C_{disk} = 640$ GB and $d = 312.5$. If the disks' speed increased by 40% per year, then $R_{disk} = 53.8$ MB/sec. Then $R_{total} \approx 16.9$ GB/sec, and $F/R_{total} \approx 595$. In other words, the relative I/O performance would be only a sixth of its previous value! To counteract this problem, it would be necessary to add more disks and perhaps reduce the amount of data per drive. Thus, in future systems the reason to add more disks will not be to increase capacity but rather to improve performance through greater parallelism. An alternative view of this trend is that the amount of data a program can store will be limited by how much time the user is willing to spend writing it, not by the amount of space available on the disks.

1.3 Understanding the Levels of I/O

Ideally, computer architects and system programmers could improve I/O performance without forcing application developers to change their programs. However, tuning the overall performance of an application requires an understanding of all the major parts of a computer's architecture, including not only the CPU, cache, and memory, but also the I/O system. The I/O system includes storage devices, interconnection networks, file systems, and one or more I/O programming libraries.

This book presents I/O from the bottom up, starting with hardware technology, moving upward through several layers of software to the I/O libraries that scientific applications commonly use, and concluding with a survey of techniques for managing large collections of data.

The design of storage devices affects the performance of all the levels above them. Chapter 2 looks at several types of storage devices. Magnetic hard disk drives receive the most attention, but magnetic tape, optical disks, floppy disks, and new holographic storage techniques are also covered. Each of these devices performs some operations more efficiently than others. Showing why this is so helps explain all the tricks and traps in the layers of software above.

Perhaps the most important development in the design of storage devices for large computers has been the advent of RAID technology, which combines many small disk drives to form large, high performance storage devices. The combination of multiple disk drives with RAID software and hardware simultaneously increases capacity, improves data transfer rates, and makes the system more reliable. RAID systems have been largely responsible for the disappearance of disk drives with dozens of huge platters, for which the original RAMAC 350 was a prototype.

Connecting storage devices to the rest of the computer system requires high speed networking. Several standard networks exist with different combinations of characteristics, such as their transmission medium (fiber or copper), their method of connecting more than two devices, and their ability to move data efficiently into user memory. Chapter 2 describes some of these networks.

The final part of Chapter 2 looks at emerging hardware technology that could alter the configuration and performance characteristics of high performance I/O systems.

The capabilities and programming interfaces of storage devices are quite primitive. For example, most storage devices don't support the notion of a file, let alone file ownership, access permissions, or directories. Chapter 3 describes *file systems*, the software that creates these familiar abstractions and makes storage devices usable to higher-level applications. File systems are also responsible for maintaining the integrity of stored data and for trying to hide some of the performance quirks of disk drives.

Parallel file systems do all these tasks for multiple processors and multiple independent storage devices. Parallel file systems are not the same as distributed file systems, such as NFS and DFS. While both types of file systems support access to shared files from multiple processes, parallel file systems must efficiently support *simultaneous* access to individual files. Distributed file systems are not designed to support this kind of fine-grained file sharing efficiently. A key challenge for parallel file systems is maintaining data integrity during the parallel access without compromising performance. Computer vendors and research groups have developed a number of parallel file systems over the years that attack these problems. Some systems use novel programming interfaces that let the user customize the system's behavior to improve performance for specific kinds of data access patterns. Others present a standard interface similar to Unix I/O and try to offer good performance over a wide range of access patterns. Research file systems have focused on novel programming interfaces or novel architectures. The growing popularity of parallel computers built from clusters of workstations has presented a number of challenges to file system designers, which several research groups have tried to address with their file systems.

Despite the best efforts of file system designers, many parallel scientific applications exhibit very poor I/O performance for certain access patterns. Chapter 4 looks at common access patterns for scientific applications on distributed memory computers. Unlike codes on vector computers with a single pool of memory, the parallel codes often write data in small, discontiguous pieces, which are difficult for file systems and storage devices to handle efficiently. To remedy this problem, a number of research groups have developed techniques for collecting small pieces of data into larger units that lower levels of the storage hierarchy can manage better. These techniques are called *collective I/O,* and a number of variations have been proposed and implemented. No single technique appears to perform best in all situations, and all the techniques have several adjustable parameters that affect their performance on different underlying I/O systems.

Another important I/O optimization is the use of *hints,* which let applications tell the I/O system about upcoming I/O access patterns. The I/O system can use this information to select optimization parameters that are likely to yield good performance. A step beyond the use of hints is to analyze the I/O access patterns of a running application and select optimal parameter settings automatically.

Both collective I/O and hints require more information from an application than they can get through a standard sequential I/O programming interface. Parallel I/O interfaces, described in Chapter 5, are more expressive than the standard sequential Unix I/O interface. They can describe I/O operations that are coordinated across multiple processes, and the operations can involve many separate pieces of data. Many interfaces also let applications pass in hints or change some of the I/O system's configuration parameters.

Chapter 5 describes three parallel I/O interfaces. It focuses on MPI-IO, the I/O interface defined in the MPI-2 message passing standard. This interface uses concepts and data structures from MPI (message passing interface) to describe parallel I/O operations, and it has been implemented on many parallel systems. The discussion includes several code examples in both C and Fortran.

Many scientific application developers prefer to program with higher-level interfaces that implement more sophisticated *data models.* These models allow programs to describe I/O operations in terms of application-level data structures, such as arrays and meshes, rather than describing blocks of undifferentiated bytes. Scientific data libraries also let applications write data in a standard format, so scientists working with different application programs and on different types of computers can share data files. Chapter 6 introduces data models and presents two popular scientific data libraries, netCDF and HDF. Both of these libraries let programs define multidimensional array data structures in a file and read or write them as whole units or in parts. Both also add users' annotations to various parts of the data structures. Several programming examples are given for both libraries, and readers can download many of the example programs in Chapters 5 and 6 from the publisher's Web site at *www.mkp.com/may.*

The netCDF data model is easy to understand, but the library that implements it does not support parallel I/O, and it places certain other inconvenient restrictions on applications. Until recently, HDF supported a number of data models suited to different kinds of applications, including regular arrays, images, and tables of unstructured mesh data. A new release of the library called HDF5 simplifies and generalizes the data model. HDF5 also supports parallel I/O as an option. Its programming interface is quite rich and complex, allowing programs to carry out various transformations on data as the software reads and writes it. Among the most important of these transformations is the ability to change the bit- and byte-level representation of numbers, so an application can write a file in a standardized representation or in the proprietary numerical representation of a different computer architecture. NetCDF also writes data in a standard numerical representation, but it doesn't allow conversions between two different proprietary representations.

Chapter 6 concludes with a discussion of a new high-level data model and of the interactions between layers of I/O software.

The parallel I/O interfaces of Chapter 5 and the scientific libraries of Chapter 6 are flexible enough to carry out many I/O tasks, but some applications can benefit from specialized interfaces that support specific operations. Chapter 7 examines two categories of I/O: out-of-core operations (sometimes called external memory operations) and checkpointing.

Applications use out-of-core methods when working with data sets that are too large to fit in main memory. General-purpose computers have used virtual memory techniques for many years to present the illusion of a data space much larger than physical memory. These techniques are convenient and nearly invisible to the user, but they don't always produce the best performance. Out-of-core methods put the application in control of moving data between main memory and disk during the course of a computation. Because the programmer can predict better than the operating system when the application will need each piece of data, out-of-core techniques can schedule data transfers to reduce the number of I/O operations and to increase concurrency between I/O and computation. Algorithms designed specifically to operate on out-of-core data often perform much better than standard algorithms that rely on the virtual memory system to simulate unlimited main memory.

Checkpointing records the state of a running program so that it can be restarted from that point later. Saving a checkpoint can help an application avoid repeating work after a system failure, and it can help computer centers move jobs on and off a machine in response to changing scheduling policies. All checkpointing systems represent a compromise between three goals: minimizing the amount of data in a checkpoint (and therefore the time needed to store it), allowing the program to be restarted on a different type of computer, and reducing the involvement of the application in storing checkpoint data. Checkpointing parallel applications presents the additional challenge of recording states of separate processes in a way that forms a consistent global view of the program. The discussion of checkpointing concludes with a description of a simple model for determining how often a program should store checkpoint data.

The final chapter of this book steps back from the mechanics of reading and writing data to look at the question of how to explore a large data collection.

Chapter 8 surveys three aspects of this problem: how to find a particular data item of interest in a collection, how to query a data set for data that meets specified criteria, and how to discover new, unanticipated information in a data set.

The first task involves both familiar tools for managing data and the emerging use of metadata to catalog and summarize large data sets. For the second task, many applications use database management systems to store and query scientific data. Chapter 8 introduces basic database technology, discussing its strengths and limitations. Relational DBMSs have been studied and used for many years, but recently two new database models, object-oriented databases and object-relational databases, have been introduced. These new models offer scientific users a more flexible way to describe data, and they promise better I/O performance than relational databases for scientific data. Three examples of scientific database projects using large DBMSs are presented.

In the area of knowledge discovery, several techniques have been developed to help users extract interesting patterns of data from large data sets. Many of these data mining algorithms have been borrowed from commercial database analysis, and they may well create exciting new possibilities for the analysis of large scientific data sets.

1.4 Summary

This chapter has introduced some of the important problems in storing data for high performance computers. Applications make a variety of demands on I/O systems, and parallel I/O can help meet these demands by increasing both capacity and I/O speed. Although many measures of computer and I/O performance are increasing exponentially, they are increasing at different rates. Specifically, the capacity of disk drives is growing much faster than their speed, so efficient techniques for reading and writing data are becoming increasingly important. This book presents a variety of these techniques, along with several I/O programming interfaces designed for performance, convenience, or both.

Chapter Two Storage Devices and Interconnects

Computers store data on a variety of media, including electronic memory, magnetic disk, optical disk, and tape. These media are often classified in a three-level hierarchy, which distinguishes them according to their volatility, cost, access time, and typical use.

Primary storage, the top level of the hierarchy, includes all types of electronic memory. Computers use primary storage to hold data and instructions for programs that are currently running. Primary storage is generally volatile: removing electric power erases its contents. Access times range from nanoseconds to microseconds, and the cost per byte of this storage is higher than the other levels. Primary storage is also called *main memory;* the latter term usually excludes cache memory.

Secondary storage includes rigid magnetic disks (hard disks) and sometimes optical media. It is nonvolatile, and data can be retrieved from it in a matter of milliseconds. Secondary storage holds programs and data not currently in use that users want to retrieve on short notice. Secondary storage can also act as a temporary staging area for active programs and data that don't fit into main memory.

Tertiary storage includes magnetic tape, some optical media, and flexible (floppy) magnetic disks. If the tape or disk is already mounted in the storage device, access times can be a few seconds. If a person or a robot must retrieve the storage medium and mount it in a drive, access times can range from seconds to days. Tertiary storage holds backup or archival copies of data and programs. It can also be used to transfer data between systems. Secondary and tertiary storage are sometimes called *external memory* or *external storage.*

This chapter will examine secondary and tertiary storage devices, as well as interconnection networks. RAID systems (redundant arrays of independent disks) have become the major form of secondary storage for large systems, and these will be described in detail. Floppy disks and rewritable optical disks are not widely used in high performance computing, so they will receive less attention.

The interconnection networks that link storage devices with computers can strongly influence I/O performance, so this chapter also describes the main features of interconnects and several common interconnection networks. The last part of this chapter reviews some new storage technologies that show promise for future systems.

2.1 Basic Characteristics of Storage Devices

Storage devices are described in terms of several important characteristics, such as capacity, transfer rate, access time, and sequentiality, among others.

Capacity is the amount of data a device can store. The basic unit of capacity is a byte or a bit. One bit is a binary digit: 0 or 1. A byte in modern computers is eight bits. The total capacity of a storage device is usually given in megabytes (MB) or gigabytes (GB). The meaning of "mega," "giga," and other prefixes is sometimes ambiguous. In the context of storage capacity, "megabyte" usually means 2^{20} or 1,048,576 bytes, rather than 10^6 (1,000,000) bytes. In 1998, the International Electrotechnical Commission adopted a new set of prefixes intended to resolve the ambiguity [164]. The familiar prefixes would retain their base-ten meanings, and the new prefixes would indicate base-two multiples. Each new prefix is formed from the first syllable of the corresponding base-ten prefix followed by the syllable "bi," producing "kibi," "mebi," "gibi," and so on. The corresponding abbreviations are "Ki," "Mi," "Gi," and so on. Table 2.1 summarizes the base-ten and base-two prefixes and their values. Since the new prefixes are not yet widely used, this book will use

Prefix	*Abbreviation*	*Base-ten*	*Base-two*
kilo, kibi	K, Ki	10^3	$2^{10} = 1024$
mega, mebi	M, Mi	10^6	$2^{20} = 1{,}048{,}576$
giga, gibi	G, Gi	10^9	$2^{30} = 1{,}073{,}741{,}824$
tera, tebi	T, Ti	10^{12}	$2^{40} = 1{,}099{,}511{,}627{,}776$
peta, pebi	P, Pi	10^{15}	$2^{50} \approx 1.1259 \times 10^{15}$
exa, exbi	E, Ei	10^{18}	$2^{60} \approx 1.1529 \times 10^{18}$

Table 2.1 *Standard base-ten and base-two prefixes. The names of the binary versions have been accepted as a standard by the International Electrotechnical Commission but are not yet widely used.*

the old versions and tolerate the ambiguity. Exact values will be specified whenever the distinction is important.

The largest computers now built come with enough disk capacity to hold tens of terabytes of data, and the largest archival storage systems now contemplated will hold petabytes of data.

Capacity is determined in part by the *areal density* of the storage medium, which is the amount of data that the medium can store per unit area. Common units are bits per square inch or bits per square millimeter. Density is specified per unit area rather than per unit volume because most storage devices record data at or near the surface of the medium. You could imagine storing data throughout the volume of a medium to improve storage density. Holographic storage devices (Section 2.8.2) are a step in this direction, but they are not yet available commercially.

The rate at which a device can read or write data is called its *transfer rate* or *bandwidth.* A common measure of transfer rate is megabytes per second (MB/sec). When referring to rates rather than capacities, "mega" and the other prefixes often imply base-ten multiples rather than base-two multiples.

When a computer issues a request to read or write data, there is always a delay before the first byte moves. This delay is the *access time.* (Another common term is *latency,* but that word has a more specific meaning in the design of disk drives.) A *random access* storage device can access every byte it stores in equal time. The set of registers in a processor is random access storage, but most other storage in modern computers is not. For example, a computer's primary storage usually has main memory and multiple levels of cache memory that hold recently accessed data. Each level down in a cache is larger and slower than the one above it, so accessing different logical addresses takes different amounts of time.

Likewise, in secondary and tertiary storage devices, the access time is not the same for all data. In disks, platters must rotate and heads must move when data is read or written. The time it takes for the head to reach the appropriate byte location determines the access time, and this time depends not only on the location of the bytes requested but also on the location of the last bytes accessed. This variability means that disks are not true random access devices, although they are often used as if they were. If disks were random access devices, many of the optimizations that the following chapters describe would be unnecessary.

The opposite of a random access device is a *sequential access* device, such as a tape drive. In these systems, the time to retrieve the first byte of a request depends strongly on the location of that byte and the location of the last byte accessed; the tape drive's head must traverse all the intervening data.

One more characteristic of storage devices is their rewritability. Magnetic disk drives can rewrite data at a given storage location repeatedly. Some optical disks are rewritable, but many can be written only once, either by the end-user or by the manufacturer. Magnetic tape can also be rewritten, but not in the same flexible way as magnetic disks.

There are other figures of merit for storage devices, such as the mean time to failure, physical size, and power requirements. However, most of these are not an immediate concern to most users.

2.2 Magnetic Hard Disk Drives

The main components of a magnetic disk drive are a set of spinning platters on which the drive stores data, the read/write heads, a set of arms that move the heads approximately along the radius of the disk, and an actuator that pivots the arms (Figure 2.1). A single drive has one or more platters on a single spindle. Disk drives usually store data on both sides of a platter, and separate heads access the data on each side.

The platter is coated with a material that responds to changing magnetic fields. To write data, the head produces a time-varying field, which polarizes tiny, arc-shaped domains on the platter in one of two directions. A sequence of these arcs forms a circular track. When the disk drive retrieves data, the read head can sense transitions between the polarity of adjacent domains. Techniques for encoding data in these transitions have evolved over the years, and better encodings have significantly improved areal density. These encodings also store extra bits that allow the disk drive to detect and correct errors that arise from corrupted domains.

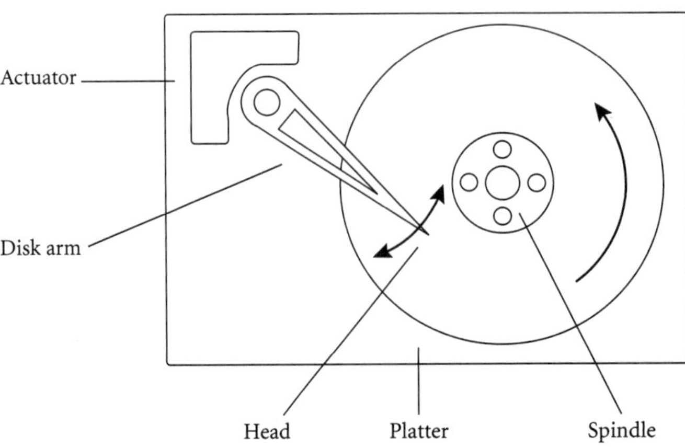

Figure 2.1 The major components of a hard disk drive. Many drives have several platters on the same spindle. Separate disk arms and heads access each side of each platter and move in tandem.

Head technology has also been improving. For many years, disks used a single read/write head. Newer designs use separate heads. Read heads are now made from a magnetoresistive material, whose resistance to a current varies in response to the changing magnetic field of the domains moving beneath it. These heads are more sensitive than their predecessors, especially at high data transfer rates. The write head is a tiny electromagnet and is wider than the read head. Making the read head narrower helps isolate it from spurious data in the tracks adjacent to the one it is reading, which improves the signal-to-noise ratio.

The drive uses a servo mechanism to position the head accurately over a particular track. The servo is an electronic circuit that senses the position of the head and makes small corrections to keep it aligned with the center of the track.

When the disk is stopped, the head is parked in contact with an otherwise unused surface of the platter. When the disk is spinning, the head flies on a layer of air 100 nanometers or less above the disk surface. A winglike device called a *slider* is mounted at the end of the arm and allows the head to fly over the platter as it spins. Keeping the head off the platter reduces wear on the head and lets the disk spin continuously at high speed without damaging the magnetic material. However, the closer the head flies over the disk, the more data it can read and write in a given area, so disk designers try to position the head as close as possible to the disk surface while avoiding actual contact. Future disks may use a coating of lubricant on the platter, so the head will ride in contact with the lubricant but off the magnetic material.

Hard disks spin at several thousand revolutions per minute (RPM). If a dust particle becomes trapped between the head and the platter, it can scratch the platter and corrupt the data. To prevent this, drives enclose the platters and heads in a dust-free chamber. Nevertheless, debris may be generated inside the chamber over the lifetime of the device, or physical shock may cause the head to crash into the platter. When this happens, the data in the damaged area of the platter is usually lost. Other data may still be available, and if the damage is minor, the disk may continue to work. If the damage is more severe and the disk no longer works, it may still be possible to recover some of the data by opening the drive and repairing the damage or moving the good platters to a new drive. These repairs must be done in a dust-free environment, so the procedure is economical only when the disk contains valuable data that cannot be recovered in any other way.

2.2.1 Organization of Data

The tracks on the disk are laid out in concentric rings (Figure 2.2). Each track consists of several *sectors* that contain a fixed number of domains and therefore a fixed number of bits. A common sector size is 512 bytes of user data. Disk sectors

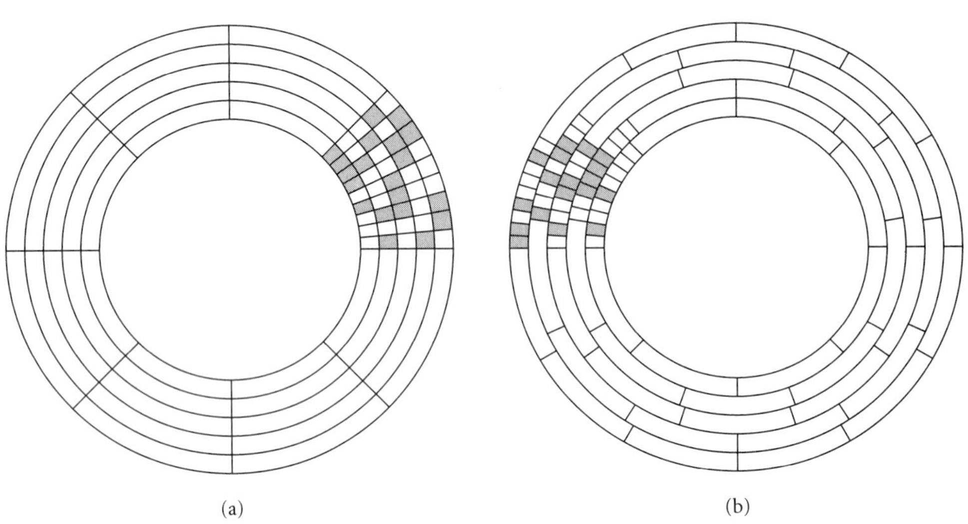

Figure 2.2 The surface of a disk platter is formatted as concentric circular tracks that contain arc-shaped sectors. Each sector consists of magnetic domains that are polarized in one of two directions (shown here by the different shading). Some formats use the same number of sectors on every track, so the outer domains are somewhat longer than the inner ones (a). More efficient formats fit more sectors in the outer tracks, so all the domains are the same length (b).

are sometimes called *blocks.* However, "block" can also refer to a fixed-size unit of data that an operating system or disk subsystem handles in an I/O operation. A block may contain the same number of bytes as a sector or a whole multiple of that number. To avoid confusion, this book will call the physical region of disk space a "sector," and a "block" will be the unit data size of an I/O operation.

Besides data, each sector contains header information, error correction bits, and possibly some domains with fixed polarity to guide the servo mechanism that positions the heads. Since the tracks near the outer edge of the platter have a larger circumference than the inner tracks, the outer tracks have room for more sectors. The layout of tracks and sectors on a disk platter is called its *format.* Some disk formats place a fixed number of sectors in each track. These formats store data less densely on the outer tracks, wasting about one-third of the theoretical capacity. Newer designs use formats that recover some of this space by storing more sectors in the outer tracks. Since the disk spins at a fixed rotational speed, the linear speed under the head is higher for the outer tracks than the inner tracks. Therefore, varying the number of sectors per track requires the disk electronics to read and write data at different rates for different tracks. In principle, the rate could be different for each of hundreds of tracks. In practice, this would make the control electronics too complex, so instead the tracks are grouped in a small number of zones. Each zone uses a different, fixed data rate for its tracks, and as few as eight zones are enough to exploit about 90% of the available density (see Ashar [7], p. 243).

Another way to pack more sectors in the outer tracks would be to change the platter's rotational speed as the head moves between tracks. This technique is used in optical disks and some floppy disks, but it is not practical for magnetic hard drives. The drive needs time to stabilize the platter speed as the head moves from track to track. Floppies and optical disks move the heads more slowly between tracks, and they often spin their disks more slowly, so they have more time to stabilize their speed than hard disk drives do. Also, the height at which the hard disk head flies over the platter depends in part on the rotational speed of the platter, since the platter carries on its surface a layer of air that supports the head. The head height must be carefully controlled, so the rotational speed of the disk cannot easily be varied.

Disk drives are designed to read and write whole sectors; they cannot access one byte at a time. If a user wishes to change a single byte in a file, the operating system must read an entire sector into a memory buffer, change the requested byte, and then write the sector back to the disk. This read-modify-write operation can slow performance severely, although the operating system can avoid it in some circumstances. Chapter 3 gives more details.

As noted above, many disk drives store data on both sides of multiple platters. Tracks at the same radial position on each platter surface form cylinders. Each surface uses a separate head, and a single actuator moves all the arms together. Therefore, all the heads access the same cylinder at the same time. Accessing data in parallel through multiple heads would seem to be an obvious optimization, but it is hard to implement in practice. Before RAID systems became popular, some high performance disks could access data through multiple heads in parallel. These devices required extra read and write electronics, and the heads needed to be aligned with each other very accurately. This was quite difficult because of vibration, thermal gradients, and mechanical imperfections in the drive. As track densities grew, alignment became even more difficult, and the advent of RAID technology has practically eliminated the demand for specialized high performance disk drives. Modern drives access data through only one head at a time.

2.2.2 Disk Performance

The capacity of a disk drive depends on the number and size of the platters and the areal density of the data. Areal density has increased rapidly over the past decades, while the platters have slowly shrunk. The number of platters is usually chosen to suit the physical size and capacity needs of the drive. However, even when space allows it, using many platters is impractical for two reasons. First, a single actuator moves all the heads, so increasing the number of heads increases the mass that the actuator must move, which in turn increases the access time. Second, the more platters a drive uses, the greater the risk that any one of them will suffer a head crash, which could potentially force expensive repairs or render the whole drive useless.

Areal density is the product of *track density* and *linear density.* Track density is the number of tracks per unit of disk radius, and linear density is the number of bits per unit length on the track. In practice, the number of bits of user data per unit area on a disk is different from the theoretical areal density. Not all tracks have the same linear density, and the disk format includes domains dedicated to marking off sectors, controlling head position, error correction, and so on. As Figure 2.3 shows, areal density is increasing exponentially, and the rate of increase turned upward around 1991. The main source of this improvement is magnetoresistive heads.

Improvements in linear density come mainly from reducing the distance between the head and the platter, from increasing the rate at which the electronics

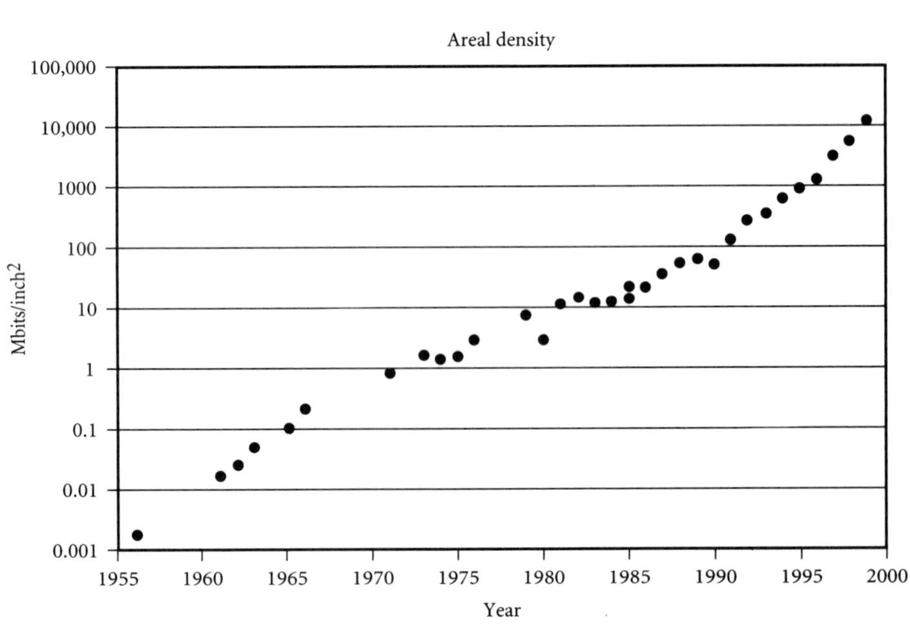

Figure 2.3 Areal density for selected disk drives introduced between 1956 and 1999. Data was taken from a list of drives compiled by DISK/TREND, Inc. The drive with the highest areal density introduced in a given year is shown. (Not all years are represented.) Around 1991, the rate of improvement grew sharply after the introduction of magnetoresistive heads.

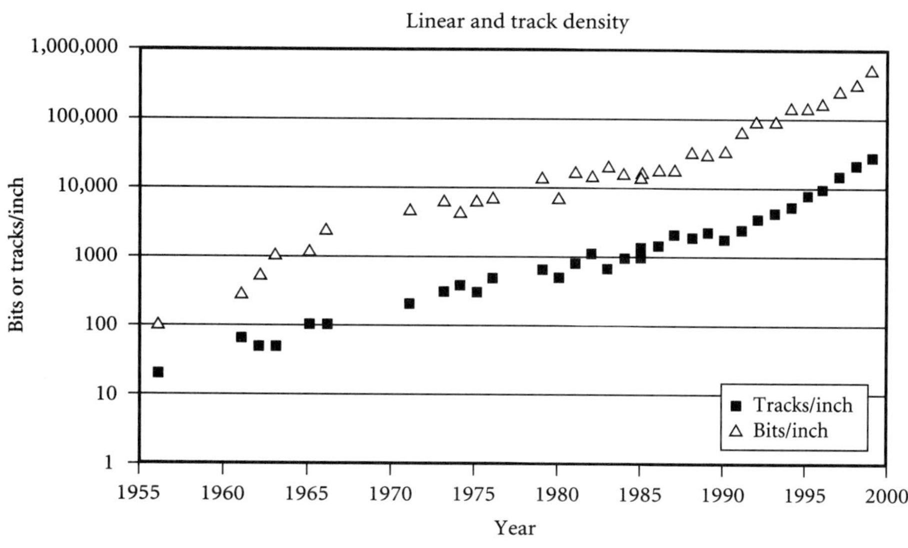

Figure 2.4 Linear density and track density for the same disk drives shown in Figure 2.3. Both parameters are increasing at exponential rates, and the product is the areal density. (Courtesy DISK/TREND, Inc.)

can read and write data, and from better magnetic coatings on the platters. Smaller head-to-platter distances also improve track density, as does more accurate control of the head position on the platter. This control, in turn, depends on the precision of the servo and on mechanical considerations like the flatness of the platters and the absence of wobble as they rotate. As Figure 2.4 shows, both track density and linear density are growing exponentially.

The transfer rate depends on the rotational speed of the platters and the density of the data. Raising the linear density moves more data past the head on each rotation.

An important limitation in the design of disk drives is that increasing the areal density by a given factor does not increase the transfer rate by the same factor. Of the two contributors to areal density—linear density and track density—only linear density contributes to the transfer rate. As shown in Figure 2.5, transfer rates have improved no faster than the linear densities, despite the fact that rotational speeds have also increased (slowly) over the years. The main limitation appears to be the head and its supporting electronics, which cannot read and write data at arbitrarily high speed. The result is that as disk drive capacity increases, so does the time required to access all the data on the drive.

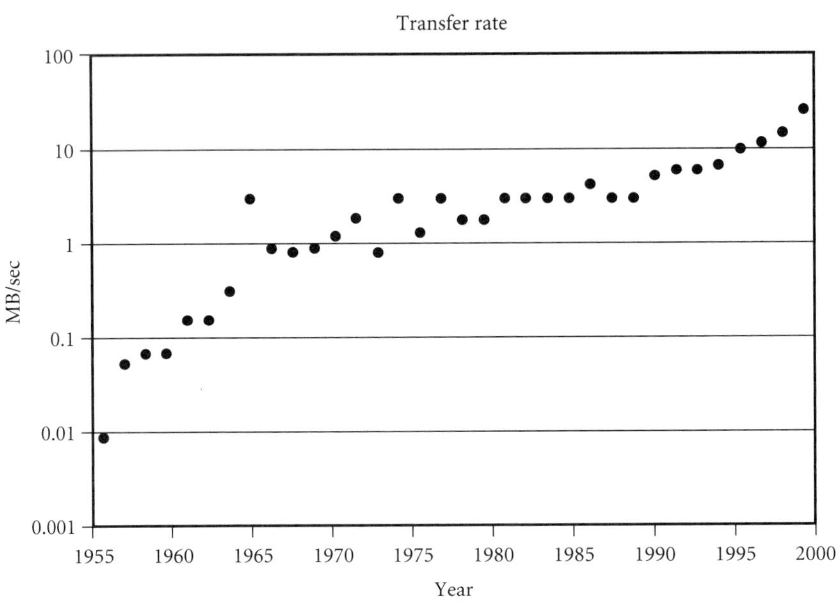

Figure 2.5 Transfer rates are improving exponentially, but not nearly as fast as total areal density. This data is for the same set of disk drives shown in Figures 2.3 and 2.4. (Courtesy DISK/TREND, Inc.)

Access time depends only on electromechanical considerations, and it has been improving even more slowly than transfer rates. The time needed to access a particular sector is

$$T_{\text{access}} = T_{\text{seek}} + T_{\text{latency}},$$

where T_{access} is the access time, T_{seek} is the time to move the head to the correct track, and T_{latency} is the time to rotate the correct sector to the head. You might at first guess that the access time was

$$T_{\text{access}} = \max(T_{\text{seek}}, T_{\text{latency}}) \text{ (incorrect)}$$

since the head moves at the same time as the disk is spinning. Recall, though, that the disk spins continuously. If the start of the requested sector arrives in the path of the head before the head reaches the track, the disk cannot stop and wait for the head. Instead, when the head arrives at the track, it must wait for the sector to come around again.

For currently available disks, the average value of T_{seek} is about 10 milliseconds (ms), and the average value of $T_{latency} = 1/(2T_{rotation})$, where $T_{rotation}$ is the rotational speed. For a disk with $T_{rotation} = 7200$ RPM, $T_{access} = 10\text{ ms} + 4.2\text{ ms} = 14.2\text{ ms}$.

Fourteen milliseconds is an eternity in high performance computing, equivalent to millions of clock cycles. Fortunately, the use of buffers can hide much of this access time. Chapter 3 describes buffering and caching techniques. Modern disk drives include a megabyte or more of their own buffer memory. Since the buffer often holds an entire disk track of data, it is sometimes called a *track buffer.* For write operations, the drive can store an incoming block of data in the buffer and report immediately that the write operation is complete. The data is held in the buffer until the head arrives over the appropriate sector, and then the data is written to the disk. Some drives use nonvolatile memory for their buffer. This type of memory continues to store data even when electrical power is removed, preventing the disk from losing data in the event of a power loss. The operating system and user applications assume that the data is safely stored once the drive reports that the operation is complete.

For read operations, the disk can attempt to predict which sectors are about to be requested, based on recent access patterns. These sectors are read into the buffer, and if a request for a predicted sector does indeed arrive, the disk can respond immediately using data in the buffer. One common prediction technique retrieves the sector immediately following each sector requested in a read operation (or the entire track containing the sector). The cost of reading the extra sectors is small, since the head is already in position as soon as it finishes reading the first sector. Moreover, since the adjacent portions of a file often reside in adjacent sectors, it is quite likely that the extra sectors will be requested shortly after the first one.

2.3 Magnetic Tape

Magnetic tape is familiar from audio and video recording. Like magnetic disks, tape drives encode digital data in the transitions between polarized domains. The main virtue of tape in modern computer systems is its low cost per byte of storage. Tapes are available in many formats, differing in size, areal density, and recording format.

2.3.1 Tape Formats

There are two basic recording formats for tapes: *helical scan* and *linear scan* (Figure 2.6). Linear scan tapes store data in one or more continuous tracks that run in

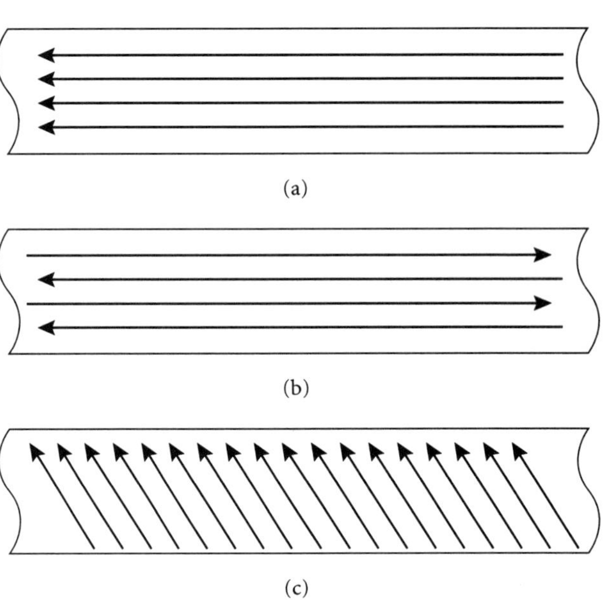

Figure 2.6 The tracks of parallel linear tape can be read and written in parallel by multiple heads (a). Serpentine linear tapes are scanned back and forth by one head that moves from track to track (b). Helical scan tapes are read and written by a rotating head; the head scans the tape at high speed, but the tape's linear speed is relatively low (c).

parallel along the tape's length, like lanes in a highway. When there are multiple tracks, multiple read or write heads can access them in parallel to improve the transfer rate. Alternatively, data tracks may be laid out in a serpentine format, to be accessed one track at a time as the tape moves first in one direction and then the other. A serpentine tape offers lower data rates but costs less to build than a parallel system. Combinations of parallel and serpentine scanning are also possible; multiple heads read a subset of the tracks in each direction.

Helical scan tapes, which were first developed for analog video recording, store data in diagonal stripes that run from one edge of the tape to the other. These stripes are created by moving the tape in a shallow spiral (hence the term "helical scan") over a spinning drum that contains the read and write heads. The main advantage of helical scanning is that the heads can move across the tape at high speed while the tape itself moves slowly. Fast-moving heads increase the data transfer rates, while slow-moving tapes allow a simple transport mechanism. Slow-moving tapes are also less likely to stretch.

Rewriting tapes is more difficult than rewriting disks. One reason is that disks store data in fixed-size sectors, but tapes often store data in variable-length records. If a record must be overwritten, the new record can be no longer than the old one;

otherwise it will overlap the record that follows. As a tape is repeatedly overwritten, the available space can become increasingly fragmented with smaller and smaller records. Also, tapes can stretch, and positioning the head accurately at a specific location on the tape is difficult. These considerations make it likely that stray data will be left over on a tape after part of it is rewritten. The stray data can be hard to distinguish from real data. Because of these difficulties, it is common practice not to rewrite individual records. Instead, outdated records are usually left in place on a tape. If they are superseded later, the new version is written elsewhere. Some tapes can be bulk-erased and reused if all the data becomes obsolete. Other tapes come from the factory with prerecorded servo data, which bulk-erasing would destroy. These tapes must be rerecorded rather than bulk-erased.

Early computer tapes were loaded on large reels, but modern tapes are enclosed in cartridges of varying sizes and shapes. These simplify handling and loading the tape.

2.3.2 Tape Libraries

Since tapes typically store little-used data for long periods of time, it's not economical to keep a single tape mounted permanently in its own drive. In most hard disks, by contrast, the storage medium and the read/write hardware are an inseparable unit. For many years, tapes were stored on racks, and the main contributor to the access time was the human operator, who had to locate the requested tape, carry it to the drive, and mount it by hand. This offline storage is still common at many sites. Offline storage allows valuable data to be kept in a safe place, out of harm's way if some disaster strikes the computer room.

Automated tape libraries use storage robots instead of human operators to retrieve and mount tapes. These systems can hold anywhere from a few tapes to a few thousand tapes. The larger systems use bar-codes to help robots identify individual tapes. The robot can find a tape, pluck it out of a storage slot, move it to an open drive, and mount it in the drive. The whole operation takes tens of seconds.

2.3.3 Tape Performance

Because tape is a sequential access medium, it works poorly for general-purpose data storage, where the user wants rapid access to any byte of any file. Instead, tapes mainly store archival data that is accessed infrequently or backup copies of data that already resides on secondary storage. These uses allow entire files or even entire directory structures to be read or written as a whole. Long, uninterrupted accesses are ideal for tapes because repeated stopping and starting takes time and can damage a tape.

The capacity of a tape depends on its areal density and its physical dimensions. As with disks, the areal density is the product of the linear density and the track density. Early computer tapes were half an inch (12.7 mm) wide and had only seven linear tracks. Modern tapes are narrower (8 mm, 4 mm, and quarter-inch are common formats) and may have over 100 linear tracks. This gain is modest compared to improvements in hard disk track density. Linear density, on the other hand, has grown faster. The newest formats approach 4000 bits per millimeter. Total capacity for current tapes can reach tens of gigabytes. Tape lengths range from tens to hundreds of meters. Thin tape substrates allow longer tapes to fit in a fixed-size cartridge, but thin tapes are delicate, so tape transport mechanisms must be designed to handle them gently. Starting and stopping a tape rapidly can damage it, but gradual speed changes can increase the overall access time. Modern tape drives partly solve this problem by using memory buffers to isolate variations in the tape speed from the drive's I/O interface.

A tape's transfer rate depends on its linear density, the degree of parallel access, and the speed of the heads over the tape. In helical scan drives, the head speed is much higher than the tape transport speed. Unlike disk drives, tape drives can increase parallelism and track density together, although parallel read/write heads cannot be situated arbitrarily close together. Also, the drive's electronics may limit transfer rate, so an increase in linear density may force a decrease in head-to-tape speed. Parallel access, high head speeds, and high linear density allow tape drives to offer transfer rates comparable to magnetic hard disk drives, as much as 10 to 20 MB/sec.

The access time, of course, is far worse. Since tape is a sequential access medium, the access time depends strongly on the location of the requested data. The average access time depends on the length of the tape and the speed of the transport mechanism. Some tape drives can move a tape faster when searching for data than they do when reading or writing it, just as videotape players support fast-forward and reverse. The fastest tape drives offer average access times under 10 seconds, assuming the tape is already mounted in the drive.

An important difference between secondary and tertiary storage is that tertiary storage media can be detached from the drive. This makes tertiary storage suitable for archiving data, but it also limits potential improvements. New technology may offer higher capacity and better performance, but for customers with a large archive of data stored on old media, new technology presents an unwelcome choice:

- Keep using older read/write technology to maintain compatibility with old media.
- Transfer all the old data to new media.
- Support several kinds of media.

The first option ties the user to obsolete technology year after year. The second can be a large and expensive undertaking, although it does offer the opportunity to clean house every few years. The third option forces system administrators to maintain an increasing variety of incompatible equipment.

2.4 Other Media

Floppy disks and optical disks are not commonly used in high performance I/O systems, but it is interesting to compare them with magnetic hard disks.

A floppy disk consists of a single platter coated on both sides with magnetic material. The heads of a floppy drive touch the surface of the disk. This is possible because the disk spins much more slowly than a hard disk, and it stops spinning when the drive is not accessing data. The 90 mm (3.5 inch) disks used in personal computers spin at 300 RPM, less than a tenth the speed of the slowest modern hard disks. The seek time for these drives is 94 milliseconds, and the transfer rate ranges from 30 KB/sec to 125 KB/sec. The floppiness of a floppy disk makes it difficult to align the head precisely on a track, so the track density is low. Some floppy drives can vary the number of sectors on a track by changing the rotational speed of the disk. Since the access time on a floppy disk is already large, the extra time to stabilize the rotational speed isn't significant.

Optical disks first appeared on the market in the form of audio compact disks (CDs). The same kind of disk stores computer data in CD-ROMs (Compact Disk Read-Only Memory). Optical disks store data in a reflective material encased in transparent plastic. The reflective material is etched with a series of *pits*. Reflective areas without pits are called *lands*. To read a disk, a CD player focuses a laser beam on the reflective material, and a photocell detects the changes in reflectance between the pits and the lands. Because the laser and the photocell don't need to be very close to the disk, there is no risk of a head crash and no need to enclose the disk in a dust-free chamber. Dust and small scratches on the surface of the disk don't usually interfere with the laser. If they do, error correction codes help the drive reconstruct the obscured data.

CD-ROMs, of course, are read-only devices. They can be written only once, either at the factory or by the user with a CD-ROM recorder. Rewritable magneto-optical disks are also available. These devices contain a material whose response to magnetic fields (coercivity) changes with moderate heating. To write data, a laser heats specific domains in the presence of a fixed magnetic field. The heated domains change their magnetic polarity and then "freeze" with this polarity when they cool off. The disk is read optically, like an ordinary CD. The variations in the magnetic polarity of the domains modulate the polarization of reflected laser light, and the photodetector sees these variations as changes in reflectance. A magneto-optical disk currently requires two passes to rewrite data: the first sets all the domains to one polarity, and the second sets specific domains to the opposite polarity in response to the modulated laser beam. The need for two-pass writes makes magneto-optical disks inherently slower to write than magnetic disks, which can overwrite data in a single pass.

The areal density of optical disks is very high. The CD-ROM format can store up to 650 MB on a disk 120 mm in diameter. The track density is 625 tracks/mm, and the linear density is 1200 bits/mm. Both figures are much higher than the typical densities for magnetic disks in the mid-1980s, when the CD format was introduced. For example, in 1985, an IBM 3380E disk drive had a track density of 54.6 tracks/mm and a bit density of 598 bits/mm. One reason for the high track density is that optical disk drives can focus a laser on a tiny area of the disk, and the optical servo mechanism that positions the beam on the track is very precise. Optical disks also waste little of their available linear density: the drives vary their rotational speed to access data at a constant linear speed. The original CD specification called for a rotational speed range of 200 to 500 RPM. The basic data transfer rate is about 150 KB/sec. CD-ROM readers in modern computers have much higher rotational speeds and transfer rates, but access times remain a problem. The CD format was designed primarily for audio recording, where the player usually reads the tracks sequentially. (In fact, CDs have spiral tracks, like vinyl audio records.) The rotational speed changes only slightly with each rotation to maintain a constant linear speed. In computer applications, however, seeking between widely separated tracks is common. These seeks require large changes in the disk's rotational speed, which takes time to stabilize. Also, the optical read/write mechanism is heavier than a disk arm, so it moves more slowly. As a result, seek times for optical disks are currently over 100 ms.

DVD (the letters stand for Digital Video Disk, Digital Versatile Disk, or nothing at all) is a newer optical disk format developed for consumer multimedia applications. The disks look like CDs, and they work essentially the same way. However, DVDs have about four times the areal density of CDs, with a maximum linear density of 2500 bits/mm and a track density of 1350 tracks/mm. More efficient encoding of data further improves capacity. DVDs can record data on both sides of two separate semireflective layers. The laser changes focus to discriminate between the layers. The basic transfer rate is almost 1.4 MB/sec. The capacity of a DVD depends on the number of layers and the number of sides. Single-side, single-layer DVDs can hold 4.7 GB (a gigabyte is 10^9 bytes in this case). Double-side, double-layer DVDs hold 17 GB. The ratio is not quite 4:1 because double-layer DVDs have a lower linear density. DVD access times are similar to those of CDs.

2.5 The Need for Parallelism

The fastest individual disk drives at the time of this writing can read and write data at about 20 MB/sec. This is far too slow for modern parallel computers, which need to access data at hundreds or thousands of megabytes per second. An obvious solution is to use parallel I/O, just as supercomputers have adopted parallel processing.

The main parallel I/O technique is disk striping (Figure 2.7). A computer writing a large quantity of data can split the data into pieces and write them simultaneously to separate disks in a disk array. Of course, in addition to multiple disks, the computer must have separate I/O channels to each disk and appropriate hardware and software to send data over all the channels simultaneously.

The data is generally divided into fixed-size blocks, and the blocks are distributed cyclically to the disks. The number of disks in this simple striping scheme is called the *stripe factor,* and the size of the blocks is the *stripe depth.* The stripe factor obviously determines the degree of parallelism and therefore the maximum aggregate transfer rate. The stripe depth can be as little as one bit or as much as several disk sectors. The appropriate choice depends on how the disk array will be used, as shown in Section 2.6.

In principle, a system could be built in this way that striped data over hundreds of disks and moved data at many gigabytes per second. The problem with a simple striping scheme is reliability. If a file is striped over multiple disks, the loss of

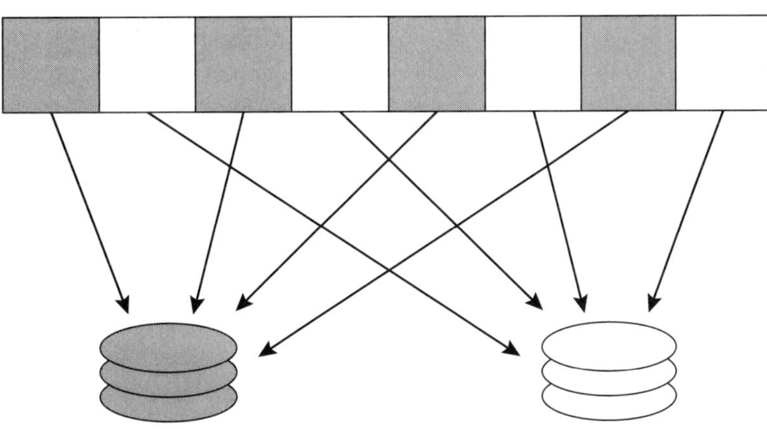

Figure 2.7 Disk striping sends alternating blocks of data in memory to separate disks in parallel. The size of the blocks is called the stripe depth, and the number of disks is the stripe factor.

even one disk could make the entire file useless, and the risk of losing a disk rises approximately in proportion to the number of disks. For large systems that store valuable data, this risk is too high.

2.6 RAID

To address the reliability problem in disk arrays and to improve I/O performance, a research group at the University of California, Berkeley, proposed redundant arrays of inexpensive disks (RAID) in 1988 [125]. "RAID" is now taken to stand for "redundant arrays of *independent* disks" because the gap between expensive, high performance disks and cheap, mass-produced disks has narrowed quite a bit since 1988. The largest RAID systems move data at more than 200 MB/sec and store over 1 TB.

The central idea in RAID is to replicate data over several disks so that no data will be lost if one disk fails. The original RAID paper described five strategies, called *RAID levels*, with different performance characteristics and different ways of replicating data. The levels are numbered one to five, but these numbers are only labels; they don't imply anything about how many disks a level uses or about differences in performance and reliability between levels. RAID has become an important area of storage research and development, and several new RAID levels have been introduced, including RAID 6, RAID 10, and RAID 53. Also, disk striping with no redundant storage is now called RAID 0. (Another common term is JBOD, short for "just a bunch of disks." It can mean either RAID 0 or a collection of disks that don't use striping.)

Except for RAID 0, all the RAID levels trade disk capacity for reliability, and the extra reliability makes parallelism a practical way to improve performance. Since disk capacity has become so cheap, trading it for reliability and performance is increasingly attractive. As a result, RAID technology has spread from large storage systems used in computer centers to compact units designed to work with desktop computers. The next few subsections describe the basic ideas of RAID technology, and later subsections present each of the major RAID levels in more detail.

2.6.1 Data Redundancy

The original RAID paper proposed three different techniques for storing data redundantly: mirroring, Hamming codes, and parity.

RAID 1 uses data mirroring. Mirrored systems replicate all data on two or more disks. If one disk fails, the data can be recovered from another. A standard RAID 1 configuration uses only two disks. Data could be mirrored on additional disks for added security, but this is not a common practice. Thus, disk mirroring usually stores one disk's worth of data on two disks, doubling capacity needed to store the data.

RAID 2 uses Hamming codes. Each group of data bits has several check bits appended to it, and these bits form Hamming code words. No two code words differ by only one bit, so if any bit is corrupted, the system can detect and correct the error. RAID 2 systems store each bit of a Hamming code word on a separate disk, so the stripe depth is one bit. If a disk fails, the system can reconstruct the missing bits using bits from the remaining disks. The number of extra disks required to store the check bits depends on the number of data bits in the code word. A word with four data bits requires three check bits, so seven drives would be needed. Four check bits can protect up to 11 data bits. If the system stored standard eight-bit data bytes, the extra capacity needed for redundancy would be 50%.

A simpler and more efficient way to protect data is parity checking. This technique relies on the properties of the exclusive-or (XOR) operator. XOR combines two input bits to produce one output bit as follows: if the two input bits are both zero or both one, the output bit is zero, but if the two input bits are different, the output bit is one. When applied to two collections of bits, such as a pair of bytes, XOR operates individually on corresponding pairs of bits. For example:

```
      01101010   (data byte 1)
XOR   11001001   (data byte 2)
--------------
      10100011   (parity byte)
```

The useful property of XOR for RAID systems is that it's reversible. Suppose the three bytes listed above were stored on separate disks, and the first disk, containing data byte 1, failed. This byte could be recovered by performing the XOR operation on the remaining two bytes:

```
      11001001   (data byte 2)
XOR   10100011   (parity byte)
--------------
      01101010   (recovered data byte 1)
```

Likewise, an entire block of parity bytes can back up two blocks of data bytes, as long as only one of the blocks needs to be recovered. In fact, a block of parity bytes can back up any number of data blocks, since the XOR operator works with any number of input bits. When multiple bits are combined with the XOR operator, the result is zero if the number of ones in the input is even, and the result is one if the number of ones is odd. For example:

```
    01101100  (data byte 1)
    10010110  (data byte 2)
    01111100  (data byte 3)
XOR 11010010  (data byte 4)
------------
    01010100  (parity byte)
```

As the number of data inputs increases, however, so does the risk that a second block will be corrupted before the first can be recovered, so large systems use more elaborate parity schemes. RAID levels 3, 4, and 5, and some of the newer RAID levels, all use parity checking. The differences among these levels are in how they store the parity data and in what kinds of I/O operations they handle best.

All these redundancy techniques incur some cost to compute the parity or store the redundant data. However, as long as the system is operating normally (that is, not reconstructing lost data), there is no extra cost to read data. Therefore, RAID systems usually read data faster than they write it.

2.6.2 Recovering Data

When a disk in a RAID system fails, there is sufficient information in the remaining disks to reproduce every byte of data on the missing disk. The system can continue to operate, completing every read and write request it receives. Eventually, the failed disk will need to be replaced; otherwise, the loss of a second disk would corrupt data. Once the disk is replaced, the system automatically reconstructs the lost data on the new disk while continuing to handle I/O requests (possibly with reduced performance). Some large RAID systems include *hot spares,* extra unused disks that are brought online automatically as soon as a failure is detected. Other systems support *hot swapping,* which allows someone to replace a failed disk while the storage system is running. *Warm swapping* requires the system to be taken offline but not powered down. *Cold swapping* requires the system to be powered off while the disk is replaced. As long as no more disks fail before the bad one is replaced, none of these systems will lose data, so they all offer high reliability. However, some applications also require high availability, meaning that the system rarely goes offline. High-availability systems usually have redundant power supplies and fans, as well as battery backup units.

2.6.3 Transfer Rates vs. Request Rates

Applications that move large blocks of data between primary and secondary storage need a high transfer rate, and disk striping helps meet this need. Other applications move relatively small pieces of data, but they issue many concurrent requests. Some scientific codes fall in the first category, while databases and other transaction-based systems fall in the second. Parallelism can help both kinds of applications in different ways. For applications that demand high transfer rates, all the disks should move data at the same time for each request. However, for applications with high request rates, it's better for each disk to work independently on a different request. These two requirements are obviously in conflict, so it's difficult to design a storage system that handles both high transfer rates and high request rates efficiently.

The choice of a stripe depth is especially important for systems with high request rates. It should be large enough that the data for a typical read request resides on only one disk. This keeps the other disks free to respond to other requests. On the other hand, if the stripe depth is too large, then separate requests for nearby data will require access to the same disk, reducing parallelism.

For high-transfer-rate applications, the stripe depth must be small enough to ensure that data for a typical request will be evenly distributed among all the disks.

2.6.4 The RAID Levels

As noted earlier, the original Berkeley paper described five levels, RAID 1 through RAID 5. The RAID Advisory Board, a trade group made up of RAID developers, vendors, and users, defines four additional levels: RAID 0, RAID 6, RAID 53, and RAID 0&1 (also known as RAID 10).

RAID 0

RAID 0 is another name for disk striping. It offers no redundancy, so the loss of a single disk will corrupt data. However, it is sometimes used in combination with other RAID levels to improve their performance. RAID 0 systems can support both high-transfer-rate and high-request-rate applications.

RAID 1

RAID 1 uses disk mirroring to back up data. For write operations, it stores each incoming block on two or more disks. (For the rest of this description, assume there are only two disks.) Usually, the writes can proceed in parallel, so the write transfer rate is about the same as it would be for a single disk. However, the access time for writes may be a little longer than it is for single disks. The write isn't complete until both disks have finished writing, and the completion time will depend on the longer latency of the two disks. The description of RAID 3 looks at this latency problem in more detail.

For reads, on the other hand, duplicating the data improves the access time. The system can issue each request it receives to the disk that is least busy at the moment. It can also improve the read transfer rate by retrieving alternate blocks from both disks in parallel, just as it would in RAID 0. Disk mirroring can be used for multiple disks, but unlike RAID 10 (see below), it does not use disk striping.

RAID 2

RAID 2 is the only RAID level that uses Hamming codes. As discussed above, this technique uses disk space less efficiently than parity-based methods, so it is rarely implemented. RAID 2 has many of the same performance characteristics as RAID 3.

RAID 3

RAID 3 uses parity-based data protection, and it is optimized for high transfer rates. Each incoming block of data is divided evenly into subblocks. The system XORs data bytes in these subblocks to form an additional subblock of parity bytes. All these subblocks are then written in parallel to the disks. If there are N disks, this is called $N + 1$ parity. Typically, N is around 4 or 5. Since disks have a fixed sector size and can only accept data in units of this size, RAID 3 requires blocks of at least N times the sector size for best performance. If the user writes less than this amount of data, the system must read some of the old subblocks before it computes the parity. (Either the subblocks to be replaced are "subtracted" out of the old parity subblock before the new ones are "added" in, or else the new subblocks are combined with the untouched old subblocks to form a new parity subblock.) Also, because RAID 3 accesses every disk in every I/O operation, it works poorly in applications with high request rates. To alleviate these problems, some RAID 3 systems treat small accesses differently from large ones, using techniques similar to RAID 5 when a request uses only a single sector.

Since RAID 3 accesses all the disks at once, the time to complete an operation will depend in part on the longest latency of any disk, just as it does for disk mirroring. However, since RAID 3 uses more than two disks, its latency problem is worse. For a single disk, $T_{\text{latency}} = 1/(2v_{\text{rotation}})$, since on average the desired sector is one-half rotation away from the head. For a request that accesses multiple disks, the latency accumulates: the desired sectors and the head position will on average be evenly spaced around a circle (Figure 2.8). The farthest sector among the N disks will on average be $N/(N + 1)$ of a rotation from its head, and this latency will delay the completion of the entire operation. Latency can accumulate even when all the disks are nominally identical because the spindles rotate at slightly different speeds. Fortunately, since RAID 3 is optimized for long transfers, the extra latency may not

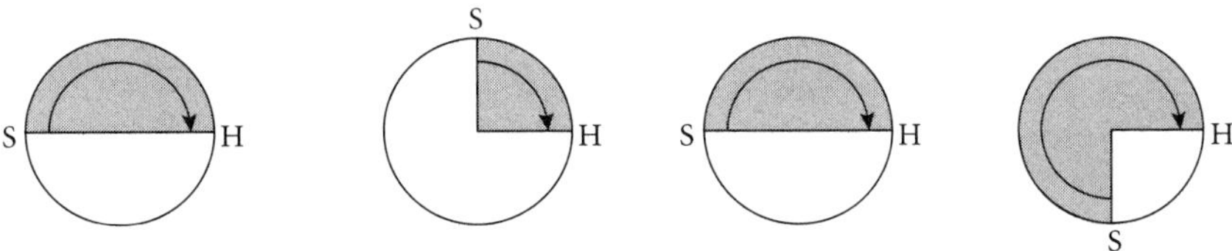

Figure 2.8 For a single disk (left), the position of a requested sector, marked S, is on average one-half rotation away from the head, marked H. For a collection of disks (three on right), the requested sectors will on average be evenly spaced around a circle with respect to their heads. The total latency will be the longest latency for all disks, the rightmost disk in this case.

add much to the total time of a typical operation. However, some RAID 3 systems eliminate latency accumulation by using circuitry that synchronizes the spindles with each other, so location of corresponding sectors remains fixed with respect to the heads on each disk.

RAID 4

RAID 4 is designed for high request rates. It is not widely used because RAID 5 does the same job better. Like RAID 3, it stores parity bytes for *N* disks on a separate parity disk, but instead of distributing every request over all the disks, it accesses disks individually. For read operations, it simply determines which disk holds the requested block and accesses only that disk. For write operations, RAID 4 must store the data bytes on the correct disk and also update the parity bytes, which reside on a dedicated parity disk. To update the parity bytes correctly, the system must have the data bytes from the block being overwritten as well as the data bytes from the new block. Therefore, a RAID 4 write consists of the following steps:

1. Retrieve the old data from the sector being overwritten.
2. Retrieve the parity block from the parity disk.
3. Extract the old data from the parity block using the XOR operation.
4. Add the new data to the parity block using the XOR operation.
5. Store the new data.
6. Store the new parity block.

Usually, the first two steps can be done in parallel, and step 5 can proceed in parallel with steps 3 and later. Nevertheless, write operations are significantly slower than read operations.

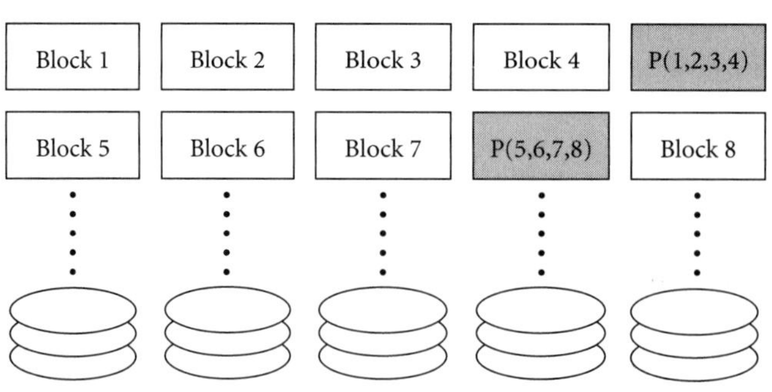

Figure 2.9 RAID 5 computes a block of parity data for each group of data blocks. The parity blocks for each group are stored on different disks so that no one disk participates in every write operation.

The problem with RAID 4 is that it stores all parity data on a single disk. Different write operations may store their data on different disks, but every write operation must read and then write the parity disk. Obviously, this disk is a bottleneck. RAID 5 corrects the problem.

RAID 5

RAID 5 eliminates the bottleneck in RAID 4 by storing parity blocks on different disks. The read and write operations are essentially the same for RAID 5 as they are for RAID 4, but parity blocks are distributed among the same disks that hold the data blocks (Figure 2.9). Every write operation still requires reading and writing two disks, but no single disk participates in every operation. Read operations require access only to the disk where the data is stored. These considerations make RAID 5 a good choice for systems with high request rates. However, because parity is updated separately each time a disk block is written, RAID 5 works poorly for applications that require high transfer rates for write operations. Systems can improve write transfer rates by caching parity and data blocks so they don't have to be reread as new data arrives.

RAID 6

RAID levels 3, 4, and 5 can tolerate the loss of only one disk without corrupting data. While the risk is relatively low that a second disk will fail in the time it takes to reconstruct the first one, some systems cannot tolerate this risk. In particular, very large RAID systems with many independent disks run a higher risk of data loss than smaller ones. RAID 6 is designed to reduce this risk. It is not a single technique like the other RAID levels, but rather a collection of techniques that allow a system to tolerate the loss of two disks without corrupting data.

One of these techniques, called $P + Q$ parity, is similar to RAID 5. However, it computes redundancy data using two different algorithms instead of one, and it stores the resulting parity blocks on different disks. One parity block is computed using the standard XOR operation; the other is computed with a different parity function. The functions must be different because if two disks fail, a single parity block won't contain enough information to reconstruct two missing data blocks. Like RAID 5, RAID 6 with $P + Q$ parity distributes parity data among several disks to avoid creating bottlenecks. However, since both parity blocks must be updated each time a data block is written, the cost of writes is even higher for RAID 6 than it is for RAID 5.

Another RAID 6 technique is two-dimensional parity (Figure 2.10). If $M \times N$ data disks are logically arranged in a two-dimensional array, the system can compute parity along each dimension and store it in $M + N$ dedicated parity disks. If two data disks fail, they will be in different rows, different columns, or both, so their data can be reconstructed from separate row or column parity disks. If two parity disks fail, they can be reconstructed from the original data. If one data and one parity disk fail, the data disk can be reconstructed from the parity disk along the other dimension, and the parity disk can be reconstructed from the good data. Two-dimensional parity requires a total of $MN + M + N$ disks, so it is less space-efficient than $P + Q$ parity. Its write performance also suffers because it writes two parity blocks for each data block. However, even though two-dimensional parity

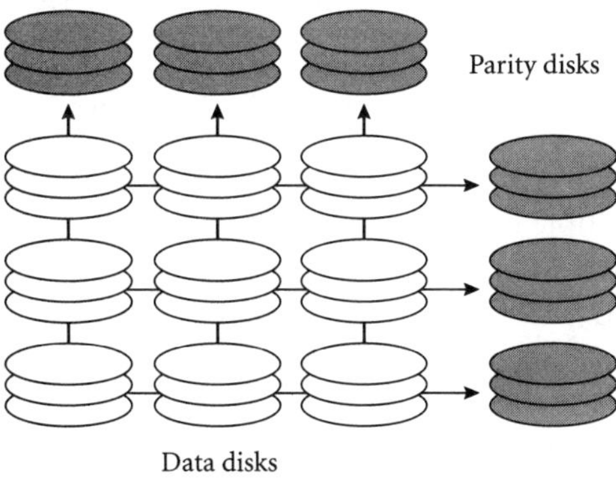

Figure 2.10 One RAID 6 strategy uses two-dimensional parity; parity is computed for each row and column and stored on a corresponding disk. RAID 6 can tolerate the loss of any two disks without corrupting data.

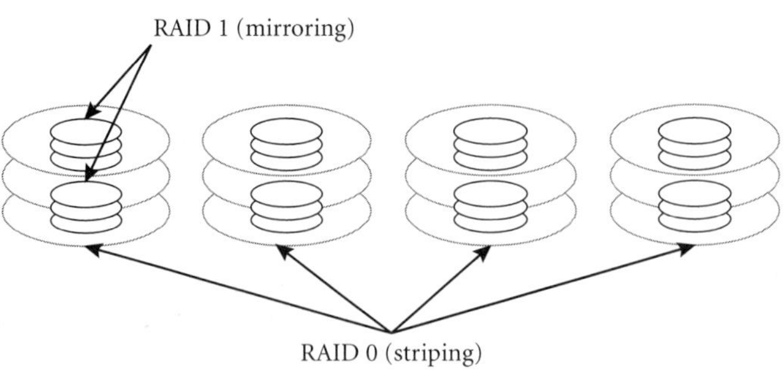

Figure 2.11 RAID 10 is a RAID 0 array of virtual disks, and each virtual disk is a RAID 1 system.

uses dedicated parity disks like RAID 4, it doesn't create a parity bottleneck. Different pairs of parity disks protect each data disk, so no disk participates in all writes.

RAID 10

RAID 10, also known as RAID 0&1, is a combination of striping and mirroring. Pairs of mirror disks act as virtual disks in a striped array (Figure 2.11). When the system is configured for high transfer rates, a block of data is distributed over all the virtual disks, and each mirrored pair stores two copies of the data. As in RAID 1, the mirrored pair can deliver better read performance than a single disk by load balancing and by reading alternate subblocks from different disks in parallel. In a high-request-rate configuration, a RAID 10 system assigns each block to a different virtual disk in the array. The usual considerations about selecting the best stripe depth apply.

The disadvantage of RAID 10 is that, like RAID 1, it doubles the capacity requirements compared to simple striping; that is, RAID 10 is a $2N$ redundancy system. The difference between RAID 1 and RAID 10 is that RAID 1 does not distribute individual files over multiple disks.

RAID 10 is implemented as an array of mirrored disks; each virtual disk in a RAID 0 array is a RAID 1 system. The inverse arrangement is not widely used. This would consist of two virtual disks mirroring each other, with each virtual disk configured as a RAID 0 array. Although its performance would be comparable to the first arrangement, its availability would not be as good. In the first arrangement, if one disk fails, the system will continue to run unless the failed disk's mirror also fails. In the second arrangement, the failure of one disk will render the entire virtual disk inoperative, so if *any* disk in the other virtual disk also fails, the entire system will be unavailable (although no data would be lost unless both failed disks held the same data). In other words, once one disk fails, the first arrangement can tolerate the failure of any one of $N-2$ other disks, while the second arrangement can tolerate the failure of any one of only $N/2-1$ other disks.

RAID 53

Like RAID 10, RAID 53 is a combination of two other RAID levels. Perhaps surprisingly, the other levels are 0 and 3, not 5 and 3. RAID 53 is a RAID 0 array of virtual disks. In this arrangement, each virtual disk is a RAID 3 array, consisting of at least three disks. (RAID 3 with only two disks would be essentially the same as RAID 1.) The outer RAID 0 array is generally configured for high request rates, while the inner RAID 3 arrays offer high transfer rates. Thus, RAID 53 is a compromise that tries to offer good overall performance. Since each RAID 3 array uses at most one-third of its capacity for data protection, RAID 53 uses disk space more efficiently than RAID 10. However, since each stripe requires its own parity disk, the system is not as space-efficient as pure RAID 3.

2.6.5 Comparing RAID Levels

Table 2.2 summarizes the RAID levels described here. Most commercial RAID systems can be configured for RAID levels 0, 1, 3, 5, and 10. Of these, RAID 5 is

RAID level	*Protection method*	*Space usage*	*Good at...*	*Poor at...*
0	none	N	performance	data protection
1	mirroring	$2N$	data protection, read performance	space efficiency
2	Hamming codes	$\approx 1.5N$	transfer rate	space efficiency, request rate
3	parity	$N+1$	transfer rate	request rate
4	parity	$N+1$	read request rate	write performance
5	parity	$N+1$	request rate	transfer rate
6	$P+Q$ or 2-dim	$N+2$ or $MN+M+N$	data protection	write performance
10	mirroring	$2N$	performance	space efficiency
53	parity	$N+$ stripe factor	balanced performance	

Table 2.2 *A summary of RAID levels. In the space usage column, N is the amount of nonredundant user data that a RAID system holds, expressed as a number of disks. An exception is RAID 6, where the capacity is MN.*

probably the most widely used. Once a system is configured, it typically can't be changed without erasing the resident data. System administrators must consider the common uses of the I/O system when choosing a RAID level and a stripe depth. Fortunately, the extensive use of caching and buffering has helped minimize the performance differences between RAID levels 3 and 5.

Systems with many disks often use one of the combination levels, such as RAID 53. These offer a good balance of request-rate and transfer-rate performance. The system administrator can often reserve some number of disks as hot spares in these systems as well, so their availability is usually very high.

RAID techniques have also been applied to tape systems. Data is streamed to multiple tape drives simultaneously, with redundancy data stored on some drives. Although RAIT systems are available from some vendors, they have not caught on as RAIDs have.

2.7 Interconnection Networks

An interconnection network moves data between a computer and a storage device or another computer. Interconnect technology is a branch of computer networking, but interconnects have special requirements that distinguish them from the local area networks (LANs) and wide area networks (WANs) that handle electronic mail, Web pages, and other traffic. Data moving between primary storage and secondary or tertiary storage often demands high transfer rates for large blocks of data. However, interconnects usually span short distances, and they don't require elaborate switching techniques because the set of communicating devices is often small and fixed. Interconnects are sometimes called system area (or storage area) networks (SANs).

This section begins by describing the features of interconnects that are important for high performance I/O. Then it looks at three common interconnects: SCSI, HIPPI, and Fibre Channel.

2.7.1 Topology and Connectivity

If an interconnect links only one computer with one storage device, the network can just be a single cable from one to the other. However, when more than two devices (or *nodes*) are involved, there are several ways to lay out the connections. The layout of a network is called its *topology*. Stars, rings, and chains are common topologies (Figure 2.12), and elaborate networks often use combinations of these patterns.

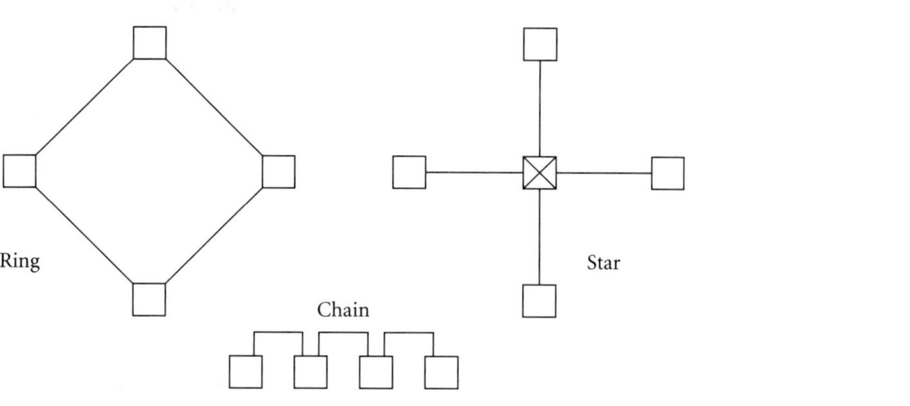

Figure 2.12 Common interconnect topologies are rings (loops), stars, and chains. The center of the star, called the *hub,* is a switch and not a computer or storage device.

However, not every interconnect permits every kind of topology. For example, a basic SCSI network can only be a chain.

A network's connectivity is closely related to its topology. An interconnect has point-to-point connectivity if it can move data between two devices without interfering with communication between any other two devices. If communication between one pair of devices blocks communication between other pairs, an interconnect has shared access connectivity. Every node in a shared access network can see every message that is sent, so the network needs an arbitration mechanism to prevent more than one node from sending messages at the same time. It also needs an addressing mechanism that tells nodes which messages are intended for them.

Star networks often use point-to-point connectivity, while chains are usually shared access. Rings (also called loops) are a hybrid: a message from a source node travels from node to node around the ring until it reaches its destination. Usually, no data travels along the return path from the destination back to the source. Many ring networks allow data to travel in both directions between each pair of nodes. This allows communication among all nodes to continue even if the connection between any two nodes breaks. Since rings need arbitration and addressing, they generally behave like shared access networks.

Point-to-point networks offer dedicated, high-bandwidth connections, and they allow multiple pairs of devices to communicate at the same time, so they work very well for high performance I/O. The center of the star in a point-to-point network is called the hub, and the connections between pairs of communicating nodes are managed by a crossbar switch at the hub. This device creates direct links between pairs of nodes for as long as they need to communicate. Crossbar switches are expensive, and increasing the number of nodes in a network may require upgrading or replacing the crossbar. Shared access networks don't require a crossbar, so they are often less expensive to build and upgrade than point-to-point networks. On the other hand, increasing the size of a point-to-point network increases its aggregate bandwidth, while adding a new device to a shared access network does not: the devices must contend for access to a fixed amount of bandwidth.

2.7.2 Interconnect Levels

Moving data over a network involves activity at many levels. The well-known Open Systems Interconnection (OSI) model of computer networking divides communication into seven layers, with the physical medium at the bottom and the user application at the top. Not all the layers apply to I/O interconnects, and many interconnects span layers. For simplicity, consider just three levels: the communication medium, the data transmission protocols, and the device commands. This division reflects a similar separation of functions in the design of interconnects over the past several years. This section will use the word "levels" to avoid confusion with OSI layers. The separation of levels is important because it allows engineers to develop these levels independently and to introduce new technology at one level without affecting the others.

Communication Media

Until the early 1990s, all interconnects used some form of copper cable to carry signals between devices. The maximum frequency at which bits can travel over a single wire (or pair of wires in some systems) is called the *signaling rate,* and it is usually stated in megahertz (MHz). The transfer rate is equal to the signaling rate times the number of bits moved per clock cycle. To reach the high transfer rates that storage devices need, copper interconnects use parallel wires rather than high signaling rates. A set of data lines may carry one, two, or four bytes in parallel, and control lines carry parity and flow control information. Some interconnect cables have 50 or 100 separate wires. This makes them somewhat bulky and difficult to handle. Moreover, the connectors on these cables must create good electrical contact that can support high signaling rates for each wire.

Some interconnects use one return wire for all the signal wires. These *single-ended* systems can use cables with relatively few wires, and they are inexpensive to build. However, they are susceptible to electrical interference, which causes errors in data transmission. The interference problem is especially troublesome for long cables and high signaling rates. *Double-ended* (or *differential*) systems use two wires for the signal line. Both wires carry the same electrical signal, but with opposite voltage. This arrangement allows the interconnect circuitry to cancel the noise. Copper interconnects with signaling rates of 10 MHz or more generally use differential signaling.

High speed parallel interconnects must also deal with bit skew. Slight differences in the length and electrical characteristics of each electrical path cause bits traveling in parallel to arrive at slightly different times. If the difference in arrival times is comparable to the signaling period, the data can be garbled. High speed parallel interconnects therefore require de-skew circuitry to compensate for the problem. Typically, the sender will periodically transmit a known bit pattern to the receiver, which will detect the pattern and adjust itself to the delays between the parallel bits.

Optical fiber solves many of the problems inherent in copper cables. A transparent fiber carries pulses of light rather than electrical signals. Fiber can support extremely high signaling rates and is immune to electrical noise. The high signaling rate allows one fiber to carry as much data as many copper wires, so there is no bit skew or bulky cable. In fact, the current limit on the signaling rate for optical fiber networks is not the fiber itself but the electronics that drive the light emitters and detectors. Techniques exist to overcome this limitation, such as wavelength-division multiplexing (WDM). However, WDM, which sends parallel data streams over a single fiber using different light wavelengths, is not currently used in interconnects.

The *extent* of an interconnect is the maximum length of a single link between nodes. For copper cables, the extent of an interconnect is usually tens of meters or less. For fiber, extents range from hundreds to thousands of meters. In large systems, interconnects with short extents can limit the options for laying out equipment in a machine room.

The many advantages of fiber have pushed it ahead of copper as the preferred medium for high speed connections. Fiber does require additional hardware to convert electrical signals to light pulses and back, but the cost of this hardware is declining, and many network protocols that were originally developed for parallel copper wiring have now been adapted to fiber.

Communication Protocols

Networks use a variety of protocols to package data in manageable pieces, move it to the correct destination, detect and correct transmission errors, and control the transfer rate. These are all important features of an interconnect design, but this discussion will focus on the protocols that affect the transfer rate. The protocols described here do not interpret the data. The bytes that form a request for a disk to read a block are treated no differently at this level from the bytes that the disk sends in return.

Whether a device is sending a single byte or many gigabytes, all protocols divide messages into units that are either a fixed size or no larger than a fixed size. These units will be called by the generic name "packets," although different protocols define this word in different ways. Most interconnects use several layers of protocols to implement error detection, routing, and so on. Each protocol defines its own packets, so a single byte in transit over an interconnect can be part of several packets at once, with each packet fitting into a larger one in a hierarchy of protocols.

The protocol that most affects transfer rate is flow control. If a device needs to send a large number of packets to a receiver, it cannot simply dump the packets into the network as fast as the network will accept them. The receiver may not be able to accept the data at full speed, or it may be too busy with another task to handle the incoming data. Flow control prevents a device from sending data over a network until the receiver is ready to accept it. In one simple form of flow control, the receiver sends a short acknowledgment message each time it has successfully read a packet from the network and is ready to accept another one. When the sender gets this acknowledgment, it sends the next packet. The problem with this protocol is that it incurs a delay equal to the round-trip transit time between the two devices for each packet. To see the effect of this delay, consider a protocol with a packet size of two bytes, a peak transfer rate of 10 MB/sec, and a round-trip delay of 300 nanoseconds. (These numbers correspond to Fast/Wide SCSI, which actually has a more sophisticated flow control protocol.) To send a 1 MB message, the simple flow control protocol would require 1 MB/(10 MB/sec) $=$ 0.1 second to move the data and $2^{20}/2$ packets $\times$ 300 ns $=$ 0.16 second for the flow control. The transfer rate has been reduced to 1 MB/0.26 second $=$ 3.8 MB/sec from a peak of 10 MB/sec. Clearly, high performance interconnects need a more efficient flow control mechanism.

One popular choice is credit-based flow control. In this protocol, the receiving device issues a series of credits to the sender. Each time the sender transmits a packet, it consumes a credit, and each time the receiver processes a packet and is ready to accept another, it issues another credit to the sender. This protocol allows the sender to continue transmitting data as long as it has credits, and if credits arrive as fast as the sender can transmit packets, the sender can transmit continuously. Of course, the receiver can only issue credits when it is prepared to accept data. If it issues, say, five credits, it must have enough buffer space and processing power to accept five packets in rapid succession. To permit the sender to transmit continuously, the receiver must initially issue enough credits (and therefore have enough buffer space) to keep the sender busy until the receiver's first acknowledgment credit arrives at the sender. This delay, from the time the sender transmits the first packet until it gets its first acknowledgment, will be at least as long as the transit time from the sender to the receiver and back. Among other things, this implies that the larger the distance between the sender and the receiver, the greater the transit time, and the more buffer space the receiver needs to support continuous transmission. High speed interconnects all support credit-based flow control or a similar protocol.

Device Commands

With a reliable, high speed link connecting it to the storage device in place, a computer needs a set of commands to request various operations. In early systems, devices from different manufacturers had proprietary command sets, but modern systems use standard commands. Some interconnects, like SCSI, include a command set as part of their definition. The commands in a set will depend on the kind of device they control. For example, SCSI defines command sets for magnetic disk drives, CD-ROMs, printers, scanners, and several other devices. HIPPI doesn't specify a command set, but HIPPI devices often use a command set called IPI-3 (Intelligent Peripheral Interface Level 3; the other two levels define an interconnect that is not widely used).

An important optimization that a command set can support is queuing. This technique allows a computer to send several requests to a peripheral without waiting for responses. A disk drive, for example, could accept requests to read several different blocks. It could then schedule the reads in an order that minimized the travel of the heads, which would greatly reduce the overall access time. Of course, the requesting device must be prepared to handle responses out of order, and the protocol must include a way to match responses with requests.

2.7.3 Interconnect Performance

From a user's point of view, the most important feature of an interconnect is its transfer rate. This value is stated in megabytes per second as with storage devices, or in megabits per second, abbreviated Mb/sec (with a lowercase *b*). Not every bit that an interconnect handles is user data; some bits transmitted are needed to support the various protocols. For parallel interfaces, specified transfer rates give the number of *user* bits or bytes per second. For serial interconnects, the raw communication link will support a higher transfer rate than the available user data rate. The higher rate includes the bits used for the protocols.

Ideally, an interconnect should move data as fast as the storage device or the computer can handle it. However, some modern storage devices, like large RAID systems, can move data faster than any available interconnect. For these situations, it is often possible to use two or more parallel links between the device and the computer. Of course, this requires both hardware and software support at each end. In particular, many computers cannot transfer data over a network interface at very high rates. Their internal bus may transfer data between memory and CPUs at gigabytes per second, but the network interface card is often connected to an I/O bus limited to 100 MB/sec or less. Moreover, many interconnects require the operating system to participate actively in a data transfer, moving bytes between the network hardware and memory. This software may be too slow to service a high speed interconnect at its maximum rate. Recent interconnect strategies address this problem using O/S bypass techniques, described below.

Interconnect performance is a function of latency as well as bandwidth. The latency for an interconnect includes the time needed to set up a transfer and move the first byte. This definition is different from the definition of latency given in connection with disk drives. Here, latency is analogous to disk access time. Latencies vary among different interconnect technologies and according to the number of devices on the network and the physical separation between them. In most cases, the interconnect latency is a microsecond or less, negligible compared to the access time of the storage device. (However, as noted above, the latency can strongly influence the transfer rate if the interconnect uses an inefficient flow control protocol.)

When a packet arrives at a computer, how it is handled depends on the interconnect protocol, the computer hardware, and the operating system. In early I/O systems, an arriving byte would either trigger an interrupt or wait for the operating system to poll an I/O register. In either case, the operating system would move the data from the register where the data arrived to the buffer location where the user wanted it stored (or possibly to an intermediate buffer with the operating system). This intimate involvement of the operating system with I/O operations was relatively slow, and it diverted the operating system and CPU from other work. An early solution to this problem is direct memory access (DMA). DMA hardware moves data directly from the I/O channel to memory (or vice versa) without involving the CPU or operating system. DMA has been used for many years in simple desktop computers. Modern systems that use DMA must contend with a few problems: The DMA hardware must ensure that data moved to or from main memory remains consistent with data in the cache. Also, the operating system must ensure that the virtual memory pages that are the source or destination of a transfer are mapped to physical memory when the transfer takes place. (See Section 7.1.1 for a discussion of virtual memory.)

A newer version of DMA is called *O/S bypass.* O/S bypass coordinates data movement in advance with the operating system to guarantee that the virtual page where data will be stored is "pinned" to physical memory. Pinned memory cannot be swapped out, so there is no risk of a page fault when data arrives over the network. The result is that data can move directly from the interconnect to user memory without involving the operating system.

The next sections look at some common interconnection networks. Several years may pass between the time a standard is publicized in draft form and the time a standards organization adopts it. Products based on draft versions of the standard often appear on the market before the standard is formally adopted, so the following descriptions give only approximate dates for these standards.

2.7.4 SCSI

The Small Computer System Interface (SCSI) was developed in the 1980s to connect high speed peripheral devices to desktop computers. Over the years, many variations of SCSI have emerged, and its bandwidth has increased steadily. SCSI is a shared-medium network that uses parallel copper cables in a chain topology. Both single-ended and double-ended versions are available. Single-ended SCSI has an extent between nodes of 6 meters; double-ended SCSI has an extent of 25 meters. The two systems are incompatible; single-ended and double-ended devices cannot be connected in the same network.

The basic SCSI standard uses eight parallel data lines and runs at a maximum signaling rate of 5 MHz, so its maximum transfer rate is 5 MB/sec. Several variations improve this rate. Fast SCSI runs at 10 MHz instead of 5 MHz. Wide SCSI uses a 16-bit or 32-bit data path instead of the basic 8-bit path. Fast/Wide SCSI therefore has a maximum rate of 20 MB/sec or 40 MB/sec; the latter version is sometimes called Ultra SCSI. Modern SCSI hardware supports synchronous and asynchronous flow control. Asynchronous flow control requires an acknowledgment after each packet. Synchronous flow control allows the sender to transmit several packets before receiving its first acknowledgment. If this acknowledgment doesn't arrive within a certain time interval, the sender stops transmitting until it receives an acknowledgment message.

The original SCSI standard (now called SCSI-1) appeared in the early 1980s and was based on earlier vendor-specific interfaces. SCSI-1 specified the communication medium, the signaling protocols, and several command sets in a single standard. The command set was unique for its time because it hid many of the details of a device from the computer that controlled it. For example, SCSI identifies disk blocks by sequential numbers instead of requiring the computer to request a specific sector, track, and head. While this abstraction and commonality made it much easier for computers to control many kinds of disk drives, it also eliminated certain opportunities for the operating system to optimize requests.

SCSI-2 was developed in the late 1980s and early 1990s. It introduced Fast and Wide SCSI with their higher data rates, as well as double-ended interfaces, synchronous flow control, and a larger command set. SCSI-2 also closed some loopholes in SCSI-1 that prevented supposedly compatible devices from working together.

SCSI-3 was introduced in the mid-1990s. Its most important feature is the separation of the interconnect levels. The standard makes it easier to use a different communication medium or a different command set with the basic SCSI protocols. The protocols themselves are more efficient, allowing higher transfer rates.

2.7.5 HIPPI-800

HIPPI (High Performance Parallel Interface) was developed in the late 1980s to offer the highest possible transfer rate between pairs of high performance computers or between computers and peripherals. Its peak transfer rate of 100 MB/sec was selected in part because it allows a visualization system to transmit video at full size (1024 × 1024 pixels per frame), in full color (24 bits or 3 bytes per pixel), and at full speed (30 frames per second). Multiplying these requirements yields a data rate of 90 MB/sec, just within the capabilities of HIPPI. Since 100 MB/sec is equal to 800 Mb/sec, the original HIPPI standard is also called HIPPI-800.

HIPPI is a point-to-point interconnect, so networks of more than two devices must use a crossbar switch. Multiple switches can be linked to increase the end-to-end extent of a HIPPI network. HIPPI-800 moves data over a 100-conductor copper cable, which consists of 50 differential pairs. It has a maximum extent of 25 meters between nodes, and data moves in parallel 32 bits at a time. (The remaining pairs of wires are used for flow control and other protocols.) The signaling rate is therefore 25 MHz. A revision of HIPPI called HIPPI-1600 uses two cables to double the data width to 64 bits, increasing the maximum transfer rate to 200 MB/sec.

The HIPPI protocol is quite simple. It supports credit-based transfers, and it is optimized for large data blocks. Unfortunately, the simple protocol and the large transfer sizes cause problems in some circumstances. If a large transfer is under way, neither the source nor the destination can handle any other messages. This blocking feature can be useful because the communicating devices are guaranteed the full interconnect bandwidth for as long as they need it. However, in a multiprocessing environment, a single job can prevent any other job on the same machine from using a shared HIPPI connection.

The HIPPI-800 signaling protocol has been implemented over a serial optical link, and the resulting interconnect is called Serial HIPPI. The optical fiber allows much longer extents, up to 300 meters or 10 kilometers, depending on the type of fiber used. The fiber cables are easier to manage than copper ones. Except for the superior extent of Serial HIPPI, the two systems appear the same to the user.

HIPPI does not specify a command set. However, many HIPPI storage devices support a command set called IPI-3, the Intelligent Peripheral Interface Level 3. Like the modern SCSI command set, IPI-3 supports command queuing to allow storage devices to optimize access sequences.

2.7.6 GSN (HIPPI-6400)

The HIPPI standard was redesigned in the late 1990s to increase the transfer rate to 6400 Mb/sec per direction. Originally called HIPPI-6400, the standard is also known as SuperHIPPI or GSN (Gigabyte System Network). GSN solves HIPPI-800's blocking problem by using a somewhat more complicated protocol. Instead of a single point-to-point channel, each GSN connection has four virtual channels. Each channel sends 32-byte "micropackets" that time-share the physical link. One of the channels, called VC0, is reserved for control messages; its packets take priority over all others. Two data channels, VC1 and VC2, carry small- to medium-size messages, and VC3 carries very large messages. The VC3 channel also implements an O/S bypass protocol called scheduled transfers, allowing high transfer rates for large messages.

GSN can use parallel copper cables with 23 differential pairs of wires. On these cables, it sends only 16 bits in parallel instead of the 32 bits that HIPPI-800 uses. The maximum extent of the copper cable is 50 meters. GSN also specifies a parallel fiber interconnect that uses 12 fibers to transmit data with four-bit parallelism. The standard specifies a parallel fiber link because the high signaling rates necessary for a serial link are not yet practical. The maximum extent of the fiber link is initially specified at 250 meters, and the standard anticipates a kilometer extent in the future.

The developers of the GSN standard are working on ways to support the higher-level protocols of HIPPI-800 and HIPPI-1600, and to multiplex several low speed HIPPI channels over a single GSN channel. However, the cables of the earlier HIPPI interconnects cannot be connected directly to GSN hardware.

2.7.7 Fibre Channel

When fiber optic networking started to become practical, engineers realized they could develop a high performance interconnection network that would replace several copper-based interconnect standards. Fibre Channel development began in the late 1980s. Its goal was to produce an interconnect standard that would support high speed data transfer between various types of computers and peripheral devices. Because its designers wanted a system that would work in many applications, Fibre Channel became a collection of carefully segregated but related standards. These standards cover various levels of the network hierarchy. The bottom level defines several physical connection media (including both copper and fiber cables) with maximum user data rates from 12.5 MB/sec to 100 MB/sec. Higher levels define various encoding, transmission, and flow control protocols. Although some of these protocols are mandatory in a Fibre Channel network, others are designed for specific applications, and engineers can choose the ones that best meet their needs. Still-higher levels of Fibre Channel define how to implement HIPPI-800, SCSI, and other protocols on top of Fibre Channel.

Fibre Channel also defines multiple topologies. Probably the most widely used is Fibre Channel Arbitrated Loop (FC-AL). This is a ring network intended for local area networks and system area networks. The variety of Fibre Channel protocols and media makes it usable in many different applications, but this range of options has also caused compatibility problems. Since Fibre Channel products need not support every protocol, system integrators must choose components carefully. SCSI has suffered from the same problem, although new versions of the standard have tightened up certain specifications to make products interoperate better.

2.7.8 Message Passing Networks

Another form of interconnect used in parallel computers is the internal message passing network that connects the compute nodes with each other and often with the I/O nodes. (See Section 3.3 for information on parallel computer I/O architectures.) Like other interconnects, message passing networks are designed for high bandwidth and low latency. For most systems, the maximum extent is a secondary consideration. These networks are designed to allow many nodes to communicate with each other simultaneously, so they use switching rather than a shared medium, and they provide redundant paths between nodes. Message passing networks often take advantage of specific architectural features of the nodes and the operating system to improve performance, and they may be designed to perform certain common operations, such as broadcasting messages, very efficiently. Because internal networks are among the major features that distinguish different vendors' parallel systems from each other, they often use proprietary designs. However, some off-the-shelf networks (such as Myrinet) have become available for use in workstation cluster parallel computers.

2.7.9 Other Interconnect Technologies

The move to separate interconnect layers allows new networking media to replace old media without requiring new software at higher layers. New networks with high bandwidth, low latency, and long extents are eliminating some differences between interconnects and other networks. One result is that network-attached storage devices, discussed in the next section, are becoming more practical.

In the past, network technologies like ATM, FDDI, and Gigabit Ethernet have been promoted as universal media that would replace many existing networks. None has succeeded so far, and it is impossible to predict which emerging networks will take hold. At present, HIPPI is widely used for high-bandwidth SANs, and SCSI is common for other applications.

2.8 Emerging Technologies

This section looks at some promising new developments in storage technology.

2.8.1 Network-Attached Storage Devices

Before networks became pervasive, most computers had one or more disk drives that belonged exclusively to them. One computer could not read or write another's secondary storage. Now, many desktop computers and most large systems have some kind of shared file system that multiple computers can access directly. Chapter 3 describes the software structure of these shared file systems, but it's appropriate here to mention some hardware technology that makes shared file systems more efficient.

The most common way for multiple computers to access a shared storage device is through a file server, a computer that acts as a gateway to the storage device (Figure 2.13a). The file server accepts requests from other computers on the network to access data stored on its disks. One server can manage many disks, but each request must go through the server. Part of the server's job is to authenticate requests and to ensure that users have permission to access the requested files. The file server can also cache blocks of data in primary storage to improve performance. However, because all the requests and all the data move through the server, the server can become a bottleneck when I/O traffic is heavy.

One way to relieve this bottleneck is to connect the disks directly to the network and bypass the server for some operations. The file server still accepts and

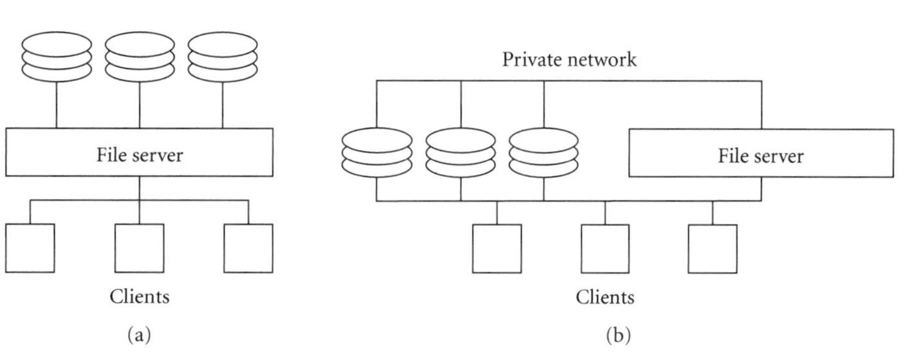

Figure 2.13 A file server architecture uses a dedicated computer to process requests from clients to read or write stored data (a). Data must travel through the file server. In a network-attached storage device (NASD) architecture, the disks are attached directly to the same network as the clients, so data can bypass the file server (b).

authenticates requests, but instead of mediating the data transfer, the file server simply instructs the disks to read or write data directly over the network. This type of storage architecture requires an intelligent peripheral called a *network-attached storage device* (NASD). (One research group working in this area uses the acronym NASD to stand for "network-attached secure disk.") An NASD system offers two important performance advantages. First, once the file server initiates the data transfer between the storage device and the client computer, its work on that transfer is done, so the server is free to handle other requests. In contrast, a traditional file server remains involved in a transfer until every byte has been moved. The second advantage of NASD is that the server is no longer a bottleneck for the data transfer. Multiple disks can move data over the network at the same time, as long as the network has enough bandwidth.

Because network-attached storage devices don't have the server to authenticate requests and protect the files from accidental or intentional corruption, systems that use them must take steps to maintain the integrity of the data. One approach to this problem is to have the server screen all requests and send commands to the storage devices over a secure, private network (Figure 2.13b). Since only the server and storage devices are connected to this secondary network, only the server can control the disks. To further protect the data, the system can encrypt data that moves over the public network between the storage devices and the client computers.

A second security technique does not require a private network. The server again receives requests from clients, and when a request is accepted, the server issues cryptographic keys to the client and the storage devices. These keys allow the client and the storage devices to communicate both commands and data securely.

The amount of intelligence that an NASD requires depends on how much of the server's functionality it takes on. At a minimum, the storage device must be able to communicate using standard network protocols, but this capability is common in modern disk drives. More sophisticated systems require the storage device to encrypt and decrypt data or to participate in key-exchange protocols. Research systems simulate intelligent storage devices by attaching one or more disk drives to an inexpensive computer with a network interface. If NASD techniques prove viable, disk manufacturers should have no trouble incorporating the necessary intelligence directly into their commercial products.

The NASD model is especially attractive for computer centers in which multiple large systems need to share access to data. If each system used its own disks, generating a file on one system and reading it on another would require the user to move the file between the systems. With shared network-attached storage devices, files would not need to be copied between machines. Of course, distributed file systems such as NFS and DFS (described in Section 3.2) also avoid this extra copy, but using NASD instead of a file server in the underlying hardware architecture could greatly improve performance. Because an NASD architecture can coordinate access to multiple storage devices connected to the network, it also offers a more natural model for file striping than server-based systems.

2.8.2 Holographic Storage

Current storage devices record data at or near the surface of their media, and most storage devices (tape is an exception) read and write these two-dimensional media only one bit at a time. Holographic media store data throughout the volume of a material. The basic unit of data transfer is a large two-dimensional array of bits called a *page.* Imagine a page as a monochrome image on a computer screen. The screen in this case is a spatial light modulator (SLM), which emits coherent, monochromatic light from its illuminated pixels. Another planar wave of laser light called a *reference beam* intersects the light from the SLM at an angle. The interaction of the light waves from the reference beam and the image create a distinctive pattern of light and dark regions in space called *interference fringes.* The details of these fringes depend on the pattern of illuminated bits in the page and the angle of the reference beam. The storage device produces these fringes within a volume of translucent, light-sensitive material. The material records the light and dark patterns much as photographic film does, but in three dimensions (Figure 2.14).

To read data out of the holographic medium, the device aims the reference beam at the material with the SLM turned off. The light and dark patterns in the material scatter the reference beam in a way that reconstructs an accurate image of the SLM on the other side of the material. A digital camera sees this image and decodes the bit pattern to reproduce the original data.

The same holographic material can record many different pages if the angle is varied between the reference beam and the light from the SLM. To retrieve a particular page, the reference beam is set to the appropriate angle.

Holographic storage systems have several interesting features. Perhaps the most important is their high data rate. Prototype systems have used pages of 1024 × 1024 bits, so each reference angle reads or writes 1 Mb of data, truly massive parallelism. Since the laser angle can be changed quickly, the readout rate is limited only by the speed at which the digital camera gathers and decodes the data. If the camera can read an image in 1 millisecond, the data rate is about 1 Gb/sec, comparable to a large RAID system. Writes take longer, however, because the holographic material needs time to record the image of the interference fringes. The storage density of the medium is limited by the minimum difference between reference angles needed to differentiate the interference patterns for separate pages.

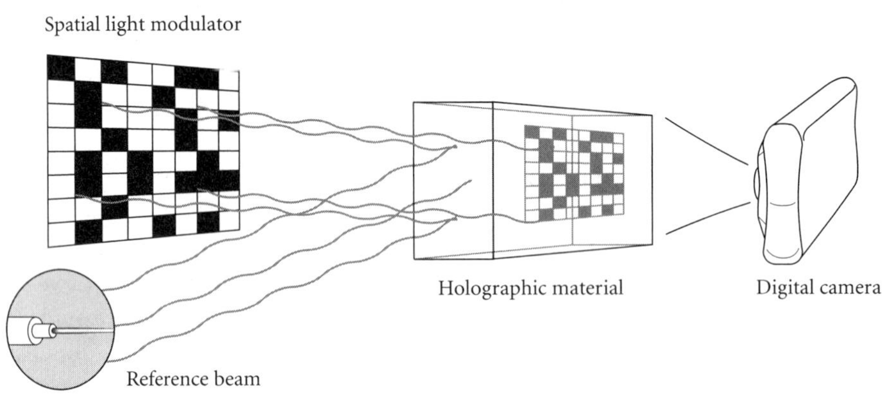

Figure 2.14 A holographic storage device records the image of a two-dimensional array of pixels projected from a spatial light modulator (SLM). The interference patterns produced by the light from the SLM interacting with a reference beam are recorded in a holographic material. To retrieve data, the reference beam shines into the holographic material with the SLM shut off. A digital camera sees an image of pixels from the SLM and decodes these as binary data.

Another interesting feature of holographic storage is that it can perform associative searches in parallel. These are searches that try to find a stored page whose bit pattern matches a certain "input page" as closely as possible. With the reference beam turned off, the SLM can illuminate the holographic material with an image of the input page. The material will then emit a number of *images* of reference beams at different angles. The brightness at each angle will be proportional to the correlation of the input page to the page stored with the reference beam at that angle. A sensor can detect which angles have the strongest correlations, and the storage device can then retrieve the pages for those reference angles.

The SLM and the camera are both expensive components, and their cost is independent of the amount of holographic material in a storage device. For that reason, the first practical holographic systems are likely to be jukebox-style machines that mount blocks of storage material in the read/write mechanism on demand, much as a tape robot does. This will make them most suitable for tertiary storage, despite their high data transfer rate and low latency.

Other designs for holographic storage systems offer less parallelism but simpler read/write hardware. One proposed design uses a smaller SLM and detector, and it stores data on a rotating disk like a CD or DVD. Unlike an ordinary optical disk, though, each location on a holographic disk would store multiple bits of data. Yet another design combines the SLM with the detector to produce a relatively simple, compact system.

2.8.3 InfiniBand

The InfiniBand architecture [77] is a proposed new standard for interconnects. It is the result of a merger between two formerly competing standards proposals, System I/O and Next Generation I/O. InfiniBand will connect memory in computers directly with storage devices and other peripherals. It will take the place of both the standard system bus and the system area network. A DMA engine will move data directly between memory to the network. The proposed standard calls for links of 1, 4, or 12 lines with data moving at 250 MB/sec in each direction on each line; thus, the maximum bidirectional transfer rates will range from 500 MB/sec to 6 GB/sec. Both copper and fiber media will be supported, and the network will use switching rather than shared access.

Many computer and network vendors support the InfiniBand standards effort, and the InfiniBand Trade Association expects the first commercial devices to be available in 2001.

2.9 Summary

This chapter has introduced a variety of I/O hardware and terminology. Storage devices, such as disk drives and tape drives, are characterized by their capacity, access time, and transfer rate, among other parameters. Fundamental design features of these devices make some types of operations, such as small accesses and random access, inherently inefficient. Striping can improve capacity, access time, and transfer rate, but the failure of a single device can corrupt files that are distributed over multiple devices. RAID techniques alleviate this problem, and a variety of RAID levels have been developed to optimize certain I/O characteristics at the expense of others.

Interconnection networks move data between storage devices and main memory. The key parameters of interconnects are their latency, their bandwidth, and their maximum extent. Shared access network topologies are generally more economical than point-to-point networks, but they can become saturated with traffic as more devices are connected.

New developments in I/O hardware include network-attached storage devices, which offer an attractive architecture for shared parallel data storage; holographic devices, which may improve capacity and transfer rates; and the InfiniBand interconnect standard, which could potentially improve interconnect latency and bandwidth.

2.10 Further Reading

Disk design is a complex topic, drawing technology from electrical and mechanical engineering, material science, physics, mathematics, and other disciplines. Two good references on the subject are Mee and Daniel's *Magnetic Storage Handbook* [104] and Ashar's *Magnetic Disk Drive Technology* [7]. Both are detailed, technical works. Mee and Daniel cover disk and tape storage systems, as well as video and audio recording. Ashar focuses exclusively on disks, and several chapters are quite accessible to the nonspecialist. A shorter technical discussion of disk technology [139] appeared in an issue of *Computer* devoted to I/O. Optical disk technology is covered in *The CD-ROM Handbook* [114], but the discussion is not very detailed. Two useful Web sites have information on the DVD format [53, 157].

The *Winn L. Rosch Hardware Bible* [137] is a comprehensive description of the technology used in personal computers. It is aimed at the nonspecialist, and much of its information on storage technology applies to large systems as well as desktop machines. Toigo's *Holy Grail of Data Storage Management* [166] covers many of the topics described in this chapter, with a focus on large storage systems. It is aimed at system administrators and planners. Ranade's 1991 book on mass storage systems [134] also has some useful information, though some of the material is out of date.

The RAIDbook [102] presents RAID technology thoroughly and clearly. It is published by the RAID Advisory Board.

Many books cover computer networks, but relatively few focus on interconnect technologies like SCSI, HIPPI, and Fibre Channel. Some manufacturers of network equipment have produced helpful introductory guides [152, 44, 43, 115]. Hoffman [71] published an early description of HIPPI-6400, outlining its differences from HIPPI-800. The High Performance Networking Forum has a Web site on HIPPI (mainly GSN) at *www.hnf.org,* and the Fibre Channel Association has a site at *www.fibrechannel.com.* Steenkiste [151] discusses network interface issues in the issue of *Computer* mentioned above. Other networking references consulted for this chapter include Jain [80], Sheldon [144], Tolmie and Flanagan [167], and Van Praag [169].

Gibson et al. describe architectures for network-attached storage devices in two papers [58, 57], and more information appears at the Web site of the National Storage Industry Consortium, *www.nsic.org.* An excellent introduction to holographic storage technology appeared in the February 1998 issue of *Computer* [133].

Chapter Three
File Systems

Most storage devices have no notion of files, directories, or the other familiar abstractions of data storage; they simply store and retrieve blocks of data. A *file system* is the software that creates these abstractions, including not only files and directories but also access permissions, file pointers, file descriptors, and so on. File systems have other duties as well:

- Moving data efficiently between memory and storage devices
- Coordinating concurrent access by multiple processes to the same file
- Allocating data blocks on storage devices to specific files, and reclaiming those blocks when files are deleted
- Recovering as much data as possible if the file system becomes corrupted

All modern file systems handle these tasks, whether they run on parallel or sequential computers. A parallel file system is especially concerned with efficient data transfer and coordinating concurrent file access. This chapter begins by describing how file systems organize blocks of data into files and directories. It then looks at buffering and caching techniques and the problem of concurrent access. Next, it describes distributed file systems, such as NFS, AFS, and DFS, and shows how these systems differ from the parallel file systems found on shared memory and distributed memory computers. After examining some of the unique problems in parallel file system design, the chapter reviews the designs of several commercial and research parallel file systems to see how they address these problems. Chapter 4 will further explore how some parallel file systems attempt to optimize the most common access patterns.

This chapter and the remaining chapters focus on I/O between primary and secondary storage. Moving data between memory and disk presents the most pressing I/O problems, and the majority of I/O research has been directed at these problems. However, Section 3.5.5 will describe some of the techniques that involve tertiary storage.

3.1 File System Operation

To see how file systems work, it's helpful to review the standard view of files that they present to programs and users. For readers who are experienced Unix programmers, the rules that define this view will seem like second nature and hardly worth repeating. However, parallel file systems often bend or break some of these rules to improve efficiency. To understand how the rules may be broken, it's important to review what they are.

3.1.1 The Unix File Access Model

In the file systems that Unix-like operating systems use, a file is a sequence of bytes numbered from zero to $N - 1$, where N is the (logical) size of the file in bytes. The file assigns no special meaning to these bytes; it's up to an application program to interpret the bytes as numbers, letters, machine instructions, and so on, and to fit the data into a higher-level structure. When a program opens a file, the file system establishes a file pointer. This pointer is an integer that indexes a location in the file, the point at which the next byte will be read or written. Initially, the file system sets this pointer to byte location zero. When a program reads or writes data, the file system automatically advances the pointer by the amount of data that was accessed. If a program reads every byte in the file (or if the file is initially empty), the file pointer will contain the value N, which is the size of the file. Since the last valid byte resides at $N - 1$, any attempt to read data at location N or greater will fail, and the file pointer will not be advanced. On the other hand, attempts to *write* data at location N or greater will succeed (as long as the storage device has enough space), and the file system will reset the size of the file to equal the new location of the file pointer after the write operation has finished.

A program can change the file pointer without accessing any data by issuing a `seek` call. A `seek` can set the file pointer to any nonnegative value, even a value greater than the size of the file. Attempts to read a file when the pointer is set beyond the end of the file will fail, but writes will succeed. In the latter case, the file will contain a "hole" between the previous end of the file and the first byte written at the new file pointer location (Figure 3.1). Reading data in this hole is legal, and most modern file systems will return zeros for file locations that lie in holes. The size of a file with holes is taken to be one plus the index of the last valid byte. A program can create a file whose apparent size is one million bytes by opening a new file, seeking to location 999,999, and writing a single byte. However, the file system will not necessarily allocate storage for one million bytes.

A program can open one file several times, and multiple processes can open a file concurrently. Each instance of the open file will have its own "file descriptor"

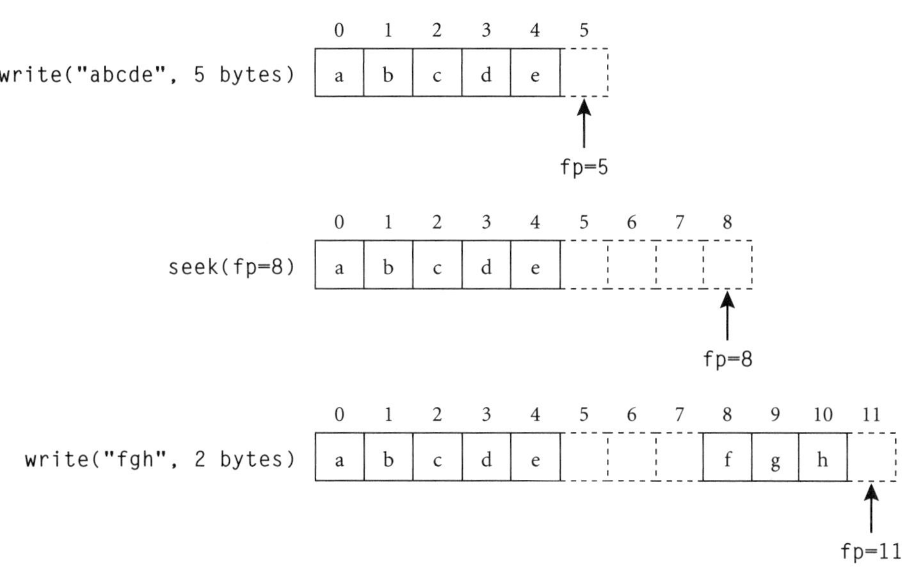

Figure 3.1 Unix-style file pointers index the *next* byte to be accessed by a read or write request. After the first five-byte write (top), the file pointer (labeled "`fp`") points to location 5 in the file. A `seek` request (center) moves the file pointer to location 8 but does not access any data. Writing three more bytes (bottom) leaves the file pointer at location 11 and creates a three-byte "hole" in the file at locations 5 through 7.

and its own file pointer. A file descriptor is an integer that indexes the file system's internal list of open files. The file system updates different file pointers for the same file independently of each other.

Multiple processes can access the same file at the same time. As long as the accesses are all read operations, there will be no conflicts. However, if two or more processes write to the file at the same time, or if one process writes while another process is reading, the file system has to guarantee that the results make sense. If the concurrent accesses involve different parts of the file, there is no problem. The difficulty arises if the accesses overlap. Consider the case of two processes writing different sequences of bytes to the same locations in the file at about the same time (Figure 3.2). What data will end up in the file? Most Unix file systems guarantee *sequential consistency;* that is, they guarantee that the result will be as if the two write operations happened in a specific order. Either the first sequence of bytes will be written or the second sequence will be written (and it's unpredictable which sequence will prevail), but in no event will bytes from the first sequence be intermixed with bytes from the second sequence. It's relatively easy for a file system to make this guarantee when the conflicting accesses happen on a single (time-shared)

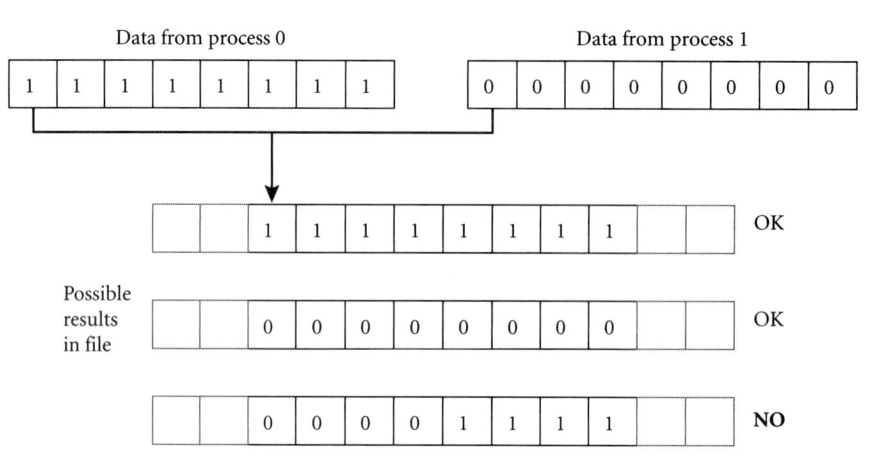

Figure 3.2 If two processes write different data to the same location in a file at about the same time, Unix semantics allow data from either process to end up in the file, but the result cannot be a combination of data from both processes.

CPU with a single disk drive, but in parallel and distributed file systems, sequential consistency is much harder to guarantee, for reasons discussed below.

3.1.2 Turning Blocks into Files

As noted in Chapter 2, disk drives read and write data in fixed-size units. File systems allocate space in blocks, which consist of a fixed number of contiguous disk sectors. To create a file, the file system selects one or more unused blocks on the disk that will hold the data. The file system must keep track of which blocks are unused, and many file systems try to allocate nearby blocks on a disk to the same file. This technique minimizes the access times as the disk reads or writes sequences of blocks. For example, some Unix implementations organize disk blocks into cylinder groups. These groups consist of one or more adjacent cylinders on a drive. For small files, the system attempts to allocate all the blocks in the same cylinder group in order to minimize the movement of the disk heads when the file is accessed. For large files, the system allocates blocks in several cylinder groups, but it tries to keep each section of the file in the same group, again minimizing head movement.

Another way that file systems (and some disk drives) minimize head movement is to manipulate the order in which they carry out requests to read or write specific blocks. A busy I/O system may have pending requests for blocks that are scattered over many cylinders. If the system responds to these requests in the order they arrive, the disk heads may move long distances as they travel from one requested block to the next. This can happen even in file systems that store adjacent blocks of a file in nearby locations because the file system may receive concurrent requests from different processes to access different files. Two alternatives to the "first come, first served" (FCFS) method of accessing blocks are "shortest seek time first" (SSTF) and the "elevator algorithm." SSTF scheduling retrieves the requested block that requires the least time to reach from the heads' current location. This method gives good performance for sequences of nearby blocks, but requests for blocks that are distant from the current location may go unfilled for a long time. The elevator algorithm mimics the behavior of an elevator in a building: As requests come in for blocks at different locations (analogous to requests for an elevator to stop at different floors), the system sorts them so that the heads continue to move in one direction until the most distant block is accessed. Then it reverses direction and carries out requests until it reaches the farthest requested block in the opposite direction. The elevator algorithm and variations on it are widely used in modern file systems.

In Unix-based file systems, the blocks that hold a file's data are listed in a data structure called an *inode* (Figure 3.3). (The *i* stands for "index.") Each inode contains the information needed to find all the blocks that belong to one file. In the classic Unix design, an inode is just a simple list of disk blocks when the file is small. The inode also contains some additional information like the file size and creation date. However, since the inode's length is fixed, it doesn't have enough space to list all the blocks for large files. Instead, the inode lists one or more indirect blocks. These are disk blocks that contain lists of additional blocks that belong to the file. The indirection can be extended to a second level (or more if necessary) to form a complete list of all the blocks in a file. A complete list of inodes for all the files in a collection resides on one or more disks. However, the file system keeps part of the inode list in memory so it can rapidly access files that are in use. Some file systems use more efficient data structures to manage the blocks in a file, but the term "inode" remains in common use.

Other operating systems use different mechanisms to keep track of the blocks that compose a file. For example, the MS-DOS file system maintained a linked list of blocks for each file in a single central data structure called a *file allocation table* (FAT). This technique conserved disk space and memory used for keeping track of the blocks in a file. However, it was inefficient for random access to files because finding the block that contained a particular file location required a linear search through the linked list of blocks. An inode structure, on the other hand, allows a more direct lookup of the file block for a given file location. The file systems described in the rest of this section are based on the Unix model.

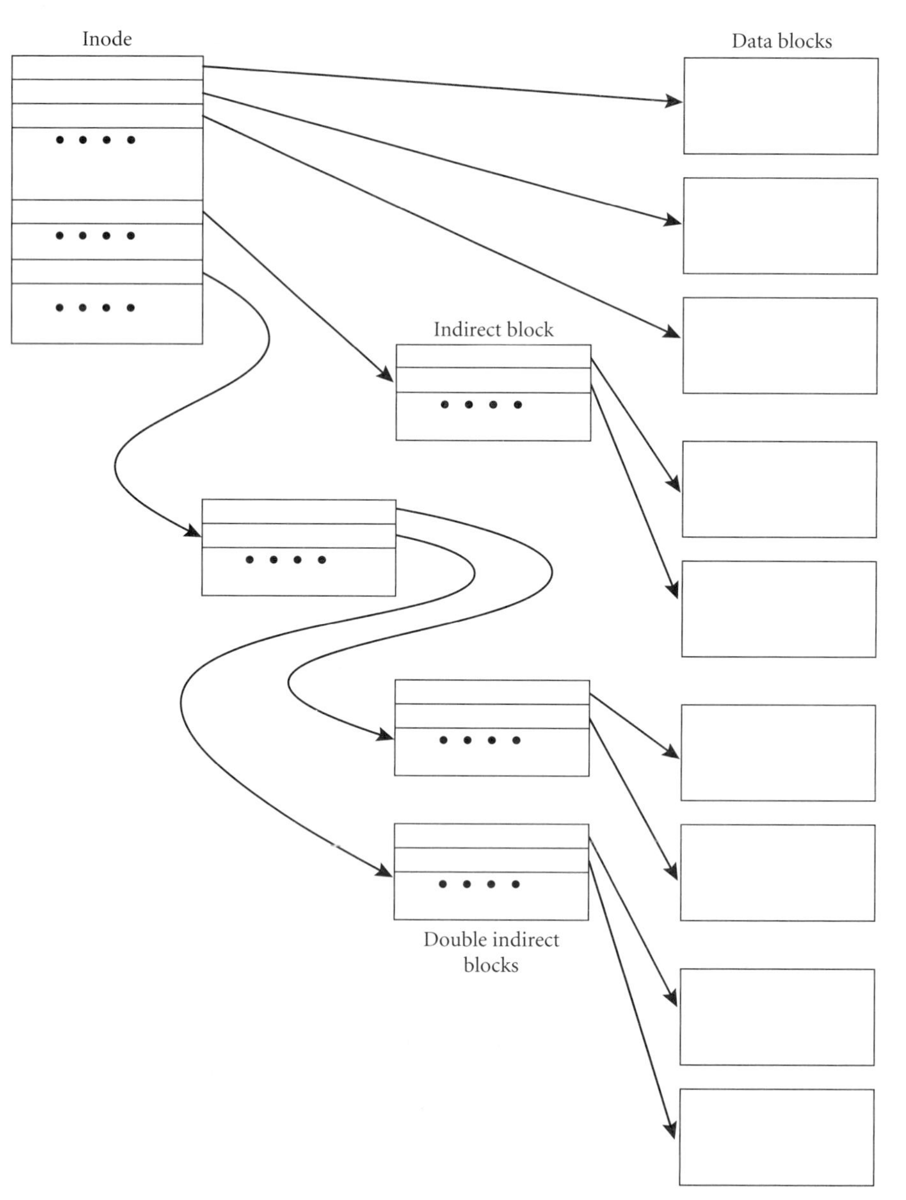

Figure 3.3 An inode contains a list of disk blocks that hold the data in a file. If the list of blocks is too long to fit in the inode, some inode entries will point to indirect blocks that contain additional list entries. The indirection can be extended to multiple levels, as shown by the double indirect blocks here. Additional information stored in the inode, such as the total file size, is not shown here.

When a program opens a file, the file system looks up the file name in a table to find the inode number for that file. Each subdirectory in a file hierarchy uses a separate table; a subdirectory is just a file that contains a table of file names and inode numbers. To locate an inode given a path name (such as /usr/include/stdio.h), the file system starts at the root directory (/) and searches its table for the first subdirectory in the path (usr). This directory is a file with its own inode, and the file system examines the inode and reads the corresponding blocks from the disk (they aren't already in memory). It then searches the table stored in these blocks to find the next subdirectory (include) and its inode. The process continues until the inode for the requested file is found. If no file with the requested name is found, the file system can (at the program's option) create a new file by allocating an inode and recording the inode number and the file name (along with some other information) in the file's parent directory. Since Unix-based file systems permit users to give the same file several names (by using "hard links,") several entries in one or more directories can point to the same inode.

To write data, a file system normally copies bytes from a user buffer into one or more block-sized system buffers. As these buffers fill up, the file system sends them to the disk. As the file grows, the file system allocates additional blocks, and it records their indices in the inode or the indirect blocks. If a file doesn't completely fill its last block, the unused space is generally filled with zeros.

To read data, a file system determines which blocks contain the requested data, reads those blocks from the disk into a system buffer, and then copies the data from the buffer into user memory.

The size of a disk block is defined in a high-level format that the file system uses to organize disk space. This format is in addition to the formatting that defines tracks and sectors on a disk. System administrators can choose the block size, which is a whole multiple of the disk's sector size, when they configure the file system. This choice has important consequences for performance and the utilization of disk space. The optimum block size depends on how the file system will be used. Small blocks work well when the file system will contain mostly small files. Since most files use at least one block, blocks that are much larger than the typical file size will waste disk space. (Some file systems store data for very small files in the inode itself.) On the other hand, large blocks allow more efficient data transfers. Disk drives and interconnection networks operate more efficiently when they move data in large chunks. Furthermore, using many small blocks to store a large file requires more entries in an inode's block list. When a file has many blocks, its inode is more likely to need indirect or double indirect blocks, which take longer to access and use more storage than a short list of large blocks. Finally, when a large file uses many small blocks, the blocks are likely to be scattered across the disk, so the drive will have to move its head frequently as it retrieves the blocks. Common block sizes range from 512 bytes to a few tens of kilobytes. At least one commercial file system, IBM's

GPFS, tries to balance the needs of small and large files by allocating large blocks and storing several small files (or the fragmentary ends of files) in a single block.

3.1.3 File Buffering and Caching

Obviously, most files don't fit exactly into a whole number of blocks, and most read and write requests from applications don't transfer data in block-sized units. File systems use buffers to insulate users from the requirement that disks move data in fixed-size blocks. Buffers also give the file systems several ways to optimize data access. File systems allocate their buffers in units the same size as a disk block. The most important benefit of buffers is that they allow the file system to collect full blocks of data in memory before moving it to the disk. If a file system needed to write less than a full block of data, it would have to perform an expensive read-modify-write operation. Write buffering improves performance even when an application writes a full block of data or more. For accesses about the size of a block, the file locations where the data will be written may cross over a block boundary, so a block-sized write may end up as two partial blocks. For larger writes, the file system can delay writing until it has several blocks to transfer. Disks can usually handle these multiblock transfers more efficiently than single-block transfers. The latter technique is sometimes called *delayed write* or *write behind.*

Similarly, when a file system reads data, it must retrieve a full block at a time. Even if the application program hasn't asked for all the data in the block, the file system will keep the entire block in memory, since the application may later request more data from the same block. This technique is called *file caching.* If a file system detects that an application is reading data sequentially from a file in small steps, it may use "prefetching" (also called "read ahead") to improve performance further: the file system reads not only the block that contains requested data but also one or more subsequent blocks in the file. The extra cost of reading the additional blocks in a single request is usually less than the cost of reading two or more blocks separately. When the program requests data from the prefetched blocks, they will already be in memory, or at least on their way. Therefore, the file system can complete these subsequent reads more quickly than the initial request. Prefetching reduces the apparent data access time for a disk, since the cost of reading the second and subsequent blocks is hidden from the application. However, prefetching works poorly when an application's read requests don't follow a simple, predictable pattern. In that case, the file system may waste time prefetching blocks that the application doesn't need right away.

The file system uses the same pool of memory for both buffering and caching. This allows it to keep the data consistent when the application writes and then reads back the same file location. These accesses will be very efficient because neither request will require access to the disk. An application can create a file, store a small amount of data, read it back, and delete the file without ever accessing a disk. Because caching and buffering are closely connected, this book will often refer to both techniques as *buffering.*

In some systems, all memory not being used by applications is allocated to the file buffer pool. Nevertheless, a file system has only a finite amount of buffer space, so it cannot keep data there indefinitely. When all the buffer blocks are in use and the file system needs a new block for a read or write request, it must reuse one of the buffer blocks currently in use. If the buffer to be reused contains data that was read from the disk, and the application hasn't written data back to that file block, then the file system can immediately use this buffer to carry out the new request. However, if the buffer contains data that the application has written but that the file system hasn't yet moved to disk, then the file system must "flush" this data to the disk before it can reuse the buffer. Buffers containing data that hasn't yet been written to disk are called "dirty."

One disadvantage of buffering data is that most buffer memory is volatile. A user who has saved data to a file may think the data is safe in the event the computer crashes, but if a crash happens before the file system has written its dirty buffers to disk, the data in those buffers will be lost. When a program closes a file or issues an explicit request to flush the data, the buffers for that file are supposed to be flushed to nonvolatile storage. However, modern file systems and modern storage devices have buffers and caches in many places to improve performance, so it is very difficult to be certain when a block of data has actually been moved to magnetic storage. These same considerations make it difficult to measure the performance of storage devices and file systems, especially for small files. With no sure way to know when a transfer has taken place, you cannot easily tell how long it took.

In some applications, buffering does more harm than good. For example, if a program writes a long stream of data to a file, the copy operation between user memory and file system memory takes time and doesn't reduce the number of disk accesses. Also, some database applications need to ensure that file accesses happen in a specific order, and buffering can alter this sequence. To meet these special needs, some file systems allow programs to bypass the system buffers and transfer data directly between user memory and disk. However, these programs must arrange their data transfers to match exactly the block boundaries of the file.

3.1.4 Nonblocking I/O

Caching and buffering improve performance in two ways: by avoiding repeated accesses to the same block on disk and by allowing the file system to smooth out bursty I/O behavior. The smoothing happens because the application can quickly write a large amount of data into file system buffers without waiting for the data to be written to disk. The file system can write these blocks to disk at a slower, steady rate while the application continues with other work that doesn't require I/O. This delayed writing can make the file system's instantaneous transfer rate much higher than its sustained rate.

Prefetching for read operations is analogous in some ways to delayed writing, in that it can hide disk access times for blocks fetched before they were requested. However, prefetching only works once the file system has correctly discerned a pattern in the user's access requests. The file system can't usually prefetch the *initial* block of a sequence of read requests because the user has not yet established a pattern. Therefore, the first request incurs the full delay of the disk access.

Nonblocking I/O gives a program control over prefetching and delayed writing. An application can issue a read request some time before it expects to need the data. Then instead of blocking the program until the data has arrived, the I/O function returns immediately, and the file system completes the request in the background while the application continues to work. When the application reaches a point where it needs the data, it can issue another request to check whether the data is available or to pause execution until the access is complete. Alternatively, some nonblocking I/O implementations can signal the application when the data arrives. An application can also issue a request to write data to a file and then continue computing while the file system moves the data from the user buffer to the disk. Since the application often knows sooner than the file system what data it will need, nonblocking I/O can be much more effective than prefetching. Also, an application can devote a specific memory buffer of exactly the right size to prefetched and delayed-write data, whereas the file system must share its buffers among all jobs and try to guess which disk blocks to keep and which to reuse.

Not all file systems implement nonblocking I/O. Those that do often use the term "asynchronous I/O" for these operations. However, this book uses "asynchronous" to include explicit nonblocking access, automatic prefetching, and delayed writing.

Obviously, all forms of asynchronous I/O work best when the computer has hardware (such as DMA) that can move the data at the same time as it computes. If a CPU manages these transfers, then it has fewer available cycles to devote to computation. Likewise, if data moving between primary and secondary storage travels over the same bus that carries data between memory and the CPU (or cache), the file access and the computation have to share the available bandwidth.

A common use of nonblocking I/O is for double buffering. Double buffering can improve performance when a program repeatedly reads data and then processes it, or produces data and then stores it. Consider the latter case. During each step of a computation, the application uses one memory buffer to store the data it produces. Another buffer of equal size contains data produced in the previous step, and this data is sent to disk in a nonblocking write operation while the first buffer is being filled. At the end of each step, the application switches the roles of buffers: it initiates a nonblocking write on the buffer holding data it just finished computing, and it begins another computation step using the buffer whose data has just been written out. Double buffering, and asynchronous I/O in general, can improve performance by no more than a factor of two (assuming there is only one outstanding request at a time). This optimum improvement happens when the background I/O request takes exactly as long as the computation it overlaps. Similarly, asynchronous I/O can increase an application's memory requirements up to a factor of two.

3.1.5 Fault Tolerance

If a disk drive fails or power is lost while an operation is in progress, the data structures that organize the disk blocks into files may be left in an inconsistent state. For example, if an application is in the process of writing a series of blocks to disk when system power is lost, the inode structure on disk may not include an up-to-date list of the blocks in a file. Data that was successfully written to disk before the failure might not appear in the file when the system is restarted. This problem is especially common when the file system buffers inodes in memory to improve efficiency.

To reduce the chance of data loss, file systems include a number of features to maintain file data and inodes in a consistent state. Most Unix-based systems have a utility program called `fsck` (for "file system check") that verifies the integrity of the inode data structures and searches for "lost" disk blocks that are neither allocated to a file nor included in the list of free blocks. Many systems are configured to run this program each time they are restarted, but running `fsck` on large file structures can take a long time.

More sophisticated file systems have better techniques to avoid corruption of the file structures. One common approach is *journaling*. In a journaled file system, each request that would affect data or the inode structures on disk is written to a log on the disk before the action is initiated. The log entries describe what is to be done, and they are kept separate from the file structure they describe. Once the log entry has been written, the file system proceeds with the actual operation. When a failure occurs, the file system retrieves the log from the disk. Starting with the beginning of the log, or the last point at which the file structures were known to be in a consistent state, the file system carries out each action in the log. Since there is no way to know exactly which operations were completed before the failure occurred, the file system and data structures must be designed so that each action is *idempotent;* that is, repeating a completed action must not corrupt the system. In normal operation, the file system must write the log data to disk immediately, but it can use buffering to delay other disk accesses. The log will capture enough information to recover any buffered data that is lost before it is written to disk. Journaling obviously requires more disk space and more time than ordinary file system operations, but it allows faster and more complete data recovery in the event of a disk or power failure.

3.2 Distributed File Systems

The file systems discussed so far are designed to run on a single CPU. Several processes may access a file concurrently, but the file system guarantees sequential consistency. It usually does this by preventing any process from writing a file at the same time as another process is either reading or writing the file.

Distributed file systems are designed to let processes on multiple computers access a common set of files. Although distributed file systems have some features in common with parallel file systems (Section 3.4), they are not a complete solution for parallel I/O. In particular, as described below, distributed file systems are not designed to give multiple processes efficient, concurrent access to the same file. Nevertheless, distributed file systems are a good point from which to begin an examination of parallel file systems.

Probably the best known distributed file system is NFS (Network File System) [59, 154], which Sun Microsystems first released in 1985. NFS allows a computer to share a collection of its files[1] with other computers on the network. The computer where the collection of files resides is called a server, and a computer that remotely accesses these files is a client. In NFS, a computer can be a server for some files and a client for others. Clients "mount" a collection of files—a directory on the server and all its subdirectories—at a particular location in their own directory hierarchy (Figure 3.4). The remote files appear to be part of the client's directory hierarchy, and programs running on the client can access them using the standard Unix naming conventions. When a client program reads a file that resides on the server, the client's file system sends a request to the server, which gets the file (or just a part of it) and sends it back to the client. The operation is invisible from the application's point of view, except that accessing a remote file takes longer than accessing a local one. Users often don't know which directories in their system are local and which are remote. In diskless workstations, all the files are remote.

Two other well-known distributed file systems are AFS and DFS. AFS [72] is based on the Andrew File System, first developed at Carnegie-Mellon University

1 A collection of files residing on a particular computer is often called a "file system." However, this book uses the term "file system" only for the software that manages the files and not for the collection itself.

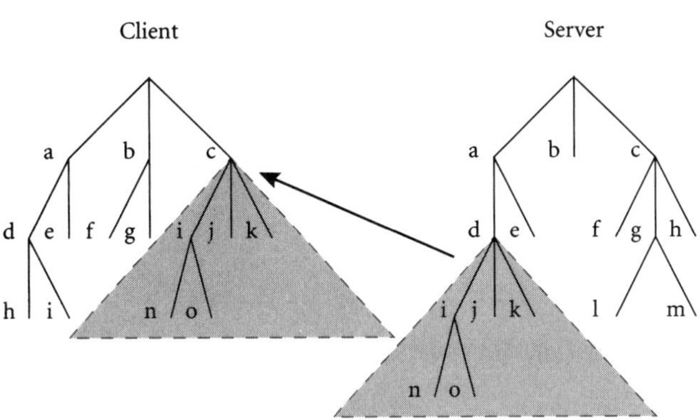

Figure 3.4 NFS, a distributed file system, lets a server computer export a subdirectory and all the files below it. A client computer can "mount" this collection of files as part of its own directory hierarchy.

in the mid-1980s and later offered as a commercial product. DFS [87, 122] is the Distributed File System, a successor to AFS developed as part of the Open Software Foundation's Distributed Computing Environment. Like NFS, AFS and DFS allow multiple computers to access a collection of files over a network, but they have different architectures and features. In particular, AFS and DFS have more sophisticated techniques for controlling user access to files: they use a structure called an *access control list* (ACL) to assign specific rights to users of files and directories. ACLs give more detailed control than Unix file permission bits.

For parallel computer users, the most important difference between NFS and the other two systems is how they maintain consistent views of a file. All three systems use some form of caching on the client, so frequently read blocks don't have to be retrieved from the server repeatedly. If a client modifies a cached block, any other client holding a copy of the same block will have an outdated view of the file. This problem doesn't arise in ordinary Unix file systems because every instance of an open file uses the same buffers. If one process writes to a cached block, the change is immediately visible to all the programs that have the file open.

NFS addresses the file consistency problem by storing with each cached block the time at which it was last compared to the server's copy of the data. When a client reads a locally cached block, it will check this time. If more than 30 seconds have elapsed, the client will request a new copy from the server; otherwise, it will use the cached copy. This technique is a compromise between never checking the cached data against the server's copy, which would increase the risk of using an outdated copy of the data, and checking the server at every request, which would produce more traffic on the network.

AFS and DFS use different techniques to maintain cache consistency. Instead of relying on the clients to check the server for modifications to their cached data, the server in AFS informs the clients whenever it receives a new copy of data that they may be caching. The clients will then discard their cached copies of the modified block and retrieve a new copy the next time they need to read it. DFS uses a distributed locking mechanism (described in Section 3.4.3) that requires a process to hold a lock on a file before it reads or writes it.

3.3 I/O Hardware Configuration

To see how parallel file systems differ from distributed file systems, it is useful to look at the configuration of I/O hardware in parallel computers.

Parallel computers are often described as having shared memory or distributed memory. The differences between these arrangements influence the design of the computer's I/O subsystem. Hybrid systems called distributed shared memory (DSM) computers combine features of both architectures. This section will examine each of these three configurations.

3.3.1 Shared Memory Computers

Figure 3.5 shows a typical shared memory parallel computer. A number of processors share direct access to a pool of memory through a bus or a crossbar switch. To

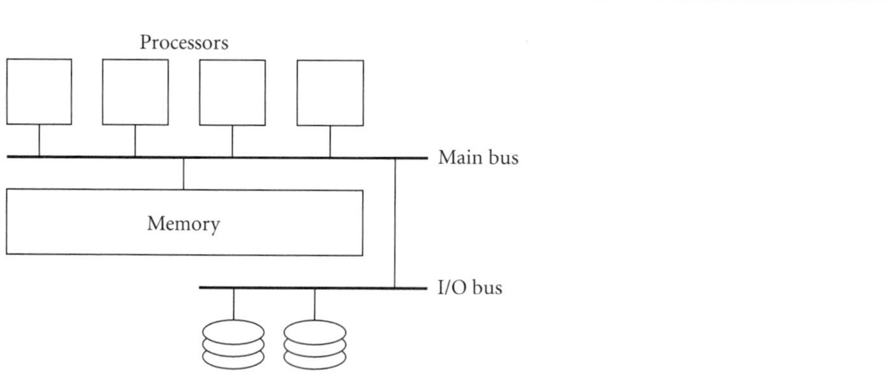

Figure 3.5 In shared memory computers, all the processors share access to a common pool of memory. Storage devices may be connected directly to the main bus or, more likely, to a secondary I/O bus connected to the main bus. Some shared memory computers use a crossbar switch in place of the main bus.

be precise, the systems described in this section are *uniform* shared memory computers (sometimes called symmetric multiprocessors or SMPs) because the access time from any CPU to any main memory location is uniform.

In bus-based systems, the bus is the main artery for data movement between the CPUs, main memory, and peripheral devices such as disk drives. Just like a shared access interconnect, a bus can move data between only two points at a time. Buses rely on high transfer rates and short packets to keep pairs of components from waiting too long for their turn to communicate. Since the bus must have enough capacity to meet the data needs of all the processors, even machines with modest parallelism (say, four CPUs) require very high bus transfer rates—at least a gigabyte per second and preferably much more. Since high-capacity buses often use proprietary designs, and since file access does not need the high transfer rates that memory access does, many bus-based parallel computers use a secondary bus for I/O. One or more of these buses may be connected to the main bus, and the secondary bus can use a standard, nonproprietary interface. Using a standard bus interface allows the I/O interconnect to be attached to the computer through a relatively inexpensive adapter instead of a custom interface designed specially for the main bus.

SMPs may also use a crossbar switch to connect processors to memory. A crossbar behaves like an interconnect with a star topology: several CPUs can access different memory locations at the same time. This parallel access allows crossbar systems to support more CPUs than bus systems because the system's aggregate memory bandwidth can be split into several moderately fast data channels instead of one very fast bus. The crossbar must be able to switch very quickly between different combinations of CPUs and memory locations, since the switching time will add to the overall memory access time. In a crossbar system, the interconnect adapter may connect directly to a crossbar. Alternatively, the system may have a separate I/O bus that links multiple adapters to the crossbar.

One or more storage devices (disks or RAID systems) can be connected through a bus or a crossbar to a shared memory system, and any CPU can read or write any storage device directly. The system may also support DMA or O/S bypass to move data directly from the interconnect interface to memory, without involving a CPU. The capacity of an I/O bus, a main bus, or a single crossbar link can limit the total I/O capacity of the system. Since SMPs have only a few dozen processors at most, the total I/O capacity doesn't usually need to be very large. Systems that do require very high I/O capacity can be configured with fewer CPUs and more I/O buses, which increases the amount of I/O bandwidth per processor.

The file system can stripe files across multiple disks, and it can even implement RAID-style data protection in software. Alternatively, the file system can store different files in the directory structure on different disks. Striping maximizes the transfer rate, so it works well on systems that run large parallel jobs that create large files. Allocating files to different disks improves concurrent access to different files, so it works best on general-purpose machines that run many unrelated tasks.

3.3.2 Distributed Memory Computers

Distributed memory computers are a collection of nodes, each of which is more or less a stand-alone computer (Figure 3.6). A node contains one or more processors, a portion of the computer's total memory, a bus or a crossbar, and some communication hardware. The nodes communicate with each other over an internal network. In most parallel computers, these networks are not standard I/O interconnects like HIPPI or Fibre Channel. Instead, vendors use proprietary, scalable designs with low latency and high aggregate bandwidth. To avoid confusion with I/O interconnects, this book will sometimes call these interconnects "message passing networks."

Although each node may itself be a shared memory computer, the number of processors per node is usually small, so the demands on each node's internal bus

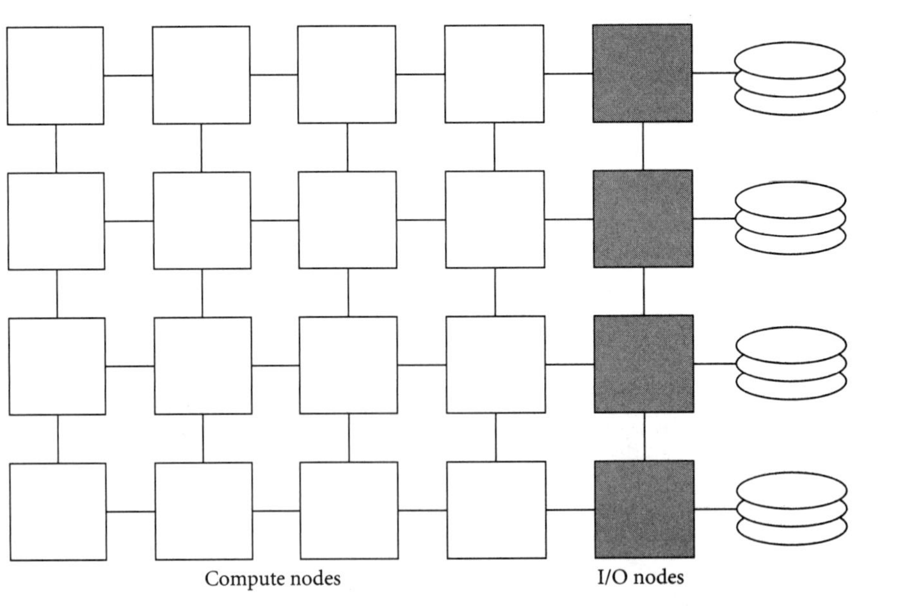

Figure 3.6 In distributed memory computers, the storage devices are connected through I/O nodes to the compute nodes. Data may travel between the I/O nodes and compute nodes over the system's regular message passing network (as shown) or on a separate I/O network.

are less than in pure SMPs. In ordinary distributed memory computers, a processor in one node cannot directly access the memory in another node; the nodes must exchange data by passing messages over the network. This restriction disappears in DSM machines.

The I/O subsystems in distributed memory computers are complex because they have to meet three separate needs:

- *General-purpose file storage.* Program source files, object files, executable programs, scripts, configuration files, and so on all need to be available to all nodes. The structure of the directory and file names should look the same everywhere; in other words, the name space should be uniform. These files don't usually need to be accessed with very high transfer rates, and any concurrent access by multiple processes (loading a program on multiple nodes, for example) is often read-only. Moreover, it's often convenient for these files to be visible to other computers, such as a front-end machine or a workstation where users edit and compile source code. A distributed file system is adequate for all these tasks.
- *High performance, scalable input and output.* The large data files that a parallel program reads or writes during execution demand the highest possible transfer rates.
- *Swap space and other temporary storage.* Each node runs its own copy of the operating system, which needs file I/O to support virtual memory and to create a variety of temporary files. Many application programs also need to create small temporary files. The main feature of this kind of storage is that it's local. No other node needs access to the data, and there is no need for a common name space among the nodes. However, this storage does need to be accessible quickly on the node that uses it. If a node has to move its virtual memory pages over the message passing network, performance of both the node and the network will suffer.

To meet these needs, many large distributed memory computers have three separate file systems: a distributed file system, a parallel file system, and a local file system running on each node. The three file systems often use three separate sets of storage devices. Each node may have one or more disks directly attached to it for local file access. A distributed file system will be available over a local area network, and a parallel file system will use special I/O nodes.

I/O nodes are like ordinary compute nodes in a distributed memory computer, but they have extra I/O interconnect hardware and storage devices. When the compute nodes read and write data through the parallel file system, they forward their requests to one or more I/O nodes, which complete the access and send the results back to the compute node. The I/O nodes can communicate with the compute nodes over the message passing network, or the system can include a special I/O network to keep the I/O traffic off the message passing network. Files are usually striped or *declustered* among the I/O nodes. Declustering is a more general form of striping (Section 2.5); unlike striped files, declustered files are not necessarily divided into fixed-size pieces. The collection of storage devices attached to all the I/O nodes behaves like a RAID 0 array: the aggregate data rate is high, but if any one disk on any I/O node fails, declustered files could be corrupted. For that reason, either the storage devices connected to the I/O nodes should be RAID systems themselves, or else the software on the I/O node should implement a RAID-like protection mechanism across its individual disks. Of course, if the I/O node fails rather than a storage device, the declustered files will be unavailable until the node is repaired. However, the data itself won't be lost. To keep data available in the event an I/O node fails, some disks have multiported (or "twin-tailed") inputs that allow two or more I/O nodes to control them. If a disk's primary I/O node fails, another node can still access the data. You could also imagine implementing a RAID-like mechanism across all the I/O nodes so that a node could fail without bringing down the whole file system. The practical problem with this idea is that it would require a lot of internode communication to compute the parity data between the I/O nodes.

The architecture of the I/O system, with I/O nodes that control storage devices connected over a network, is similar in some ways to the NASD design discussed in Section 2.8.1. An important difference is that NASD is designed as an open system, which can serve a heterogeneous collection of compute nodes that may not trust each other. The I/O systems for distributed memory computers are typically designed to be tightly integrated with the rest of the machine. They may rely on specific features of the interconnection network and the operating system software running on the compute nodes to improve performance. However, in future systems, I/O architectures may begin to look more like NASD designs, allowing them to share files between systems more effectively.

What should be the ratio of compute nodes to I/O nodes? To answer this question, you must consider several variables: the speed of the compute nodes (often expressed in FLOP/sec), the amount of data stored per operation (bytes per FLOP), the transfer rate of the message passing network, the rate at which an I/O node can move data between the message passing network and the I/O interconnect, the transfer rate of the storage device, and the number of storage devices attached to each I/O node. These hardware considerations don't account for the performance of the software that moves the data, and they assume that the application does I/O continuously and not in bursts. Despite these simplifications, the following numbers produce a reasonable approximation. They don't represent any particular computer, but they are typical at the time of this writing.

- FLOP rate (F): 500 MFLOP/sec per CPU. (This is a theoretical peak; the actual observed application performance ranges from a few percent to more than 50% of this value.)
- Data storage rate (R_{compute}/F): 0.05 bytes per peak FLOP. (The U.S. Department of Energy's Accelerated Strategic Computing Initiative [ASCI] has used this ratio in planning its supercomputer acquisitions.)
- Message passing network transfer rate: 100 MB/sec.
- I/O node internal transfer rate: 100 MB/sec.
- I/O interconnect transfer rate: 100 MB/sec.
- RAID system transfer rate: 100 MB/sec.

The rate at which a compute node generates data to store will be $R_{\text{compute}} = F(R_{\text{compute}}/F) = (500\ \text{MFLOP/sec})(0.05\ \text{bytes/FLOP}) = 25\ \text{MB/sec}$, assuming one CPU per node. The message passing network can support this rate both leaving the compute node and entering the I/O node. The internal transfer rate of the I/O node—how fast it can take data from the message passing network and move it to the I/O interconnect—is also sufficient. If it weren't, the communication network would be a poor match for the nodes. The I/O interconnect rate assumes a single (perfect) HIPPI connection. The transfer rate of the RAID system is slower than the fastest current commercial products, but since the I/O node can't move data faster than that, any extra bandwidth would be wasted. In this situation, then, the ratio, C, of compute nodes to I/O nodes should match the rate at which compute nodes produce data to the rate at which the I/O nodes can accept data, $R_{\text{I/O}}$. Therefore, $C = R_{\text{I/O}}/R_{\text{compute}} = (100\ \text{MB/sec})/(25\ \text{MB/sec}) = 4$ for this example.

Of course, there is considerable uncertainty in these numbers, especially in the amount of data stored per peak FLOP, which varies widely among scientific applications. One byte per 20 FLOPs is at the high end of the spectrum; most applications will probably generate less. On the other hand, this estimate assumed only one CPU per compute node; many distributed memory computers have more.

A study by Baylor, Benveniste, and Hsu [13] took a different approach to determining the ideal ratio of compute nodes to I/O nodes. They computed the I/O performance on simulated parallel computers with 16 to 512 nodes. That study, somewhat remarkably, also concluded that a 4:1 ratio was optimal. However, very few large parallel computers have only four compute nodes per I/O node. Ratios of 10:1 or higher are common. In these systems, many parallel jobs do not use all the available compute nodes. An application that runs on only 32 nodes of a system that has 120 compute nodes and eight I/O nodes would stripe its files across all eight I/O nodes and apparently have the benefit of a 4:1 ratio. However, other parallel jobs running on the remaining 88 compute nodes will also contend for access to the same eight I/O nodes, so the apparent benefit disappears on a fully loaded system.

3.3.3 Distributed Shared Memory Computers

A DSM computer is similar to a distributed memory computer in that it consists of a collection of nodes that communicate over a message passing network. However, DSM computers have additional hardware and software that gives every CPU direct access to every memory location. CPU requests to access memory in another node are transformed into messages, which the system sends over the message passing network to the node where the data resides. Since these remote memory accesses take longer than accesses to local memory, some memory locations appear more distant from a CPU than others. These machines are sometimes called *nonuniform memory access* (NUMA) architectures. Two variations on this strategy are ccNUMA (cache-coherent NUMA) [91] and S-COMA (simple cache-only memory architecture) [141]. The variations don't generally affect I/O, so they aren't considered here. Examples of DSM architectures include the SGI Origin 2000 [93] and the Cray (formerly Tera) MTA [158].

The I/O configuration of DSM computers is often a hybrid of SMP and distributed memory techniques. For example, the Origin 2000 has compute nodes that each contain two CPUs and hardware to connect I/O adapters, either directly to a crossbar or through a standard I/O bus. There are no separate I/O nodes. Since all the memory in the system is directly accessible from every node, DMA hardware in each node can move data between an I/O adapter and any memory location.

The Cray MTA takes a different approach. Unlike most other current computers, it has no cache memory. Instead, it presents programs with a large address space in which all data can be accessed in approximately equal time. Although the latency is relatively large, the MTA compensates by supporting very efficient switching between threads. When sufficient threads are active, the latency of each memory access request by a thread is hidden by computation that can proceed in other threads. The system demands a high bandwidth between memory and the CPU, but it can tolerate a long latency. The MTA has dedicated I/O nodes, which contain HIPPI hardware to communicate with RAID storage devices. Like the Origin, the MTA can move data directly from the I/O interconnect to memory anywhere in the system. Typically, though, the MTA's I/O operations move data to and from file system buffers that reside on the I/O node. The operating system can transfer ownership of these buffers to an application, which accesses the buffers directly. The combination of direct memory access and ownership transfer allows the MTA to avoid the cost of copying data from the I/O buffer to user memory.

3.4 Parallel File Systems

A distributed file system does only part of what a parallel file system needs to do. Distributed file systems manage access to files from multiple processes, but they generally treat concurrent access as an unusual event, not a normal mode of operation. The design of a parallel file system must deal with several important questions:

- How can hundreds or thousands of processes access the same file concurrently and efficiently?
- How should file pointers work?
- Can the Unix sequential consistency semantics be preserved?
- How should file blocks be cached and buffered?

Each of these questions is considered below. Even though parallel file system development is quite advanced, many parallel applications continue to use one of two alternative types of I/O: pure sequential file access, in which a program sends all of its file accesses through a single task, and multiple file access, in which each task writes its own file.

Pure sequential access works well in a shared memory computer. A single thread can copy data between global memory and one or more I/O channels. The file system can automatically arrange to stripe data over multiple storage devices, and with appropriate DMA hardware, data can move in parallel between different regions of memory and storage. However, pure sequential access is much less suitable for a distributed memory computer. Data being written to a file from each process must move into the memory of the I/O process before it goes to a storage device. Collecting data from several parallel processes into one place is called a "gather" operation. The inverse operation is called a "scatter." For read operations, the I/O process reads data from disk into its own memory before scattering it to the other processes.

Sequential access in distributed memory computers does have two attractive features. First, all the data resides in one file, so it is easy to manage. In particular, the user can copy the file as a single unit to tertiary storage or to another computer. Second, sequential access is likely to produce contiguous file accesses that the storage devices and file system can handle efficiently. This advantage is clearest when the program accesses a modest amount of data. Reading or writing a block of data from a single process is often more efficient than having many separate processes access small amounts of data from the same file.

Sequential access also has some important drawbacks in distributed memory computers. A single process running on a single node may not have enough memory to hold all the data that the parallel job needs to read or write. To work around this problem, the program must access the file in several steps, separated by gather or scatter operations. More importantly, the total transfer rate is limited to what a single node can support. For moderately large parallel programs, sequential file access is too slow.

Multiple file access is an alternative to sending all the data to one process. For this technique, used mainly in message passing programs, each process writes data to a separate file. If the files reside on the nodes' local disks, file access will be very fast because the data won't need to travel over the computer's message passing network, and the data transfer is perfectly parallel. If the files are temporary or if the user doesn't need a single combined data set, multiple file access is an excellent choice. However, many applications do need to produce a single data set. The postprocessing required to collect many separate files into one large file can easily wipe out the performance benefits of multiple file access. On systems where local disks are not accessible to other nodes, merging files will require another parallel program that runs on the same set of nodes as the program that generated the data.

Parallel file systems try to address the main drawbacks of both sequential access and multiple file access. They combine the high performance and scalability of multiple file access with the convenience of collecting data in single files. To do this, they must allow multiple tasks to access a file at the same time, though not all the tasks will necessarily access the same locations in a given file.

3.4.1 Concurrent File Access

The first challenge for a parallel file system is to support concurrent access from several processes. Since parallel file systems usually stripe files over multiple disks (connected to different I/O nodes), the file system has to manage two separate data mappings: the mapping from multiple compute nodes to a shared file and the mapping of the shared file to multiple I/O nodes and storage devices. Figure 3.7 shows two examples of these mappings with four compute nodes and two I/O nodes. The top row in each diagram shows four compute nodes, each with two blocks of data. (Numbers in all the blocks show which compute node produced the data.) The middle rows of the diagrams show how these blocks fit into the logical structure of the file. The bottom rows show how the file is striped over the I/O nodes. In the top example, the distribution of data among the compute nodes matches the file's striping, so each compute node can send whole blocks of data to just one of the I/O nodes. In the bottom example, the data distribution doesn't match the file striping, so compute nodes must send partial and whole blocks to both I/O nodes, which will be less efficient. Although the diagram shows the mapping from the compute nodes to the logical file layout to the I/O nodes, in reality the data moves directly

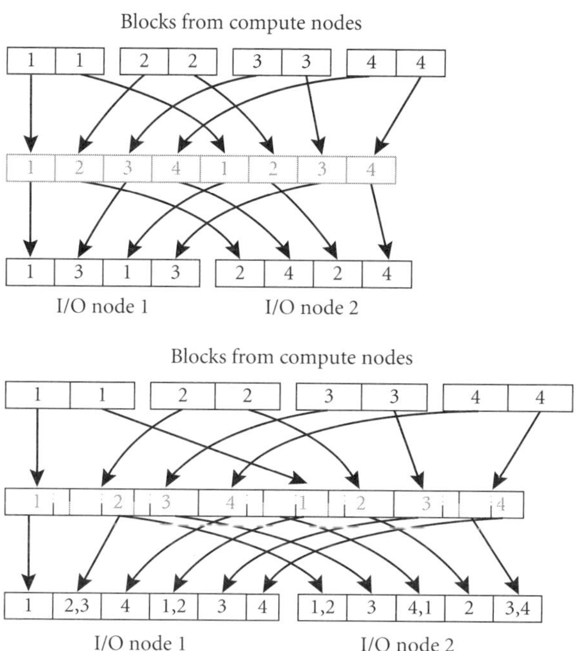

Figure 3.7 Mapping of blocks from compute nodes to logical files to I/O nodes. See the text for a description.

between the compute nodes and I/O nodes; it never resides all in one place as shown in the middle rows.

To access a file in parallel, each process begins by opening the file. In a sequential system, the file system translates the file name to an inode number as described in Section 3.1.2. In parallel file systems, each I/O node manages a subset of the blocks that make up a file, so every file has an inode (or a similar data structure) on every I/O node. The file system needs a way to look up each of these inodes when it opens a file. It's possible to have each I/O node maintain its own directory information and look up its own inodes. Another solution is to use a central name server, a process that file system software on all the nodes can call to look up inode numbers using file names. This avoids the need to replicate the directory data on each I/O node. The name server typically resides on an I/O node.

Some file systems fix the stripe factor and stripe depth when the system is configured; others allow users to specify these parameters separately for each file. When a file is first created, the file system chooses the I/O node that will store the first block of the file. Varying this location distributes the work among the I/O nodes; if the location were fixed, all short files would reside at the same I/O node. Subsequent blocks go to the other I/O nodes in a fixed or pseudorandom order.

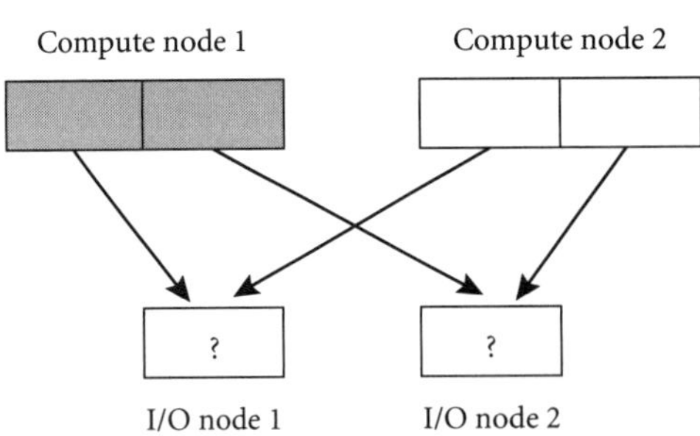

Figure 3.8 If two compute nodes write different data concurrently to the same range of locations in a file, and the range spans two or more I/O nodes, sequential consistency requires that the distributed file end up as if the I/O nodes all wrote data from the two requests in the same order.

Once each process knows the striping pattern and the initial block for a file, it can determine on its own which I/O node is responsible for each byte location of a file. When reading or writing a file, the compute nodes simply calculate which I/O node will handle each piece of data to be moved. They can send requests to the I/O nodes in parallel, and of course the I/O nodes can carry out the requests in parallel, since they are accessing data on storage devices that they control exclusively. As long as processes on different compute nodes don't try to access the same part of the file, striping is easy to manage.

Problems arise when the system has to enforce sequential consistency. Suppose two processes write to the same range of locations in a file, and the range spans two blocks on different I/O nodes (Figure 3.8). Sequential consistency requires that the two I/O nodes write their portions of the data in the same order, ensuring that the write requests *appear* to occur in a well-defined sequence. How will each I/O node know what the other is doing? One solution is to use a locking mechanism on the file that prevents more than one process from writing a file at the same time. This solution prevents parallel file access, and it is essentially what sequential Unix does. The problem with locking the whole file is that it prevents parallel access even when the processes are not writing overlapping regions of a file. Most applications rarely write the same file location concurrently from separate processes, so maintaining the Unix model of sequential consistency using file locking needlessly ruins parallel performance for common access patterns. As a result, some parallel file systems offer the user a choice of access modes: one that guarantees sequential consistency at the expense of parallel performance and another that allows concurrent access by relaxing the consistency semantics. In the latter case, the application is responsible for preventing different processes from writing data concurrently to the same location.

Some file systems help applications enforce this separation by partitioning the file. Each process can access only one partition, and the partitions don't overlap; therefore, no conflicts can occur. A single partition need not be a contiguous range of file locations. It can be a series of separate locations throughout the file, interleaved with other partitions. Together, the partitions cover the whole file. Applications can define partitions when they open the file, or they can define them dynamically with each file access. Partitioning is a simple and efficient form of concurrency control.

A more sophisticated form of concurrency control is token passing. This mechanism guarantees that all I/O nodes will complete their requests in the same order. For example, the token passing mechanism in IBM's Vesta parallel file system [33] works as follows: The I/O node that stores the first block of a file (called the base node) is notified of every I/O access request that the compute nodes generate for that file. The base node receives a notification whether or not it manages any of the file blocks involved in a particular request. For each request, the base node generates a short numbered message called a *token*. The number reflects the sequence in which the base node received the request. If the base node needs to access some blocks for the request, it does so and then it passes the token to the next I/O node in the file's stripe sequence. Meanwhile, the other I/O nodes queue the requests they receive from the compute nodes. When a node receives a token, it checks to see if the token number is one higher than the last token it received for that file. If so, and if the corresponding request has arrived, the I/O node carries out that request. If a token arrives out of order (perhaps because the message passing network allows messages to overtake each other), the node holds it until any tokens that should precede it arrive and the corresponding requests are dispatched. A token is forwarded from one I/O node to the next until it reaches the end of the stripe sequence. An I/O node doesn't need to wait for a request to complete before it forwards the corresponding token, so the I/O accesses are not sequentialized. However, a node does have to hold requests until all preceding requests have been completed. This technique guarantees that all the I/O nodes will carry out requests on a given file in the same order as the base node. This guarantee is sufficient to enforce sequential consistency. Although token passing restores parallelism to parallel I/O, it does incur overhead, so some systems that support it let programs turn token passing off and forego sequential consistency. This can be dangerous, however, if two independent programs access a file concurrently. Each program may avoid overlapping accesses, but there may be overlap between the programs that neither could detect on its own.

3.4.2 File Pointers

Programs that write a single file concurrently from several processes need special support for file pointers. In Unix semantics, each process that opens a file will have its own file pointer that the file system updates independently of the other processes. Consider again the access pattern in Figure 3.7. Each process writes some data to the file, then uses a seek request to skip past the part of the file that other processes are writing, writes some more data, skips again, and so on. To avoid overlapping file accesses, each process needs to know what part of the file the others will use. Although it requires careful programming, this access pattern is feasible with ordinary Unix file pointers, as long as all the tasks know in advance the planned pattern of access.

Now consider a different way to access a file. An application may need to generate a log of errors or unusual events that happen as it works. The events happen unpredictably in different processes, but the user wants a single, time-ordered record of them. This kind of log would be easy to generate in a sequential program because a single process would write out the events one after another, automatically updating the file pointer after each one. In a shared parallel file, though, all the processes usually have separate file pointers, so each time a process writes some data, it might obliterate data that another process wrote earlier. To prevent this problem, all the processes need a common view of the current location of the file pointer, so when any process writes data, the file system will update the pointer on all the other processes. A similar problem arises if several processes need to read a single file that contains a list of tasks to do: it may not matter which process does which task, but exactly one process must read every task.

Several file systems offer shared file pointers, which allow this kind of coordinated access. However, shared file pointers are hard to implement efficiently. The file system must give all the processes access to the file pointer, but it must allow only one process at a time to update it. A common solution is to store the shared pointer in one server process and have that process coordinate all requests from compute nodes to read or update the file pointer. Obviously, using a shared file pointer reduces (but doesn't necessarily eliminate) parallel access to a file, so programs should use them only when necessary.

The discussion so far has considered parallel programs that use message passing rather than shared memory. It's important to remember, though, that in a shared memory program, shared file pointers are quite common. Whenever a program stores a file descriptor in a variable that more than one thread can access, the file pointer corresponding to the descriptor will be shared. Any updates to the file pointer through the shared descriptor will affect all the threads that use the descriptor. This sharing can work in unexpected ways. For example, suppose two threads write data to a file at about the same time, each at a specific location.

Thread 1:	***Thread 2:***
`seek(location = 100)`	`seek(location = 200)`
`write(..., length = 50)`	`write(..., length = 150)`

Both threads will issue a seek request followed by a write. If both calls in Thread 1 happen before either call in Thread 2 (or vice versa), the operations will complete as the user expects. However, because the seek and write operations are not an atomic unit, requests in separate threads can interleave. For example, both seeks could happen before either write. The first write will then happen at the location of the second seek, and the second write will be placed immediately after the first. For the concurrent accesses shown here, there are six possible outcomes, and only two are what the user wanted. (These two produce the same file output but leave the file pointer in different locations.)

The problem of file pointer atomicity happens whenever concurrent tasks (processes or threads) share access to a file pointer. Some programs use both message passing and multithreading at the same time, so what looks like a local (nonshared) file pointer to the message passing part of the program could be a shared pointer in the multithreaded part. Atomicity problems also occur when programs read data. Although the file will not be affected, unexpected interleaving of seeks and reads may cause the program to read the wrong data.

To address the atomicity problem, Unix has added read and write calls (`pread` and `pwrite`) that let the application specify the file location (also called a "file offset") explicitly. Some parallel file systems have a similar mechanism. In these functions, the program passes in a file offset, and the file system begins the access at this point instead of using the location currently stored in the file pointer. Explicit offset functions don't update the file pointer, so the application program is responsible for computing where in the file each successive access should begin.

A separate problem with file pointers in parallel programs has to do with how the file system updates them. Sequential Unix systems update file pointers after each request completes, and they increment the file pointer by the actual number of bytes read or written. For example, if a program tries to read 100 bytes, but only 50 bytes remain between the current file pointer location and the end of the file, then the read access will return only 50 bytes, and the file pointer will be incremented by 50.

Now suppose several processes in a parallel program are reading a file using a shared file pointer. Under standard Unix semantics, since the file pointer is a shared resource, the processes will sequentialize their I/O requests. Each will first read the pointer's current value, then read data from the file at the pointer's current location, and finally update the pointer by the amount of data read. The file pointer will remain unavailable to other processes during the entire operation, so this method of updating the shared pointer prevents parallel access to the file because no process can begin reading until the previous process updates the shared pointer.

Most of the time, each process will get exactly the amount of data it requested, so a process could update the file pointer immediately after reading it. The process would simply increment the pointer by the amount of the request. A second process could then read the new pointer value and begin reading its portion of the data in parallel with the first process. The problem with this "eager update" technique is that when a process tried to read past the end of a file, it would update the file pointer by the wrong amount. The pointer would then point past the end of the file. If another process tried to write beginning at that location, it would leave a gap in the file between the previous end of the file and the location stored in the file pointer. Since the eager update technique doesn't maintain a correct file pointer at all times, it violates Unix semantics. At least one parallel file system (IBM's Vesta but not PIOFS, both described in Section 3.5.2) relaxes these semantics to allow eager updates of file pointers.

A similar problem occurs in file systems that support nonblocking file access. If a program tries to access a file while a separate nonblocking access to the same file is under way, the second access won't have a usable file pointer unless the nonblocking access updates the pointer eagerly. Of course, if the accesses use explicit file offsets instead of file pointers, this problem doesn't arise. The nonblocking I/O mechanism in Unix systems uses explicit offsets.

A final potential problem with file pointers is their size. For many years, the standard Unix file pointer was 32 bits long. This size limited files to no more than 2 GB. (In fact, 32 bits is enough to address 4 GB, but the customary Unix limit is 2 GB.) Since the applications that run on large parallel computers can easily generate files longer than 2 GB, this limit is no longer acceptable. Modern parallel file systems use longer file pointers, and they can manage files of a terabyte or more. In some file systems, the programmer must use a special compiler flag or give some other indication that the system should use long file pointers. Compatibility problems can arise in applications that store file pointers as ordinary 32-bit integers instead of specially typed file pointer variables.

3.4.3 Buffering

Parallel file systems, like sequential ones, use caching and buffering to reduce the need for disk accesses. In systems with separate I/O and compute nodes, buffering can happen in both places. Buffering at the compute nodes is called *client buffering,* and buffering at the I/O nodes is called *server buffering.* Some file systems use only client or server buffering; others use both.

File systems with client buffering manage a pool of buffer space on each compute node. As in sequential file systems, data to be written to a file is copied from the user's address space into the buffer, and the file system might not send the buffer to the I/O node until some time after the write request appears to the application to have completed. Read requests copy data from I/O nodes into the buffer, and subsequent read requests from the same disk block can be satisfied without further communication with the I/O node.

The problem with client buffering is similar to the caching problem in distributed file systems. If a process writes data to a file, and the data remains in a buffer on the compute node for some time, a process on another compute node trying to read the same location in a file won't see the changes the first node made. This problem is more severe than the sequential consistency problem noted earlier because it can happen even if the two processes access the data in a well-defined order (i.e., not concurrently). File systems use a variety of approaches to address the problem. Some offer a relaxed consistency model that requires the program to synchronize the file explicitly to make changes visible to all processes. Another solution is to implement a cache coherence protocol that allows processes to keep track of which nodes are reading and writing each location in a file. A process can lock all or part of a file for writing; then no other process can read or write the specified region until the writing process releases the lock. Likewise, one or more processes can acquire a lock for reading; then no process can write data to the locked region until all of the readers are finished. When a writing process releases a lock, it must flush its data to the I/O nodes so that other processes can see it. When a reading process acquires a lock, it can cache the locked data with assurance that no other process will change the data.

Parallel and distributed file systems often use token passing to implement locking. The basic idea is for a server process to keep track of what processes are reading and writing different parts of a file (or the whole file). When a process needs a lock that it doesn't already hold, it sends a request to the server, which determines whether the lock is available (i.e., whether another process is currently accessing the requested region of the file). If one or more processes already hold a lock that is incompatible with the requested lock, the server can contact those processes directly, acquire the lock from them, and then return the lock to the requesting process. DFS uses this technique. Alternatively, the server can give a list of processes that hold the lock to the requesting process, and the requesting process then communicates directly with the other processes to get the lock. The latter strategy minimizes the burden on the server, but it requires a level of trust among the clients that may not exist in all systems. An IBM research file system called Calypso [107] uses this strategy, as does a commercial IBM file system, GPFS (Section 3.5.3).

The granularity of locks is an important performance consideration. If a single lock covers the entire file, the processes cannot write data concurrently, which is a severe limitation on a parallel file system. Alternatively, the file system could lock and unlock every byte of a file individually. This would give the processes maximum concurrent access, but the cost in processing time, memory, and communication of such an arrangement would be large. An obvious compromise is to lock file blocks. Since each block resides on only one I/O node, locking files at this level doesn't prevent parallel access to separate file stripes. A drawback of block-level locking is that two processes may try to write different file locations that reside on the same file block. Even though the regions don't overlap, only one process can write at a time. If the processes each make a series of small writes to their separate regions, they will trade the lock back and forth. Each process will continually force the other to flush and then update its copy of the block. This phenomenon is called *false sharing*, and it happens in caches for shared memory as well as in file systems. The problem becomes more severe as block sizes increase. File systems can partly avoid false sharing by locking file ranges with flexible boundaries. If each process locks the specific range of bytes in the file that it intends to use, then another process should be able to access any bytes outside that range. Byte range locking has the flexibility of individual byte locking, but it incurs less overhead. In practice, the strategy has limits because file systems cache and buffer entire blocks, and the system must eventually merge updates to different parts of the same block before writing the block to storage.

The alternative to client buffering is server buffering. In this strategy, I/O nodes buffer blocks locally and use the buffered data to satisfy requests from all compute nodes. Since there is only one buffered copy of a block, server buffering avoids the cache consistency problem. Also, when multiple compute nodes access a file, data buffered on the server can be shared among them. If several processes want data from the same disk block, the I/O node need only read the block once (as long as the requests arrive at about the same time). If several processes write data to different parts of the same block, the requests can be merged into a single disk access.

The main disadvantage of server buffering is the traffic it creates on the message passing network. Every access request from a compute node must travel to an I/O node. A series of small requests to access contiguous file locations could be handled very efficiently with client buffering, but with server buffering each request will generate network traffic.

File systems that combine client buffering and server buffering gain some of the benefits and some of the drawbacks of both systems. The use of compute node buffers eliminates the extra network traffic server buffering creates, but the file systems must still manage the cache coherence issues. Server buffers help the system avoid extra disk access when multiple compute nodes read or write the same block, but these buffers must now be kept coherent with the client buffers.

3.5 Commercial Parallel File Systems

This section looks at some of the parallel file systems that computer vendors have developed to address the problems discussed so far in this chapter. Some of these systems are no longer actively supported, but they are instructive because they represent unique or pioneering technology. Later, this chapter will look at some of the parallel file systems developed in academic institutions, mainly for workstation clusters.

3.5.1 Intel PFS

Intel's PFS (Parallel File System) [79] was a significant early parallel file system. Intel developed PFS for its Paragon supercomputers. The company used an earlier file system called CFS (Concurrent File System) [108] in the Paragon's predecessor, the iPSC. Although Intel has left the supercomputer market, PFS was the subject of several studies and optimization efforts throughout the late 1990s.

The Paragon is a distributed memory parallel computer with I/O nodes that manage access to parallel files. The Paragon also supports NFS files and ordinary sequential Unix files (called UFS files, for Unix File System). NFS and PFS subdirectories are typically mounted in a UFS directory hierarchy. PFS stripes files over multiple I/O nodes. The system administrator configures the striping parameters, and they apply to all the files that PFS manages in a hierarchy.

PFS manages concurrency and file pointers through six I/O modes. Each mode gives programs a different set of file access semantics and performance characteristics. For example, a program can choose a mode that offers maximum concurrency with relaxed consistency semantics, or it can select a mode with shared file pointers and somewhat lower performance. Each open file in a program can use a different I/O mode, and a program can change I/O modes without reopening the file. Different programs can access a file with different modes at the same time.

PFS I/O modes let the user vary three separate parameters: the type of file pointer, whether one or all processes participate in each file access, and how atomicity is managed. Table 3.1 summarizes these parameters, which are described further below.

- **M_UNIX** gives Unix file pointer and atomicity semantics. The file system carries out concurrent access requests one at a time, so the results are sequentially

I/O mode	*File pointer*	*Access type*	*Concurrency control*
M_UNIX	local	independent	serialization
M_LOG	shared	independent	serialization
M_SYNC	shared	collective	serialization
M_RECORD	local	collective	partitioning
M_GLOBAL	shared	collective	identical access
M_ASYNC	local	independent	none

Table 3.1 *The Intel PFS I/O modes allow programs to choose combinations of performance and semantic characteristics. Collective operations require all the processes in a parallel program to participate in each file access; independent operations can be done by one process at a time. See the text for an explanation of the atomicity mechanisms.*

consistent. This mode is the most compatible with standard Unix I/O, but it does not give processes concurrent file access.

- **M_LOG** uses shared file pointers, and it sequentializes access requests to ensure that they are atomic. Since the accesses are sequential, the system can update the file pointer by the amount of data actually accessed.
- **M_SYNC** is similar to M_LOG in its use of shared file pointers with sequential access, but in this mode all processes in the parallel job must participate in every read and write operation. This requirement makes M_SYNC a *collective* mode. PFS performs the accesses in the order of the process numbers.
- **M_RECORD** is also a collective mode. Furthermore, every process in a given access must read or write the same amount of data, although the access size can vary from one request to the next. The order of these fixed-size records in a file is determined by the process number, although the actual file accesses can proceed in parallel. The data size restriction lets PFS compute the file location that each process will access in a request, and every node can calculate this location independently. Since the records for each process reside in fixed, nonoverlapping file locations, PFS doesn't need to serialize accesses from different nodes to maintain sequential consistency. Each process maintains a separate file pointer, but since the processes all access the same amount of data in the same order, they update the local pointers in lockstep, so the pointers all have the same value. PFS doesn't verify that all the processes access the same amount of data in each request; violating this restriction is likely to corrupt the file.
- **M_GLOBAL** is useful when all the processes need to read or write the same data. For example, a file may contain a problem description that is identical for every process. This mode uses a shared file pointer, and since all the processes make the same accesses at the same time, the data is by definition consistent. PFS implements this mode by having only one process do the actual data access. For writes, data from other processes is ignored; for reads, the node that does the access broadcasts its data to all the others.
- **M_ASYNC** is similar to M_UNIX, but it doesn't try to maintain sequential consistency. Each process has a local file pointer and can read or write any amount of data at any time. The program must ensure that no two processes try to access overlapping file regions concurrently. M_ASYNC offers maximum parallelism for programs that don't need full Unix semantics.

These modes are designed for use with files that PFS manages, but the Paragon lets programs use them with UFS files as well. The semantics of each mode will be the same as for PFS, but the parallel modes (M_RECORD and M_ASYNC) won't give better performance than M_UNIX. For NFS files, the Paragon manual states that parallel I/O operations may give poor performance or unexpected results.

The programming interface for PFS is an extension of the Unix interface. Most programs written with Unix I/O calls will work correctly, but they won't do parallel I/O. PFS adds several new functions that let processes open a file, set the I/O mode, and access data in parallel. PFS also lets programs do nonblocking I/O. The system imposes various synchronization rules to avoid the problems with file pointer update semantics described earlier in the chapter. Although the PFS programming interface is compatible with Unix, PFS doesn't support all the file operations that Unix does. In particular, PFS cannot write core files or run executables because it does not support standard Unix file operations that map the contents of a file to a range of memory locations.

3.5.2 IBM Vesta and PIOFS

IBM developed the Vesta parallel file system [33] as a research project. A central feature of Vesta is that it abandons the Unix model of a file as a linear sequence of bytes. When IBM turned Vesta into a commercial product, it renamed the system PIOFS (Parallel I/O File System) [76]. The two file systems are similar but not identical. This book will refer to them together as PIOFS and will point out significant differences explicitly.

PIOFS was designed for the IBM SP series of parallel computers. These are distributed memory machines with separate I/O nodes. IBM has replaced PIOFS as its standard parallel file system with GPFS (see Section 3.5.3). Nevertheless, PIOFS is interesting because of the unique file model it defines to improve parallel I/O performance.

Unlike the Unix one-dimensional array of bytes, the PIOFS file model is two-dimensional (Figure 3.9). A file consists of several cells, and each cell contains an arbitrary number of basic striping units (BSUs). The designers of PIOFS consider a cell to be a virtual I/O node, in the sense that files are striped over cells. Each cell is assigned to a physical I/O node, so each physical I/O node stores one or more cells. A BSU is the smallest unit of data access that a file will use. Essentially, the number of cells corresponds to the stripe factor, and the BSU size corresponds to the stripe depth. PIOFS lets applications define these striping parameters for each file when it is created. The PIOFS model lets programs tailor the file striping to give optimal parallelism.

PIOFS further partitions its two-dimensional file structure into one or more subfiles. A subfile is a collection of BSUs, usually defined as a regular pattern in the two-dimensional array. When a process opens a file, it passes PIOFS a set of four parameters that define how the file is partitioned into a group of subfiles.

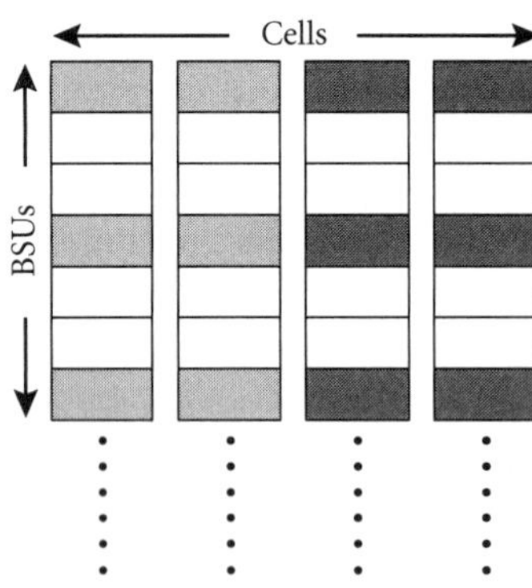

Figure 3.9 PIOFS files have a two-dimensional striping pattern of cells and basic striping units (BSUs). The number of cells is fixed when the file is created, but the number of BSUs grows with the file. Each process can define one or more subfiles, which give them partitioned access to the file. Two possible subfiles are shown in different shades of gray. (Adapted from Corbett and Feitelson [33].)

A fifth parameter selects a particular subfile from the group. If all the processes open a file with the same initial four partition parameters, the subfiles will not overlap. If each process accesses a different subfile, then PIOFS can handle concurrent file accesses without concern for sequential consistency. Although an application fixes the cell and BSU sizes when it creates a file, the program is free to use different subfile parameters each time it opens the file. A single process can also access the same file through different subfiles at the same time. The subfile abstraction lets an application choose the order in which it accesses a file's data without having to compute file locations explicitly. The definition of a subfile specifies the order in which BSUs are accessed.

An application can define overlapping subfiles by using different subfile parameters on each process. It can also access the same subfile on different processes. In both cases, PIOFS can enforce sequential consistency. It does this using a token passing mechanism (described earlier) that forces all the I/O nodes to handle requests in the same order. A program can turn this mechanism off if it doesn't need it. PIOFS uses only server buffering, so it doesn't need a cache coherence protocol.

PIOFS supports both local and shared file pointers. File pointers define a location in a subfile, not a global file location. Vesta (unlike PIOFS) has no explicit seek function. The read and write calls include an atomic seek operation, to avoid the interleaving problem that can arise when multiple access requests use the same file pointer. Also, Vesta updates file pointers by the amount of data requested without waiting for the request to complete, so requests that use the same file pointer can proceed concurrently. PIOFS updates pointers using normal Unix semantics.

In addition to its unique file model, Vesta manages directories differently from typical Unix file systems. The user sees a familiar hierarchy of files, but Vesta does not look up inodes by searching a series of directory files. Instead, it computes a file ID number by hashing the full path name. The data describing each file resides on one of the I/O nodes, and the hashed value identifies this master node. The file's record on the master node contains information about the layout of the file's cells on I/O nodes. There is no single inode that contains a list of all the file's blocks; the system manages file blocks at the level of cells. Cell block lists are stored in a balanced tree structure rather than the direct and indirect block lists that typical inodes use. Each compute node can calculate which cells on which I/O nodes will be involved in a data access, and the compute node sends a separate request to each cell.

If Vesta used only hash tables to record file information, it could not produce directory listings, since it would have no records that associated files with a particular directory. To provide this important service, Vesta stores records called Xrefs. Like a directory, an Xref contains a list of files and subdirectories. However, when a user needs to list a directory, Vesta does not traverse the path name from the root downward as a regular Unix file system does. Instead, it hashes the path name of the directory in the same way it does for files. It uses the hash code to find the Xref for that particular directory, and the Xref contains a list of the directory's contents. The hashing mechanism for files and Xrefs is efficient and scalable, but it interferes with some common Unix functionality, such as hard linking, directory search permissions, and directory renaming.

As a research system, Vesta was free to abandon compatibility with the standard Unix programming interface. However, PIOFS was a commercial product that needed to work with existing programs, so its interface is closer to standard Unix than Vesta's is. PIOFS files by default work like ordinary Unix files; there is a single subfile that covers the whole file, and all the processes share access to it. The file is striped over multiple I/O nodes, and the PIOFS token passing mechanism lets multiple processes access it concurrently. Users who wish to improve parallel I/O performance can call specialized PIOFS routines to create customized striping patterns and subfiles, and they can turn off the token passing mechanism.

3.5.3 IBM Tiger Shark and GPFS

IBM's successor to PIOFS is GPFS (General Parallel File System) [11], introduced in 1998. GPFS is based on another IBM file system called Tiger Shark [65]. Tiger Shark was designed specifically for multimedia applications, such as video-on-demand. It includes a number of features to help it stream audio and video data at high, guaranteed transfer rates. It also has a number of special features to ensure data integrity. Since high transfer rates and data integrity are also valuable in file systems for parallel computers, IBM adapted Tiger Shark to work in a general-purpose, high performance computing environment. Like Vesta and PIOFS, Tiger Shark and GPFS have similar designs, so this section will describe them together and refer to them both as GPFS.

GPFS represents an interesting departure from the trend that PFS, PIOFS, and some other parallel file systems established. Instead of offering a standard Unix interface for compatibility and specialized extensions for high performance, GPFS has only a standard interface. All its special features to support high performance concurrent I/O lie below the interface, essentially invisible to the user. Its designers apparently determined that GPFS could offer strict Unix semantics without reducing performance unacceptably. The exact cost of this trade-off cannot be measured, since there is no way to relax Unix semantics.

Like other file systems for distributed memory computers, GPFS accesses data through I/O nodes. It uses client buffering with a distributed locking mechanism to maintain cache coherence. Although GPFS doesn't implement server buffering directly, it is designed to access storage devices through IBM's Virtual Shared Disk (VSD) software, which does its own buffering. This software runs on the I/O nodes and controls multiple physical storage devices; it presents a uniform view of these devices to higher-level software like GPFS.

For both cache coherence and concurrency control, GPFS relies on byte range locking. No process can access a range of bytes while another process is writing that range. When a process opens a file, it acquires a lock. Both the GPFS software on a node that holds a lock and a central token manager server keep track of locks. If another node needs access to the file, it contacts the token manager server (which resides on one of the compute nodes) to request access to the file. If a lock is available, the server grants it; if not, the server returns to the requesting node a list of other nodes that hold locks (multiple nodes can hold read locks). The requesting node then negotiates directly with the other nodes to acquire the lock it needs. If the other nodes are using only part of the file, they may grant a lock for a specific range that is not in use, so multiple nodes can access a file concurrently if they access disjoint ranges.

The GPFS directory and inode structures are similar to those in standard Unix systems. One significant feature of GPFS is its large block size: 256 KB is the default. This choice reflects the origin of GPFS as a multimedia file system. The system can manage large blocks more efficiently than small ones, so large blocks contribute to high transfer rates. Since multimedia files are usually quite large, most large blocks are completely filled. However, for general-purpose use, 256 KB blocks would waste too much space, so GPFS collects small files and the ends of large files into single blocks. This allows it to use disk space about as efficiently as systems that use small blocks.

GPFS can stripe files in the usual way over a fixed sequence of I/O nodes. It can also use one of two randomized striping techniques. In these modes, GPFS determines the I/O node at which it will store each successive file block by generating pseudorandom numbers. The advantage of this technique is that the system can easily be reconfigured to use a different number of I/O nodes. If a file with N blocks is striped over k I/O nodes and a new node is added, any $\frac{N}{k(k+1)}$ blocks can be moved from each of the existing nodes to the new node. To restripe a file that was distributed sequentially, it would be necessary to move nearly all the blocks. The disadvantage of random striping is that it requires GPFS to maintain more information about block locations, and managing this information can reduce the transfer rate. The two random modes differ in the way they choose I/O nodes for each block. One method ensures that every node gets the same number of blocks; the other relies on the pseudorandom selection of nodes to balance the distribution stochastically. The system administrator determines the striping mode and stripe parameters; the user cannot change them.

GPFS supports high reliability and availability by avoiding single points of failure. The system uses journaling to log actions that affect the file system's records of the directory and file structure on disk, and the system always stores two copies of the log. As an option, it can also replicate the inode structure and data blocks, essentially implementing RAID 10 data protection. To protect the system from the failure of an I/O node, GPFS (and VSD) can use twin-tailed disks.

GPFS differs from Tiger Shark mainly in its support for general-purpose computing. Although Tiger Shark has a standard Unix interface, it is optimized specifically for multimedia workloads, which tend to read long streams of data and do little concurrent writing. GPFS added byte range locking to Tiger Shark's file locking, and it uses more sophisticated algorithms for prefetching data.

3.5.4 SGI XFS and CXFS

XFS [155, 47, 37] is the standard file system on Silicon Graphics computers. Since these machines are all shared memory or distributed shared memory computers, XFS does not have to deal with many of the problems that arise in the other parallel file systems discussed so far. In particular, there are no separate I/O nodes and no replication of buffers. As a result, concurrency control is relatively simple. XFS uses standard Unix-style I/O calls, with a few extensions for special services, and it supports Unix consistency semantics.

XFS does not manage storage devices directly. Instead, it calls a lower layer of software called XLV (the LV stands for logical volume), which in turn manages the disks. This arrangement is similar to the relationship between GPFS and VSD on IBM systems. XLV aggregates access to multiple storage devices so they appear to XFS as a single device. XLV can implement striping and mirroring to improve performance and data protection. Application programs cannot control the striping parameters.

Like GPFS, XFS was designed to support multimedia. To support this application, the system lets programs reserve a fixed amount of file I/O bandwidth, so data will flow at a guaranteed transfer rate. However, guaranteed-rate files must reside in a special data volume that the file system manages separately from regular files. Files in the normal, general-purpose directory structure do not support guaranteed-rate I/O.

XFS tries to maximize transfer rates by allocating contiguous file blocks for adjacent data. Although XFS doesn't control physical disk space directly, if it can allocate blocks in groups rather than one at a time, it improves the opportunity for XLV to store blocks on adjacent disk sectors. XFS delays flushing buffered blocks as long as possible to increase the probability that the application will write additional data to nearby file locations. As a result, XFS can send large, contiguous chunks of data to XLV. Delaying writes also lets it fulfill subsequent read requests for buffered data without accessing a disk.

For applications that access data in block-size units, XFS can disable buffering entirely. In this "direct I/O" mode, the interconnect adapter moves data directly to and from the application's own data buffer using DMA hardware. This eliminates a data copy operation between the file system buffer and the user buffer, but it forces the application to access data in units that are whole multiples of the file block size and to align the accesses to file block boundaries.

Like standard Unix systems, XFS uses directories and inodes, but it stores them in data structures called B+ trees. The system can search these structures more efficiently than ordinary inode lists. B+ trees also keep track of unused storage space and other file system internal data. Like GPFS, XFS uses journaling to restore the integrity of file system data in case of a disk failure.

Since XFS buffers reside in shared memory, XFS has no need for a cache coherence mechanism (beyond what the underlying hardware already provides). However, the system must still enforce sequential consistency between multiple concurrent I/O calls. For buffered I/O, XFS simply locks the whole file whenever a task is writing to it, so there is no parallel access. For direct I/O, XFS supports parallel access but does not enforce sequential consistency between accesses that span multiple file blocks.

CXFS (cluster XFS) [82] is an SGI extension to XFS that supports clusters of shared memory computers. A cluster consists of 2 to 16 computers (nodes) communicating over a private network. The nodes are also connected to a SAN that gives them access to a shared collection of storage devices. The structure is similar to what is used for network-attached storage devices (Section 2.8.1). One of the nodes acts as a server to mediate access to storage by the other nodes, but, as in the NASD model, the server centralizes only control, not data movement. All nodes see a common directory hierarchy and can access files concurrently. Each node can buffer data, and CXFS maintains coherence between the buffers.

Although CXFS is based on XFS and shares many features with it, CXFS does not support guaranteed-rate I/O. CXFS also does not efficiently support concurrent writing of the same file by multiple processes on different nodes, except in direct I/O mode.

3.5.5 HPSS

HPSS (High Performance Storage System) [173, 73] is very different from the parallel file systems described so far. Strictly speaking, it isn't a file system at all; it's an archival storage system, designed mainly for storing very large files and moving them quickly between primary, secondary, and tertiary storage. HPSS has a number of programming interfaces, one of which is based on Unix. Programs can access data directly on HPSS without going through the computer's native file system, but HPSS is not designed for general-purpose file storage. Although HPSS is an IBM product, it also runs on other vendors' hardware. It was developed jointly by IBM and several U.S. national laboratories, including Lawrence Berkeley, Lawrence Livermore, Los Alamos, Sandia, and Oak Ridge.

HPSS consists of a library of client interface functions that run on the compute nodes and a collection of servers that typically run on other nodes or on separate computers (Figure 3.10). Each server is responsible for a different HPSS operation.

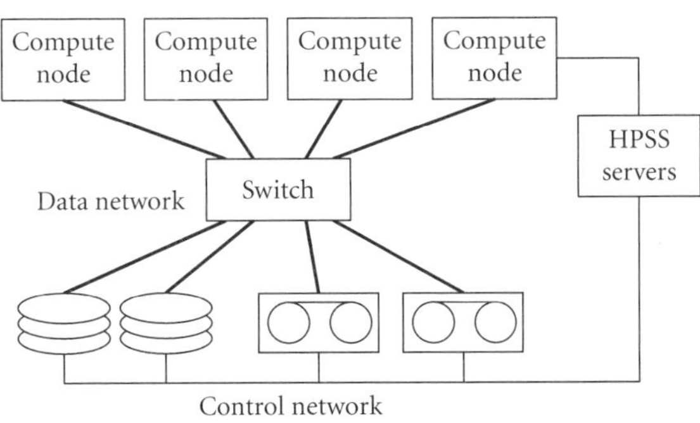

Figure 3.10 HPSS connects compute nodes to storage devices (both disks and tapes) through a high speed interconnect like HIPPI. Servers usually run on a different computer or node from the application. They accept requests from the compute nodes and control the storage devices through a separate network.

For example, the name server looks up file names and maps them to bitfile IDs, which correspond to Unix file descriptors. The bitfile server interprets data access requests and generates requests to the storage server, which is responsible for managing parallel I/O over a collection of volumes. Volumes are virtual or physical storage devices, which can be disk drives, RAID systems, or tape drives. Other servers are responsible for managing these individual devices (for example, mounting and unmounting tapes).

Data travels between the compute nodes and the storage devices over an external I/O network such as HIPPI. Control information traveling between the client software, the servers, and the storage devices often moves over a separate network such as Ethernet. A single HPSS installation can manage files for multiple computers.

To access a file, an application calls an HPSS function, which issues a remote procedure call to the bitfile server. The bitfile server interprets the request and forwards it to the lower layers of software, which in turn send commands over the control network to the storage devices. Data then travels between the compute node and the storage device. The actual data transfer is managed by a pair of "mover" tasks, one for the client node and one for the storage device. HPSS does not use client buffering because the large transfers it manages offer little opportunity for data reuse, and copying the data in and out of a buffer on the compute node would slow the transfer. HPSS does implement a form of caching and buffering, but not in memory. Instead, HPSS uses disks to store frequently accessed files that normally reside on tape. Programs can control this caching by requesting HPSS to "stage" a file from tape to disk shortly before the program expects to read it. Conversely, when a program does not expect to use a file, HPSS can migrate it to tape and then purge it from disk. HPSS can also do these operations automatically.

Users cannot control striping parameters directly, but the system administrator can define several classes of service, which define a number of parameters such as striping, whether the file should normally reside on disk or tape, and the maximum expected size of a file. A program can then request a particular class of service when it creates a new file.

Since HPSS doesn't cache data on the compute nodes, it doesn't need to manage cache consistency. It enforces sequential consistency by performing only one request on a given file at a time. In most file systems, this restriction would eliminate the opportunity for multiple processes to access a file in parallel. However, HPSS supports a specialized interface that does support parallel access. A process can construct a request that lists a collection of memory locations in the application processes and a collection of locations in a single file. The request also defines a mapping between the two lists of locations. One of the compute nodes sends this request to the HPSS servers, which split the request into components that the storage devices can carry out in parallel. Of course, the external I/O network must be designed to support parallel data movement between multiple storage devices and multiple compute nodes.

Because parallel transfers require the application to issue a single request to HPSS, the application needs a mechanism to collect individual requests from each process and merge them into one request. Initial versions of HPSS relied on the application to provide this mechanism, but the system now includes an MPI-IO interface (see Chapter 5) that gives applications a standard way to specify these collective requests. The ability of one process to issue a request that moves data between a storage device and another process is called *third-party transfer*, because the issuing process is neither the source nor the destination of the transfer.

In addition to its Unix-style interface, its third-party transfer interface, and its MPI-IO interface, HPSS also supports an FTP (file transfer protocol) interface that can move data in parallel between a local file system and HPSS. It's also possible to mount a collection of HPSS files in another file system's directory hierarchy.

Because each HPSS request travels from the client through a series of servers to the storage devices, usually traversing two network links, the request latency is high. For large file transfers, this delay is minimal compared to the overall transfer time, but the high latency clearly makes HPSS unsuitable for small requests and small files.

3.6 Cluster File Systems

Clusters of workstations are a popular alternative to integrated parallel systems designed and built by a vendor. Well-known cluster projects include the Berkeley Network of Workstations (NOW) [4], NASA's Beowulf [14], and Sandia National Laboratory's Cplant [60]. The architectures of these systems vary, but they are all built from off-the-shelf components, presumably at a lower cost than an integrated system with equivalent hardware. Workstation clusters consist of a collection of PCs or other workstation computers (which usually include disk drives) connected by some kind of message passing network. The systems typically run a standard operating system such as Windows or Linux, and they have additional software to manage communication between the nodes. Some systems are designed to scavenge unused computing power from workstations that normally run sequential jobs for individual users. Other clusters use workstations that are dedicated exclusively to the parallel system. The same type of workstation can work in either kind of system, but dedicated parallel clusters can be designed specifically to run parallel jobs efficiently. For example, they may have faster message passing networks instead of an ordinary LAN connection between nodes.

The general architecture of a cluster is similar to a distributed memory parallel computer; it consists of multiple nodes that exchange data over a message passing network. Therefore, parallel file systems for clusters must address many of the same problems as distributed memory file systems. These include consistency control and the choice between client and server buffering. In addition, cluster parallel file systems must contend with heterogeneity at several levels: individual clusters differ from each other; the hardware within a cluster may be heterogeneous; and the configuration of a cluster can change even while a program is running. Cluster file systems manage the first two kinds of heterogeneity by using standard programming interfaces. Some implement file service on top of the native file system running on each node. Managing files when the cluster configuration can change is more difficult. Some cluster file systems try to adapt to changing environments; others simply ignore the problem and assume that the cluster configuration will remain stable.

Many cluster computers make do with a distributed file system rather than a parallel one because existing distributed systems like NFS and DFS can already work in heterogeneous, dynamic environments. Although many research projects have developed parallel file systems for cluster computers, no one system has emerged yet as a de facto standard. The next section looks at some of the design issues for cluster file systems, and the following section describes a few research systems in more detail.

3.6.1 Issues for Cluster File Systems

Many clusters have no dedicated I/O nodes, so file systems have to distribute their file management functions over the compute nodes. A cluster file system may logically divide its functions between a client interface library and several server tasks, but the servers often run on the compute nodes and access the local disks. The systems often use client buffering, and they use partitioning or token passing for concurrency control, just as file systems for integrated machines do. Because the message passing networks are often relatively slow, the benefits of using client buffering are substantial. Most systems enforce locking at the level of file blocks, although at least one system, PIOUS [112], uses byte-level locking.

In clusters where nodes come and go unpredictably, the departure of a node can disrupt file service or make stored data unavailable. Most cluster systems replicate at least some of their file management data and functions over many or all of the nodes. A few, such as Berkeley's xFS [5] and River [6], replicate file data using RAID-like techniques so the loss of one node doesn't corrupt files. (Berkeley's xFS, with a lowercase *x*, is unrelated to SGI's XFS.) Another approach, which BFXM [95] uses, is to migrate data off a node when it leaves the cluster; this assumes that the node is still accessible but is busy with a sequential job.

A final problem for cluster file systems is how to stripe data. Since every node can act as both a compute node and an I/O node, the number of storage devices is often equal to the number of compute nodes. The arrangement offers a large aggregate I/O bandwidth. However, striping the data over many nodes can require excessive data movement over the network, and it increases the risk of data loss if a node fails or leaves the cluster. The second problem can be handled through replication as described above. The xFS file system handles the first problem by partitioning the storage resources into stripe groups to limit the number of disks over which it stripes each file. BFXM tries to store each file block on the node that generates it; a map of each file records the current location of every block.

3.6.2 Example Cluster File Systems

Many research groups have developed cluster file systems. This section will look at a few of these to see how individual systems handle the issues described above.

xFS

The xFS file system was developed at Berkeley for their NOW project. As noted above, xFS stripes files over stripe groups, and each stripe group forms a RAID unit controlled in software. There are no separate servers; file management software runs on all of the compute nodes, and each file is managed by one node. The manager's tasks include keeping track of the file's blocks both on disk and in replicated caches. The system uses token passing to maintain cache consistency. Because xFS locks files at the block level, false sharing is a potential problem.

PVFS

PVFS (Parallel Virtual File System) [23, 97] is a research project at Clemson University. It is aimed at Beowulf-class clusters. Unlike xFS, PVFS uses I/O server processes that can run on separate I/O nodes. However, the system also allows the server software to run on compute nodes. The system focuses on file partitioning for concurrency control. It offers several interfaces that let processes define their own nonoverlapping subsets of a file. The model is similar to PIOFS subfiles. Applications can define striping parameters individually for each file they create. PVFS does not manage file blocks directly; instead, it relies on the local native file system at each I/O node to handle this task. Although PVFS doesn't do buffering directly, there may be buffering in the underlying file system; if so, its effects would be similar to server buffering.

River

River is another Berkeley project with a different focus from xFS. It is designed specifically for a dataflow programming model, in which the programmer defines a collection of independent tasks and links them with input and output ports. In this programming model, file I/O works like a producer of data when a program reads a file and a consumer when a program writes. River concerns itself with managing parallel I/O resources so that a disk or node running slower than the others won't unduly affect the whole system. The inherent parallelism of the dataflow model helps avoid bottlenecks because the system can assign independent units of work in a way that keeps all nodes equally busy.

The system balances the I/O workload using two mechanisms. The nodes computing data write their results to a distributed queue at full speed, with no concern for which disks will actually store the data. The individual disks take data from this queue and store it as they are able. The fastest disk will automatically do more I/O than the slowest one. However, the system can arrange for every block of data to be mirrored on two disks. The mirroring allows a second mechanism, graduated declustering, to balance the load when nodes read data. Since every block resides on two disks, a node has a choice of sources for its data. Normally, each node gets half of its data from each source, but if one of the disks slows down (perhaps because the physical data layout is fragmented), the system can rebalance the load so that the slower disk receives fewer requests. Of course, the aggregate bandwidth of all the disks will be lower as long as one disk is running slow, but the system can balance the I/O load over all the disks so that the slowdown affects all the nodes equally.

Because the file system rather than the application controls the placement of data in files, I/O accesses are contiguous and do not overlap. Of course, to benefit from the performance available in this programming model, application developers must adopt a new way of writing their code.

3.7 Other File System Research

Two other parallel computing projects of interest are Legion and Globus. These systems focus on widely distributed networks of heterogeneous computers. Legion [61] defines a programming model and an architecture for linking machines over long distances (i.e., across the country) to form a unified metacomputing environment. The Legion programming model anticipates the need to store large data sets using parallel techniques, and it can define objects with different semantics to support sequential consistency or concurrent access, as the application requires. However, the Legion architecture does not define a specific implementation for a parallel file system.

Globus [54] is another wide area computing project. It has defined a storage system called GASS that gives multiple processes access to a common group of files.

However, GASS is not a general-purpose parallel file system. In particular, it does not allow multiple processes to write at arbitrary locations in a file at the same time, nor does it allow one process to read a file that another process is writing. The system caches entire files rather than individual blocks, which is a sensible approach when a process needs to access a file stored on a different system a long distance away. GASS does permit limited sharing of files in what its designers expect to be common cases. Processes can jointly append data to log files, read a file concurrently without changing it, or write separate versions of the same file. In the last case, writes are sequentially consistent across the entire file, so multiple processes can't write the same file in parallel.

Because of their low cost, cluster architectures are especially popular at universities. It seems likely, then, that academic research on file systems will focus increasingly on clusters. However, research also continues on file systems for integrated parallel computers. Much of the interesting work in this area explores novel programming interfaces to improve I/O performance. Later chapters will look at some of these research systems.

3.8 Summary

This chapter has shown how file systems organize raw data blocks on storage devices into the familiar view of files and directories. File systems use caching and buffering to improve performance, especially for accesses to small amounts of data and for bursty access patterns. Distributed file systems give programs running on different computers access to a shared collection of files, but they are not designed to handle concurrent file accesses efficiently. Parallel file systems do handle concurrent accesses, and they stripe files over multiple I/O nodes to improve bandwidth.

Sequential Unix-based file systems have traditionally defined the semantics of read and write operations in a way that makes concurrent file accesses by separate processes appear to occur in a well-defined order. Maintaining these semantics in parallel and distributed file systems is difficult, so some systems relax the traditional semantics to improve performance. Other systems use various techniques to maintain standard Unix consistency semantics while endeavoring to offer good parallel performance.

Distributed memory parallel computers often route file access requests through specialized I/O nodes. Some parallel file systems do "server buffering" on these nodes, while others do "client buffering" on the compute node. Both approaches have strengths and weaknesses.

Computer vendors and researchers have developed many parallel file systems, some with novel programming interfaces. The trend in current commercial parallel file systems appears to be toward offering standard Unix semantics rather than specialized parallel I/O interfaces.

3.9 Further Reading

Many textbooks on operating systems describe file system design in detail. For this chapter, I consulted Bach [10] and Silberschatz and Galvin [145]. A brief but useful comparison of distributed file systems appears in a paper by Többicke [165]. A collection of papers edited by Jain, Werth, and Browne [81] covers many topics in parallel file systems. Feitelson et al. [52] published a useful review of parallel I/O subsystems in 1995. Information on specific file systems comes from user documentation and research papers; see the references noted for each system. The bibliography also includes several papers on file systems not discussed here [45, 56, 106, 112, 131].

Chapter Four
Access Patterns and Optimizations

Storage devices and file systems perform best when they transfer large, contiguous blocks of data, but these large transfers are not the way many parallel applications access data. This chapter will examine the I/O patterns of parallel scientific codes and how to handle those patterns efficiently.

Studies of parallel I/O workloads have shown that access patterns vary widely between applications. Many applications generate long sequences of requests that each access only tens or hundreds of bytes. Even when an application moves data in large blocks, the configuration of the I/O hardware and software (including the file system's caching and buffering policies) may cause the system to deliver much better performance for some access patterns than others. For example, performance improves in some file systems when compute nodes match the size and alignment of their file accesses to the striping parameters of a file. Developers can modify applications to generate efficient I/O requests, but the job is tedious, and the resulting code may perform well only for a specific system configuration on one parallel computer.

Some I/O systems can transform I/O requests from a form that is convenient for application developers into a form that improves I/O performance. *Collective I/O* (Section 4.4) is a technique that coordinates I/O requests from multiple processes, merging many small requests into a larger one. *Hints* (Section 4.5.1) are information that the application program passes to the I/O system that describe the properties of upcoming access requests. The I/O system can then adjust its configuration to improve performance for the specified access pattern.

4.1 I/O in Scientific Applications

Large scientific codes need to move large data structures between primary and secondary storage. Miller and Katz [105] divided supercomputer application I/O into three categories: required, checkpoint, and data staging. Required I/O includes reading input data and writing final results. Checkpoint I/O is the data a program writes periodically as insurance against a hardware or software failure. If the program halts before completing its computation, it can resume near where it left off by reading the checkpoint data and restarting the computation. Staging I/O supports applications whose data does not fit in memory. The application moves subsets of a large data structure between primary and secondary storage as the computation proceeds. In systems that support virtual memory, the operating system manages data staging with no help from the application. However, some supercomputers do not support virtual memory, so applications must manage data staging themselves using "out-of-core" techniques. Even on systems that do have virtual memory, some applications stage data explicitly because they can determine better than the operating system what data to fetch and store. Applications that do staging often read more data than they write because they read data from the disk several times before updating it.

The details of scientific data structures depend on the application, of course, but two examples represent the common cases. Consider first a program that manages a multidimensional rectangular array. Individual array elements may be single numbers or a collection of related values (tuples), such as the temperature, pressure, and velocity of a fluid at a given point in space. In the latter case, some applications store these values in memory as separate arrays, while others maintain a single array of tuples. The smallest logical unit of data that a program accesses in an I/O operation is called a *record*. For this multidimensional array, a record could be a tuple or a single number.

In memory and in most file systems, a multidimensional array is stored as a one-dimensional array of bytes. Therefore, two array elements that are logically contiguous (e.g., they reside in the same row and adjacent columns) might not be stored in adjacent memory or file locations. This is not usually a problem when an application accesses the whole array because it can access the array in the underlying storage order. However, accessing only a portion of an array can produce requests to read or write *discontiguous* (separate) regions of a file or memory (Figure 4.1). This kind of access is especially common in out-of-core programs, since these codes routinely read and write subsets of a large data structure. However, despite being discontiguous, these accesses follow a regular pattern. For example, a program that reads one column of a two-dimensional array stored in row-major order will issue a series of read requests at regularly spaced file offsets. A sequence of accesses at fixed

1	2	3	4	5	6	7	8
9	10	11	12	13	14	15	16
17	18	19	20	21	22	23	24
25	26	27	28	29	30	31	32
33	34	35	36	37	38	39	40
41	42	43	44	45	46	47	48
49	50	51	52	53	54	55	56
57	58	59	60	61	62	63	64

```
read(..., offset=21, length=2)
read(..., offset=29, length=2)
read(..., offset=37, length=2)
read(..., offset=45, length=2)
```

Figure 4.1 A two-dimensional matrix is stored in a file as a one-dimensional array (the numbers correspond to indices in the one-dimensional array). Reading a subblock of the matrix requires a series of discontiguous requests for small amounts of data.

intervals is called a *strided access;* the stride is the number of elements (or bytes) between the start of successive elements.

A more complicated data structure is an irregular grid. Regular grids define points in a computational space at fixed intervals. Irregular grids have nodal points at arbitrary locations. An irregular grid can be represented as a set of arrays that list nodes, edges, surfaces, volumes, and so on (Figure 4.2). Adjacent nodes in an irregular grid may be stored at arbitrary intervals in an array, so accessing a subset of the grid requires a series of random accesses rather than strided accesses.

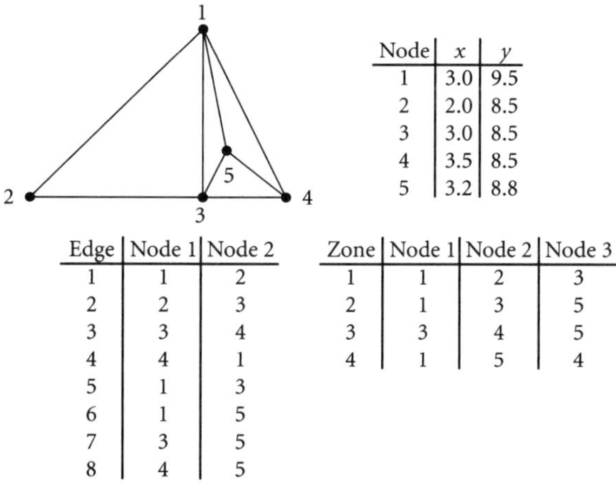

Node	x	y
1	3.0	9.5
2	2.0	8.5
3	3.0	8.5
4	3.5	8.5
5	3.2	8.8

Edge	Node 1	Node 2
1	1	2
2	2	3
3	3	4
4	4	1
5	1	3
6	1	5
7	3	5
8	4	5

Zone	Node 1	Node 2	Node 3
1	1	2	3
2	1	3	5
3	3	4	5
4	1	5	4

Figure 4.2 A simple two-dimensional unstructured grid and the data structures that define it.

All these considerations apply to both sequential and parallel programs. Distributed memory parallel programs must also deal with the distribution of data structures among the processes. Regular grids are often partitioned in a regular pattern, so each process computes on a fixed-size subset of a global grid. A common distribution technique is to partition each dimension of a rectangular array in one of two ways: as a set of equal-size blocks (*block distribution*) or as a repeating series of strips (*cyclic distribution*). Each strip in a cyclic distribution can be one element or several elements wide. Different dimensions use block or cyclic distributions, or none at all. (See Figure 5.1 in Chapter 5 for diagrams of some example data distributions.) Depending on the distribution, a program that reads or writes a whole array from a collection of processes may produce a series of discontiguous accesses at each process. This happens because although the program as a whole is accessing the entire array, individual processes must skip through the file to access array elements in the individual rows or columns assigned to them.

Irregular grids have more complex distributions, and these often change as the program runs. The description of how a portion of a grid at one process fits into the global structure is called a *local-to-global mapping.* This mapping specifies a location in the global grid for each point in a processor's local grid. Any access to a globally shared data structure in a file will use this mapping. In applications that use regular grids with regular distributions, each process can determine the local-to-global mapping with a simple algorithm that produces strided access requests, as shown in Figure 4.3.

Irregular grids cannot use simple algorithmic mappings. Instead, each process must store the local-to-global map explicitly. To read or write an unstructured grid in a shared file, each process must traverse a list, as shown in Figure 4.4.

The two forms of access both look simple, but describing the regular mapping requires only four parameters: the number of records, the record size, the local

```
bytes = record_size
for i = 0 to n_records - 1
    offset = proc_num * record_size
        + i * record_size * num_procs
    write(..., bytes, offset)
end
```

Figure 4.3 This pseudocode for a cyclic (or "round-robin") local-to-global mapping computes file offsets based on the process number, the record size, and the number of processors. The algorithm will produce repeated sequences of records, with one record from each process in each sequence.

```
bytes = record_size
for i = 0 to n_records - 1
    offset = global(i) * record_size
    write(..., bytes, offset)
end
```

Figure 4.4 For irregular data distributions, the application must produce an array, `global`, that lists the global location for each record of the local array. This pseudocode shows how the application can then write each record to its correct file location.

processor number, and the total number of processors. The irregular grid mapping requires an array whose size is proportional to the number of records.

4.2 Access Patterns

Efforts to improve I/O performance must begin with an understanding of I/O access patterns. Studies of sequential Unix systems (e.g., Ousterhout et al. [123]) have found that many files are small and temporary, being created and then removed within a short time. Also, many sequential Unix files are read more often than they are written. Most are read or written in sequential order and all the way through. For these access patterns, caching and buffering work well. Unfortunately, high performance computer applications are not typical Unix programs, and vector computer I/O patterns differ from distributed memory I/O patterns.

4.2.1 Vector Computer I/O Patterns

On vector supercomputers, long accesses to large files are the rule. For example, a 1991 study by Miller and Katz [105] of seven applications running on a Cray Y-MP vector computer found that codes used files that were tens to hundreds of megabytes long. The applications tended to access data in chunks ranging from 32 KB to 512 KB. For each application, the access sizes were relatively constant. Over time, the accesses were cyclic and bursty; that is, periods of little I/O activity alternated with periods of intense activity. Furthermore, the ratio of data read to data written varied widely among the applications, from 11:1 down to 0.09:1. A study by Pasquale and Polyzos [124] in 1994 also found regular patterns of large data access on a Cray C90.

In these applications, caching and buffering are ineffective. The writes are large enough to fill a whole block, so buffers do not eliminate read-modify-write sequences. For out-of-core applications, buffers are too small to cache data written temporarily to storage; if a buffer were large enough to hold a significant amount of out-of-core data, its memory could be used more effectively in the application itself.

4.2.2 Distributed Memory I/O Patterns

I/O patterns on distributed memory computers differ from both sequential Unix and vector computer applications. Indeed, distributed memory applications differ quite a bit from each other. Two instructive distributed memory I/O studies examined applications running on machines no longer widely used: the Connection Machine CM-5, the Intel iPSC/860, and the Intel Paragon. However, application programming models and the general I/O architecture of distributed memory computers have changed little enough that the results of these studies remain useful for understanding I/O access patterns. Few, if any, I/O workload studies are available for shared memory or distributed shared memory computers. Unfortunately, this means that it is difficult to compare the performance of various I/O access patterns on current parallel file systems.

The SIO Study

The Scalable I/O Initiative (SIO) [130] was organized to address a number of parallel I/O problems. As part of this effort, Smirni and Reed [149] measured the I/O characteristics of five scientific applications. The codes are MESSKIT and NWChem, both of which compute the electron density around a molecule using the Hartree-Fock method; QCRD, which computes quantum chemical reaction dynamics; PRISM, a computational fluid dynamics code; and ESCAT, which calculates scattering in electron-molecule collisions. The SIO researchers added code to these applications that records each open, close, seek, read, and write request, and they ran the applications on an Intel Paragon. All the applications except PRISM use out-of-core techniques.

The study found that data access sizes vary greatly. Even within individual codes, the sizes could range from tens of bytes to tens of thousands of bytes. In many applications, the majority of the requests were for small amounts of data (less than a few thousand bytes), but the majority of the total data moved was part of a few large requests. Smirni and Reed note that this disparity demonstrates the importance of optimizing both the access time, which dominates the cost of small requests, and the transfer rate, which dominates the cost of large requests.

In both MESSKIT and NWChem, each process in a job uses a separate file for its data staging I/O. The processes write data consecutively to their files (so each write begins where the previous one left off). Then several times during the subsequent execution, each process reads back data consecutively from the same file. The programs route all their input and final output (required I/O) through a single process. QCRD and ESCAT, on the other hand, use interleaved access patterns; processes share access to one or more files that hold global data structures. To access its portion of the data, each process must repeatedly seek and then read or write a small amount of data. PRISM does both consecutive and interleaved I/O.

Figure 4.5 shows how I/O operations contributed to the total execution time in five SIO applications. Taken together, the I/O operations contributed from less than half a percent to more than 75% of the total time. In three applications, the read requests accounted for the majority of the I/O time; in one, the write requests dominated. In the fifth application, QCRD, seek requests accounted for 93% of the I/O time and nearly 30% of the total execution time. These seeks are part of the interleaved access pattern described above. The other two codes that do interleaved access, PRISM and ESCAT, also spent a significant amount of time seeking (11% and 18% of I/O time). At least one of the latter codes used the PFS M_ASYNC mode instead of the M_UNIX mode (see Section 3.5.1 in the last chapter). Evidently, PFS serializes all accesses to the same file in the M_UNIX mode, including seeks on local file pointers, and this accounts for the high cost of the operations. It is not clear whether all this serialization is necessary to maintain sequential consistency, or if a different implementation of PFS could have avoided it. Nevertheless, the disparity shows how the choice of access modes can affect performance for similar operations.

The SIO group further demonstrated how an application's use of I/O can affect performance in a study that focused on ESCAT and PRISM [148]. The researchers measured the I/O performance of these codes on the Paragon as several I/O optimizations were added. At the outset, both codes used only M_UNIX (the default) for all their I/O operations. All the processes read their initial data from an input file. Further I/O operations included data staging, checkpointing, and required output, and each application routed all its I/O through one process.

To improve the performance, the researchers first noted in both applications that all processes were reading data from one file at start-up. Sharing the file in M_UNIX mode caused PFS to serialize the read requests. The developers of the two codes solved this problem in different ways. ESCAT was changed to make one process read the input data and broadcast it to the other processes. PRISM was changed to use M_GLOBAL for shared input data and M_RECORD for process-specific data. Both modes give all the processes efficient access to a shared file.

A second optimization in ESCAT was to use PFS parallel access modes for data staging. The application switched to M_ASYNC for its interleaved write operations,

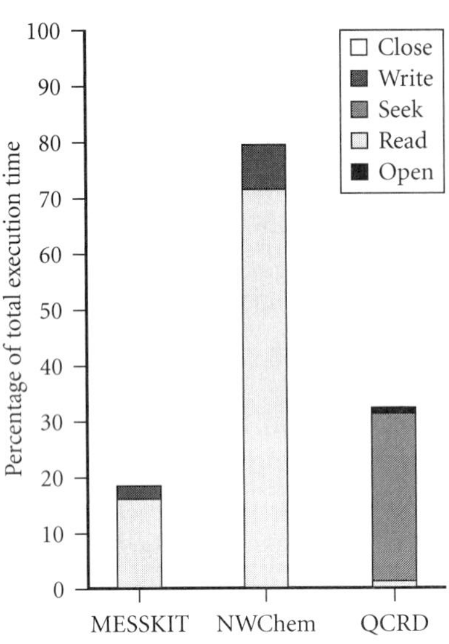

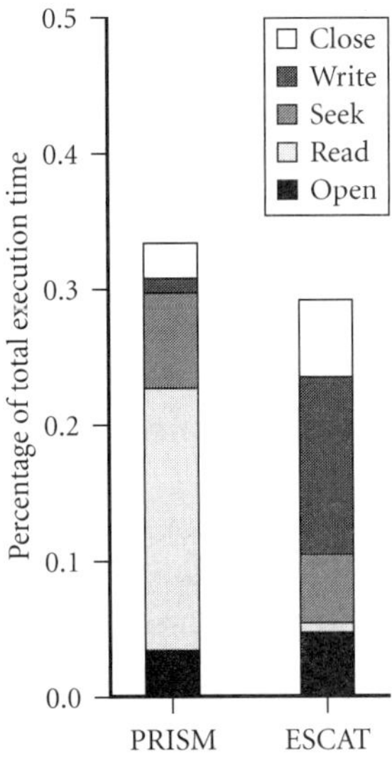

Figure 4.5 Smirni and Reed's data show the contribution of various I/O operations to the total execution time of five scientific applications. Note the different scales on the two graphs. In QCRD, the seek operation accounted for almost all of the total I/O time. (Adapted from Smirni and Reed [149].)

which reduced the cost of seeking and writing. To read the data back, the application used M_RECORD, and each process accessed data in whole multiples of the stripe width. Using M_RECORD lets the processes access data in parallel, and accessing data in whole multiples of the stripe width lets the I/O nodes move data in whole blocks.

These optimizations reduced the execution time of ESCAT by about 20% and PRISM by about 27%, both for relatively small problem sizes. The SIO researchers believe that for larger problem sizes, the I/O demands would grow rapidly, so the effect of the optimizations would be even larger.

The CHARISMA Study

While the SIO researchers instrumented applications to measure I/O characteristics, a study called CHARISMA [120] instrumented I/O libraries. The CHARISMA group modified the I/O libraries on two parallel computers that were running a range of scientific applications. All the applications that used these libraries automatically generated records of their I/O access patterns. This approach gave the researchers information for many applications, but since they didn't have direct access to the codes, they had to infer from the access patterns what the codes were trying to do. The studies recorded access patterns on an Intel iPSC/860 at NASA Ames Research Center and a Thinking Machines CM-5 at the National Center for Supercomputing Applications. The iPSC was running CFS rather than PFS, which has a smaller selection of I/O modes. The CM-5 was running a parallel file system called SFS, and applications on that machine were coded either in a data parallel language called CM Fortran or with a message passing library called CMMD. (The CMMD applications used the instrumented I/O package only if the user chose it explicitly; CM Fortran and iPSC users got the instrumented package automatically when they linked their codes.)

The study focused on applications that used the parallel file system on the Intel machine and the RAID storage device on the CM-5. This helped eliminate sequential jobs from the data. Without access to the codes, the researchers could not be certain whether any particular I/O operation represented required I/O, data staging, or checkpointing. However, certain access patterns suggested specific uses. For example, files that were written but never read back were probably checkpoints or required output files. Temporary files (those that jobs created and then deleted within a single run) were likely used for either data staging or checkpointing. In the latter case, the applications removed the files because they had completed successfully. Unlike the SIO study, the CHARISMA project found little apparent use of data staging. Temporary files accounted for fewer than 1% of the files on the iPSC and fewer than 5% of the files on the CM-5.

	Traced jobs	*Files read*	*Files written*	*Average MB read/file*	*Average MB written/file*
CFS	470	14,540	44,500	3.3	1.2
CMF	1760	1,271	2,286	27.8	25.2
CMMD	127	257	596	117.5	110.2

Table 4.1 *Applications using the iPSC's CFS accessed a large number of small files compared to applications on the CM-5 using either the CM Fortran (CMF) or CMMD programming model. (Data from Nieuwejaar et al. [120].)*

CHARISMA found a greater skew toward small access sizes than the SIO group did. For example, on the iPSC, 96% of read requests and 90% of write requests accessed fewer than 100 bytes. However, these requests accounted for 2% and 3%, respectively, of data transferred. The predominance of small accesses on the CM-5 was less extreme, but roughly 90% of reads and writes were under 1000 bytes.

The study found that many files were accessed consecutively. This was especially true of files that were only written. When applications did access files nonconsecutively, they often read or wrote fixed amounts of data at regular intervals, which indicates an interleaved access pattern. The study also detected multiple levels of interleaving, where applications would alternate among several fixed patterns. The interleaving suggests that applications were distributing large, regular data structures such as matrices among multiple processes. This sharing of data in a file was much more common for read operations than for write operations.

Finally, the study found that on the iPSC, applications tended to access a large number of relatively small files, especially for write operations. Table 4.1 shows the disparity in both the number and size of the files. (The study considered concurrent open operations on the same file by multiple processes as a single open on the iPSC. CMMD and CM Fortran support a global open operation, so they do not need this correction.) The authors infer that the programmers of the CM-5 do more I/O because that machine had better storage capacity and bandwidth.

4.2.3 The Need for Optimizations

These two parallel I/O studies establish no typical I/O pattern; instead, they demonstrate a range of patterns. The studies also show that users are willing to change the access patterns of their codes to suit the I/O performance of their machines.

Although none of the studies cited above followed the same application from a vector processor Cray machine to a CM-5 to a Paragon, all these machines were running general scientific workloads, and the large fixed-size accesses seen in both Cray studies were not common on the Intels or the CM-5. It seems likely that in developing or modifying their applications for the distributed computers, developers adapted their I/O patterns to the machine at hand. Differences appeared even between different types of distributed memory computers. Of course, these variations are possible because an application can do its I/O in many different ways. For checkpoint I/O, users can adjust the number of checkpoints written according to the I/O performance of the machine. They may also determine the amount of "required" output in a program based on a target machine's I/O performance. They may even choose to recompute data as the program runs rather than store it on disk between uses. This malleability of I/O access patterns means that characterization studies do not necessarily expose applications' fundamental I/O needs.

Despite this flexibility, users have good reason to prefer standard programming interfaces, since high performance computers become obsolete so quickly. Although programming models and the general architecture of distributed memory computers are not changing rapidly, the implementations of file systems are. The changes that improved the performance of the SIO applications are useless on systems that don't support the Intel PFS interface: they won't improve performance, and they must be disabled before the code can be compiled for another system. Scientific codes often evolve over many years, outlasting several generations of computers. Furthermore, at any given time, users can often run their codes on a variety of parallel systems.

Thus, application developers face a dilemma. They can improve performance by adapting their I/O calls to use specific features of a parallel file system, or they can write code that uses standard Unix or Fortran I/O calls to keep their code portable. A further difficulty is that using the special file system features requires an understanding of the details of the file system configuration. The ESCAT code noted above is an example: it must be aware of the file stripe depth and stripe factor to achieve good performance.

A general-purpose parallel file system must manage both small access and large ones, both consecutive and interleaved accesses, and both shared and local files. Optimizing one case can reduce performance in another. For example, caching and buffering work well for small access, but they slow down large transfers by imposing an unnecessary copy operation. Moreover, the characterization studies show that the access pattern most difficult to handle efficiently, small disjoint accesses, has become quite common. Figure 4.6 shows how performance varies with access size on a typical system.

To address these problems, researchers have developed techniques to improve I/O performance in parallel applications and to simplify parallel file access. Some techniques are implemented directly in a parallel file system; others use a layer

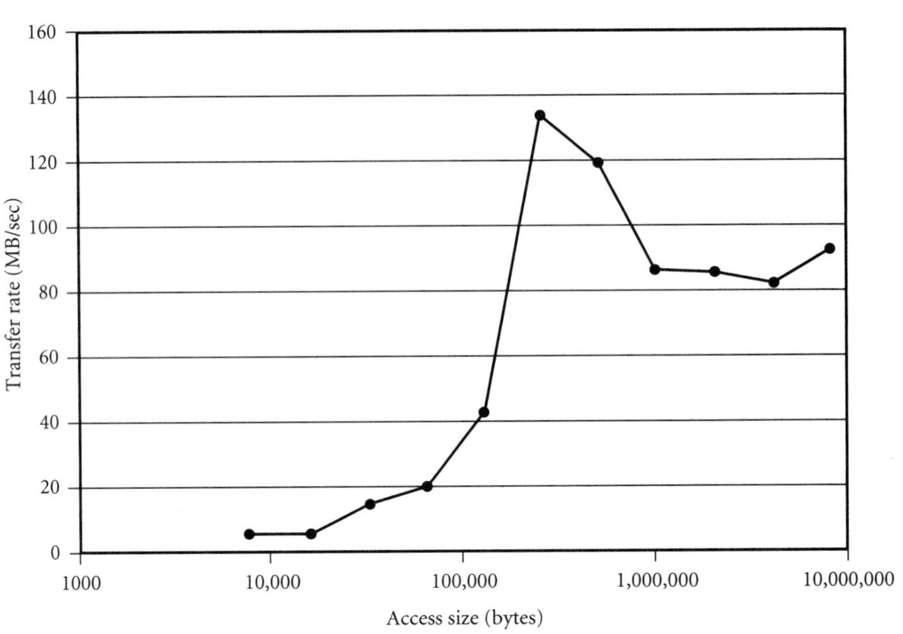

Figure 4.6 Performance for small, discontiguous accesses is much worse than for large accesses. Here, 16 compute processes on an IBM RS6000/SP write a single 1 GB file on GPFS with four I/O nodes. The accesses are interleaved, and each process uses standard Unix calls to seek and then write data. The performance peak at 256 KB corresponds to the GPFS block size.

of software that resides between the application and a file system. In both cases, the software that implements these techniques is called the "I/O software." The techniques fall into three general categories: discontiguous access methods that read or write separate parts of a file in a single request; collective I/O, which treats requests from multiple processes as a single operation; and adaptive methods, which tell the I/O software what kind of accesses an application will perform so the system can configure itself to give better performance. At present, these techniques require the application to use special I/O subroutines with interfaces that differ from standard Unix or Fortran I/O. The standard interfaces simply cannot give the I/O software all the information it needs to carry out the optimizations. However, as Chapter 5 shows, new standard interfaces do support parallel I/O optimizations. The advantage of these interfaces over a vendor file system interface like PFS or PIOFS is their independence from any specific I/O software implementation. They tell the system what kinds of optimizations are possible, but they don't specify how to carry them out.

4.3 Discontiguous Access

Distributed memory applications often share a global file among processes. As shown in Figure 4.1, each process may need to issue a series of short requests to read or write this data. Small accesses are inefficient by themselves, but combining them into a single request can improve performance. Discontiguous accesses merge requests for separate chunks of data into a single operation. One advantage of these merged requests is that the I/O software can send a group of small requests or data items between a compute node and an I/O node as a single message, reducing the communication cost. Minimizing the number of separate requests is especially important in systems that do not use client buffering. Since client-buffered systems move whole data blocks between the compute nodes and I/O nodes regardless of the request size, grouping nearby requests for discontiguous data avoids separate messages.

A second advantage of combining requests is that it can improve the scheduling of disk accesses. For example, if a compute node reads a long series of widely separated records in a file, the I/O software may not be able to prefetch data effectively if it receives the requests individually. The records may be separated by one or more disk blocks that contain no requested data, so prefetching blocks sequentially would be wasteful. However, if the I/O software receives a request that describes the entire access pattern, it need only prefetch those blocks that contain useful data.

I/O interfaces can support discontiguous access in two ways: as an algorithmic description or as an explicit list. Algorithmic descriptions work well for accesses that follow a regular pattern, and lists are appropriate for irregular accesses. One form of algorithmic description includes in each I/O request a set of parameters that describe the individual chunks of data. For example, the Galley file system [119] (described below) uses this function to read strided blocks of data:

```
gfs_read_strided( file, buffer, offset, record_size,
    file_stride, memory_stride, quantity)
```

This function reads `quantity` records from `file` starting at `offset` and continuing every `file_stride` bytes. The records are stored in `buffer` at intervals of `memory_stride`. As this example shows, accesses can be discontiguous in both the file and memory.

An alternative to specifying the access pattern in each I/O request is to partition the file logically for each process. This approach defines a template through which each process accesses data in the file. All the processes can use the same template, or they can use interleaved templates. PIOFS is an example of this approach. The templates are PIOFS subfiles. A process can access only the data that is visible through its template. Therefore, accesses that appear contiguous from the perspective of a process are discontiguous in the file. Templates have the advantage that the application developer need only worry about the local-to-global mapping when opening a file and not at every I/O operation. However, templates define accesses that are discontiguous only in the file, not in memory.

A list-based I/O request includes a series of descriptors that define individual accesses. For example, the Unix list I/O interface uses a series of C structures that include the following fields:

```
struct aiocb {
    int aio_filedes;     /* file descriptor */
    void *aio_buf;       /* memory buffer */
    size_t aio_nbytes;   /* size of chunk */
    off_t aio_offset;    /* file location */
    /* ... several other fields omitted */
};
```

As shown here, each structure lists the target file descriptor, the location in memory where the data is to be read or written, the corresponding location in the file, and the number of bytes to be moved. Each of these structures describes a single contiguous data transfer. Applications pass the Unix list I/O function an array of pointers to these structures, with one for each element in the transfer. A list-based interface works for both regular and irregular access patterns, but since an algorithmic interface can describe a long series of transfers compactly, the I/O software can communicate algorithmic descriptions between compute nodes and I/O nodes more efficiently than lists. Therefore, algorithmic interfaces are better than list-based interfaces for regular transfers.

Applications use local-to-global mapping data for purposes other than I/O, and it is not always convenient for them to maintain the mapping in the format that the list I/O interface requires. Therefore, building the descriptor list incurs some computational overhead, which is proportional to the number of records in the list. This step must be done before every access if the data distribution changes or if the application cannot afford the memory needed to store the list of I/O descriptors between uses.

The Galley I/O system demonstrates the power of discontiguous data accesses. Nieuwejaar and Kotz [119] developed this system to improve performance for the typical I/O patterns they observed in the CHARISMA study. Galley uses a multidimensional model of file storage, similar to PIOFS and Vesta, and its programming interface supports list-based descriptions and two kinds of algorithmic descriptions. (The Galley interface presented above describes simple strided access patterns; the second algorithmic interface describes more complicated regular patterns.) The researchers measured the performance of Galley on an IBM SP2. They used 16 compute nodes and 4 to 64 I/O nodes with simulated disks. The tests simulated the performance of disk drives instead of accessing real disks because the IBM file system that managed the real disks masked the performance variations that the experiment was trying to expose. The simulated disks mimicked the access time and bandwidth of real physical drives.

The experiment measured read and write performance for both contiguous and interleaved access patterns for record sizes ranging from 64 bytes to 64 KB. When the tests used a series of separate read or write requests to move the data, the performance followed a pattern similar to Figure 4.6: the transfer rate was low for small records and grew steadily as the size increased. When the tests were done with the two algorithmic interfaces, the performance for small records increased dramatically, especially for read requests. In some cases, the transfer rate for 64-byte accesses was essentially the same as the rate for 64 KB accesses. These tests showed the benefits of grouping accesses. The test code wrote in parallel from multiple processes, and the good performance depended in part on the fact that interleaved requests from multiple processes arrived at the I/O nodes at about the same time. This temporal locality allowed Galley to coordinate requests from multiple compute nodes and thereby minimize the number of disk accesses. However, this coordination is implicit; Galley takes advantage of the locality when it is available but does not enforce it.

4.4 Collective I/O

Collective I/O, like discontiguous access, is a class of optimizations that improve performance by merging separate I/O requests. However, unlike discontiguous access, collective I/O merges requests across multiple processes. In many cases, collective I/O enforces temporal locality so the I/O software can explicitly coordinate requests.

Collective write operations gather data from multiple processes into large, contiguous chunks before storing it to disk. Collective read operations retrieve large chunks from disk and distribute this data to multiple requesting processes. This reduces the number of disk accesses and makes each access more efficient. False sharing (accessing data in the same block but at different locations) and sequentialization of accesses are both eliminated. Although in principle collective I/O algorithms need not synchronize the participating tasks, in practice most collective operations have the effect of a barrier: no task will finish the operation until all the tasks have started. Many parallel scientific applications already operate in synchronized phases. All the tasks gather initial data, compute a time step, exchange data, compute another time step, and so on. At each time step, or after some number of time steps, all the tasks do I/O. This may be required I/O (the data computed for a particular time interval of a simulation), data staging, or a checkpoint. In some applications, writing data for a time step is equivalent to a checkpoint. A phased structure works well for collective I/O; all the tasks are doing I/O at about the same time, so the tasks are already synchronized independent of the I/O operations.

On the other hand, parallel applications that are not at least loosely synchronous gain no benefit from collective I/O. For example, consider an algorithm in which tasks independently test possible solutions to an optimization problem. Some solutions may take longer to test than others, so the program balances the load among the tasks by having each one read and test candidate solutions independently of each other. If a tested solution is promising, the task writes a record of it to a globally shared file. Tasks will access both the input and the output files at unpredictable intervals, so trying to coordinate the accesses will impose a synchronization that will idle some processes while others are still computing. Any benefit that the application gains from accessing data in large blocks will be lost in the cost of synchronizing the tasks.

Collective I/O techniques fall into two categories: client-based collective I/O, which gathers small requests into larger blocks on the compute nodes, and server-based I/O, which gathers the requests at the I/O nodes. Since the performance of these systems is their most important measurable feature, the next section briefly discusses the question of how to measure collective I/O transfer rates. Then the following two sections look at collective I/O techniques in more detail.

Although collective I/O techniques have existed for several years, and a number of I/O research projects implement these techniques, no current commercial parallel file system implements collective I/O.

4.4.1 Measuring Collective I/O Performance

Because a collective operation involves multiple compute processes, there are several ways to define its duration (Figure 4.7).

- *Earliest start to latest finish* ($T_{\text{e-to-l}}$). This is the most conservative measurement. The elapsed time is the interval from the time the first process initiates an operation to the time the last process completes it. Such a measurement requires a globally synchronized clock to ensure that timestamps on different processes are comparable. This measurement shows the total effect of the collective operation on the application. If the synchronizing effect of a collective operation is a concern, this measurement will expose it.

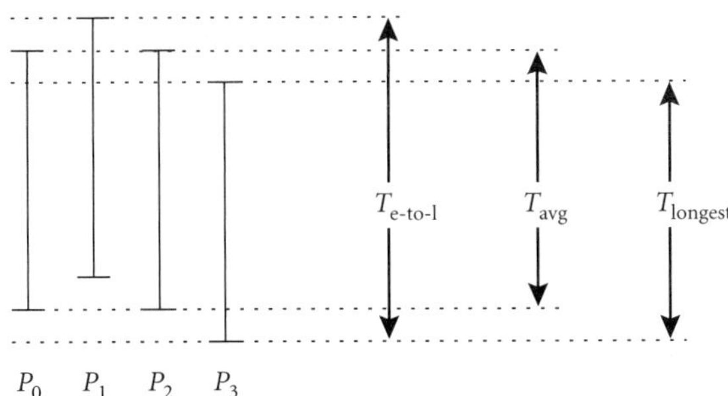

Figure 4.7 The four vertical bars on the left show the durations of write operations on processes zero through four; all have length T_{par}. Three ways to measure the overall time of the operation are: earliest start to latest finish ($T_{e\text{-}to\text{-}l}$), average elapsed time (T_{avg}), and longest elapsed time ($T_{longest}$). In this example, T_{par} is the same for all processes, so $T_{longest} = T_{par}$.

- *Longest elapsed time of any process* ($T_{longest}$). Like the earliest-to-latest measurement, this will expose synchronization effects, but it doesn't require a globally synchronized clock.
- *Average elapsed time* (T_{avg}). This measurement produces the highest apparent transfer rates. An average time measurement gives the most accurate view of the quantity of computing resources that an operation used, but it conceals the effect of synchronization and unbalanced workloads on the rest of the program.

To see the differences in these measurements, consider two applications running with P processes: one sends data from all processes to Process 0, which outputs the data and then continues. The other has each process write data to a separate file. Suppose that both applications write a total of N bytes, that the first application takes T_{seq} seconds to write the N bytes sequentially from Process 0, and that the second application takes T_{par} seconds on each process to write the N/P bytes in parallel. (T_{par} is measured separately on each process.) Assume that the transfer rates from nodes to storage devices are the same for both applications, and ignore the communication time.

To compute the overall I/O performance of the parallel access using the average transfer time, $T_{avg(par)}$, observe that all the processes take T_{par} time to write, so $T_{avg(par)} = T_{par}$. For the sequential write, $T_{avg(seq)} = T_{seq}/P$. But $T_{seq}/P = T_{par}$, so $T_{avg(seq)} = T_{avg(par)}$. The average time measurement fails to distinguish between sequential and parallel I/O. On the other hand, a measurement that uses the longest elapsed time will report $T_{longest} = T_{seq}$ for the sequential case and $T_{longest} = T_{par}$ for the parallel case. A measurement that uses the earliest-start-to-latest-finish method will report a time that depends on how closely synchronized the processes were before the I/O operation began.

If all processes access the same amount of data, the parallel transfer rate is the total number of bytes moved divided by the time needed to perform the operation. If each process moves a different amount of data, expressing the performance as a single parallel transfer rate is probably meaningless.

A final consideration is the effect of caching and buffering on I/O performance. For small accesses, these techniques can allow I/O operations to complete very quickly. If you are interested only in the performance of short I/O operations, then measurements that use small data sets are appropriate. However, extrapolating these results to predict performance for larger data transfers usually produces incorrect results because long transfers benefit less than short ones from caching and buffering. Many test programs that measure performance conclude each write operation with a flush operation to force the data out of the buffers. However, some file systems don't respond to flush requests immediately, so this technique is not always effective. Therefore, the most reliable way to compute I/O performance for large data transfers is to use large data sets in the measurements. Caching and buffering can also affect the scalability of I/O operations. Systems with client buffering will have a larger aggregate buffer pool as the number of compute nodes grows. Similarly, systems with server buffering will gain buffer space as the number of I/O nodes grows. In both cases, if the total number of bytes moved remains fixed as the size of the machine grows, a larger proportion of the data will fit in the buffer. The result is better performance even if there is no increase in the parallelism of the actual data transfer. These effects further demonstrate the need to measure performance using data sets that are much larger than the available buffer space.

4.4.2 Client-Based Collective I/O

Client-based collective I/O uses the parallel computer's message passing network to rearrange data between a layout that suits the application's needs and a layout that improves I/O performance. The exchange of data is called a *shuffle.* Processes writing data will first shuffle the data among themselves to form larger blocks and then send the blocks to the I/O nodes (Figure 4.8). For read operations (Figure 4.9), the processes first determine among themselves the total range of data to be accessed. Then each process reads a subset of this data in large blocks. When the data arrives, the processes each have some data that other processes requested, so they shuffle the data to send it to the correct destination. Several variations exist on this basic technique. It is simplest to describe them in terms of write operations, but the same ideas apply to read operations.

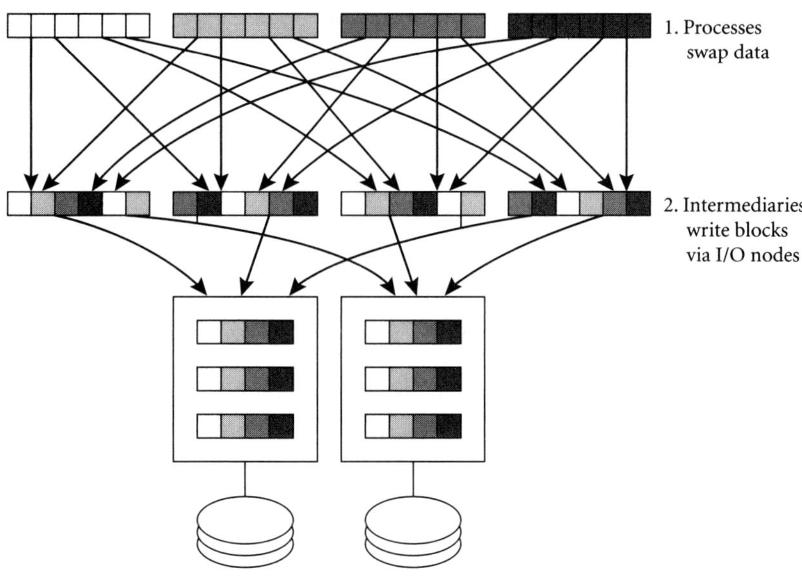

Figure 4.8 A client-based collective write operation shuffles data into blocks that will be sent to the I/O nodes. In this example, all the compute processes act as intermediaries, and they shuffle the data in a single step. The shuffle operation does not work perfectly here; some of the larger blocks created on the intermediaries must be broken up and sent to separate I/O nodes.

To distinguish the two steps in client-based collective I/O operations, it is convenient to call the participating processes "compute processes" when they are computing data or initiating collective I/O operations and "intermediary processes" when they are collecting data in blocks and communicating with the I/O nodes. However, they are really the same processes. Some versions of client-based I/O use all the processes writing data as the intermediaries; other versions use only a subset of the processes that are writing data. For example, the number of intermediary processes could be chosen to match the number of I/O nodes.

Another variable is the amount of buffer space that the intermediaries dedicate to the collective operation. Suppose that 16 processes write a total of 1 GB of data, and all the processes act as intermediaries. Each process will have 64 MB of data to store. To complete the shuffle, each node needs an additional 64 MB of buffer space to hold its portion of the data after the shuffle. In memory-bound applications, the extra buffer space may not be available. The problem is more severe when there are fewer intermediaries than compute processes, since each intermediary needs a larger share of the 1 GB buffer space. One solution is to use smaller buffers and shuffle the data in stages. Instead of communicating all the data among the

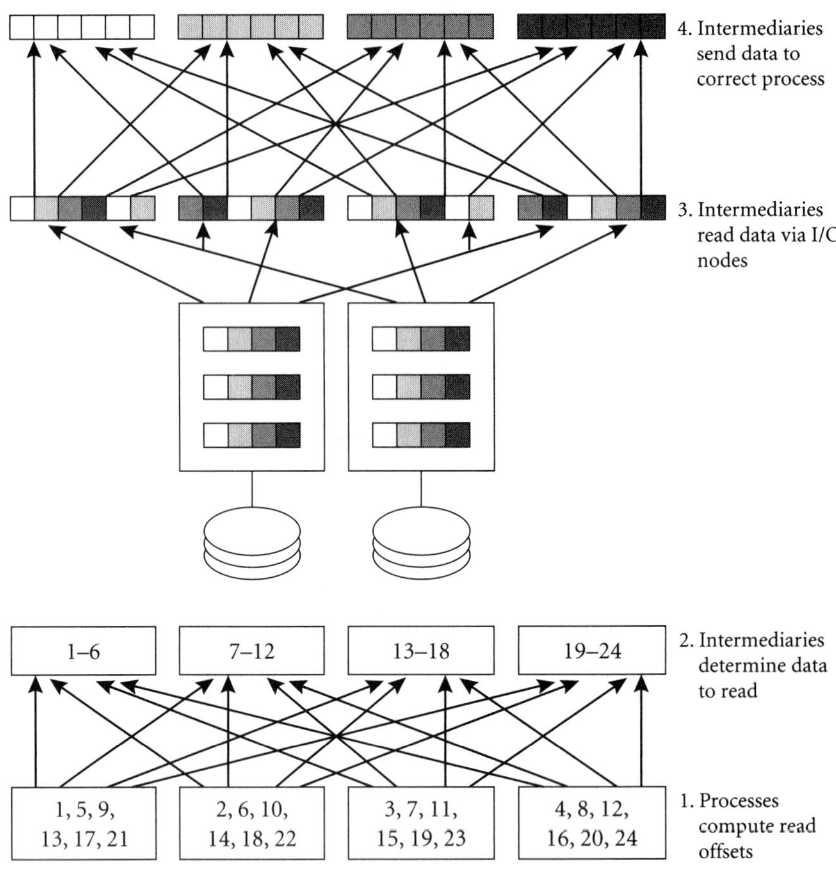

Figure 4.9 Client-based collective reading begins with the compute processes exchanging information about the data they need to read (bottom). The intermediaries read large blocks from the file through the I/O nodes and scatter it to the requesting processes.

processes at once, the collective I/O call can repeatedly shuffle smaller amounts of data, writing out the buffers between each stage. With sufficient memory, the intermediaries can use double buffering to write data from one stage of the shuffle operation while gathering data in the next stage.

The distribution of data among the intermediaries is yet another possible variation. A simple choice is to shuffle data among all *P* processes to form *P* contiguous blocks. However, the length of these blocks may not match the file striping parameters. For example, if the block size is equal to the stripe depth times the stripe factor of the parallel file system being accessed, then all the intermediaries will simultaneously send data to the first I/O node, then to the second, and so on.

Access to I/O nodes will then be sequential instead of parallel. An alternative arrangement is to match the number of intermediaries to the number of I/O nodes, and to have each intermediary collect blocks for only one I/O node. Then each intermediary can send a long, continuous stream of blocks to exactly one I/O node, which should produce excellent transfer rates.

Since client-based collective I/O communicates all the data to an intermediary buffer before sending it to an I/O node (or after receiving it from an I/O node in a read operation), it incurs communication and copying costs that do not arise in ordinary parallel I/O. The central premise of client-based collective I/O is that the improved I/O performance available by reading and writing large blocks outweighs the communication and buffering costs. However, this premise is not always true. When an application writes blocks of data that are much larger than the stripe depth of the file, shuffling the data can reduce the transfer rate instead of improving it. As shown below, the communication cost can also outweigh the improved I/O performance when the data blocks are very small.

Several research projects have implemented client-based collective I/O. Here are some examples.

Two-Phase I/O

Bordawekar et al. [18] proposed an early version of client-based collective I/O called *two-phase I/O* (2PIO). The two phases are the shuffle and the I/O operation. This version of 2PIO rearranged various global array distributions (such as block-block, row-major, column-major, etc.) into a distribution that matched the file striping. The researchers had observed that certain combinations of striping parameters (also known as file layouts) and array distributions matched badly, so that each process made many separate I/O requests. Other distributions matched file layouts well and required fewer requests. Their goal in developing 2PIO was to make all kinds of distributions equally efficient for I/O purposes.

The group modified CFS on an Intel Touchstone Delta parallel computer so that applications could describe global array distributions in a form similar to what HPF and other parallel Fortran variants use. The description distributes each dimension of a rectangular array over an array of processors using either a block or cyclic distribution. The interface also gave applications the flexibility to determine the striping parameters of each file. The 2PIO implementation chose the number of intermediaries and the size of data blocks to match these parameters.

Although the system implemented both two-phase reading and two-phase writing, the original paper reports only read performance. The researchers tested two array sizes (5 K × 5 K and 10 K × 10 K) and two sets of compute processes (16 and 64). They compared performance for four different array distributions, using both 2PIO and direct calls to CFS. The 2PIO operations improved the I/O time by factors ranging from 10% to several hundred. The improvement was greater for the tests on 64 processors than for 16 processors, but the smaller data arrays showed the larger gains. The proportion of time spent on the shuffle step as compared to the I/O step was larger for their larger arrays. The growing cost of communication with array size suggests diminishing returns for this implementation on massively parallel systems. Perhaps the most encouraging result of these measurements is the difference between the most favorable and least favorable data distributions for each class of measurement. Without collective I/O, the read times for different array distributions varied by factors of hundreds. 2PIO brought the worst cases to within a factor of two of the best cases for all array sizes and processor groups.

In a later study, Bordawekar [17] implemented a different version of 2PIO in PFS on an Intel Paragon. He found that collective I/O was better than ordinary PFS calls that used M_UNIX mode. However, more often than not M_RECORD performed better than 2PIO. The study attributes this result to the high cost of interprocessor communication on the test system. Also, this version of 2PIO made no attempt to match the number of intermediaries and their access pattern to the striping parameters of the file.

Extended Two-Phase I/O

Thakur and Choudhary's extended two-phase I/O (E-2PIO) strategy [160] includes further optimizations, mainly to improve performance for collective accesses to a subset of a distributed array.

The researchers observed that although ordinary 2PIO implementations can be configured to access files with different combinations of intermediaries and block sizes, a given configuration uses only one such combination for a particular file or parallel job. Extended two-phase I/O dynamically chooses a block size and a distribution to intermediaries, so that all intermediaries participate in every file access. The benefit of this optimization appears when an application collectively reads or writes only a subset of a distributed array. In that case, some of the intermediaries in ordinary 2PIO may access less data than others. With a dynamic access pattern, the I/O software computes a balanced access pattern for each request, so it uses more of the available parallelism. Balancing the load in this way also equalizes the buffer space requirement between the intermediaries, so the I/O software can complete the transfer in fewer steps. Of course, the striping pattern of the file does not change, so the varying access patterns generally won't match the file layout.

Even with collective I/O, reading only a subset of an array can produce small, disjoint file accesses. For example, consider a two-dimensional array stored in column-major order. If a collection of processes together reads only the even-numbered rows, the resulting access pattern will read every other array element. Caching on the server will allow the file system to avoid reading each element from disk individually. However, since 2PIO is a client-based operation, each intermediary still needs to request each of its assigned elements separately. Extended two-phase I/O merges these requests using a technique called *data sieving*. The intermediaries compute the total extent in the file of the individual data items they need and then read that entire range. Then they pick out only the requested data and forward it to the compute processes in the shuffle phase. In the example of reading only the even-numbered rows, the intermediaries together would read the entire file (except possibly the first row) and throw away odd-numbered rows. Although data sieving appears to read more data than is needed, in many cases the disks will have to transfer all the data anyway. Data sieving simply avoids the latency of issuing separate I/O requests to the I/O nodes. Data sieving handles disjoint write requests by performing a read-modify-write operation on the contiguous file ranges that contain the data to be updated.

Thakur and Choudhary measured the performance of their optimizations on a collection of array access patterns chosen to match typical out-of-core file accesses. In some read access patterns, the compute processes read partially or fully overlapping regions of the file. The remaining read access patterns and all write access patterns accessed disjoint regions of the file. They ran their tests on up to 128 processors of an Intel Touchstone Delta running CFS with 32 I/O nodes. Like ordinary 2PIO, E-2PIO performed much better than direct access and reduced the large differences in performance between different access patterns. Dynamic access patterns produced much better performance than static access patterns (up to a factor of five), but the static patterns used every process as an intermediary and did not match the file layout. Unlike the implementations of ordinary two-phase I/O noted above, the E-2PIO implementation demonstrated *better* performance relative to direct I/O as the number of processors increased. Thakur attributes the improvement to careful use (and avoidance) of buffering and communication in his implementation [159].

Collective Buffering

Independently of the 2PIO projects, Nitzberg and Lo [121] developed a similar group of client-based collective I/O optimizations. Their work examined the performance of different distributions of data among the intermediary processes, and they described four variations on client-based collective I/O.

- **CB-B:** Collective buffering with block distribution uses all the compute processes as intermediaries and simply shuffles the data to form a distribution of single equal-size data blocks. CB-B shuffles the data in a single step, so it requires intermediate buffer space equal to the total size of the data access.

- **CB-FL:** Collective buffering with file layout distribution matches the number of intermediaries and the access pattern to the file striping parameters. Also, it shuffles the data in steps, so it uses less buffer space than CB-B for large transfers.
- **CB-C:** Collective buffering with cyclic distribution is a generalization of CB-B and CB-FL. CB-C supports any number of intermediaries with any fixed intermediate block size. Like CB-FL, CB-C can shuffle the data in steps.
- **CBx:** Collective buffering with scatter-gather is an implementation of CB-C that uses scatter-gather operations in the message passing library to improve communication performance. Scatter-gather operations combine many small communication requests into a large one.

Nitzberg and Lo measured the performance of several collective buffering variations on an Intel Paragon and an IBM SP2. The Paragon had 208 compute nodes and six I/O nodes, and it ran PFS. The SP2 had 150 compute nodes, eight I/O nodes, and a beta version of PIOFS. These tests used M_ASYNC mode on the Paragon and the standard Unix interface (with none of the Vesta extensions) on the SP2. The tests measured only the write performance of various access patterns. The size of individual records that the compute processes requested in these tests ranged from 64 bytes to either 256 KB or 1 MB, depending on the file size.

A general characteristic of most of the tests is that write performance is poor for small records both with direct access (i.e., no collective buffering) and with most forms of collective buffering. The accesses that use collective buffering improve fairly rapidly compared to direct access as the record size increases, with the greatest difference appearing for records of a few kilobytes. Then direct access performance improves rapidly and converges with collective buffering performance for records larger than a few tens of kilobytes. The size at which the performance converges is close to the file's stripe depth. A somewhat surprising result is that CB-FL did not always give the best performance. On the Paragon, CB-FL was indeed the fastest, but on the SP2, PIOFS performed better with larger buffers than CB-FL used. For some distributions, CB-B was best; for others, certain variations of CB-C were slightly faster than CB-B. In all cases on the SP2, CB-FL was at least 30% slower than the alternatives. The researchers believe that PIOFS performs best when the amount of data accessed and the number of accessing clients are both large. The significance of this result is that no one data distribution for client-based collective I/O works best in all situations.

The study did not test the performance of CBx directly because of limitations in the message passing library that the test code used. However, a version of the test that simulated the performance of the scatter-gather operation on the Paragon showed promising results. The performance for small record sizes was nearly as good as it was for large records. The simulated transfer rate for 128-byte records was within about 10% of the rate for large records and at least a factor of 10 better than CB-FL at that size.

4.4.3 Server-Based Collective I/O

Client-based collective I/O clearly improves performance over direct access to parallel files, but it has several apparent drawbacks: it requires additional buffer space in the intermediary processes for the shuffle operation, it moves the data twice over the interconnection network (once in each phase), and it requires a good intermediate data distribution for optimal performance. Server-based collective I/O attempts to address these problems. Like client-based I/O, server-based I/O collects and merges small requests from multiple compute processes into larger I/O requests. However, instead of shuffling the data on the compute nodes as a separate phase from the I/O, it gathers small requests directly on the I/O nodes.

For a write operation (Figure 4.10), the compute processes send a description of the transfer (but not the actual data) to all of the I/O nodes. However, before they do this, each node prepares itself to receive requests from the I/O nodes for portions of the actual data. Depending on the implementation, the preparation may involve setting up a socket or posting a nonblocking request to receive a message. Once an I/O node has received a description of the transfer from all the compute nodes, it

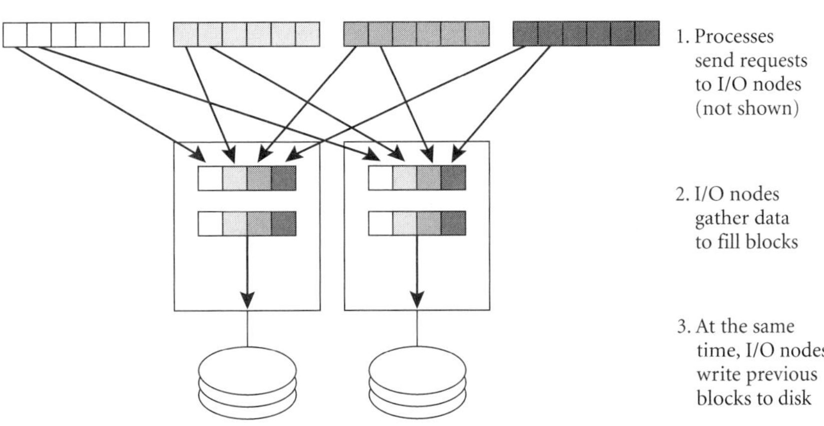

Figure 4.10 Server-based collective I/O does not shuffle data. Instead, for write accesses, compute processes send their requests directly to the I/O nodes, which retrieve data from these processes and fill file blocks one at a time. When each block is full, the I/O node writes it to disk while gathering data for the next block. Read operations are similar.

determines which file blocks under its control it must write. Then it determines which compute nodes hold the data that will fill each block. Often, several compute nodes hold data for the same block. For each block, the I/O node requests the data from the compute nodes (possibly in parallel) and fills the block as the data arrives. Once the block is full, the I/O node can write it to disk and begin working on the next block. To save time, an I/O node can fill several blocks at once, or it can use double buffering to write out one block while filling the next one. However, the total amount of buffer space on each I/O node is small because the I/O nodes transfer data from the compute nodes only as needed. The compute nodes require no system buffer space at all.[1] However, they must be prepared to transfer data in whatever increments the I/O nodes request and to receive requests from multiple I/O nodes concurrently.

A read operation also begins with the compute nodes preparing for connections with the I/O nodes. Then, as in a write request, the compute nodes send their requests to the I/O nodes. The I/O nodes determine which file blocks to read, and once the data has arrived from the disks, they distribute it to the waiting compute nodes. Again, the operation can use double buffering, and the requirements for buffer space are the same as for write operations.

By managing the rearrangement of data from processor layout to file layout on the I/O nodes, server-directed I/O eliminates the need for extra buffer space on the compute nodes, and it requires relatively little buffer space on the I/O nodes. The amount of buffer space can be tailored to optimize the performance of the disk (since many disks handle multiple concurrent requests more efficiently than a series of single requests). Data travels over the interconnection network only once, but server-based I/O does have a potential drawback compared to client-based I/O: multiple records in the same file block can move between an I/O node and a compute node in a single message, but many server-based I/O techniques are designed to handle only a few blocks at a time (thus minimizing buffer space requirements); therefore, it requires multiple messages between each pair of communicating compute and I/O nodes for large transfers. Client-based collective I/O can face the same problem, but as noted above, using scatter-gather operations to combine many small messages can greatly improve performance. Scatter-gather is only partly effective with server-based collective I/O because it transfers only a few blocks at a time.

Kotz [89] devised server-based collective I/O and used it as a component of a strategy called *disk-directed I/O*. Others have adopted and modified server-based I/O in separate projects.

---

1 Depending on how the system transfers data, a compute node receiving subsets of its requested data in arbitrary order might require a small amount of buffer space and an extra copy operation to store the data correctly. However, the space needed is likely to be small.

Disk-Directed I/O

The central feature of disk-directed I/O (DDIO) is that it arranges read and write accesses to match the physical layout of data on the disk. By using server-based collective I/O, the strategy transforms collective operations into a series of requests for whole file blocks at each I/O node. For read operations, the I/O node minimizes access time by requesting the blocks in an order that minimizes disk head movement. Rather than reading all the blocks from disks into I/O node buffers and then sending the data to the compute nodes in file order, each I/O node distributes the data in each block as it arrives from the disk, telling the compute nodes which part of the request they are receiving. Of course, the compute nodes must be prepared to accept the data in this apparently arbitrary order and store it correctly in the application's data structures.

Likewise, write operations can build and move blocks in an order that optimizes disk performance. For newly created files on newly formatted disks, blocks can be written contiguously. However, for updates to existing files and for fragmented disks, the optimal access order may not match the logical file order.

Kotz compared the performance of disk-directed I/O with both client-based collective I/O and a generic simulated parallel file system. (The study refers to client-based I/O as two-phase I/O. However, the only version of 2PIO tested was equivalent to CB-B.) The tests were run on a simulated parallel computer with simulated disks. These tests permit controlled, repeatable measurements, but they may overlook subtle characteristics of real machines. Furthermore, Nitzberg and Lo's experiments showed that the relative performance of different strategies varies between systems.

The tests simulated a parallel computer with 16 compute nodes and 16 I/O nodes. The parallel file system used server buffering and did not sequentialize concurrent accesses. The tests measured performance for a series of access patterns on a distributed two-dimensional array with record sizes of 8 bytes and 8 KB.

Table 4.2 summarizes the results of the tests. In the median case, reordering the data accesses to match the layout of blocks on disks accounted for essentially all the

	Minimum	*Geometric mean*	*Maximum*
DDIO with reordering	1.00	1.64	18.10
DDIO no reordering	1.00	1.18	5.88
CB-B	0.44	1.20	17.83

Table 4.2 *Ratios of the simulated performance of disk-directed I/O and CB-B to the performance of a simulated parallel file system. Values greater than 1 indicate higher performance than the parallel file system. (Data from Kotz [89].)*

improvement of DDIO over CB-B. However, even without reordering, DDIO was never slower than direct access; CB-B, on the other hand, was much slower in the worst case.

Server-Directed I/O

A parallel I/O research project called Panda adopted a version of server-based collective I/O [143] and implemented it on an IBM SP2, a network of workstations, and other systems. Panda manages multidimensional distributed arrays using collective I/O. The Panda group points out that while client-based collective I/O can be implemented separately from the underlying file system, DDIO as proposed by Kotz requires low-level control of disk accesses [25]. They argue that sequential file systems already optimize low-level disk control quite well, so parallel I/O software should confine itself to transforming application requests into a form that lower-level file systems can manage efficiently.

Separating disk control from parallel optimization certainly simplifies the design of parallel I/O software. As Chapter 3 notes, some vendor file systems adopt this approach. However, Kotz's simulation data suggests that low-level optimization is the key to DDIO's performance advantages.

The Panda researchers implemented a technique called *server-directed I/O* (SDIO), which is essentially DDIO without the reordering of disk block accesses. Instead, each I/O node writes data to an underlying sequential file system. Because the Panda I/O library is not itself a file system, the parallel files it writes are really a collection of sequential files. Panda can access these files as a single logical unit from within an application. Outside an application, though, the user must manage these files as separate units.

The Panda group notes that the disk access can happen concurrently with the communication between the I/O nodes and compute nodes. Double buffering is most efficient when the operations on the two buffers take equal time, so the amount of data in a disk access should be chosen to match the communication and I/O times. Of course, the optimum buffer size will depend on many factors, such as the disk performance, the message passing network performance, and the size and number of messages that the I/O nodes and compute nodes exchange. Indeed, the researchers found very different optimal buffer sizes for reads and for writes. On one IBM system, reads performed best with a buffer size of 16 KB to 64 KB, while writes performed best with buffers of 512 KB to 4 MB. The difference arises because the underlying (sequential) file system uses its own delayed-write buffering, so the apparent transfer rate for writing is much higher than for reading; as a result, write operations require more data to match the I/O time with the communication time.

The Panda group also found that DDIO contains a communication step that is unnecessary for SDIO [27]. Recall that for writes, DDIO has the I/O nodes request data from the compute node in an order that matches the physical layout of blocks on disks. Since Panda doesn't attempt to optimize the order of disk accesses, the I/O nodes can accept data from each compute node in a predictable order. Therefore, at the beginning of each write operation, the compute nodes and the I/O nodes each determine in advance the pattern of data transfers. Then the compute nodes send the data to the appropriate I/O nodes in nonblocking messages. The I/O nodes receive these messages without having to request them first. Using nonblocking messages allows each compute node to make data available to all the I/O nodes without having to wait for each transfer to finish. Nonblocking messages also allow the I/O nodes to accept data from the compute nodes in the order it arrives. The Panda group calls this modified communication pattern client-server-directed I/O, and they have found that it works especially well for fine-grained transfers that involved many I/O nodes. In these situations, the amount of message traffic is large compared to the number of disk accesses at each I/O node, so eliminating a communication step is important.

Modeling the Performance of DDIO

In Kotz's simulations of DDIO performance, the model parallel computer had relatively slow disks and a relatively fast message passing network. Moore and Quinn [109] point out that on a machine with fast disks and a slow network, the performance of ordinary DDIO suffers. For a read operation, DDIO first fills a buffer at an I/O node with data from the disk and then transmits portions of this data to various compute processes. While the I/O node is scattering this data, it can simultaneously read another block from disk. For slow disks, reading a new block takes at least as long as scattering data from the old block. However, on many computers, the scatter operation is sequential: the I/O node can send data to only one compute node at a time. If the network latency is large, and if each block contains data destined for many different nodes, the time needed to scatter the data can exceed the time needed to read the next block. When that happens, the benefit of reordering the sequence of disk accesses disappears.

This is essentially the same point that the Panda group made about the importance of matching the disk transfer time to the communication time. However, Moore and Quinn attack the problem in a different way. Rather than choosing a buffer size that balances the I/O and communication times, they propose three variations on DDIO that improve its network performance. They have also developed analytical models (for read operations only) that show how these variations compare to ordinary DDIO.

The first variation uses discontiguous access techniques so that I/O nodes can send (or receive) fewer messages for each disk block. Instead of sending a separate message for each contiguous group of records in a block, the system collects all the records in a block that are destined for a particular compute node and sends them in one message (or "packet"). The technique is called *packet-based DDIO* (PB-DDIO). This optimization works best when blocks contain small, discontiguous records that go to the same compute node. PB-DDIO incurs an extra cost compared to ordinary DDIO: collecting records into a packet and scattering them (if necessary) at the other end. When there are many records per block, this cost is significant.

An obvious extension of PB-DDIO is to packetize records for several blocks at a time. Instead of distributing each block as it is read, the I/O node reads several blocks and packetizes all the records bound for each compute node. Meanwhile, the I/O node can read multiple data blocks from disk. The benefit of reducing the number of messages in multiple-block DDIO (MB-DDIO) is proportional to the number of blocks. However, using too many blocks incurs a separate penalty at the compute nodes, according to Moore and Quinn. If the node must unpack too much data at a time, excessive misses in the memory cache and the translation lookaside buffer (TLB) degrade performance. (The TLB is a special type of memory cache included in most computers that stores mappings from virtual to physical page addresses; see Section 7.1.1 for more information on virtual memory.)

A third variation on DDIO adopts the shuffle operation from client-based collective I/O. Two-phase DDIO (2P-DDIO) is similar to CB-FL. The I/O nodes read blocks of data and send them (using double buffering) to an equal number of compute nodes acting as intermediaries. Then the intermediaries perform the usual shuffle operation to move data to the right locations.

Two-phase DDIO seems at first to be a step backward from the other types of DDIO, especially in a system with slow message passing. However, Moore and Quinn's model exposes an important difference between the techniques. In DDIO, each I/O node sending data to the compute nodes incurs the message passing network latency (l) once for each record in each block. The network bandwidth does not enter into this model because the same amount of data is moved between the I/O nodes and compute nodes in all cases. If B is the number of blocks that each I/O node handles, and each block contains r records, then DDIO will incur a total latency on the message passing network of

$$L_{\mathrm{DDIO}} = Brl.$$

This discussion focuses on the latency and the time to set up the packets because these parameters show most clearly the differences between the models. There are other contributions to performance, such as the message passing network bandwidth; see Moore and Quinn [109] for the details. PB-DDIO incurs

$$L_{\mathrm{PB\text{-}DDIO}} = BPl + T_{\pi},$$

where T_π is the time needed to packetize the data and P is the number of compute processes (this calculation assumes that all nodes receive data from each block). With buffers of M blocks,

$$L_{\text{MB-DDIO}} = \frac{B}{M} Pl + T_\pi .$$

On the other hand, with 2P-DDIO the message passing latency between an I/O node and compute node is incurred only once (at the start of the double-buffered transfer of blocks). The shuffle step incurs latency on each intermediary for each compute process to which it sends data. The intermediaries send their data in parallel, just as the I/O nodes do, so 2P-DDIO incurs a latency of

$$L_{\text{2P-DDIO}} = l + Pl + T_\pi + T_{\text{read}} .$$

T_{read} is the time to read the data from the disk; with 2P-DDIO, this operation does not overlap the data redistribution (shuffle) step. When $P \ll B$ (and the message passing time is large compared to the disk access time), 2P-DDIO should perform well because it incurs latency once per process instead of once per block. An equivalent solution would be to use MB-DDIO with $M = B$; in other words, read all the blocks into the I/O nodes before distributing them. Of course, 2P-DDIO and to a lesser extent MB-DDIO increase the buffering requirements. 2P-DDIO requires buffer space in the intermediaries equal to the size of the collective data access, just as CB-FL does.

Moore and Quinn's models, more detailed than those presented here, compute the performance of DDIO and the three variations. Their calculations compare the simulated parallel machine from Kotz's paper with a real computer, a Meiko CS-2, that has fast disks and slower message passing than Kotz's simulated machine. They show that the variations perform much better than ordinary DDIO in most cases. The relative performance of 2P-DDIO and MB-DDIO depends on the record size, the disk and message passing performance, and the time needed to packetize data. They computed performance for records as small as 8 bytes (equivalent to one double-precision floating-point number). The relative ordering of PB-DDIO, MB-DDIO, and 2P-DDIO changes drastically as the record size increases from 8 to 16 bytes; above that size, the relative performance is stable. In general, 2P-DDIO performs best for small records, fast disks, and a high ratio of I/O nodes to compute nodes. MB-DDIO, PB-DDIO, and ordinary DDIO benefit greatly from low-latency message passing.

4.4.4 Comparing Collective Methods

Few obvious trends emerge from the comparisons of optimization techniques presented here. Moreover, since the test programs, computer architectures, and system configurations varied between studies, their results cannot be compared directly. Different implementations of the same technique can also perform differently.

Clearly, some form of collective I/O is better than direct access parallel I/O for small access sizes (less than a few tens of kilobytes) in synchronous programs. Collective I/O depends on the high performance of a message passing network to make up for the poor performance of a disk access. Since the latency of a disk access is roughly 1000 times the latency of sending a message (several milliseconds versus several microseconds), it would appear that avoiding even one disk access is worth the cost of many messages. However, the performance models of Moore and Quinn and the escalating communication costs seen in some collective I/O implementations demonstrate that collective I/O models cannot afford to waste communication resources.

4.5 Adapting to Access Patterns

The performance of any collective I/O technique depends on machine parameters, application parameters, and the implementation quality of the I/O library. No user can sort through these considerations and decide for each application on each machine (and even for each different I/O call) what form of collective I/O works best. For I/O software to perform well in many different situations, it must adapt to changing circumstances; no single configuration of an I/O system works best in all situations. Therefore, some I/O software gathers information from the application that helps it adjust to the planned patterns of access. A *hint* is information that an application passes explicitly to the I/O software to improve performance. Some I/O software can also discern for itself the patterns of access and adapt itself automatically.

4.5.1 Hints

Hints span a wide range of techniques for configuring an I/O system. Some hints impose semantic requirements on a program: if the program issues a request that contravenes earlier hints, the request will operate incorrectly. For example, if an application asserts that it will never write to overlapping file regions from different processes, and then it proceeds to do so, the contents of the resulting file may be garbled. Other hints affect only performance and not correctness. If an application tells the I/O software that it will read a file consecutively from beginning to end, the I/O software may aggressively prefetch blocks from disk. If the application then fails to read consecutively, performance will suffer because the I/O system will waste time reading unneeded blocks, but the application will still receive the correct data.

Hints can be at a high level, describing an application's intended access patterns and leaving it to the I/O software to select appropriate optimizations, or they can be at a low level, directly controlling a specific aspect of the system's configuration. The file systems described in Chapter 3 include many examples of low-level hints. The atomicity modes in PIOFS and the M_UNIX and M_ASYNC modes in PFS affect concurrency control. The direct I/O mode in XFS disables buffering, and PFS has a similar hint called Fast Path I/O. PIOFS and some other file systems have hints that affect file striping. The programmer must choose low-level hints based on an understanding of how the program's access patterns will perform on a given file system and hardware configuration.

High-level hints tell the I/O software *what* the application will do, and the I/O software determines *how* to adapt its configuration for best performance. Table 4.3 lists some high-level hints. The best choice of optimizations for a given set of high-level hints may be obvious, or it may require sophisticated analysis. I/O software can use a rule-based algorithm to find the appropriate settings, or it can compute the likely performance of an application with different combinations of settings to determine the best choice.

Hint	*Possible optimizations*
Read-only	Prefetch blocks aggressively.
Write-only	Turn off prefetching.
Consecutive access	Prefetch blocks in sequence for read-access files; replace least-recently-used cache buffers; write out buffers as soon as they fill.
Strided access	Prefetch according to strided pattern (if known); delay writing if other processes will fill in data.
Random access	Turn off prefetching; use largest possible cache and buffer; delay writing as long as possible.
Large consecutive access	Turn off caching and buffering.
No overlapping access	Turn off automatic concurrency control.

Table 4.3 *Some high-level hints and possible optimizations.*

Transparent Informed Prefetching

Patterson et al. [126] presented an example of using hints to control prefetching in their Transparent Informed Prefetching (TIP) system. They modified a file system to accept hints that allow applications to predict their upcoming file access requests. These hints are passed in through the Unix `ioctl` (I/O control) interface. Programs can assert either that they will be reading an entire file sequentially or that they will be reading specified portions of it discontiguously.

The file system has a fixed amount of cache and buffer space available to it, so prefetching has the disadvantage of tying up some of this space from the time the prefetch operation completes to the time the program actually needs the data. If the file system could have used this space more productively for caching and buffering other I/O requests, the result of prefetching could be a net performance loss even if performance for a particular access improved. Therefore, TIP uses a performance model to estimate the costs and benefits of prefetching a given request. Individual requests then bid against each other for the right to use some of the fixed available buffer space.

Tests on a large single-processor system in 1995 with a variety of applications showed execution times decreasing with TIP by 20% to 80% compared to using the standard file system.

Madhyastha et al. [100] extended this work in 1999 by suggesting that prefetching could take the place of collective I/O for read operations. They pointed out that if all the processes in a parallel job provide advance information about their upcoming access requests, the system can merge these requests and arrange to carry them out in an order that optimizes performance. Essentially, hints for prefetching stretch out the window of temporal locality that Galley (Section 4.3) exploits to improve performance when multiple requests arrive from different processes at the I/O server at about the same time.

The researchers carried out a limited study of this approach, with file sizes of only a few megabytes and access sizes no smaller than disk blocks. They compared prefetching to disk-directed I/O and found that they performed similarly. Of course, prefetching only applies to read operations.

4.5.2 Automatic Adaptation

A step beyond explicit hints are systems that analyze the access patterns of a particular program and select a configuration automatically. The system may adapt itself dynamically based on recent accesses in the current execution of a program, or it may use data from earlier executions of the same program to determine the access patterns. Systems that adapt dynamically are convenient and self-contained, but they can perform poorly during the time they spend determining the appropriate configuration. At worst, they can lag continually behind rapidly changing patterns of access, switching to a new configuration after it's too late for the application to benefit.

The first adaptive systems concentrated on prefetching. Simple prefetching algorithms assume that an application will read a file consecutively, so they read blocks in the logical order of a file, even before the application has requested them. This technique works badly when a program reads data nonconsecutively, but if the I/O software can find a pattern in the accesses, it can adjust its prefetching algorithm to read the correct blocks even when the application requests them out of file order.

More recent adaptive methods vary several configuration parameters. Two I/O research projects, PPFS and Panda, demonstrate the techniques.

PPFS

PPFS (Portable Parallel File System) [75, 147] was developed by the same group that carried out the SIO study of parallel file access patterns. PPFS works either as a layer above Intel PFS or as a parallel I/O system that stripes files over multiple sequential file systems.

Initially, PPFS used hints to control caching, prefetching, and data layout. These hints were passed in through a programming interface that allowed applications to describe a wide range of access patterns. The application's choice of access mode helped determine the caching mechanism that PPFS would use for the operation. Applications could also select striping parameters for each file separately. Tests of this version of PPFS showed that the wide range of choices, combined with sophisticated caching mechanisms, improved performance for a benchmark code and two applications. However, the user was responsible for choosing the right parameters.

Later work has helped automate these choices. Madhyastha and Reed [101] analyzed application runs to detect specific kinds of access patterns. Three independent variables define their "access pattern space": sequentiality (with several levels ranging from consecutive access to random access), read/write (i.e., read-only, write-only, or read and write), and request uniformity (fixed size or variable size). Based on the combination of characteristics their algorithms find in an access pattern, PPFS selects the most appropriate of the six PFS access modes. For example, if a series of accesses is read-only, fixed size, and strided at fixed intervals on each process, then PPFS chooses M_RECORD. The system must collect and classify information locally at each process and then forward this data to a global classifier that determines the access mode all processes will use for a given file.

Madhyastha and Reed used two techniques to analyze access patterns: an artificial neural network (ANN) and a hidden Markov model (HMM). The ANN works online, watching access patterns as the program executes. The neural net is trained on a variety of access patterns, and it assigns a classification to each new pattern it sees. The HMM, using data from previous test executions of the application, predicts access patterns in the optimized executions. The HMM computes the access patterns offline, after gathering data from the test runs and before the optimized runs. Therefore, when the application is running, the HMM can determine the likely access pattern at the moment a file is opened. As a result, PPFS can set the appropriate PFS mode from the outset. The ANN, on the other hand, must observe several accesses for each file before deciding on a mode.

The researchers tested their adaptive methods with a simple I/O benchmark that performed many accesses, so ANN had plenty of time to observe a pattern. PPFS performance with automatic classification ranged from about twice as fast to more than 25 times as fast as the default M_UNIX mode in PFS. The speedups were generally greatest for smaller access sizes (1 KB). For two real applications (PRISM and QCRD, described in Section 4.2.2), both ANN and HMM improved performance compared to M_UNIX, and both chose the same mode. Because HMM was able to set the optimal mode sooner, it produced better performance in the applications than ANN did.

Madhyastha and Reed use ANN and HMM to assign patterns to general categories. Simitci et al. [147] are further refining PPFS (now called PPFS II) so it can predict an application's specific access pattern. Using a statistical technique called Autoregressive Integrated Moving Average (ARIMA), the researchers have been able to predict accurately the latter half of a rather complex (but regular) access pattern based on a trace of the first half. This information could help the system prefetch data accurately. However, their initial work required offline computations to predict the pattern.

PPFS II also supports adaptive striping and caching mechanisms. Both techniques use "sensors" in the application code that report access patterns to an ANN classifier. The classifier forwards its results to a central decision server, which manipulates the cache sizes and replacement policies. Adaptive striping stores each file several times with different stripe parameters. The system uses an analytic performance model based on access patterns, system load, and striping parameters to determine which copy of the file will offer the fastest access for a given request. In general, when a system is lightly loaded, PPFS II can quickly access files that are striped over many disks. However, as the load increases, more jobs contend for access to each disk, so files striped over fewer disks may offer faster access.

Panda

Chen et al. [26] have developed an optimization mechanism for Panda that uses either explicit hints or execution analysis to select three parameters: the communication strategy, the file layout of a global array, and the I/O node buffer size. The options for the communication strategy (server-directed vs. client-server-directed) were described earlier, as was the choice of the I/O node buffer size. The choice of an array layout determines how a multidimensional distributed array is partitioned and striped on disks. This choice is similar to the options in PIOFS for defining subfiles. As in PIOFS, an obvious consideration is that a partition that matches the disk layout to the distribution of the array among the processes will allow the I/O system to move data between compute nodes and I/O nodes in larger pieces. However, this conforming distribution is not always ideal. Consider an application that stores a whole array and then reads back a subset of it from several processes. These processes may contend for access to an array subset that resides on a single storage device. Read performance could be poor in this case even though write performance was optimal. If read operations are more frequent than writes, a better distribution might divide the data more finely so that multiple nodes can access a subset of the data in parallel.

Applications can tell Panda their intended access patterns through a hint mechanism, or Panda can determine the access patterns for itself during a sample program run. The optimization system uses a combination of rules and performance prediction. The rules apply to combinations of read and write accesses for each distributed array. If the file is written and never read (as checkpoint or output files may be), then Panda can use a conforming layout. A conforming layout is also best when each process reads and writes the same portion of an array. Finally, if the application reads an existing file, Panda uses its existing layout.

The complex cases arise when different combinations of processes read and write subsets of an array. To compute an appropriate layout, Panda uses an I/O performance model that estimates the total I/O time for all requests on a given array. The model includes both the application's access patterns and the performance of the I/O and communication hardware. Panda estimates the performance for a variety of layouts, communication strategies, and buffer sizes. Usually, Panda cannot fully evaluate all possible combinations in a reasonable length of time, so the optimization algorithm uses a well-known heuristic technique called *simulated annealing* to construct a likely optimal choice from the many possibilities. Since simulated annealing works well in parallel, Panda runs the optimization algorithm across all the I/O nodes. The compute nodes are not involved, so when an application begins running, Panda can begin computing the I/O parameters on the I/O nodes while the application proceeds on the compute nodes with its initial calculations (if they require no significant I/O). In tests on two different IBM parallel computers, the optimization computations required from a few seconds to a few minutes. The resulting parameters were found to be the same ones that would have been chosen by an exhaustive search of all possible combinations.

The optimizations were quite successful. Benchmarks run with parameters chosen automatically always performed better than those run with default parameters or those run with parameters that a human chose based on experience. Differences ranged from a few percent up to a factor of two. These improvements were over a version of Panda that was already using collective I/O. However, the improvements do not include the cost of computing the optimization, since this could be done on the I/O nodes. The optimizer chose different array layouts for the two different parallel computers, even though all other parameters of the benchmark were the same, demonstrating again how no single configuration of an I/O system performs optimally in all situations.

4.6 Trends in Optimization

This chapter has presented several parallel I/O optimizations. Although collective I/O techniques have demonstrated significant performance gains over direct parallel I/O, application developers have been slow to adopt them. There are several reasons for their reluctance. First, many of the techniques in this chapter are available only in research I/O systems and not in commercially supported products. Second, collective I/O techniques require specialized programming interfaces. These interfaces require extensive recoding of existing applications, and users need assurance that the performance benefits will be worthwhile and that their applications can use the same interface across different systems and for several generations of hardware and software. Finally, many users are willing to continue using either sequential I/O or multiple-file parallel I/O until a better solution arrives that does not require extensive recoding.

One drawback of the message passing model that has dominated parallel programming over the past several years is that it places too much burden on application developers to manage the distribution of large data structures like matrices and finite-element meshes. Compilers and run-time systems cannot easily optimize global operations like parallel file accesses because these operations are difficult to discern. Sequential optimizations are easier because the compiler or run-time system has good information about what a program is trying to do, so it can replace an inefficient series of operations with more efficient operations that are semantically equivalent. Transformations of this kind at a global level, such as replacing independent I/O operations with a collective operation, require global information about the intended purpose of the operations. Clever I/O software might recognize a series of independent file access requests as a global operation, but by the time a pattern is visible, it is too late to set up a complete collective transfer. As Galley demonstrates, I/O nodes can use caching and buffering to improve performance of parallel operations. Essentially, these operations are implicitly collective because they rely on the operations' fortuitous temporal locality. However, the best performance is possible when the I/O software has clear information about the program's intent from the outset of an operation.

Researchers have devised many novel parallel programming models that take a global view of a program. These models enable automatic optimizations in both communication and I/O, but they often require even more significant code changes than collective I/O techniques, so they appear unlikely to overtake message passing anytime soon.

The trend for hint-based optimizations is more promising. It is possible for I/O software to determine for itself what parameters to set. However, the most effective techniques require advance information.

Nearly all the techniques in this chapter are designed to optimize performance for a single parallel job. Real parallel computers run multiple jobs that issue concurrent I/O requests. A buffer on an I/O node that performs well for a single application may become fragmented when it has to serve many jobs, since the effective buffer space for each job becomes smaller. With multiple jobs contending for access to disks and communication networks, their performance is harder to predict and fluctuates over time. As a result, optimal I/O software configurations are much harder to determine. Future research in parallel I/O will need to account for these effects.

4.7 Summary

This chapter began by reviewing I/O access patterns in scientific programs. There is no one standard pattern, especially in parallel programs. However, many codes include sequences of small access requests from multiple processes, which standard sequential file systems handle poorly. Several techniques have been developed to improve performance for these operations. Discontiguous accesses merge requests from the same process to reduce the overhead of moving small pieces of data separately. Collective I/O is a set of techniques that merge requests from multiple processes in a parallel job. Collective I/O methods fall into two categories: those that merge requests on the compute nodes and those that merge them on the I/O nodes. While these techniques can improve I/O performance in many situations, no single collective I/O algorithm works best in all cases.

Because it is impossible to optimize a file system to handle all types of requests well given a single set of configuration parameters, some systems use hint mechanisms. These allow the application to tell the system what kinds of requests to expect so the system can adjust its configuration for better performance. Researchers are developing more advanced techniques that allow systems to adjust automatically to various access patterns, but these are still in the research stage.

4.8 Further Reading

Most of the material for this chapter comes directly from research papers. Proceedings of the Supercomputing Conference series and the Workshops on I/O for Parallel and Distributed Systems (IOPADS) contain many I/O optimization papers. Both Panda and the Pablo group (which performed the SIO characterization studies and developed PPFS) are based at the University of Illinois at Urbana-Champaign. Their Web site, *www.cs.uiuc.edu,* has links to many more papers on these projects. Dartmouth College hosts a parallel I/O Web site, *www.cs.dartmouth.edu/pario,* that has links to parallel I/O research projects around the world. The site also has an extensive annotated bibliography of parallel I/O research papers.

Chapter Five Low-Level I/O Interfaces

Discontiguous I/O, collective I/O, and hints all require specialized application programming interfaces (APIs). Standard Unix I/O includes a list-oriented interface that can access discontiguous regions of files and memory, but it's inconvenient for strided file accesses because the program must list every contiguous element of the transfer separately. The Unix file control interface (`fcntl`) could be used more extensively for hints, but so far it does not support the kind of high-level hints described in Chapter 4. Fortran's standard I/O interface lacks even these abilities. Neither Unix nor Fortran I/O can identify a group of processes participating in a collective operation.

This chapter describes three interfaces that support parallel I/O: High Performance Fortran (HPF), the Scalable I/O Initiative's Low-Level API (SIO LLAPI), and the MPI-2 I/O interface (MPI-IO). Although these interfaces work at different levels of abstraction, they are all low-level interfaces in the sense that they do not record any information about the meaning of the data they store, and the application must keep track of where data elements (individual records or whole data structures) reside in a file. These three interfaces were chosen for inclusion in this chapter because they have all been proposed as standard APIs for parallel I/O and because they were designed to be independent of any particular underlying implementation. Chapter 6 describes I/O programming interfaces that manage data at a higher level of abstraction. Chapter 7 reviews some APIs designed specifically for out-of-core and checkpoint I/O.

It is important to distinguish an I/O interface from the implementation of an I/O library or a file system. In vendors' parallel file systems like IBM PIOFS and Intel PFS, the interface is designed to expose the special capabilities of the underlying system. However, HPF, SIO LLAPI, and MPI-IO were designed to let applications use the same API on a variety of platforms.

To offer this portability, the interface designers made certain compromises. Sometimes these compromises produce function semantics that are either vague or unusually restrictive. For example, in nonblocking write operations, the standard interfaces do not allow applications to read data from a buffer that is being written out. Reading data while it is being written is harmless in some implementations, but other systems require this restriction for correct operation. Since standard interfaces must operate uniformly on all systems, they sometimes specify the most restrictive semantics. In other cases, they define the details of certain operations vaguely to permit a variety of implementations. For example, MPI-IO and LLAPI define collective interfaces but don't require any particular version of collective I/O to be supported; indeed, they don't require a collective interface to perform collective I/O at all.

Any standardization effort faces a conflict between exploiting the best features of the most sophisticated systems and maintaining compatibility with the least sophisticated ones. Often, the designers of a standard resolve conflicts by defining operations so that an underlying system can implement them in either a sophisticated or a simple way. For example, MPI-IO supports nonblocking I/O, but at the time MPI-IO was defined, not all operating systems had the necessary mechanisms to perform I/O concurrently with computation. Therefore, the standard was defined so that an implementation could perform "nonblocking" I/O by delaying the start of a transfer until the application tested for completion of an operation. Alternatively, a standard can define optional features, which a valid implementation can simply omit if they are too difficult to implement on a particular machine. Both HPF and LLAPI have optional features.

Permissive semantics and optional features both have drawbacks. A program designed to run on the widest possible range of systems must restrict itself to using features that are available everywhere, possibly foregoing the benefits of certain optional features. Alternatively, it can test whether a specific feature is available and choose a code path depending on the result. An implementation that takes advantage of permissive semantics to implement a sophisticated feature inefficiently will discourage application developers from using that feature *anywhere,* since a program cannot easily tell in advance whether the feature will work well or poorly on a given system. The result of these difficulties is that while standard programming interfaces let programmers write portable code, writing portable code that performs well everywhere remains difficult.

Another issue for portable interfaces is how much support they require of their programming and run-time environments. MPI-IO is part of MPI and uses features of that system. Therefore, it's poorly suited to parallel programs that don't otherwise use MPI. Similarly, the HPF I/O interface is only available to HPF programs. SIO LLAPI does not depend on any communication system, but it only has a C language programming interface.

Of the three interfaces this chapter presents, MPI-IO receives the most attention. The HPF I/O interface is minimal, although it implicitly supports parallel I/O. SIO LLAPI is designed for system programmers rather than application developers, and it has been implemented less widely than MPI-IO. MPI-IO is a complicated interface, but it is available on many parallel computers, at least in partial implementations.

5.1 HPF I/O

HPF is a set of extensions to Fortran through which application developers can tell a parallelizing compiler how to distribute data and parallelize loops. The programming model is mainly data parallel, which means that each process in a parallel job performs the same operations on different portions of a distributed data set. Although this model is more restrictive than message passing or shared memory parallelism, it greatly simplifies parallel I/O optimizations because the compiler and run-time system can easily identify global I/O operations.

Two major versions of the HPF standard have been published. The original, HPF 1.0 [69, 88], appeared in 1993, with updates and corrections published as HPF 1.1 in 1994. Both are called HPF-1 here. HPF-1 defined a base language and a set of optional features that compilers need not implement. This caused some confusion about what constituted a valid HPF-1 program. The second major version, HPF 2.0 [70], was published in 1997. HPF-2 defines an official language and a set of "approved extensions," which are not part of the language. Implementors of HPF-2 compilers may include these features at their discretion, and the features will be considered for inclusion in future versions of HPF. Defining nonrequired elements of the language as approved extensions rather than optional features emphasizes that these elements are experimental.

HPF-1 deals only with regular arrays and data decompositions. An application can partition a multidimensional array among a collection of processes using block or cyclic (or no) distribution along each dimension (Figure 5.1). Programs can apply decompositions at compile time or at run time, but unlike message passing programs, HPF exposes the global array structure in the program. Because of the explicit data distribution and the data parallel programming model, the HPF designers determined that no special interface was needed to implement parallel I/O. The HPF-1 standard was published before most of the work on collective optimizations discussed in Chapter 4. However, a Fortran `write` operation on a global array contains all the information necessary to implement a collective operation. Unfortunately, few HPF implementations have taken advantage of this opportunity. Most simply route all `read` and `write` operations through a single process.

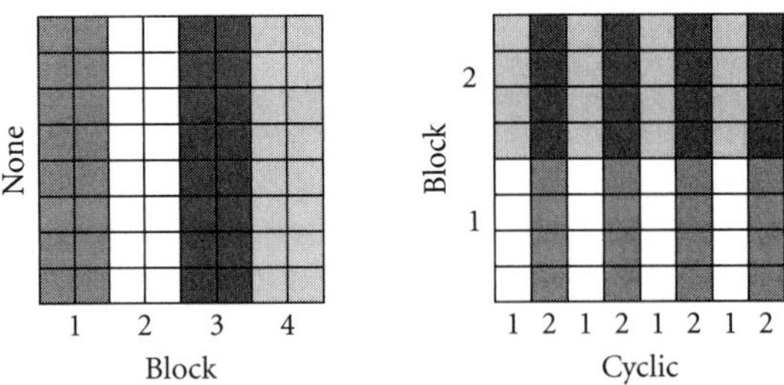

Figure 5.1 HPF can use a different distribution pattern for each dimension in a multidimensional array. The array on the left is partitioned four ways in a none-block distribution. The array on the right is partitioned four ways in a block-cyclic distribution.

Extensions in HPF-2 support more complicated array distributions and nonblocking I/O. Rectangular arrays can be partitioned along each dimension in strips of unequal width. Irregular grids can be distributed using mapping arrays: for each element in a data array (such as an array of grid point locations), a corresponding element in a mapping array specifies the process in which the data element should reside.

The nonblocking I/O extension defines some new controls to be used in `open`, `read`, `write`, and `inquire` statements, and a new `wait` statement. A program does nonblocking I/O as follows (some operations not affecting I/O are omitted and described in the comments):

```
real*8 x(100, 100)
!hpf$ processors p(2,2)
!hpf$ distribute (block,block) onto p :: x
integer istat, iaio

open(unit=5, file='sample', status='new', &
     form='unformatted', access='direct', recl=8, &
     asynchronous, iostat=istat)
! Check open status, fill array x with data
write(unit=5, asynchronous, rec=1, id=iaio) x
! Do something else while array x is being written
wait(id=iaio, iostat=istat)
close(5)
```

The new controls here are `asynchronous` and `id=`. The `asynchronous` control must appear in the `open` statement for any file on which a program will perform nonblocking I/O. Individual read and write calls may use either nonblocking or blocking I/O. Nonblocking calls use the id= control to get an identification number for the nonblocking operation; this number is passed to the matching wait statement. Nonblocking read and write statements must use a record number (so the file location is unambiguous), and they may not use either formats or function calls. The wait statement blocks until the I/O operation is complete. Alternatively, the program can periodically test for completion using the inquire statement.

```
! Other declarations as above
logical notdone

! Open file and initialize x as above
write(5, asynchronous, rec=1, id=iaio) x
notdone = .true.
do while (notdone)
    ! Do something else while x is being written
    inquire(unit=5, id=iaio, pending=notdone, iostat=istat)
end do
close(5)
```

Here, the inquire call uses the new pending= control to determine whether the I/O operation is complete. Either the wait or the inquire call must appear in the same instance of the same program unit as the call that initiated the request. Systems that do not support nonblocking I/O can perform the entire transfer before the initiating call returns, but wait and inquire must still work correctly.

5.2 Scalable I/O Initiative Low-Level API

The SIO project defined its Low-Level API [34] in 1996 as a proposed addition to POSIX. POSIX (portable operating systems interface) [78] is a standard programming interface for a variety of operating system functions; it is based on various versions of the Unix operating system. The goal of SIO LLAPI was to define a portable interface with enough expressive power to support many kinds of parallel I/O. The designers deliberately sacrificed ease of use to make the interface powerful yet reasonably small. For example, the one nonblocking read function supports a combination of list-based and algorithmic discontiguous file access. There is no simpler read function for ordinary contiguous accesses. The designers also avoided tying LLAPI to any particular communication model: LLAPI doesn't require MPI, multithreading, sockets, or any other specific communication library. (However, collective file access does require *some* form of interprocess communication.) On the other hand, LLAPI has an extensive hint mechanism and explicit control of caching, so programs can change the file system configuration in many ways.

Like HPF, LLAPI has a set of core functions that an implementation must support if it claims to conform to the standard. Two optional extensions support collective I/O and fast copying of files (for checkpointing or managing multiple file versions). The standard also defines how implementations can extend the hint mechanisms. Programs can determine at compile time or at run time whether a particular extension is available.

The designers intend LLAPI to be a system programmer's interface on which more sophisticated parallel I/O capabilities are built. Useful capabilities that the standard doesn't define, such as local and shared file pointers, are supposed to be implemented at a higher level. Only a C language interface is defined. LLAPI uses defined data types (such as `sio_count_t`) extensively, even for simple integer values.

5.2.1 Opening and Controlling Files

The LLAPI function for opening a file has an ordinary-looking interface except for its last two arguments:

```
sio_return_t
sio_open( int * fd,
          const char * name,
          sio_mode_t mode,
          sio_control_t * control_ops,
          sio_count_t control_ops_count );
```

Opening a file is not a global operation as it is in PFS; each process using a file must open it separately, and processes opening a file do not communicate with each other.

The `control_ops` parameter lets programs set or check a number of file characteristics and perform certain operations on files. The `control_ops` argument is an array whose length is given in the last parameter. Each element of the array is a structure that defines one control function. Control functions include reading and changing the following parameters, which are described in more detail below: logical size, preallocation size, striping, caching mode, and label. Control functions can also read (but not change) the physical size and the granularity at which data consistency is enforced. Finally, control functions can bring multiple cached copies of data into a consistent state. LLAPI can perform control operations on closed files (using `sio_test`), on open files (using `sio_control`), and at the time a file is opened.

Some functions are feasible only at certain times; for example, it makes no sense to set the cache parameters on a closed file, and it may be impractical to change a file's striping parameters once it has been written.

LLAPI defines the size of a file in three ways. The *logical size* corresponds to the Unix definition of file size: the offset of the last accessible byte, plus one (e.g., the size of a file containing a single byte at offset zero is one). The *physical size* of a file is the amount of space its data occupies in storage. This will typically be a whole multiple of the file block size. Programs cannot directly control this size. Finally, files have a *preallocation size*. This is the amount of space that has been reserved for a file in storage. LLAPI allows programs to reserve space for a file so they will be guaranteed sufficient storage capacity as the computation proceeds. The preallocation size may be smaller than the physical size of a file; if the file is truncated, LLAPI does not guarantee that the file can grow back to its previous size unless space is preallocated for it. Of course, a program could allocate space simply by writing out dummy data, but in file systems that support preallocation, reserving space is much faster than writing data. Seeking to a very large file offset and writing a single byte does not necessarily preallocate all the space below that offset, since a file system might only reserve blocks for portions of a file that contain valid data.

LLAPI defines striping parameters in the usual way—in terms of a striping factor and stripe depth. Although the interface allows applications to set these parameters separately for each file, the underlying I/O system is not required to honor these requests, or even to reveal the striping parameters that it uses.

A file label is a short piece of data that programs can store separately from a file's contents. For example, the label may contain information about the file's data format or a link to another file that contains descriptive information about the data. The benefit of keeping the label separate from the main data is that some programs define a strict format for the contents of a file. The programs expect to find certain information at specific byte locations, and placing a label in the file would make the data appear corrupt.

Cache control is described in Section 5.2.4.

LLAPI has the usual function for closing a file, and LLAPI can also remove (unlink) files from a directory. However, it has no functions for managing a directory hierarchy or for modifying file access permissions. Since the LLAPI designers intended the interface to become part of POSIX, they have left these operations to the existing POSIX standard.

5.2.2 Reading and Writing

The LLAPI interface for accessing data supports both list-based and algorithmic operations, and both the file and memory can be accessed discontiguously. LLAPI supports blocking and nonblocking calls in the base standard. Support for collective I/O is available only in an extension to LLAPI, and this interface is described in Section 5.2.5.

The LLAPI function for blocking reads is

```
sio_return_t
sio_sg_read( int fd,
             const sio_file_io_list_t * file_list,
             sio_count_t file_list_count,
             const sio_mem_io_list_t * mem_list,
             sio_count_t mem_list_count,
             sio_transfer_len_t * bytes_moved );
```

The "sg" in the name of the function stands for "scatter-gather," since the operation gathers data from file locations and scatters it in memory. The write function, `sio_sg_write`, has identical parameters to `sio_sg_read`. In both functions, two arrays of structures define lists of accesses to the file. The structure in the `file_list` array is defined as follows:

```
typedef struct {
     sio_offset_t offset;
     sio_size_t   size;
     sio_size_t   stride;
     sio_count_t  element_cnt;
} sio_file_io_list_t;
```

Each structure can define a strided access. The `offset` is the location in the file where the access begins, the `size` is the amount of data in each record, the `stride` is the number of bytes between the first bytes of successive records, and `element_cnt` is the number of records to access. With an array of these structures, a read or write operation can define an arbitrary sequence of strided and nonstrided accesses. To specify a purely list-based access, a function would define an offset and a size in a sequence of `sio_file_io_list_t` structures with `element_cnt` set to one. For a simple strided access, a function would use an array containing just one `sio_file_io_list_t` element, and a contiguous access would use one structure with `element_cnt` = 1.

The declaration of `sio_mem_io_list_t` is identical to `sio_file_io_list_t` except the first member of the structure is

```
void * addr;
```

The individual elements in the `file_list` and the `mem_list` do not need to match: an operation could read two groups of 150 bytes from a file and store them as three groups of 100 bytes in memory. The lists can specify locations in any order, and a given file or memory location can be read (but not written) more than once. (Allowing applications to write the same location multiple times in a single operation would require LLAPI to define some kind of sequential consistency semantics, which could reduce opportunities for parallelism.) However, the two lists must specify the same total number of bytes. Once the access is finished, the function sets `bytes_moved` to the correct value. If the operation fails partway through, `bytes_moved` is set to a value less than or equal to the number of bytes actually transferred.

Nonblocking operations use a similar interface:

```
sio_return_t
sio_async_sg_read( int fd,
                   const sio_file_io_list_t * file_list,
                   sio_count_t file_list_count,
                   const sio_mem_io_list_t * mem_list,
                   sio_count_t mem_list_count,
                   sio_async_handle_t * handle );
```

When the function initiates an operation, it stores a value in `handle`. A program tests for completion of an operation by calling

```
sio_return_t
sio_async_status_any( sio_async_handle_t * handle_list,
                      sio_count_t handle_list_count,
                      sio_count_t * index,
                      sio_async_status_t * status,
                      sio_async_flags_t flags );
```

This function checks one or more outstanding requests, but it returns results for only one request at a time. If any request has finished (or been cancelled), the index of that request in the `handle_list` is returned in `index`. The `status` parameter is filled in with the status of the operation, and `flags` can be set to request that the function either block until at least one request is complete or return immediately regardless of the completion status of the requests.

5.2.3 Hints

LLAPI supports two kinds of hints. Ordered hints tell the file system exactly what sequence of accesses a program will request. Unordered hints describe the anticipated pattern in more general terms, such as "sequential," "ordered," "random," and so on. An implementation is free to ignore this information, but a correct application may not access a file in a way that conflicts with hints it has given. However, a program may cancel hints if it needs to access files in an unanticipated pattern.

Two functions convey both ordered and unordered hints: one for open files and one for unopened files.

```
sio_return_t
sio_hint( int fd,
          sio_hint_class_t hint_class,
          const sio_hint_t * hints,
          sio_count_t hint_count );

sio_return_t
sio_hint_by_name( const char * file_name,
                  sio_hint_class_t hint_class,
                  const sio_hint_t * hints,
                  sio_count_t hint_count );
```

The `hint_class` argument is a flag that states whether the hints being given are ordered or unordered. LLAPI implementations can define additional hint classes, but these will not be portable. The `hints` are a list of `sio_hint_t` structures, which have the form

```
typedef struct {
    sio_hint_flags_t flag;
    sio_file_io_t *  io_list;
    sio_count_t      list_count;
    void *           arg;
    sio_size_t       arg_len;
} sio_hint_t;
```

The `flag` member is a collection of bits. One of these bits states whether the hint applies to a read or a write operation. Another bit can indicate that the current hint is a cancellation of one or more previous hints; programs use this flag to revoke hints. In unordered hints, additional bits describe the general access pattern. These bits describe access sequences and whether the program will access the whole file or only part of it. Unordered hints do not use the remaining members in `sio_hint_t`. Ordered hints describe specific future access patterns in `io_list` using the same format as read and write calls. The `arg` and `arg_len` members are unused in the standard version of the interface, but implementations may define hints that receive additional information through these fields.

5.2.4 Cache Control

The cache control mechanism in LLAPI operates only on client caches, since server caches are relatively easy to keep consistent. The file control operations can set one of three client caching modes: strong consistency, weak consistency, or no client caching at all. Implementations can define additional caching modes.

Strong consistency requires the file system to keep any duplicate cached or buffered copies of data consistent with each other. For example, if one task writes data to a file location, and another task reads that location a short time later, the file system must ensure that the second task sees what the first one wrote. However, race conditions are possible if the two accesses happen at about the same time.

Weak consistency relies on the program using LLAPI to ensure that cached data remains consistent. A task writing data can make it visible to other tasks by calling `sio_control` on the file with an `SIO_CTL_Propagate` command. A task reading a file can retrieve the most current version of cached data using an `SIO_CTL_Refresh` command. To guarantee that a task's refresh command will get the data that another task has propagated, the tasks must somehow synchronize to ensure that the refresh happens after propagation. For example, the writing task can send the reading task a message after it has propagated the data, and the reading task can refresh its copy after receiving this message. File systems manage consistency at a level of granularity called the *cache consistency unit* (also called the *cache coherence unit*). This unit may correspond to a file block, a memory cache line, or a single byte. When two tasks write (with weak consistency) into the same consistency unit, the file system might not correctly store the data from both tasks, even if they don't access overlapping file locations. Instead, the writes from only one of the tasks may appear in the file. This would happen if the file system maintained separate buffers for the same consistency unit on different compute nodes, and the system flushed the two buffers sequentially without merging their contents. Programs cannot control the size of the consistency unit, but they can determine this size from a preprocessor constant or by calling a file control function with the `SIO_CTL_GetConsistencyUnit` command.

Implementations need not implement weak consistency semantics if they automatically enforce strong consistency or if they use no client caching at all.

5.2.5 Collective I/O

The LLAPI specification includes a collective I/O interface only as an extension to the basic standard. LLAPI's design constraints give its collective interface a somewhat unusual form. In most other collective interfaces, each participating process calls a collective I/O function, and the underlying system uses an internal communication mechanism to match the calls from different tasks, usually through synchronization.

Without such a mechanism, the I/O system would not know which processes were participating in the operation, especially if a program issued several collective requests at about the same time. LLAPI avoids synchronization and dependence on any specific communication system, so it needs a way to match tasks explicitly. To do this, one task calls a function to generate a 64-bit handle that uniquely identifies a collective operation. The program (not the LLAPI library) distributes this handle from the task that created it to all the other tasks that will participate in the operation. Each of these tasks includes the handle in its collective call, and the I/O system uses the handle to match the tasks.

The function to generate the handle is

```
sio_return_t
sio_coll_define( int fd,
                 sio_coll_iteration_t num_iterations,
                 const sio_file_io_list_t * file_list,
                 sio_count file_list_count,
                 sio_size_t iteration_stride,
                 sio_mode_t read_write,
                 sio_coll_participant_t num_participants,
                 sio_coll_handle_t * handle );
```

The process generating the handle specifies the complete set of data that the operation will access in the `file_list`, as well as the number of tasks that will participate and whether the operation will read or write data. The LLAPI designers determined that successive collective operations on a file often access data in identical patterns at different file locations. To simplify this kind of access, they put an iteration count and a stride in the description of an operation. Then a single handle can describe a sequence of collective operations, with each iteration advancing `iteration_stride` bytes in the file from the previous one.

Once the program has distributed the handle to all the participating tasks, each task initiates its portion of the collective operation by "joining" the access:

```
sio_return_t
sio_coll_join( int fd,
               sio_coll_handle_t * handle,
               sio_coll_participant_t participant,
               sio_coll_iteration_t iteration,
               const sio_file_io_list_t * file_list,
               sio_count file_list_count,
               const sio_mem_io_list_t * mem_list,
               sio_count_t mem_list_count,
               sio_async_handle_t * handle );
```

Collective I/O operations in LLAPI do not block, and the `sio_coll_join` interface is similar to the nonblocking read and write interfaces. In joining an operation, each task specifies the subset of the data listed in the `sio_coll_define` call it will access. Although the I/O software automatically updates a handle's `file_list` for each iteration during a sequence of collective accesses, the individual tasks must explicitly update their local `file_list` and `mem_list` on successive calls. The I/O software can initiate the file access as soon as the first task joins the collective operation. Since the system has a complete list of the data to be accessed, read operations can prefetch data for tasks that have not yet joined. Alternatively, the I/O software can wait for all the participating tasks to join before accessing any data. Tasks complete collective operations using the same `sio_async_status_any` function they use for noncollective operations.

5.2.6 Fast Copy

Finally, LLAPI defines an extension for rapidly copying files. One use of this feature is for checkpointing files (not memory). An out-of-core application could save a copy of its disk-based data structures before proceeding with updates that might leave them in an inconsistent state if the program crashed. After such a crash, the application could recover the data from the checkpoint file and resume its computation.

The intended implementation of a fast copy operation is for the file system to replicate only the source file's inode structure (or equivalent information) and not the actual data blocks. Then as the program alters blocks in the original file, the system creates new copies of just those blocks. By duplicating only the inodes and the blocks that differ between files, the file system could save time compared to duplicating every block. Of course, a file duplicated in this way offers little protection from a disk failure, since any corrupted blocks that were shared would appear in both copies of the file.

Programs initiate a fast copy through the file control function, passing in the `SIO_CTL_FastCopy` command and the file descriptor of the source file. The file on which the command is issued becomes a copy of the source file.

5.3 MPI-IO

MPI-IO began as a research project at IBM in 1994, and researchers at other sites subsequently contributed to it. The design began with the observation that parallel I/O optimizations require two basic abstractions that the MPI interface [150] for message passing already includes: the ability to define sets of processes (MPI communicators) and the ability to specify complex access patterns (MPI datatypes[1]). Using communicators and datatypes as a foundation, the MPI-IO designers created an interface that supports many parallel I/O operations and optimizations. The MPI-2 Forum (an ad hoc standards committee) adopted the MPI-IO interface in 1996 as the initial draft of its parallel I/O chapter and then made several changes over the next year. In 1997, the committee approved the MPI-2 standard [63], which includes the I/O chapter and several new message passing features. The I/O portion of MPI-2 is usually called MPI-IO, but since MPI-IO existed as an independent research project before the MPI-2 Forum standardized it, early papers on MPI-IO describe an interface that differs from the MPI-2 standard.

Because MPI-IO uses many features of MPI, any program that uses MPI-IO must have an MPI library available. However, MPI-IO was designed to be implemented separately from the main MPI library. All the features it needs from MPI, such as the ability to interpret datatypes or to initiate nonblocking requests, are available through standard MPI function calls. Much of the functionality that MPI-IO needs is available in MPI-1, so many early implementations of MPI-IO did not require a complete MPI-2 library. These implementations could run with only MPI-1 libraries and emulated the few missing MPI-2 functions they needed.

File access and message passing are analogous in many ways. In particular, both involve moving data from one address space to another. Traditional message passing is a two-sided operation (one process explicitly sends data and another explicitly receives it), but several message passing interfaces, including MPI-2, support one-sided operations. In these operations, an initiating process stores or retrieves data in the address space of a target process without the explicit participation of the target process. An obvious extension of one-sided communication would be to treat file access as a one-sided operation, with the file as the target. However, the details of file access differ enough from message passing that using the same function calls for both operations would be awkward and would offer little benefit to the user. MPI-2 supports both one-sided communication and file access, but these operations use separate interfaces.

5.3.1 Basic MPI-IO Abstractions

As noted above, MPI-IO borrows two basic abstractions from MPI: communicators and datatypes. A communicator is a set of processes and a "context." Contexts

1 This book uses "datatype," with no space, for specific MPI and HDF constructs and "data type" for the general concept of a type.

help programs distinguish unrelated operations involving the same processes, but they don't affect I/O operations, so there is no need to discuss them further. The set of processes in a communicator can be all the processes in a parallel job, just one process, or any intermediate set. MPI defines two special communicators: `MPI_COMM_WORLD` consists of the processes in the current parallel job, and `MPI_COMM_SELF` consists of just the process that refers to it. Thus, `MPI_COMM_WORLD` is the same communicator in every process of a job, but `MPI_COMM_SELF` is a different communicator in each process. MPI numbers processes in a communicator consecutively starting from zero. The number of a process is also called its "rank." The "size" of a communicator is the number of processes it contains. A program specifies a communicator when it opens a file. Every open operation is collective over the communicator; that is, every process in the communicator must call the function to open the file, generally with identical parameters. Of course, a single process can open a file by specifying `MPI_COMM_SELF`. Once the file is open, operations on the file can be collective or independent. Collective operations require all the processes in the original communicator to participate. Independent operations can be done by individual processes.

MPI datatypes define a pattern of data access in memory or a file. A *basic type* is one of several predefined datatypes in MPI that correspond to the fundamental datatypes in C and Fortran: integers, characters, floating-point numbers, and so on. For C programs, the basic types include `MPI_INT`, `MPI_CHAR`, `MPI_FLOAT`, and so on. For Fortran programs, the types include `MPI_CHARACTER`, `MPI_INTEGER`, `MPI_REAL`, and so on. MPI defines several other basic types, including `MPI_BYTE`. This type can refer to anonymous, untyped data in memory or a file. MPI also supports *derived types,* which are collections of basic types at specific positions relative to each other (see Figure 5.2). A derived type is defined by a *type map* as follows:

$$\text{type map} = \{(\text{type}_0, \text{disp}_0), (\text{type}_1, \text{disp}_1), \ldots, (\text{type}_{n-1}, \text{disp}_{n-1})\}$$

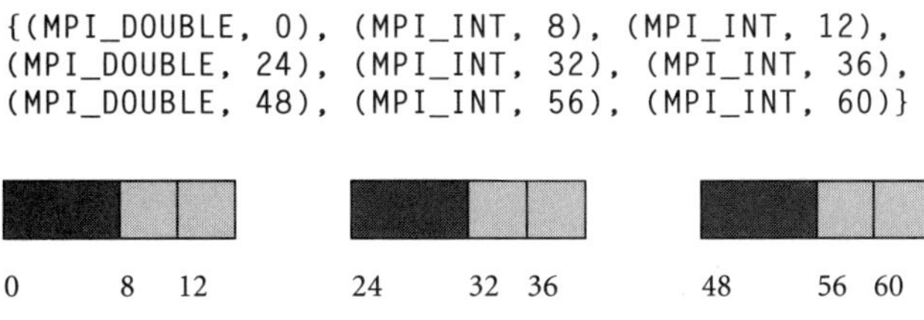

Figure 5.2 An MPI type map and a block diagram of the corresponding type. Dark blocks represent `MPI_DOUBLE` types and light blocks represent `MPI_INT` types.

where type_i is an MPI basic type and disp_i is an integer displacement that gives the starting location of the type in bytes. By themselves, the displacements are not relative to any particular location; the specific value of the displacement is only meaningful when a type is applied to a memory buffer or file. However, the displacements do specify the locations of basic types relative to each other. A basic type is defined to have a type map consisting of itself with a displacement of zero. To describe datatypes, it is useful to define both their *size* and their *extent.* The size of a datatype is the total number of bytes in its constituent basic types. The extent of a datatype is the span in bytes from the beginning of the type with the lowest displacement to the end of the type with the greatest displacement. On some systems, the extent may be rounded upward to produce a correct data alignment. The datatype shown in Figure 5.2 has a size of 48 bytes and an extent of 64 bytes. The elements in a general type map need not appear in order of increasing displacement, and they may overlap; that is, the displacement of one element may fall within the extent of another element. However, some valid MPI type maps may not be used in certain MPI-IO operations.

A *type signature* is a type map without the displacements; it is an ordered list of MPI basic types.

$$\text{type signature} = \{\text{type}_0, \text{type}_1, \ldots, \text{type}_{n-1}\}$$

Some operations require two types to have matching signatures but not necessarily matching type maps. MPI includes a number of functions for defining commonly used datatypes, such as contiguous arrays, strided arrays, and arbitrary sequences of the same basic type. These functions are called *datatype constructors.* Although the terminology of MPI datatypes is similar to C++ terminology, the concepts in the two systems are not analogous. For example, MPI datatypes don't have member functions or inheritance.

You can visualize a datatype (basic or derived) as a template that can be applied to a file or to memory. The underlying data is assumed to match the corresponding MPI basic types, but the MPI library cannot usually verify this. MPI-IO applies datatypes to both files and memory.

Processes use MPI datatypes to define *file views,* which define the parts of a file that are visible to a given process. All processes can share a common view, views can partly overlap, or views can be disjoint. A view is defined by a *displacement* and a datatype (Figure 5.3). Starting at the file location given by the displacement, a view applies the datatype repeatedly beginning at the displacement and continuing to the end of the file. A datatype used to construct a view is called a *file type.* The displacement allows a view to skip over headers or unneeded data at the beginning of a file. It is always given in bytes. When a file is first opened, every process views the file as a contiguous series of bytes, starting at file offset zero. This view is equivalent

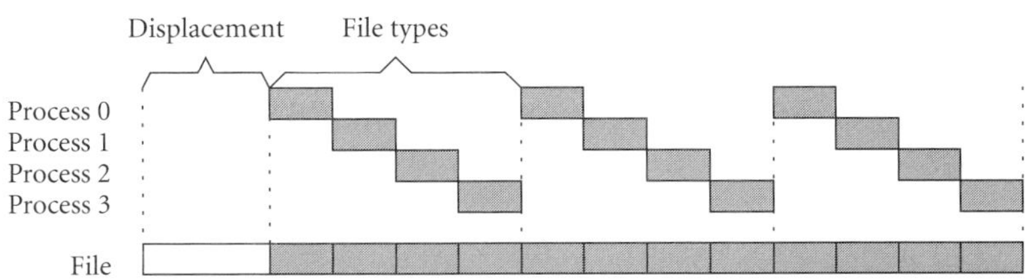

Figure 5.3 File views in different processes can interleave to cover a contiguous region of a file. The displacement moves the starting point of the view to any location in the file. The processes use complementary file types, which MPI-IO automatically repeats to the end of the file.

to the standard Unix view of a file. Once a file is open, processes can change the view as needed. The view is not a property of the file itself, and MPI-IO does not store any information about views in the file. Rather, the view is specific to each process's instance of the open file. A process can have multiple instances of the same file open with different views. Although views in different processes may overlap each other, the elements in a type map of a file type that defines a single view must not overlap, and their displacements must increase monotonically. These last two requirements simplify the translation of MPI-IO file offsets to actual file locations and vice versa.

The file type used in the definition of a view is an ordinary MPI datatype, but it consists logically of a series of *elementary types,* also called *etypes.* An etype corresponds to a file record; it is the basic unit of data that the program will access through the view. In the simplest case, the etype and file type are identical; for example, in the default view, both the etype and file type are `MPI_BYTE`. However, the etype can also be a derived MPI datatype, which might correspond to a collection of data like a C language structure. A file type always consists of one or more whole etypes (Figure 5.4).

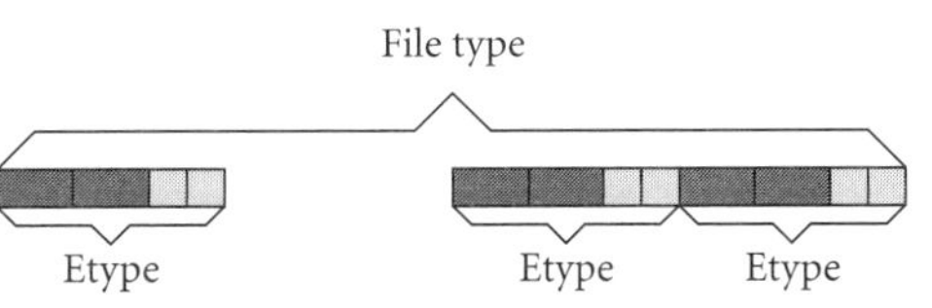

Figure 5.4 A file type consists of one or more copies of an etype, which may itself be a derived MPI datatype. The file type here consists of three etypes, with a gap between the first two.

MPI-IO supports many variations on file access operations, and applications can supply hints, control the consistency semantics, and translate between data formats within read and write operations. The standard defines programming interfaces in C, C++, and Fortran. The following sections describe these features and how they are used.

5.3.2 Basic Operations

Programs open files by calling `MPI_File_open`. The C function interface is

```
int
MPI_File_open( MPI_Comm comm,
               char * filename,
               int amode,
               MPI_Info info,
               MPI_File *fh );
```

In Fortran, the interface is

```
mpi_file_open( comm, filename, amode, info, fh, ierror )
    character*(*) filename
    integer comm, amode, info, fh, ierror
```

Where C uses defined types extensively, the Fortran interface uses only built-in types. Throughout MPI, the C and Fortran interfaces use the same initial sequence of arguments, but since the Fortran calls are subroutines rather than functions, they do not return an error code directly. Instead, the value that a C function would return is passed out through the final `ierror` argument in Fortran. Successful operations return the code `MPI_SUCCESS`, which MPI defines to be zero. Operations that encounter errors may return error codes, halt the program, or take some other action as defined by the user. See the MPI-1 and MPI-2 standards for details on error handling.

The C++ interface is

```
static MPI::File
MPI::File::Open( const MPI::Intracomm& comm,
                 const char * filename,
                 int amode,
                 const MPI::Info& info );
```

The C++ interface defines all functions within the `MPI` name space. A `File` is a class within that space, and `Open` is a static member function. It must be static because there is no `File` object for it to operate on until after the function is called. In that sense, the function behaves like a C++ constructor. The MPI designers chose not to use constructors to initialize objects because doing so would break the symmetry among the names of operations in C, C++, and Fortran. The other C++ functions that operate on open files are members of the `File` class. Whereas the C and Fortran interfaces pass a file handle as the first argument to a function, the C++ interfaces call a member function on a `File` object. Also, the C++ interfaces do not return error codes directly; instead, they can either throw exceptions in case of error or use the standard MPI error handling mechanism.

The remaining discussion will not list the C, C++, and Fortran interfaces separately for each function. Instead, the function interfaces will be given in C, and examples will be presented in C or Fortran. The full MPI-2 standard lists all the functions in each language.

Programs pass `MPI_File_open` an MPI communicator to specify the processes opening the file. The `amode` states whether the file is to be opened for reading, writing, or both, and it also defines several other options. The `info` argument is a hints interface, described in Section 5.3.7. In C and Fortran, the function returns the file handle in the `fh` argument; the C++ version returns the file handle directly.

Figure 5.5 illustrates opening, writing, reading, and closing a file. The program uses noncollective data access to write and then read 100 bytes from each process at different locations in the file.

The basic `MPI_File_write` and `MPI_File_read` functions work much like their Unix counterparts. They are independent operations that use local file pointers to determine where in the file to access data. In the MPI functions, the program specifies a datatype for each access. This type applies to the memory buffer and is sometimes called the *buffer type.* The buffer type can be a basic MPI type or a derived type, so access to memory can be discontiguous. The `count` argument that precedes the buffer type states the number of buffer type units of data to access. The file view determines the type of the data in the file. In this example, since the program did not set a view, all processes view the file as a contiguous array of `MPI_BYTE`. The type that the view specifies and the buffer type must match, although implementations do not necessarily check this. More formally, the type signature of the datatype passed to a data access function must match the type signature of some number of copies of the view's etype. However, `MPI_BYTE` in either the etype or the buffer type matches any type in the other. MPI-IO does not convert automatically between types. If the etype is `MPI_INTEGER` and the buffer type is `MPI_REAL`, the file access operation will either fail or produce undefined results.

This simple example does little more than ordinary Unix I/O. MPI-IO includes about 60 functions, many of which are more sophisticated variations on the basic read and write operations.

```
MPI_File fh;
MPI_Status status;
MPI_Comm comm = MPI_COMM_WORLD;
int count, rank;
char outdata[100];
char indata[100];

/* ... fill in outdata buffer ... */

MPI_File_open(comm, "sample",
    MPI_MODE_RDWR | MPI_MODE_CREATE,
    MPI_INFO_NULL, &fh);

/* Figure out where to write the data */
MPI_Comm_rank(comm, &rank);
MPI_File_seek(fh, rank * 100, MPI_SEEK_SET);

MPI_File_write(fh, outdata, 100, MPI_CHAR, &status);
MPI_Get_count(&status, MPI_CHAR, &count);
if(count != 100)
    printf("Wrote only %d of %d bytes!\n", count, 100);

MPI_File_seek(fh, rank * 100, MPI_SEEK_SET);
MPI_File_read(fh, indata, 100, MPI_CHAR, &status);
MPI_Get_count(&status, MPI_CHAR, &count);
if(count != 100)
    printf("Read only %d of %d bytes!\n", count, 100);

MPI_File_close(&fh);
```

Figure 5.5 Opening, writing, reading, and closing a file with MPI-IO. Some code not affecting I/O operations has been omitted.

5.3.3 Setting a View

Read and write functions define the pattern of access in memory, but the pattern of access in a file is determined by the file view, which the program sets separately. To set a file view, each process must first select or define an etype and a file type. When an application uses the same view for every process, the etype and file type are often basic MPI types. To interleave access, however, each process must define a file type that has its visible segments correctly interspersed with gaps. A common technique for creating interleaved views is to define a set of file types with the same extent on each process and to place etypes at the correct location within the extent for each process. Figure 5.3 illustrates the resulting views. To mark the beginning and end of an extended datatype, MPI defines two special basic datatypes, `MPI_LB` and `MPI_UB`. (*LB* and *UB* stand for lower bound and upper bound.) These types have zero extent and size, and programs can place them in a type map to create gaps to mark the beginning or end of a derived type.

Figure 5.6 shows code that creates the file types for the views in Figure 5.3, and then it opens the file and sets the view. It works for any number of processes.

In the call to `MPI_File_set_view`, the string "native" indicates that the I/O library should not convert between numeric data formats as it accesses the data. See Section 5.3.9 for details on this feature.

An alternative method of creating this view would have each process construct the same file type, equivalent to the one that Process 0 constructs. Then each process would define its view using this file type and different displacements.

The example uses only MPI-1 functions to create the file type. These functions work on systems where an MPI-IO library is implemented over a library that does not support the full MPI-2 standard. MPI-2 defines several new functions for manipulating datatypes. Some, like `MPI_Type_get_extent` and `MPI_Type_create_struct`, are slightly modified versions of their MPI-1 counterparts, but the MPI-1 functions continue to work (for now).

Other new datatype functions help define complex views. Consider a program that stores a multidimensional array in a shared file and has each process access part of this array. Building a file type to define the appropriate views would require several steps and a series of intermediate datatypes. The `MPI_Type_create_darray` function automates this task. The function adopts the HPF model of data distribution, mapping an array of data to an array of processes using block or cyclic distributions.

```
int
MPI_Type_create_darray( int size,
                        int rank,
                        int ndims,
                        int array_of_gsizes[],
                        int array_of_distribs[],
                        int array_of_dargs[],
                        int array_of_psizes[],
                        int order,
                        MPI_Datatype oldtype,
                        MPI_Datatype * newtypc );
```

```
int procs, rank;
MPI_Aint extent;
MPI_Datatype etype;
MPI_Datatype filetype;
MPI_Offset initialdisp;
MPI_Comm comm = MPI_COMM_WORLD;
MPI_File fh;
int blocklens[3];
MPI_Aint displacements[3];
MPI_Datatype types[3];

etype = MPI_DOUBLE;
initialdisp = 16;

/* Define the file type */
blocklens[0] = blocklens[1] = blocklens[2] = 1;

MPI_Comm_size(comm, &procs);
MPI_Comm_rank(comm, &rank);
MPI_Type_extent(etype, &extent);
displacements[0] = 0;
displacements[1] = extent * rank;
displacements[2] = extent * procs;

types[0] = MPI_LB;
types[1] = etype;
types[2] = MPI_UB;

MPI_Type_struct(3, blocklens, displacements, types, &filetype);
MPI_Type_commit(&filetype);

/* Open the file */
MPI_File_open(comm, "sample",
    MPI_MODE_RDWR | MPI_MODE_CREATE,
    MPI_INFO_NULL, &fh);
```

Figure 5.6 MPI-IO code to create the views shown in Figure 5.3. Error checking has been omitted for clarity.

```
/* Set the view */
MPI_File_set_view(fh, initialdisp, etype, filetype,
    "native", MPI_INFO_NULL);

/* ... access the file ... */

MPI_File_close(&fh);
MPI_Type_free(&filetype);
```

Figure 5.6 *(Continued)*

The function is not collective, but the intent is that every process in the communicator that was used to open the file will call this function, creating a set of complementary file types. The `size` and `rank` arguments should contain the appropriate values from the communicator. The `rank` selects a subset of the global array. Figure 5.7 shows how the function parameters define the mapping. The

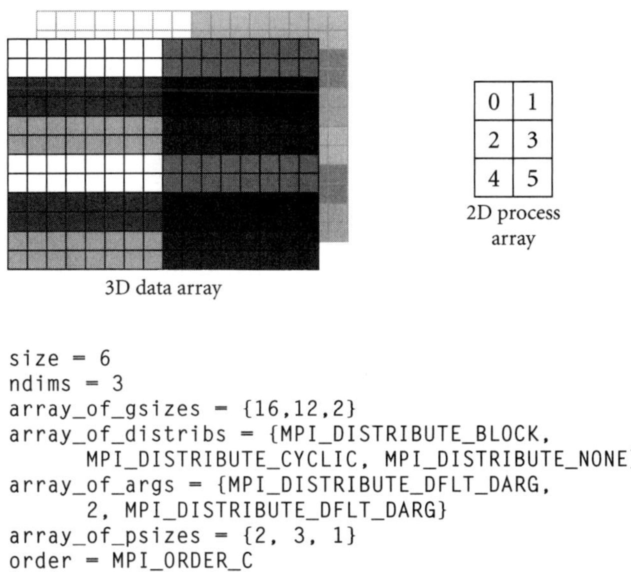


```
size = 6
ndims = 3
array_of_gsizes = {16,12,2}
array_of_distribs = {MPI_DISTRIBUTE_BLOCK,
      MPI_DISTRIBUTE_CYCLIC, MPI_DISTRIBUTE_NONE}
array_of_args = {MPI_DISTRIBUTE_DFLT_DARG,
      2, MPI_DISTRIBUTE_DFLT_DARG}
array_of_psizes = {2, 3, 1}
order = MPI_ORDER_C
```

Figure 5.7 The `MPI_Type_create_darray` function produces a datatype that defines an HPF-style distribution. Here, the three-dimensional data array is partitioned over a two-dimensional array of processes in a mapping equivalent to (block, cyclic(2),*) in HPF (though the array here uses C-style row-major ordering).

array_of_gsizes gives the dimensions of the global array, array_of_distribs gives the type of distribution for each dimension (block, cyclic, or none), array_of_args lists any parameters for the distributions (either a default of MPI_DISTRIBUTE_DFLT_DARG or an integer value), and array_of_psizes gives the dimensions of the processor array on which the global array will be mapped. Logically, the process array always has the same number of dimensions as the data array, but setting the size of any dimension to one eliminates that dimension. The oldtype parameter specifies the etype, and the file type is returned in newtype. After calling MPI_Type_commit on the new type, a program can pass it to MPI_File_set_view to create a new view. Since a view repeats the file type to the end of the file, the view for this type will correspond to a series of distributed arrays. If the file contains arrays of different sizes or the program uses different distributions on successive arrays in a file, the program must set the view with the correct file type and displacement before accessing each array. Alternatively, if the program knew in advance the series of arrays and distributions in the file, it could construct a file type that concatenated several of these distributed array types to match the layout of all the arrays in the file.

5.3.4 Specifying File Offsets

File locations in MPI-IO are called *file offsets,* and data access functions can specify offsets in one of three ways: through local file pointers, shared file pointers, or explicit offsets. Since a view is a template through which a process sees a file, offsets are relative to the view. Also, offsets are in units of etypes. For example, in Figure 5.3, the first record accessible in Process 0's view would be considered offset zero, and the next record, which is really four records away in the file, would be at offset one. Likewise, Process 1 also considers the first record visible in its view to be offset zero, and so on. Thus, the same offset refers to different records in different views. For that reason, processes using shared file pointers must have identical views of the file. MPI-IO sets local and shared file pointers to zero whenever a program changes its view of a file.

The basic read and write functions shown earlier use local file pointers. These work much as they do in Unix, with read or write operations updating the local pointer independently on each process. One subtle difference from Unix semantics occurs when a program tries to read past the end of a file. In Unix, the file pointer is incremented after the operation completes by the number of bytes actually read. MPI-IO updates the file pointer before the access begins, so it can be used by another concurrent operation. A program can detect when the amount of data read is less than the amount requested by inspecting the status object that the data access function fills in. Similar update rules apply when a write operation fails to store all the data requested.

Shared file pointers let several processes coordinate access to a file. These pointers are generally less efficient than local file pointers because the I/O library must coordinate pointer updates across multiple processes. MPI-IO data access functions that use shared file pointers have the suffix `_shared` for noncollective operations. For example, `MPI_File_read_shared` is similar to `MPI_File_read` except that it uses a shared file pointer instead of a local one. Collective operations have the suffix `_ordered` instead of `_all`. In addition to using a shared file pointer, ordered operations *appear* to read or write data in the order of the processes' communicator ranks. For example, if the shared pointer indexed file location 0 at the outset of the operation, and each process requested 100 bytes, then Process 0 would access bytes 0 through 99 in the file, Process 1 would access bytes 100 through 199, and so on. However, the implementation would be free to schedule the actual accesses in a different order, so long as each process accessed the correct range of data.

Data access functions can also specify offsets directly. These variants have the suffix `_at` in both their collective and noncollective forms, and they have an extra parameter to specify the offset. For example:

```
int
MPI_File_read_at( MPI_File fh,
                  MPI_Offset offset,
                  void * buf,
                  int count,
                  MPI_Datatype datatype,
                  MPI_Status * status );
```

Explicit offsets, local pointers, and shared pointers all work independently, and programs can freely intermix their use on the same open file (with the restriction that shared file pointers require identical views on all processes). MPI-IO has seek functions for both local and shared file pointers. The version for shared pointers is a collective operation. There are also functions to query the local and shared file pointers and another function to translate an offset that is relative to a view into an absolute byte location in a file. This last function is useful when resetting the view; a program can query the current file offset, convert it to a byte location, and use that value as the displacement for a new view.

5.3.5 Collective Operations

MPI-IO blocking collective operations are designed to look as much as possible like their noncollective counterparts. In the example above where a program opens a file, writes 100 bytes from each process, and then reads the data back, the following collective calls could replace the noncollective calls:

```
/* seek the the correct file location */

MPI_File_write_all(fh, outdata, 100, MPI_CHAR, &status);

/* check the status, seek back to the previous location */

MPI_File_read_all(fh, indata, 100, MPI_CHAR, &status);
```

The only difference between the collective and noncollective calls here is that the collective calls have the suffix `_all`. Collective calls with explicit file offsets have this form:

```
MPI_File_write_at_all(fh, rank * 100, outdata, 100,
    MPI_CHAR, &status);

/* check the status */

MPI_File_read_at_all(fh, rank * 100, indata, 100,
    MPI_CHAR, &status);
```

Of course, the explicit-offset versions don't need the seek calls. For data access functions that use either local file pointers or explicit offsets, there are only two semantic differences between the collective and noncollective versions. Every process that opened the file must call the collective operation (as they do in the earlier example even for the noncollective version), and the collective operations may impose a barrier synchronization among the participating processes, although they are not required to do so. Collective functions allow the I/O software to optimize the file access, but they do not specify *how* to optimize it. Indeed, MPI-IO allows collective functions to behave identically to noncollective ones, except for the shared pointer versions. (These, as noted above, impose an order on the accesses.) However, as the next section shows, the nonblocking versions of the collective calls are somewhat different from their nonblocking, noncollective counterparts.

5.3.6 Nonblocking Operations

MPI-IO uses different structures for collective and noncollective calls that do not block. The noncollective versions follow the same pattern as the functions described so far; they have slightly different names and a similar set of arguments. There are versions for all three methods of specifying file offsets. Figure 5.8 illustrates a nonblocking function used to double buffer output data in a sequential code.

```
integer fh, req, err, count
integer status(MPI_STATUS_SIZE)
integer bufsz
parameter (bufsz = 1000)
real*8 buffer1(bufsz), buffer2(bufsz)
logical done

call mpi_file_open(MPI_COMM_SELF, 'sample', &
    MPI_MODE_WRONLY+MPI_MODE_CREATE, MPI_INFO_NULL, fh, err)
call mpi_file_set_view(fh, 0, MPI_REAL8, MPI_REAL8, &
    'native', MPI_INFO_NULL, err)

! compute fills in the buffer.  It sets done to .true.
! and returns immediately if there is no more work to do.
call compute(buffer1, done)
do while (.not. done)
    call mpi_file_iwrite(fh, buffer1, bufsz, MPI_REAL8, &
        req, err)
    call compute(buffer2, done)
    call mpi_wait(req, status, err)
    call mpi_get_count(status, MPI_REAL8, count, err)
    if (count .ne. bufsz) then
        write(*,*) 'wrote only ', count, ' of ', bufsz
        exit
    end if
    if (done) exit

    call mpi_file_iwrite(fh, buffer2, bufsz, MPI_REAL8, &
        req, err)
    call compute(buffer1, done)
    call mpi_wait(req, status, err)
    call mpi_get_count(status, MPI_REAL8, count, err)
    if (count .ne. bufsz) then
        write(*,*) 'wrote only ', count, ' of ', bufsz
        exit
    end if
end do

call mpi_file_close(fh, err)
```

Figure 5.8 Using nonblocking, noncollective MPI-IO calls.

The noncollective, nonblocking calls use an "i" prefix on the name of the operation, following the MPI convention for nonblocking messages. (The "i" stands for "immediate return.") Programs test or wait for completion of an I/O operation using the same functions that MPI defines for nonblocking message passing.

A Problem with Nonblocking Collective I/O

The MPI-2 Forum considered defining nonblocking collective operations in a similar way, but collective operations did not fit well into the existing nonblocking model. Many forms of collective I/O require communication among the processes both before and after the disk access. For computation to overlap a disk access, the second round of communication must happen after the call that initiates the nonblocking operation returns. A multithreaded implementation could carry out this communication in the background, but the MPI Forum did not want to require multithreading as a prerequisite to implementing the standard. Another alternative would be to communicate when processes posted their `MPI_Test` or `MPI_Wait` commands. But MPI-1 defines these functions to be noncollective, and using them to complete a collective operation would effectively give them collective semantics: all participating processes would need to call one of these completion functions to ensure correct operation. Making an MPI function collective in some circumstances and not in others would be confusing and error-prone.

Another problem with applying the MPI model of nonblocking operations to collective I/O is that it would bring existing MPI rules into conflict. MPI permits multiple nonblocking requests to be active on the same communicator. In MPI-IO, the file handle plays a role similar to a communicator, so by analogy a program should be able to request multiple nonblocking operations on the same file. For noncollective operations, concurrent I/O requests present no problem. However, MPI forbids concurrent *collective* operations on a communicator because of the risk of deadlock; if two such operations tried to synchronize all the processes, some processes could wait indefinitely in one operation while the remaining processes waited in the other operation. Therefore, MPI on the one hand should permit concurrent collective nonblocking requests, but on the other hand it forbids them. It might have been possible to design nonblocking collective operations that could work around these conflicts, but the MPI-2 Forum chose instead to design a restricted form of nonblocking collective I/O that is separate from the other MPI nonblocking operations.

Split Collective Data Access

The restricted model is called *split collective* data access. It uses collective calls both to initiate and to complete nonblocking data access. Figure 5.9 illustrates

```
call compute(buffer1, done)
do while (.not. done)
    call mpi_file_write_all_begin(fh, buffer1, bufsz, &
        MPI_REAL8, req, err)
    call compute(buffer2, done)
    call mpi_file_write_all_end(fh, buffer1, status, err)
    call mpi_get_count(status, MPI_REAL8, count, err)
    if (count .ne. bufsz) then
        write(*,*) 'wrote only ', count, ' of ', bufsz
        exit
    end if
    if (done) exit

    call mpi_file_write_all_begin(fh, buffer2, bufsz, &
        MPI_REAL8, req, err)
    call compute(buffer1, done)
    call mpi_file_write_all_end(fh, buffer2, status, err)
    call mpi_get_count(status, MPI_REAL8, count, err)
    if (count .ne. bufsz) then
        write(*,*) 'wrote only ', count, ' of ', bufsz
        exit
    end if
end do
```

Figure 5.9 This split collective MPI-IO operation assumes that the program has already opened the file collectively and set an interleaved view so that each process sees a separate portion of the file. Variables are the same as those declared in the noncollective nonblocking I/O example.

their use. This example uses the nonblocking collective write subroutine with local file pointers. Analogous versions exist for shared pointers (with ordered access) and explicit offsets and for the corresponding read operations. Each uses its own matched pair of begin/end calls. MPI-IO permits only one collective data access operation of any kind to be active on a given file at one time, so a program could not perform a blocking collective operation between begin/end operations on the same file. However, a program can access a file noncollectively while a split collective operation is under way. The split collective operations require the program to pass the buffer to both the `_start` and `_end` subroutines. This unusual requirement avoids certain optimization problems in Fortran programs. Passing the buffer explicitly to the `_end` subroutine warns the compiler that the buffer contents may have changed

Positioning	*Blocking?*	*Noncollective operations*
Local pointer	blocking	MPI_File_read MPI_File_write
	nonblocking	MPI_File_iread MPI_File_iwrite
Explicit offset	blocking	MPI_File_read_at MPI_File_write_at
	nonblocking	MPI_File_iread_at MPI_File_iwrite_at
Shared pointer	blocking	MPI_File_read_shared MPI_File_write_shared
	nonblocking	MPI_File_iread_shared MPI_File_iwrite_shared

Table 5.1 *MPI-IO noncollective data access functions. (Adapted from the MPI-2 standard [63], Chapter 9.)*

after the subroutine returns. C compilers generally don't need this warning, but the C versions of these functions still use the buffer parameter in the _end functions for consistency.

The split collective operations complete the collection of MPI-IO data access functions. Tables 5.1 and 5.2 list all these functions.

5.3.7 File Hints

MPI-2 includes a mechanism for passing hints to the I/O system. The basis of this mechanism is an object of type MPI_Info, which holds a list of *keys* and *values*. A key is the name of a configuration parameter in the I/O system or the message passing system, and the associated value specifies the desired setting of the parameter. Programs pass both keys and values to MPI as text strings. Using strings instead of named constants avoids compiler errors when programs that use nonstandard hints are compiled on systems that don't define those hints. Of course, the system will not be able to respond to the nonstandard hint, but the program will still compile and run correctly. Hints in MPI affect only performance and not the meaning of a program. MPI-IO libraries are free to ignore hints, and programs are free to contravene hints they have given.

MPI-IO defines several standard hints. Implementations need not support the features these hints control, but if they do, the features must work as defined in the standard. The standard hints include controls for striping files, selecting the

Positioning	*Blocking?*	*Collective operations*
Local pointer	blocking	`MPI_File_read_all` `MPI_File_write_all`

	split	`MPI_File_read_all_begin`
		`MPI_File_read_all_end`
		`MPI_File_write_all_begin`
		`MPI_File_write_all_end`

Explicit offset	blocking	`MPI_File_read_at_all` `MPI_File_write_at_all`

	split	`MPI_File_read_at_all_begin`
		`MPI_File_read_at_all_end`
		`MPI_File_write_at_all_begin`
		`MPI_File_write_at_all_end`

Shared pointer	blocking	`MPI_File_read_ordered` `MPI_File_write_ordered`

	split	`MPI_File_read_ordered_begin`
		`MPI_File_read_ordered_end`
		`MPI_File_write_ordered_begin`
		`MPI_File_write_ordered_end`

Table 5.2 *MPI-IO collective data access functions. (Adapted from the MPI-2 standard [63], Chapter 9.)*

number and configuration of I/O nodes, configuring client-based collective I/O, and stating expected patterns of access. Programs can also use the info mechanism to retrieve file information that they cannot change, such as the file name and fixed striping parameters. As previous examples have shown, programs can specify hints when opening a file and when setting a view. They can also call `MPI_File_set_info` on open files. Figure 5.10 shows how a program can request specific striping parameters on a newly created file. Then the program prints out all the hints that are active on the file, which may include more or fewer items than the program explicitly set.

Programs with no hints to give when opening a file or setting a view can pass in the dummy value `MPI_INFO_NULL`, as shown in earlier examples.

5.3.8 File Control and Concurrency

MPI-IO has controls for setting the file size, preallocating data, and querying various parameters. The standard includes separate functions for each of these operations.

```
MPI_File fh;
MPI_Status status;
MPI_Info infoin, infoout;
int nkeys, n, key_is_set;
char key[MPI_MAX_INFO_KEY], value[256];
/* MPI defines the maximum key length to be no more than
 * 256 bytes.  The maximum value length can be much larger,
 * so although MPI defines MPI_MAX_INFO_VAL, it does not
 * recommend declaring a string of this length.
 */

/* Create and initialize an MPI_Info object.  The
 * striping unit is equivalent to the stripe depth
 * discussed elsewhere in this book.
 */
MPI_Info_create(&infoin);
MPI_Info_set(infoin, "striping_factor", "16");
MPI_Info_set(infoin, "striping_unit", "4096");
MPI_Info_set(infoin, "access_style", "write_once,sequential");

MPI_File_open(MPI_COMM_WORLD, "sample",
    MPI_MODE_RDWR | MPI_MODE_CREATE, infoin, &fh);

MPI_File_get_info(fh, &infoout);
/* infoout is initialized automatically here */

MPI_Info_get_nkeys(infoout, &nkeys);
for(n = 0; n < nkeys; n++) {
    MPI_Info_get_nthkey(infoout, n, key);

/* Read each info item.  MPI truncates value strings
 * longer than that specified (256 byte) length.
 */
    MPI_Info_get(infoout, key, 256, value, &key_is_set);

/* key_is_set is nonzero if the key has been set on
 * this info object.  Since the key came from a call
```

Figure 5.10 Using MPI-IO hints to request striping parameters on a file.

```
         * to MPI_Info_get_nthkey, it should always be valid.
         * However, a program can also call MPI_Info_get with
         * a key of its own choosing to see if it has been set.
         */
        if(key_is_set) printf("%s = %s\n", key, value);
        else printf("Error! MPI returned a bad key: %s\n", key);
}

MPI_Info_free(&infoout);
MPI_Info_free(&infoin);
/* ... use the file ... */
MPI_File_close(&fh);
```

Figure 5.10 *(Continued)*

Programs can also control the file consistency semantics. These semantics affect not only how MPI-IO handles write accesses to overlapping file locations but also how the program ensures that data written by one process becomes visible to another. By default, files are opened in nonatomic mode, which means that programs are responsible for synchronizing conflicting file accesses. Programs can get stricter consistency semantics (possibly with poorer performance) by accessing the file in atomic mode, which they activate by calling `MPI_File_set_atomicity` with a flag set to `true`. Atomic mode guarantees sequential consistency between accesses that use "related" file handles, that is, those created in the same collective open operation. It does not guarantee sequential consistency between accesses on unrelated file handles.

When files are open in nonatomic mode or when accesses use unrelated file handles, MPI-IO defines a series of rules that programs must follow to ensure sequentially consistent access. These rules depend on whether file operations are collective, whether they access overlapping regions of a file, and whether they happen concurrently. In MPI-IO, two file access operations *conflict* when the operations access at least one file location in common and at least one operation is a write. The operations may happen on the same or different processes, and they need not be concurrent. If no accesses on a file conflict, then MPI-IO can trivially guarantee sequential consistency.

For noncollective accesses that conflict, programs can guarantee sequential consistency by ensuring that accesses are not concurrent. They do this by bracketing sequences of nonconflicting accesses with `MPI_File_sync` calls (`MPI_File_open` and `MPI_File_close` are also acceptable here) and separating conflicting sequences with

```
! The following code runs on Process 0.
call mpi_file_open(MPI_COMM_WORLD, 'sample', ..., fh, & err)
call mpi_file_write_at(fh, 0, buf, 100, MPI_BYTE, & status, err)
call mpi_file_sync(fh, err)
call mpi_barrier(MPI_COMM_WORLD, err)
call mpi_file_sync(fh, err)
! Data is now available to Process 1; Process 0 can
! continue using the file.
call mpi_file_close(fh, err)

! The following code runs on Process 1.
call mpi_file_open(MPI_COMM_WORLD, 'sample', ..., fh, & err)
call mpi_file_sync(fh, err)
call mpi_barrier(MPI_COMM_WORLD, err)
call mpi_file_sync(fh, err)
call mpi_file_read_at(fh, 0, buf, 100, MPI_BYTE, & status, err)
call mpi_file_close(fh, err)
```

Figure 5.11 A sync-barrier-sync sequence used for ensuring sequential consistency.

some kind of temporal synchronization. The standard technique is a sync-barrier-sync sequence, shown in Figure 5.11.

The first call to `MPI_File_sync` flushes to storage any data that Process 0 has buffered locally. The second call to `MPI_File_sync` refreshes any cached copy of the file data at Process 1. The intervening barrier ensures that the update on Process 1 occurs after the flush on Process 0. You might be tempted to remove the second synchronization in Process 0 and the first one in Process 1, since neither appears to be necessary. However, `MPI_File_sync` is a collective call, so MPI would try to match the remaining two synchronization calls, which may act as a barrier in some implementations. The file synchronizations could then create a deadlock with the barrier operation. The extra call on each process to `MPI_File_sync` could be eliminated if the two processes had opened the file with `MPI_COMM_SELF`, since the file synchronizations would then be "collective" over just the local process.

For collective file accesses, the consistency rules are ambiguous. When processes collectively write and then read back data in a file, a sync-barrier-sync sequence ought to guarantee sequential consistency. However, a strict interpretation of the standard appears to exclude this option. The only certain ways to guarantee sequential consistency when collective file accesses conflict with each other are either to use atomic mode or to close and reopen the file between the conflicting accesses.

The semantics for nonatomic access in MPI-IO are quite relaxed in that they permit a wide range of caching strategies. Some implementations can efficiently enforce atomic semantics, or something approaching them, even in nonatomic mode. Programs developed on these systems may work correctly even if they don't follow the MPI-IO rules for file consistency; however, these programs may not run correctly when moved to other systems.

5.3.9 Conversion of Data Representations

A standard API allows programs to run on a variety of computers, but it doesn't guarantee that the files they write will be portable. Differences in byte ordering and the representations of floating-point numbers can make binary data files written on one machine useless on another. MPI-IO addresses the problem of data portability in two ways. First, it defines a standard data representation that is guaranteed to be readable by all standard MPI-IO libraries. Second, it offers programs a mechanism to insert user-defined data conversion functions into data access operations. Neither technique defines a standard file format, which might specify how arrays are laid out; they operate only at the level of individual basic types. Also, MPI does not automatically store any information about the data format in the file. A program must know what data representation it will be reading. Of course, programs writing data can easily put this information in a file header.

Both the standard data representation and the user-defined representations are selected through the `datarep` argument in `MPI_File_set_view`. Like hints, data representations are identified by text strings. MPI-IO defines three built-in representations. The "native" representation is whatever format the host computer uses internally. Data read and written in this format undergo no translation, so the native representation gives the best performance. Programs that run on a network of heterogeneous workstations may not have a single native representation. On these systems, writing data to a single file in native format from multiple processes could produce an unreadable file if the processes have different native data representations. The "internal" format forces the processes to write data in a format that is consistent across the application and that allows it to read back the file. MPI-IO does not define a specific data representation, and implementations must specify to what extent the file can be used in other environments. Finally, the "external32" representation defines a specific format for each of the basic MPI types. Files written in this format are portable to any other MPI-IO implementation. (The "32" refers to the size in bits of a single-precision floating-point number. The MPI Forum considered but decided against defining another standard representation with 64-bit single-precision values.) The external32 format is based on existing standards

(IEEE, Unicode), and on some systems it is equivalent to the native format. Other systems require conversion as they read and write external32 data. The file view (or the buffer type) is essential to this process, since it identifies not only the location and size of data to be accessed but also its type. Without this information, an implementation could not determine what transformations, if any, it should apply to the bytes as it moves them between the file and memory.

For programs that only need to read and write data in a portable format, the external32 representation is sufficient. However, in some circumstances, it is useful to transform data between two specialized formats. For example, consider a program that generates data that a visualization system on another computer will read many times, and suppose the two computers have different native data representations. The first computer could store the data in external32 format, but if this format required a conversion on the second computer, the visualization program would pay the conversion cost whenever it read the data. A better solution might be for the first computer to store the data directly in the native format of the second computer. MPI-IO user-defined data representations allow this kind of conversion. Other uses for this facility include storing data in a specialized format that will be read by a non-MPI program and compressing data (possibly sacrificing some resolution) before storing it. The latter use is somewhat restricted, since MPI-IO conversions operate only on single data elements. For example, they could not be used for run-length encoding, which compresses sequences of identical values to just the value and the sequence length.

Programs implement customized data conversions by defining three *callback functions* with specific interfaces. These are functions supplied by the application that MPI-IO calls to complete specific tasks. One of these functions converts from native format to user format, and another converts from user format to native format. The third function returns the extent in the user format of any MPI basic type. Programs register these functions with MPI by calling `MPI_Register_datarep`. Along with pointers to the callback functions, the program gives a text string containing the name of the conversion. When a subsequent call to `MPI_File_set_view` selects the user-defined representation with this name, the MPI file access functions will invoke these callbacks to convert data.

A simple design for a converter would pass in a single data item and its designated MPI type; the function would convert this value and return it in an output buffer. Such a design would be inefficient because it would incur the cost of a function call for every basic data item read or written. Instead, for a read operation, the MPI-IO library reads data from a file into a large intermediate buffer (Figure 5.12). The library passes this to the callback function, along with the buffer type from the data access function call and the user buffer where the data is to be stored. The callback must decode the buffer type to determine what data is in the intermediate buffer, then convert each item and store it at the appropriate location in the user

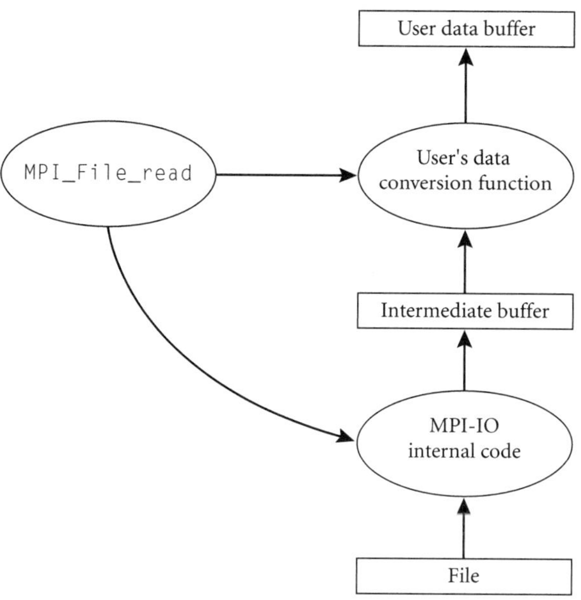

Figure 5.12 In the MPI-IO data conversion mechanism, a read operation moves data from the file to an intermediate buffer. Then the MPI-IO library calls a user-defined converter to translate data in the intermediate buffer and store it at the correct location in the user buffer.

buffer. Write operations reverse this process. This design greatly complicates the conversion functions because they must not only convert individual data items but also decode MPI datatypes and determine where to read or write data in the user buffer. A further complication arises when the MPI-IO library cannot allocate an intermediate buffer large enough to store all the data being accessed. In that case, it must access the data in stages and make successive calls to the callback function. With each call, the library tells the callback how far along it is in the data access so the callback will use the correct segment of the buffer type to convert and store the data.

A complete example of a data conversion callback function would cover several pages. Interested readers can find an MPI test program [103] on the Web that converts between native format and plain text.

5.3.10 MPI-IO Performance

Several implementations of MPI-IO are available for a variety of parallel computers. One of these is ROMIO, developed at Argonne National Laboratory by

Thakur et al. [163]. It is designed to be portable across computers and file systems while offering good collective I/O performance. The developers of ROMIO compared its performance across five parallel computers for reading and writing both regular and unstructured grid data [162]. They looked at four "levels" of access patterns for data structures that consist of multiple chunks of data scattered over many processors. Level 0 uses multiple independent I/O requests to move small, contiguous units of data, just as a program would do with a standard Unix read/write interface. Level 1 uses collective I/O for multiple contiguous requests. Level 2 uses a noncollective request on each process to move a collection of discontiguous data, and Level 3 uses a single collective request across all the processes to move all the data. Figures 5.13 and 5.14 illustrate the striking results for write performance. For reading, the differences between the levels are significant but less pronounced.

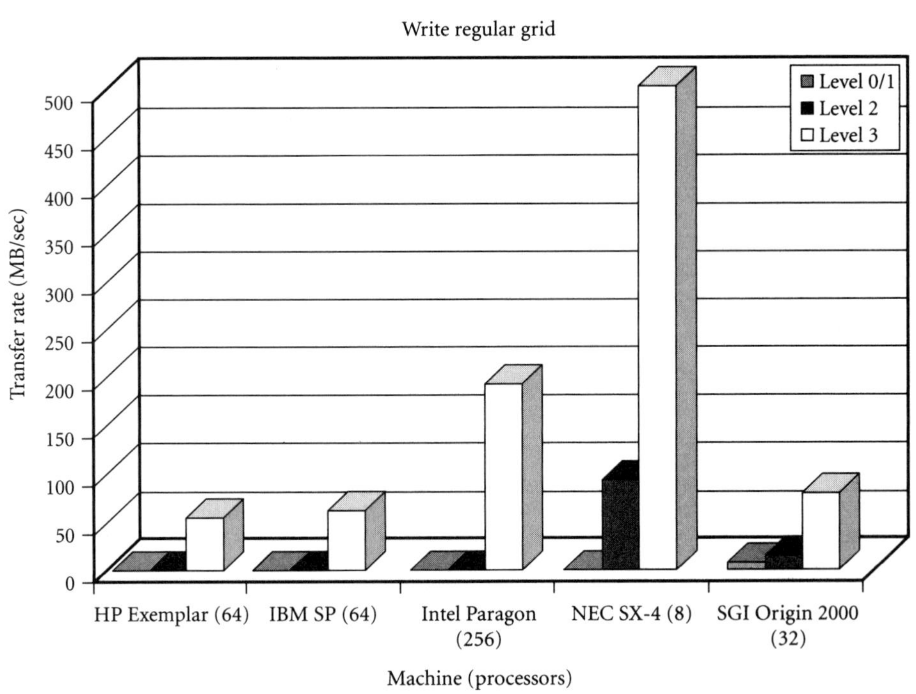

Figure 5.13 Write performance for a distributed three-dimensional array using the ROMIO implementation of MPI-IO. Total file size is 512 MB. See the text for a description of the levels. Levels 0 and 1 perform identically for this MPI-IO implementation, so they are reported together. The IBM system used PIOFS, not GPFS. Data for the different systems is not necessarily comparable because the I/O system hardware and configurations vary. Also, performance may benefit from file buffering effects, since no flush operation was performed after the write calls. Data from Thakur et al. [162].

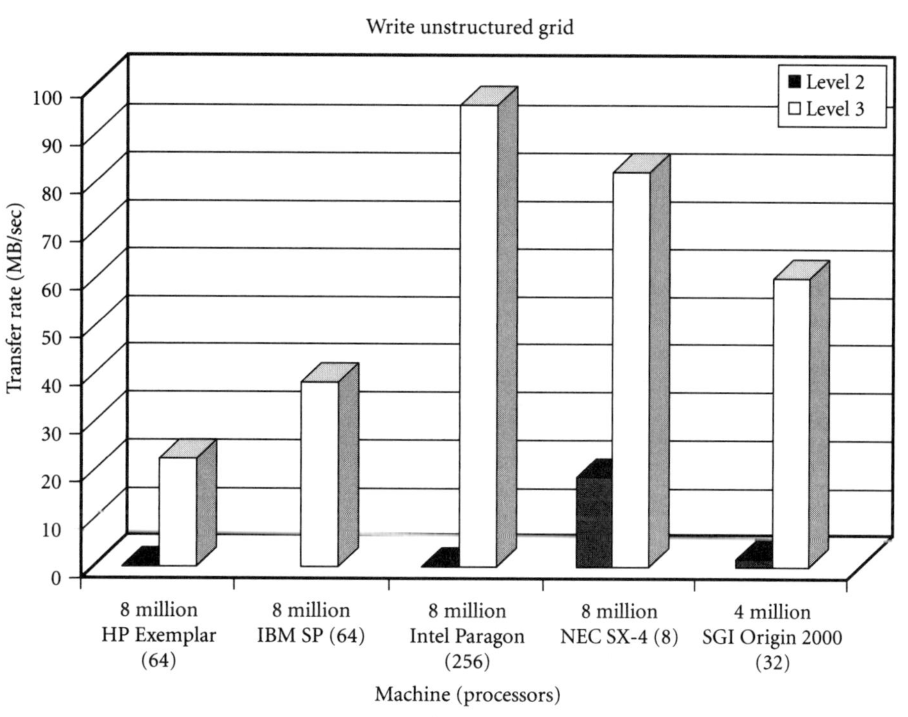

Figure 5.14 Write performance for a test program simulating an unstructured grid application. All systems wrote a file with 8 million grid points except the SGI, which wrote a file with 4 million grid points due to memory limitations. The size of a grid point was not reported. Level 0/1 performance was so poor that it was not practical to measure for these file sizes. Because of a limitation in PIOFS, performance for Level 2 on that system was comparable to Level 0/1 and was not reported. See the caption of Figure 5.13 for further comments on test conditions. Data from Thakur et al. [162].

ROMIO uses data sieving and two-phase I/O (both described in Chapter 4) to achieve this good performance for collective operations.

5.4 The Prognosis for Low-Level Interfaces

All three interfaces presented in this chapter were designed to meet the need for standard parallel interfaces. HPF is available on many systems, though compilers have been slow to implement parallel I/O for distributed arrays. The SIO Low-Level API has not been widely implemented. Although it is designed as a system programmer's interface rather than a user interface, it competes in some ways with MPI-IO. Developers of I/O systems can choose to implement either LLAPI or MPI-IO, but most would rather not implement both. Application developers need a general-purpose parallel I/O interface, and MPI-IO meets this need more directly than LLAPI, so most I/O system developers have focused on MPI-IO. MPI-IO is certainly the most complex of the three interfaces presented here, but it has become available on many systems. Argonne National Laboratory and NASA Ames Research Center have both developed free, portable implementations of MPI-IO. A number of vendors, including IBM, Fujitsu, Sun, and Hewlett-Packard, have also developed experimental or production versions of the library, and Lawrence Livermore National Laboratory has developed an MPI-IO interface for HPSS. Because the standard is so complex, many of the initial implementations offered only a subset of the features, but the implementations have continued to mature.

Whether MPI-IO will become as popular as the original MPI interface is not clear. When MPI arrived, the message passing model already dominated parallel computing, so it gave developers standard functions to implement a programming model they were already using. Parallel I/O, by contrast, is not as widely used as message passing. Many developers wishing to use MPI-IO (or LLAPI) must learn a new I/O model along with a new interface. Also, as the next chapter describes, MPI-IO does not offer all the features that some developers want in an I/O interface.

5.5 Summary

This chapter has described three standard low-level programming interfaces for parallel I/O. Unlike standard sequential Unix I/O, these interfaces allow applications to specify file accesses in ways that permit the underlying I/O system to implement optimizations like collective I/O and hints. Unlike vendor file system interfaces, they are not tied to any particular I/O system implementation. HPF's I/O interface assumes that the compiler has enough information from the program's data layout declarations to implement collective I/O automatically. However, it's not clear that any existing compiler actually does this. SIO's LLAPI is designed for flexibility and economy—its designers deliberately left out redundant functionality and simpler versions of complex functions in order to produce a small but expressive API. MPI-IO, the most widely implemented of the three interfaces, is an extension of the MPI standard that borrows the concepts of "communicators" and "datatypes" from MPI to describe a wide range of parallel I/O operations. In addition to collective

I/O and hints, MPI-IO supports a limited form of automatic translation between numeric representations.

5.6 Further Reading

Virtually all the information in this chapter comes from the reference material for HPF, SIO LLAPI, and MPI-IO. Citations for these references appear in the corresponding sections within the chapter.

Chapter Six Scientific Data Libraries

PIOFS, PFS, Unix I/O, and most of the other I/O systems described so far use very simple *data models*. A data model defines the data types and structures that an I/O library understands and manipulates directly. One simple data model is the Unix view of a file as a linear sequence of bytes. The MPI-IO data model is somewhat more sophisticated, since programs can specify data types such as integers and floating-point numbers, and they can access data in strided or irregular patterns. However, MPI-IO stores no information in its files about the type of the data or its structure; a program could write a two-dimensional array of floating-point numbers and then try to read the data back as a character string, and MPI-IO would never know the difference.

Scientific data libraries manage data at a higher level. Programs can manipulate complex data structures directly, and the library automatically records type information and other useful metadata. Scientific data libraries offer several other useful features. For example, applications can query files to determine the size and shape of data structures before reading them into memory. This allows an application to allocate the right amount of space to hold the data. Scientific libraries also record information on the numeric format of data in a file, so that a file written on one machine can be read on another. (This ability is a step beyond MPI-IO's data representation conversion feature, since scientific data libraries not only convert between data representations but also record the representation used in the file.) Finally, scientific libraries allow applications to read and write data structures by name instead of by file location. An application can open a file, find the names of the structures stored in the file, select a structure of interest, and retrieve it, all without knowing how the data is laid out in the file.

This chapter describes several data models and then presents two scientific data libraries, netCDF Version 3.4 and HDF Version 5. (HDF Version 5 differs greatly from its predecessors, so this chapter refers to it specifically as HDF5. Changes between successive netCDF versions have so far been evolutionary.) It concludes with a description of research into new data models for scientific programs.

6.1 Data Models

Chapter 2 showed how disks store data in fixed-size blocks. This block structure is the data model of a disk drive. The data model of Unix files, a linear sequence of bytes, is built upon this model, and higher-level scientific data models are generally built upon the Unix file model. Chapter 3 showed the inefficiencies that can arise in the conversion between the byte sequence data model and the collection-of-blocks model; for example, access to individual bytes can be less efficient than access to whole blocks.

The byte sequence model has both advantages and disadvantages. Any data structure that can be stored in a computer's memory can be represented as a byte sequence, since most computers' primary storage also uses a byte sequence model. However, in this data model, each application is responsible for interpreting the bytes correctly. A program that tries to read a file in an unknown format cannot easily tell what the bytes represent.

Higher-level data models define specific data types and collections of types, and some allow users to add descriptive annotations (or "attributes") to data structures. These annotations are often text, but they can also be numeric data. The MPI (and MPI-IO) data model is represented by a type map. Recall that a type map is a list of basic data types placed at specific locations in an address space. The MPI datatype constructor functions build type maps that represent certain common structures, such as arrays, array sections, lists of array elements, and so on. The MPI data access functions (both for message passing and file access) use the general type map model to represent all of these structures. The MPI-IO data model does not include annotations.

A more sophisticated data model than MPI's type maps is the typed, annotated multidimensional array that the netCDF scientific data library uses. Applications using netCDF define data structures as arrays, and all but one of the array dimensions must be fixed when the array is defined. (The first or last dimension may either be fixed or grow as data is added to the structure.) All the elements of the array have the same type, such as integer, real, and so on. NetCDF permits annotations on files, arrays, array dimensions, and individual array elements. These annotations may describe the units of measurement, the meaning of each dimension, the conditions in which the data was generated, and so on. Libraries that support an

I/O system	*Data models*
Unix	Sequence of bytes
MPI-IO	List of typed data elements
netCDF	Annotated multidimensional arrays of typed elements
HDF4	Annotated multidimensional arrays of typed elements Lists of multielement records Raster data (for images) Hierarchical groups of objects
HDF5	Annotated multidimensional arrays of multielement records Hierarchical groups of objects

Table 6.1 *Some I/O systems and their data models.*

array-structured data model usually let applications access subsets of any array, such as a slice along one dimension or a bounded slab of data within the array. MPI-IO also supports these subset accesses through its specialized datatype constructors, but higher-level libraries support subset accesses directly through function calls.

A variation of the array-structured data model permits each array element to be a collection of data objects instead of a single object. For example, an array could consist of elements that contained several values for a single point in space (e.g., temperature, pressure, fluid velocity, and so on). HDF5 supports this model. It also supports a data model that consists of a tree-structured collection of items, similar to a Unix-style file directory. Earlier versions of HDF supported other models; Section 6.3 describes these briefly. Table 6.1 summarizes some scientific data models and the I/O systems that support them.

The advantage of higher-level data models is that they closely match the data structures that scientific applications use. A program that needs to read from a file all the temperature values for a particular two-dimensional slice through a three-dimensional data set can do so easily. A program using a lower-level library could read the same data, but it would have to compute the location in the file of each required data element. To do this, the program would have to know the exact layout of data in the file, the size of the data elements, and the numeric format in which they were stored.

A further advantage of high-level I/O libraries is that they store metadata in addition to the basic data in a file. Metadata includes the annotations that programs add to their data as well as information that the library records automatically about the contents and structure of a file. (See Section 8.1.1 for a broader definition of metadata.) Metadata lets users create self-describing files, which help them share files freely. Metadata and standardized file formats also allow developers to create general-purpose data analysis tools.

On the other hand, a data model may be so closely matched to a specific class of applications that it is not useful in other application areas. For example, a data model developed to support the data structures used in aerodynamic simulations would probably work poorly for a genetic database.

Since files are ultimately stored on disk or tape, any high-level model is built upon the basic data model of the storage medium, either directly or by way of the byte sequence model of a Unix file. An I/O library that implements a high-level model must translate between the high level of abstraction that it presents to the user and the lower-level model of the storage system. Another translation occurs within primary storage between the byte sequence model of the computer memory and the high-level model that the I/O library presents. These translations can be inefficient if they require conversion between data formats, rearrangement of data, or a series of small file accesses. For example, consider a library that supports a multidimensional array data model. If a program requests a slice of data from a three-dimensional array stored in a file, the program must compute the file location of each requested element, read in the data (which may be scattered over several file blocks), possibly convert the data from a standard numeric format to the native format of the computer, and store it in appropriate locations in the computer memory. Computing file locations and reading in data represents a translation from the byte sequence and disk block data models of the file to the array model that the library defines. Converting the numeric format and storing the data in memory represents a translation from the array model to the byte sequence model of primary storage. Thus, a disadvantage of using a high-level data model compared to more direct I/O techniques is that it can increase the cost of data transfers. The program would incur this cost whether it used a scientific data library or implemented the high-level model itself. In effect, the flexibility of the high-level model makes it easy for programs to request operations that are potentially inefficient. A further potential inefficiency is that some scientific libraries do not support parallel I/O, so only one process at a time can access a given file.

The next two sections examine netCDF and HDF5 in detail. Unlike MPI-IO, which is a specification of an interface for which several implementations exist, netCDF and HDF5 are actual software libraries. Each is both a definition and an implementation of a programming interface.

Readers should note that netCDF and HDF5 define the term "dataset" in specific but different ways. A netCDF dataset is a collection of individual data objects ("variables") stored in a file. An HDF5 dataset is a single data object and its metadata. In this book, "dataset" (one word) refers to a netCDF or HDF5 construct, while "data set" refers more generally to a collection of data.

6.2 NetCDF

NetCDF [135, 136] was developed at the Unidata Program Center in the late 1980s. ("NetCDF" stands for Network Common Data Form.) One of its goals was to define a file format through which atmospheric scientists could exchange data, independent of any particular machine architecture. Since its introduction, netCDF has found wide use beyond the atmospheric sciences. It has programming interfaces in C, C++, Fortran, and Perl. A Java interface is under development. The library is available free of charge from the Unidata Program Center. An important feature of netCDF is that its files are portable; all data is written in a standard format. However, netCDF is not a parallel I/O library, so a parallel program must either direct all I/O requests through a single process or coordinate accesses so that multiple processes do not write a file concurrently. (Concurrent reading is allowed, though the program must open the file in `NC_SHARE` mode.) Another limitation of netCDF is that its files cannot exceed 2 GB.

6.2.1 NetCDF Data Model

As noted earlier, the netCDF data model is a multidimensional array of basic-type elements. Arrays can have an arbitrary number of dimensions, but when a program defines an array in netCDF, it must fix the size of all but one dimension. (The sample netCDF file that Figure 6.2 will show illustrates the data model.) Although netCDF stores data in binary form, it also defines a text format suitable for presenting data to human readers. This format is called CDL (Common Data form Language), and there are tools to convert between CDL and the binary netCDF file format. CDL is an example of a "data description language."

Consider an application that computes the temperature at various locations on the surface of a flat object. The computation can use a two-dimensional grid, and the program will generate data for a series of time steps until the temperature reaches equilibrium. It is not known in advance how many time steps this computation will require. Furthermore, the spacing between the points at which the temperature is computed need not be uniform, as long as the points form a rectangular grid. Figure 6.1 illustrates this grid.

To store the temperature grids for a sequence of time steps, the program can define a netCDF data object with the structure shown in Figure 6.2.

This example shows how netCDF defines the dimensions of an array first, then a collection of variables that use one or more of those dimensions, and finally the data that fills in the arrays. A variable is a container for data. It may be empty, partly full, or completely full.

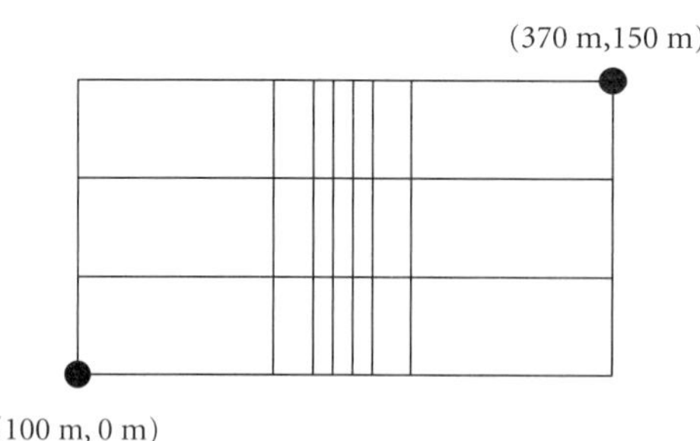

Figure 6.1 Example grid defined in netCDF. The grid is rectangular, but the spacing is variable along one dimension. A value is stored for each grid point at each time step.

Programs can associate a one-dimensional array with each dimension in a dataset. These arrays can store a physical location for each point along the dimension. Using this technique, programs can define rectangular grids with nonuniform spacing. Also, programs can store annotations (attributes) for each variable and for the dataset as a whole.

```
netcdf tempseries {
// CDL description of a sample netCDF file
// Files always contain dimensions, followed by
// variables, followed (optionally) by data
dimensions:
    height = 4 ;
    width = 8 ;
    time = UNLIMITED ; // (6 currently)
variables:
    // Arrays based on the dimensions declared above.
    float temperature(time, height, width) ;
        temperature:units = "kelvin" ;
    // The following array variables define the physical
    // dimensions of the grid.  Note that these variables
    // have the same names as the dimensions; this is not
    // required in netCDF but it is a convention to use
    // matching names when the variables are coordinates.
```

Figure 6.2 Text-formatted (CDL) description of a netCDF file.

```
    int height(height) ;
        height:units = "meters" ;
    int width(width) ;
        width:units = "meters" ;
    float time(time) ;
        time:units = "seconds" ;

// global attributes:
    :title = "Computational simulation of surface temp" ;
data:

 temperature =
  350.7, 326.6, 317.3, 313.3, 310.6, 310.1, 307.1, 307.4,
  325.3, 318, 315, 311.9, 312.5, 310.4, 310.1, 310.8,
  317.8, 314.8, 312.9, 312.7, 312.5, 313.7, 313.3, 313.5,
  313.3, 313.5, 313.8, 313.8, 315.1, 314.5, 316.7, 318.2,
  // Data for remaining time steps omitted for brevity
  ;

 height = 0, 50, 100, 150 ;

 width = 100, 200, 220, 230, 240, 250, 270, 370 ;

 time = 0, 10, 20, 30, 40, 50 ;
}
```

Figure 6.2 *(Continued)*

Once a program has defined a set of dimensions, it can use them in different combinations to form variables. For example, a program could define a pair of three-dimensional arrays over the same dimension parameters to store both temperature and pressure at each point in a grid. A third array over two of the dimensions could record a boundary condition on one side of the grid.

6.2.2 Writing NetCDF Files

A program creates netCDF data objects in two phases: First, it opens a netCDF file and defines a set of dimensions and variables. Then it stores data in the variables. These phases correspond to two mutually exclusive netCDF modes: define mode and data mode. NetCDF must be in the appropriate mode for each kind of operation. The sequence of steps to create a netCDF file is

1. Create the dataset. The netCDF `nc_create` command opens the file and puts it in define mode.
2. Define the dimensions that the variables will use.
3. Define the variables using one or more dimensions.
4. Store attributes associated with the variables or the entire dataset.
5. Switch from define mode to data mode.
6. Store data into the variables.
7. Close the dataset.

The code in Figure 6.3 illustrates these steps. Comments in **bold type** point out where each of the steps listed above begins.

Objects in netCDF—files, dimensions, variables, and so on—have both a text name and an integer identification number. Most of the functions that manipulate these objects work with the identification numbers. However, as shown in an

```
/* netcdf-write.c */

#include <netcdf.h>
#include <string.h>
#define WIDTH 8
#define HEIGHT 4
#define TITLE "Computational simulation of surface temp"
#define METER_TEXT "meters"
#define SEC_TEXT "seconds"
#define KELVIN_TEXT "kelvin"

int compute(float temp[], int timestep, float * timeval);

void main()
{
    float temps[WIDTH * HEIGHT];
    int heightvals[HEIGHT] = {0,50,100,150};
```

Figure 6.3 Writing a netCDF file. Error handling is omitted for clarity.

```
int widthvals[WIDTH] = {100,200,220,230,240,250,270,370};
float timeval;
int heightdimid, widthdimid, timedimid;
int heightvarid, widthvarid, timevarid;
int tempid;
int dims[3];
int ncfile;
int done;
unsigned long timestep;
unsigned long starts[3], sizes[3];

/* Step 1: Create the file, enter "define" mode;
 * the NC_CLOBBER flag causes netCDF to destroy any
 * existing file with the same name.
 */
nc_create("tempseries.nc", NC_CLOBBER, &ncfile);

/* Step 2: Define the dimensions */
nc_def_dim(ncfile, "height", HEIGHT, &heightdimid);
nc_def_dim(ncfile, "width", WIDTH, &widthdimid);
nc_def_dim(ncfile, "time", NC_UNLIMITED, &timedimid);

/* Step 3: Define the variables (temperature, height,
 * width, and time)
 */
dims[0] = timedimid;
dims[1] = heightdimid;
dims[2] = widthdimid;

nc_def_var(ncfile, "temperature", NC_FLOAT, 3, dims, &tempid);
nc_def_var(ncfile, "width", NC_INT, 1,
    &widthdimid, &widthvarid);
nc_def_var(ncfile, "height", NC_INT, 1,
    &heightdimid, &heightvarid);
nc_def_var(ncfile, "time", NC_FLOAT, 1,
    &timedimid, &timevarid);
```

Figure 6.3 *(Continued)*

```
/* Step 4: Store the attributes */
nc_put_att_text(ncfile, NC_GLOBAL, "title",
    strlen(TITLE), TITLE);
nc_put_att_text(ncfile, tempid, "units",
    strlen(KELVIN_TEXT), KELVIN_TEXT);
nc_put_att_text(ncfile, heightvarid, "units",
    strlen(METER_TEXT), METER_TEXT);
nc_put_att_text(ncfile, widthvarid, "units",
    strlen(METER_TEXT), METER_TEXT);
nc_put_att_text(ncfile, timevarid, "units",
    strlen(SEC_TEXT), SEC_TEXT);

/* Step 5: Switch to data mode */
nc_enddef(ncfile);

/* Step 6: Store the data */

/* First store the fixed-dimension variables */
nc_put_var_int(ncfile, heightvarid, heightvals);
nc_put_var_int(ncfile, widthvarid, widthvals);

/* Now do the computations and store the data for each
 * time step.  The following array initializations
 * identify the 2D slice of the array to be stored at
 * each time step.
 */

starts[1] = starts[2] = 0;
sizes[0] = 1;
sizes[1] = HEIGHT;
sizes[2] = WIDTH;

/* Compute the data until the temperature reaches
 * equilibrium and store the data for each time step.
 */
timestep = 0;
do {
    done = compute(temps, timestep, &timeval);
    starts[0] = timestep;
```

Figure 6.3 *(Continued)*

```
        nc_put_vara_float(ncfile, tempid, starts, sizes,
            (float*)temps);
        nc_put_var1_float(ncfile, timevarid, &timestep, &timeval);
        timestep++;
    } while(!done);

    /* Step 7: Close the file */
    nc_close(ncfile);
}
```

Figure 6.3 *(Continued)*

example in Section 6.2.3, a program can look up an identification number for an object given its name.

When the program defines the `temperature` variable, it specifies the three dimensions (`time`, `width`, and `height`) in a particular order. As an unlimited dimension, `time` must appear first in the list of dimensions when netCDF is called from a C program. The remaining dimensions appear in order from slowest-varying to fastest-varying. In this example, a two-dimensional array (`WIDTH` × `HEIGHT`) is stored as a one-dimensional array in memory. For each width value, the data for all heights is stored together, so the height dimension varies fastest. Therefore, the height dimension is given last. This convention is reversed in Fortran programs: dimensions are listed from fastest-varying to slowest-varying, and any unlimited dimension appears last. Each array has a basic type, such as `NC_INT` or `NC_FLOAT`. The basic types in netCDF are character, byte, short integer, integer, float, and double.

After defining the variables, the program creates a number of attributes. These are optional, but they can help future users of the file understand the data it contains. Attributes can be attached to variables and to the file as a whole, as shown in the example. An attribute can be of any type, but text attributes are typical. Although netCDF doesn't interpret these attributes in any way, some data analysis programs that can read netCDF files do interpret attributes, so conventions have arisen about the names and meanings of certain attributes. Both "units" and "title," which the example program defines, are standard attributes.

The program has now defined its variables, but it has written no data into them. To do this, it must switch from define mode to data mode. It can then write data in several ways. If all the values for a variable are available at once, as they are for the `width` and `height` dimension variables, the program can store the entire array using the functions `nc_put_var_xxx`, where `xxx` stands for the type of data in memory to be stored. This type need not match the data type that was defined for the variable. For example, the `width` and `height` arrays could have been defined as type `NC_FLOAT` instead of `NC_INT`. Then writing out integer data from memory to these variables using `nc_put_var_int` would initiate an automatic conversion between the integer data and the floating-point data representation used in the file. Conversion from a floating-point type to an integer type is also possible; nonintegral values will be truncated toward zero.

For variables with an unlimited dimension, the `nc_put_var_xxx` functions are not appropriate because the size of the array is unknown. Instead, the program above writes the data a slice at a time as each time step generates new data. The functions to write a portion of an array are called `nc_put_vara_xxx`. Programs specify which portion of the array to write through a pair of input vectors: one gives the starting indices of the array section to be written, and the other gives the number of elements along each dimension. The length of each vector is the same as the number of dimensions in the variable, but programs can write array sections of lower dimensionality by giving a `count` of one for one or more dimensions. The example program writes successive slices of the `temperature` array using this technique. It could also use this function to write the successive time values in the `time` array. However, since the program writes only one value to this array at each time step, it uses `nc_put_var1_float`, which stores a single value at a specific array location. Both the `vara` and `var1` functions also work on fixed-dimension variables. Additional programming interfaces support strided access to arrays and more complicated mappings between arrays in files and in memory.

Although only one dimension in the dataset can be unlimited, several variables can use this dimension (`time` in this example). However, the *current* size of an unlimited dimension must be the same for all variables that use it.

Once a program has written a netCDF file, a user can display it in the CDL format (without most of the comments that were added to Figure 6.2 for illustration) using a program called `ncdump`. A user can create a netCDF file given a CDL description using `ncgen`. The `ncgen` program will also generate C or Fortran source code to produce a given file. Thus, one way to begin writing a program to generate a netCDF file with a particular set of dimensions and variables is to write a sample CDL file with the desired objects (though possibly without the data) and then have `ncgen` produce the corresponding source code. The programmer can then modify or generalize this code to suit the application. Both `ncgen` and `ncdump` are included in the netCDF package.

6.2.3 Reading NetCDF Files

When a program reads a netCDF file, it may know the names of the dimensions and variables in advance. If so, it can look up the corresponding identification numbers through the netCDF library and then read the data. Alternatively, the program may know nothing about the contents of a file (except that it is in netCDF format). In that case, the program can query the file to find out how many objects of different types the file contains and then look up information on each object in turn.

As long as a program isn't changing the contents of a file, it does all query and access operations in data mode. The sequence of steps for reading a file whose dimension and variable names are known is as follows:

1. Open the dataset.
2. Look up the identification numbers for the dimensions.
3. Look up the identification numbers for the variables.
4. Read the attributes.
5. Read the variables.
6. Close the dataset.

The program in Figure 6.4 carries out these steps. This program opens the netCDF file with the flag `NC_NOWRITE`, which asserts that no other process will write the file while the current process is reading it. NetCDF uses this information to select

```
/* netcdf-read.c */

#include <netcdf.h>
#include <stdlib.h>
#include <stdio.h>

void main()
{
    float * temps;
    int * widthvals;
    int * heightvals;
    float * timevals;
    int widthdimid, heightdimid, timedimid;
    int widthvarid, heightvarid, timevarid;
    int tempid;
    size_t widthdim, heightdim, timedim;
    size_t attlen;
    int ncfile;
```

(continued)

Figure 6.4 Reading a file with netCDF.

```
char * title, * timeunits, *tempunits;
char * widthunits, * heightunits;
int t, w, h;

/* Step 1: Open the file */
nc_open("tempseries.nc", NC_NOWRITE, &ncfile);

/* Step 2: Look up the dimensions */
nc_inq_dimid(ncfile, "width", &widthdimid);
nc_inq_dimid(ncfile, "height", &heightdimid);
nc_inq_dimid(ncfile, "time", &timedimid);
nc_inq_dimlen(ncfile, heightdimid, &heightdim);
nc_inq_dimlen(ncfile, widthdimid, &widthdim);
nc_inq_dimlen(ncfile, timedimid, &timedim);

/* Step 3: Look up the variables */
nc_inq_varid(ncfile, "width", &widthvarid);
nc_inq_varid(ncfile, "height", &heightvarid);
nc_inq_varid(ncfile, "time", &timevarid);
nc_inq_varid(ncfile, "temperature", &tempid);

/* Step 4: Read the attributes */
nc_inq_attlen(ncfile, NC_GLOBAL, "title", &attlen);
title = (char *)malloc((attlen+1) * sizeof(char));
nc_get_att_text(ncfile, NC_GLOBAL, "title", title);
title[attlen] = '\0';

nc_inq_attlen(ncfile, widthvarid, "units", &attlen);
widthunits = (char *)malloc((attlen+1) * sizeof(char));
nc_get_att_text(ncfile, widthvarid, "units", widthunits);
widthunits[attlen] = '\0';

nc_inq_attlen(ncfile, heightvarid, "units", &attlen);
heightunits = (char *)malloc((attlen+1) * sizeof(char));
nc_get_att_text(ncfile, heightvarid, "units", heightunits);
heightunits[attlen] = '\0';
```

Figure 6.4 *(Continued)*

```
nc_inq_attlen(ncfile, timevarid, "units", &attlen);
timeunits = (char *)malloc((attlen+1) * sizeof(char));
nc_get_att_text(ncfile, timevarid, "units", timeunits);
timeunits[attlen] = '\0';

nc_inq_attlen(ncfile, tempid, "units", &attlen);
tempunits = (char *)malloc((attlen+1) * sizeof(char));
nc_get_att_text(ncfile, tempid, "units", tempunits);
tempunits[attlen] = '\0';

/* Step 5: Read the variables */
widthvals = (int *)malloc(widthdim * sizeof(int));
nc_get_var_int(ncfile, widthvarid, widthvals);

heightvals = (int *)malloc(heightdim * sizeof(int));
nc_get_var_int(ncfile, heightvarid, heightvals);

timevals = (float *)malloc(timedim * sizeof(float));
nc_get_var_float(ncfile, timevarid, timevals);

temps = (float *)malloc(widthdim * heightdim * timedim
                        * sizeof(float));
nc_get_var_float(ncfile, tempid, temps);

/* Step 6: Close the file */
nc_close(ncfile);

printf("%s\n", title);
printf("temperature values in %s\n", tempunits);
printf("width in %s, height in %s\n", widthunits, heightunits);

for(t = 0; t < timedim; t++) {
    /* Print a header for each time step */
    printf("\ntime = %f %s\n\n", timevals[t], timeunits);
    printf("      ");
    for(w = 0; w < widthdim; w++) {
```

Figure 6.4 *(Continued)*

```
            printf("%6d", widthvals[w]);
        }
        printf("\n");

        for(h = 0; h < heightdim; h++) {
            printf("%5d:", heightvals[h]);
            for(w = 0; w < widthdim; w++) {
                printf("%6.1f",
                    temps[(t * heightdim + h)
                    * widthdim + w]);
            }
            printf("\n");
        }
    }

    free(temps);
    free(timevals);
    free(temps);
    free(heightvals);
    free(widthvals);
    free(title);
    free(tempunits);
    free(timeunits);
    free(heightunits);
    free(widthunits);
}
```

Figure 6.4 *(Continued)*

a buffering strategy. If multiple processes were going to access the file (which a program would indicate with the NC_SHARE flag), then netCDF would enforce sequential consistency on the file by minimizing its use of caching and buffering. Multiple processes can write a netCDF file sequentially, but netCDF is not designed to support parallel I/O, which would require a more sophisticated technique for concurrency control.

Reading objects from the file is straightforward. The program never needs to seek to a specific file location to find a piece of data; netCDF finds it automatically. The general technique is to look up the identification number of an object given its name and then to use this number in calls to get further information about the object. Attributes work somewhat differently, however. Although netCDF has functions to look up attribute identifiers, the inquiry functions use the attribute names. The reason for the difference is that attributes can be deleted, and the identification numbers of the remaining attributes can change as a result.

Reading the text attributes in a C program requires a bit of care because netCDF does not store the usual null character at the end of a text string, and it does not include this character in the length it reports for the attribute. The netcdf-write.c program, which wrote the file, could have stored a null character with the text by incrementing the string length it computed for the attributes. However, netcdf-read.c should not depend on finding a null character. Instead, it uses the safer technique of allocating space in memory for the null character and writing this character explicitly after it reads the attribute.

Although the `time` dimension is defined to be unlimited, any particular variable will have a specific current size. Programs can query this size and allocate the correct amount of memory for the `time` and `temperature` variables. It reads them using `nc_get_var_float`. The `vara` version of the function is not required because the program is reading an entire array that has a specific current size. However, a program could use the `var1` and `vara` variants to read a single value or an array slice. These functions work similarly to the corresponding functions shown in netcdf-write.c.

After closing the file, the program demonstrates one way to use the dimensions, attributes, and variables that it read from the file. The three-dimensional array of temperatures is stored in memory as a one-dimensional array, so the program must do some arithmetic to compute the right index for a given value. The program produces the output shown in Figure 6.5 when it reads the file written by netcdf-write.c in Figure 6.3.

A program that uses the data in a file for some specific purpose, such as initializing one computation with the results of another, will likely know something about the contents of the file. Other programs don't necessarily interpret the data in a file but simply translate it to another form or present it for a human to interpret. The netCDF utility `ncdump` is an example of this kind of program. It must be able to read any netCDF file, but it doesn't do anything with the data other than write it out as text. Reading unknown data from a file requires more effort than reading known data because the program must be prepared to handle any number of variables with any number of dimensions. These are the steps:

1. Open the dataset.
2. Determine how many dimensions, variables, and global attributes the dataset contains.
3. Get information about each dimension.
4. Get information about each variable.

```
Computational simulation of surface temp
temperature values in kelvin
width in meters, height in meters

time = 0.000000 seconds

        100   200   220   230   240   250   270   370
   0: 350.7 326.6 317.3 313.3 310.6 310.1 307.1 307.4
  50: 325.3 318.0 315.0 311.9 312.5 310.4 310.1 310.8
 100: 317.8 314.8 312.9 312.7 312.5 313.7 313.3 313.5
 150: 313.3 313.5 313.8 313.8 315.1 314.5 316.7 318.2

time = 10.000000 seconds

        100   200   220   230   240   250   270   370
   0: 326.5 317.1 314.4 310.6 309.5 308.3 306.6 307.3
  50: 317.2 313.4 311.8 310.9 310.8 310.7 310.3 310.2
 100: 313.4 312.5 311.3 312.6 311.7 313.4 312.2 313.9
 150: 310.5 310.1 311.9 312.0 314.5 314.1 315.8 317.3

... remaining time steps omitted ...
```

Figure 6.5 Portion of the output produced by netcdf-write.c in Figure 6.3.

5. For each variable, get the names of the attributes.
6. For each attribute on a variable, get its value.
7. For each variable, get its value.
8. Close the dataset.

An example of a completely general program to read any unknown netCDF file would be lengthy and complicated. The example in Figure 6.6 shows just the first few steps in reading an unknown file and describes the rest of the process in comments. Once the program knows what a file contains, the remaining steps are similar to those in netcdf-read.c.

NetCDF assigns object identification numbers sequentially starting at zero, so once the program has determined that a dataset contains n objects of a particular kind, it can assume that the identifiers are the numbers 0 to $n - 1$. Attributes on variables are numbered in a separate sequence for each variable. The example program shown here discards information about variables soon after reading it.

```
/* netcdf-query.c */

#include <netcdf.h>
#include <stdlib.h>

void main()
{
    int ncfile;
    int ndims, nvars, ngatts, unlim;
    char name[NC_MAX_NAME];
    size_t * dimlens;
    nc_type vartype;
    int * vardims;
    int varndims;
    int varnatts;
    int id, attid;

    /* Step 1: Open the file */
    nc_open("somefile.nc", NC_NOWRITE, &ncfile);

    /* Step 2: Query the file */
    nc_inq(ncfile, &ndims, &nvars, &ngatts, &unlim);

    /* Step 3: Get information about each dimension */
    dimlens = (size_t *)malloc(ndims * sizeof(size_t));
    for(id = 0; id < ndims; id++) {
        nc_inq_dim(ncfile, id, name, &(dimlens[id]));
        /* It may be useful to record the name too,
         * but this isn't necessary.
         */
    }

    /* Step 4: Get information on the variables */
    for(id = 0; id < nvars; id++) {
        /* Each variable may have a different number of
         * dimensions, so we must determine this number
         * and allocate an array of the correct size.
         */
```

(continued)

Figure 6.6 Querying a file with netCDF.

```
        nc_inq_varndims(ncfile, id, &varndims);
        vardims = (int *)malloc(varndims * sizeof(int));
        nc_inq_var(ncfile, id, name, &vartype, 0, vardims,
            &varnatts);

        /* Step 5: Get the names of the attributes */
        for(attid = 0; attid < varnatts; attid++) {
            nc_inq_attname(ncfile, id, attid, name);

            /* Step 6: Read each of the attributes by its
             * name. This requires looking up the attribute
             * type and length and allocating space as
             * needed. This step is omitted here.
             */
        }

        /* Step 7: Read the variable.
         * This requires allocating the right amount of
         * space based on the dimension lengths (which can
         * be found as shown in netcdf-read.c) and
         * allocating an array of the right type.  One way
         * to allocate the right type of array is to use
         * a switch-case statement keyed on the variable
         * type returned above.
         */
        free(vardims);
    }

    /* Step 8: Close the file */
    nc_close(ncfile);
}
```

Figure 6.6 *(Continued)*

A real program might save this information so it had a complete record of all the objects in the file. However, saving the data is not strictly necessary, since netCDF loads all the file information (but not the actual data) into memory as soon as it opens a file. Therefore, querying an open file does not incur any I/O costs.

6.2.4 Changing a NetCDF File

The examples so far have treated objects in a file as being fixed once a program writes them. NetCDF permits programs to change files in certain ways, but some of these changes can be expensive because they require netCDF to rearrange the layout of data in a file.

Programs can rename or add dimensions, variables, and attributes, and they can delete attributes. To make a change that increases the size of a file, a program must place the file in define mode by calling `nc_redef`. The sequence of steps is

1. Open the dataset.
2. Switch the dataset to define mode.
3. Make desired changes.
4. Switch to data mode.
5. Read or write variable data.
6. Close the dataset.

The program in Figure 6.7 illustrates some of these steps. In this example, the program must open the file in `NC_WRITE` mode before it can make any changes. Since the new name for the temperature variable is longer than the old one, the netCDF library must rearrange the file to make room for the new text; it doesn't keep any unused space in the file to absorb changes. However, netCDF delays this expensive reorganization operation until the program switches from define mode to data mode. That way, it can accommodate all the changes at once.

Although netCDF is used widely because it offers a useful yet relatively simple data model and because it creates portable files, the system has several limitations that make it less than ideal for massively parallel computing. The most obvious of these is its sequential programming interface. Also, its 2 GB file size limit has become increasingly inconvenient as the size of computations has grown. Finally, netCDF can use primary storage inefficiently in some situations; this is especially troublesome for large variables.

6.3 HDF

HDF (Hierarchical Data Format) [66, 67] is a more comprehensive and complex I/O library that serves the same purposes as netCDF and more. It was first developed in 1988 at the U.S. National Center for Supercomputing Applications (now called

```
/* netcdf-alter.c */

#include <netcdf.h>
#include <stdlib.h>
#include <stdio.h>

void main()
{
    int tempid;
    int ncfile;

    /* Step 1: Open the file; it will be in data mode */
    nc_open("tempseries.nc", NC_WRITE, &ncfile);

    /* Step 2: Switch to define mode*/
    nc_redef(ncfile);

    /* Step 3: Make changes */
    /* New dimensions, variables, and attributes can be
     * added using the techniques shown earlier.
     */

    /* Change the name of a variable. */
    nc_inq_varid(ncfile, "temperature", &tempid);
    nc_rename_var(ncfile, tempid, "surface_temperature");

    /* Step 4: Switch to data mode */
    nc_enddef(ncfile);

    /* Step 5: Read or write data */
    /* Any changes to data already written can be made
     * in data mode; just use the regular netCDF
     * nc_put_var... functions.
     */

    /* Step 6: Close the file */
    nc_close(ncfile);
}
```

Figure 6.7 Changing a netCDF file.

the National Computational Science Alliance) at the University of Illinois. Since then, HDF has grown to support several data models and formats. Some versions can read (but not write) netCDF files. HDF Version 4 (HDF4) data models include annotated multidimensional arrays (called scientific data sets) similar to those in netCDF, as well as raster files for image data and lists of records (called vdatas) for unstructured grids. HDF4 has C, Fortran, and Java programming interfaces. Like netCDF, HDF4 does not support parallel I/O, and files are limited to 2 GB.

HDF4 and its predecessors are widely used, and several third-party tools (such as data visualizers) can read HDF files. However, as HDF grew, it became quite complex, and the lack of parallel I/O support became an increasingly significant problem. HDF Version 5 (HDF5) was designed to address the limitations in HDF4 and to simplify the programming interface. HDF5 was developed in the late 1990s, and it represents a major departure from earlier versions. Its file format and programming interfaces are new, and it replaces several specialized data models with a single, more comprehensive model. HDF5 can work with much larger files than HDF4, and it supports parallel I/O. An initial version of HDF5 was released in 1999, but not all the planned features had been implemented. This section describes the initial release of HDF5 and some of the features expected to be available shortly. The initial version of HDF5 has only a C language interface.

6.3.1 HDF5 Data Models

HDF5 supports two complementary data models, a *dataset* and a *group*. An HDF5 dataset is similar to a netCDF variable. A collection of HDF5 datasets is called a group, which is similar to a Unix file directory. Each group can contain datasets and other groups in a hierarchical structure. A file can also contain attributes, which are similar to the attributes in netCDF. HDF5 attributes consist of a text name and a small collection of data, which can be an array or scalar quantity of any type (including text). HDF5 also allows programs to store comment text in a file.

A dataset consists of a header and data. The header, in turn, includes a name, a datatype, a dataspace, and a storage layout. The name is just a text string that identifies the dataset. The datatype is either a basic (atomic) type or a collection of atomic types (a compound type), similar to a C language structure. An important difference between an atomic type and a compound type is that a program can access an atomic type only as a whole unit, but it can access a portion of a compound type. HDF5 atomic types are more general than the basic types in systems like netCDF and MPI. In addition to specifying a class (such as integer, floating point, string, etc.), an atomic type has properties such as size, precision, and byte ordering. A subset of the atomic types are native types, which correspond to the basic types supported by the compiler on a given machine. HDF5 has predefined names for these types, such as `H5T_NATIVE_FLOAT`.

A dataspace is an array of untyped elements. It defines the size and shape of a multidimensional rectangular array, but it does not define the datatype of the individual elements. Thus, a complete specification of a dataset must include both a datatype and a dataspace. The dimensions of a dataspace can be either fixed or unlimited. Unlike netCDF, HDF5 supports more than one unlimited dimension in a dataspace.

Finally, a storage layout specifies how multidimensional arrays are arranged in a file. The simplest choice is to store the data in the same order as it appears in memory; this is called a contiguous layout. Arrays can also be *chunked* to improve access times for certain operations.

6.3.2 Splitting Data into Chunks

Both HDF4 and HDF5 support chunked data. To see the uses of this technique, consider a two-dimensional array stored in a file. A contiguous layout would store the data in this array row by row (or column by column); that is, the data would be written to a Unix file as a sequence of bytes representing all the elements in the first row of the array, followed by all the elements of the second row, and so on. This storage order gives programs efficient access to the data when they read or write the whole array or when they access individual rows. However, a program that accesses an individual column of data could incur a high I/O cost because the single column of data is scattered throughout the file. For example, a 512×512 array of eight-byte floating-point numbers will occupy 2 MB of storage. If each file system block is 8 KB, then the array fills exactly 256 blocks, and each pair of rows (assuming row-major storage order) occupies one block (Figure 6.8). Reading a single row of the array requires reading one whole block from the disk. On the other hand, reading a single column requires the I/O system to fetch all 256 file blocks! A larger array, say, 2048×2048 elements, would occupy 4096 blocks. Each row would span two blocks, so reading a whole row would cause the system to access two blocks. Reading a whole column would require access to 2048 blocks, since each element in the column would reside on one of the two blocks for a given row (Figure 6.9).

An alternative to storing an array in this contiguous layout is to store rectangular regions together (Figure 6.10). Each of these "chunks" contains a short sequence of partial rows (and columns). For example, if the chunk size is equal to the file block size (8 KB), then each chunk will contain a 32×32 block of the array. Now whether a program reads a whole row or a whole column, the system must access the same number of blocks—16 for the 512×512 array and 64 for the 2048×2048 array. Of course, chunking also works with arrays of more than two dimensions.

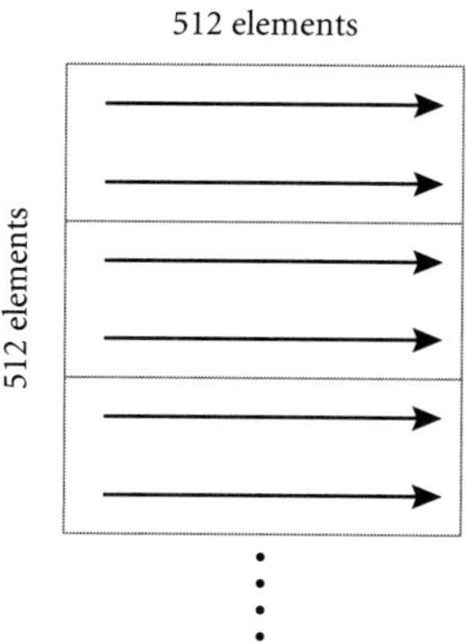

Figure 6.8 In a contiguous file layout, elements in a 512 × 512 array are stored row by row. Arrows show the sequences of array elements stored in the disk blocks, represented here by boxes. Reading a whole row requires the I/O system to access only one disk block, but reading any column requires access to all the blocks.

The technique balances performance for different operations by sacrificing the efficiency of row-wise access to improve column-wise access. However, chunking has other performance benefits.

First, chunking allows HDF to increase the size of an array along any dimension. In netCDF, only one dimension could be unlimited because increasing the size of the "major" dimension (e.g., rows in a row-major array) would require rearranging the data in the file to make room for new elements in each row. However, the chunks

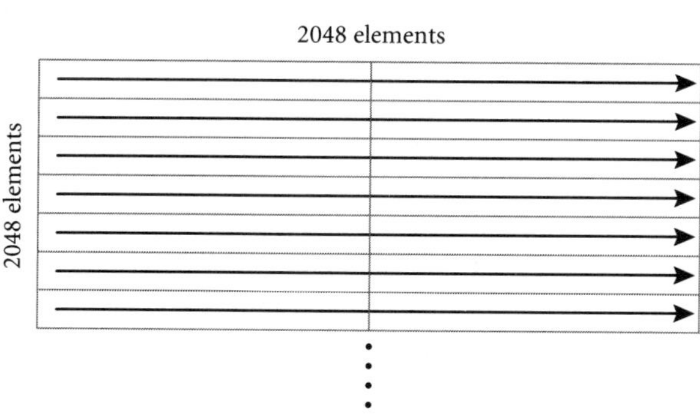

Figure 6.9 For a large array, a contiguous layout requires more than one block per row, but reading a whole row still requires access to many fewer blocks than reading a whole column.

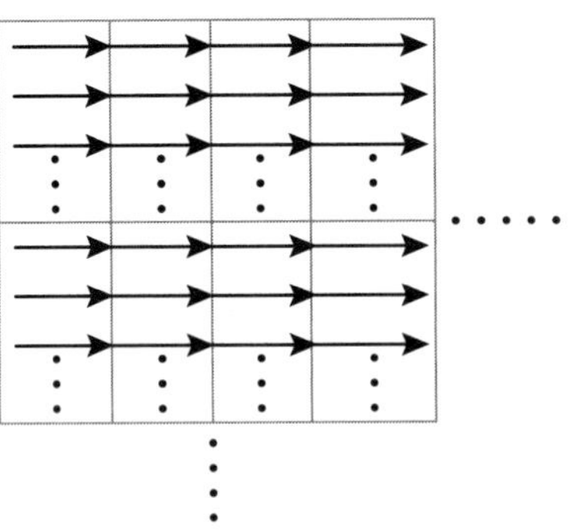

Figure 6.10 A chunked array is stored with several partial rows and partial columns in each chunk. Separate chunks can be stored in any order in the file. This layout improves efficiency for many operations, but reading whole rows (or the whole file row by row) is less efficient with a chunked layout than a contiguous layout.

that make up an HDF5 array can be stored in the underlying Unix file in any order, so new chunks can be added to the end of the file no matter what portion of the array they contain. Therefore, any dimension can be increased simply by allocating new chunks at the end of a file to cover the extended dimension. HDF5 manages chunks much as a file system manages disk blocks: it can allocate them as needed and store them in whatever location (in the file) is convenient, but it must also keep track of how the chunks fit together to form the structures supported by the data model. Just like small blocks in a file system, small HDF5 chunks offer greater flexibility in storing data than large chunks. However, they also require more metadata than large chunks and may cause data structures to become fragmented within a file.

A second advantage of chunking is that sparse arrays can be stored more efficiently. If no data is stored in a particular array chunk, that chunk need not be allocated in the file.

Finally, chunking can improve the performance of caching and buffering. Suppose an application is reading an array one column at a time. With a contiguous layout, each block could be cached in memory as the system read it in. However, since each column requires access to so many different blocks, a block containing the first element of the first column would likely be evicted from memory by subsequent blocks before the program could reuse it to access the first element in the second column. On the other hand, if the data were chunked, a cache might hold all the chunks containing the first 32 columns of the array. As the program read the 2nd through the 32nd columns, it would find all the data already in cache. Caching would also work for a program reading an array by rows. Although it would incur a greater I/O cost when reading the first row than it would for a contiguous layout, this cost would be amortized as the program read subsequent rows from the cache.

In effect, chunking improves performance by matching the storage layout of the HDF's high-level data model to the low-level data model supported by the disks, circumventing the artificial data model presented by the Unix file system. Of course, if a programmer expects that data will be read in a particular order (row-wise or column-wise) most of the time, it would probably be better simply to store the data in that order.

HDF allows programs to choose whether a file is stored in chunked or contiguous format. However, programs can increase the size of objects only when they are stored in chunked format. Programs can choose the size of chunks to optimize access efficiency.

6.3.3 Writing HDF5 Files

The HDF5 programming interface is organized into categories of functions, according to the type of information or operation the function manages. Each function name begins with `H5`, and the third character identifies its category. For example, functions starting with `H5G` manipulate groups; `H5S` functions manage dataspaces; and so on. Like netCDF, HDF uses integers to identify various objects.

Here are the general steps in writing a simple file (comparable to the file used in the netCDF examples):

1. Create the file.
2. Create a group, if desired.
3. Define one or more dataspaces.
4. Define or choose the datatypes.
5. Create the datasets.
6. Write the attributes.
7. Write the data.
8. Close all the objects.

Although the steps here are superficially similar to the netCDF example, the HDF5 version is more complex because of HDF5's more general data model and the variety of options it supports. HDF5 defines default values for many options. A common technique for selecting a nondefault value is to call an HDF5 function that duplicates a predefined object representing a set of standard or default parameters, and then to call another function to modify the duplicate object to reflect the desired changes. For example, the HDF5 code in Figure 6.11, hdf5-write.c, must use chunking to create an array that is extensible like the one in the netCDF example.

```
/* hdf5-write.c */

#include <hdf5.h>
#include <string.h>

#define WIDTH 8
#define HEIGHT 4
#define TIMECHUNK 100
#define MAXSTRING 80
#define TITLE "Computational simulation of surface temp"
#define UNITS_TEXT "units"
#define METER_TEXT "meters"
#define SEC_TEXT "seconds"
#define KELVIN_TEXT "kelvin"

int compute(float temp[WIDTH][HEIGHT], int timestep,
    float * timeval);

void main()
{
    float temps[WIDTH][HEIGHT];
    int heightvals[HEIGHT] = {0,50,100,150};
    int widthvals[WIDTH] = {100,200,220,230,240,250,270,370};
    float timeval;
    hid_t group;
    hid_t tempspace, timespace;
    hid_t heightspace, widthspace;
    hid_t temptype;
    hid_t tempset, timeset;
    hid_t heightset, widthset;
    hid_t tempchunkprops, timechunkprops;
    hid_t memspace, timevalspace;
    hsize_t dims[3];
    hsize_t maxdims[3];
    hssize_t starts[3];
    hsize_t sizes[3];
    hsize_t timechunk = TIMECHUNK, timelength;
```

Figure 6.11 Writing a file with HDF5.

```
hid_t h5file;
hid_t stringtype, attrspace;
hid_t widthattr, heightattr;
hid_t timeattr, tempattr;
int timestep, done;

/* Step 1: Create the file */
h5file = H5Fcreate("tempseries.h5", H5F_ACC_TRUNC,
    H5P_DEFAULT, H5P_DEFAULT);

/* Step 2: Create a group */
group = H5Gcreate(h5file, "tempseries", 0);

/* Step 3: Define the dataspaces */
dims[0] = 1; /* this dimension will be extended */
maxdims[0] = H5S_UNLIMITED;
dims[1] = maxdims[1] = WIDTH;
dims[2] = maxdims[2] = HEIGHT;
tempspace = H5Screate_simple(3, dims, maxdims);
memspace = H5Screate_simple(2, &(dims[1]), maxdims);
timevalspace = H5Screate(H5S_SCALAR);
timespace = H5Screate_simple(1, &(dims[0]), &(maxdims[0]));
widthspace = H5Screate_simple(1, &(dims[1]), NULL);
heightspace = H5Screate_simple(1, &(dims[2]), NULL);

/* Step 4: Define the datatype */
/* Write the data as IEEE format 32-bit floating-point
 * values with big-endian byte ordering.
 */
temptype = H5T_IEEE_F32BE;

/* Step 5: Create the dataset */
/* The first two are not extensible arrays */
widthset = H5Dcreate(group, "width", H5T_STD_I32BE,
    widthspace, H5P_DEFAULT);
heightset = H5Dcreate(group, "height", H5T_STD_I32BE,
    heightspace, H5P_DEFAULT);
```

Figure 6.11 *(Continued)*

```
/* These two arrays are extensible, so we have to
 * modify the creation parameters to use chunking.
 * For the temperature array, we choose a chunk size
 * equal to the dimensions that don't change, since
 * all (write) accesses will be this size.  For the
 * time array, we'll pick a reasonably large size
 * so we don't have to extend the array at every
 * time step.
 */
tempchunkprops = H5Pcreate(H5P_DATASET_CREATE);
H5Pset_chunk(tempchunkprops, 3, dims);
tempset = H5Dcreate(group, "temperature",
    temptype, tempspace, tempchunkprops);

timechunkprops = H5Pcreate(H5P_DATASET_CREATE);
H5Pset_chunk(timechunkprops, 1, &timechunk);
timeset = H5Dcreate(group, "time", H5T_IEEE_F32BE,
    timespace, timechunkprops);

/* Step 6: Write the attributes */
attrspace = H5Screate(H5S_SCALAR);
stringtype = H5Tcopy(H5T_C_S1);
H5Tset_size(stringtype, MAXSTRING);

widthattr = H5Acreate(widthset, UNITS_TEXT,
    stringtype, attrspace, H5P_DEFAULT);
H5Awrite(widthattr, stringtype, METER_TEXT);

heightattr = H5Acreate(heightset, UNITS_TEXT,
    stringtype, attrspace, H5P_DEFAULT);
H5Awrite(heightattr, stringtype, METER_TEXT);

timeattr = H5Acreate(timeset, UNITS_TEXT,
    stringtype, attrspace, H5P_DEFAULT);
H5Awrite(timeattr, stringtype, SEC_TEXT);

tempattr = H5Acreate(tempset, UNITS_TEXT,
    stringtype, attrspace, H5P_DEFAULT);
H5Awrite(tempattr, stringtype, KELVIN_TEXT);
```

Figure 6.11 *(Continued)*

```
H5Gset_comment(group, "temperature", TITLE);

/* Step 7: Write the data */
/* Fixed-dimension arrays */
H5Dwrite(widthset, H5T_NATIVE_INT, H5S_ALL,
    H5S_ALL, H5P_DEFAULT, widthvals);
H5Dwrite(heightset, H5T_NATIVE_INT, H5S_ALL,
    H5S_ALL, H5P_DEFAULT, heightvals);

starts[1] = starts[2] = 0;
sizes[1] = WIDTH;
sizes[2] = HEIGHT;
sizes[0] = 1;
timestep = 0;
timelength = 0;
do {
    hssize_t timeindex[1][1];
    done = compute(temps, timestep, &timeval);

    /* Extend the datasets to hold the new data */
    dims[0] = timestep + 1;
    H5Dextend(tempset, dims);

    starts[0] = timestep;
    H5Sclose(tempspace); /* free the old id */
    tempspace = H5Dget_space(tempset);
    H5Sselect_hyperslab(tempspace, H5S_SELECT_SET, starts,
        NULL, sizes, NULL);

    H5Dwrite(tempset, H5T_NATIVE_FLOAT, memspace,
        tempspace, H5P_DEFAULT, temps);

    if(timestep >= timelength) {
            timelength += TIMECHUNK;
            H5Dextend(timeset, &timelength);
    }
    H5Sclose(timespace);
    timespace = H5Dget_space(timeset);
    timeindex[0][0] = starts[0];
```

Figure 6.11 *(Continued)*

```
        H5Sselect_elements(timespace, H5S_SELECT_SET, 1,
            (const hssize_t **)timeindex);
        H5Dwrite(timeset, H5T_NATIVE_FLOAT, timevalspace,
            timespace, H5P_DEFAULT, &timeval);

        timestep++;
    } while(!done);

    /* Step 8: Close all objects (order doesn't matter) */
    H5Sclose(timespace);
    H5Sclose(tempspace);
    H5Sclose(widthspace);
    H5Sclose(heightspace);
    H5Sclose(timevalspace);
    H5Sclose(attrspace);
    H5Sclose(memspace);
    H5Dclose(widthset);
    H5Dclose(heightset);
    H5Dclose(tempset);
    H5Dclose(timeset);
    H5Aclose(widthattr);
    H5Aclose(heightattr);
    H5Aclose(timeattr);
    H5Aclose(tempattr);
    H5Pclose(tempchunkprops);
    H5Pclose(timechunkprops);
    H5Gclose(group);
    H5Fclose(h5file);
}
```

Figure 6.11 *(Continued)*

HDF5 defines a standard set of chunking parameters, and hdf5-write.c sets new chunking parameters by copying an object representing default dataset parameters and then modifying the chunk size.

When the file is created, it contains only a "root" group. Programs can store datasets in that group, or they can create additional groups, as hdf5-write.c does. A group identifier can then be used just like a file identifier in calls that create dataspaces. After creating the group, the program defines dataspaces for both the file and memory. Memory dataspaces are needed only when the program is reading or writing a partial array; they allow a program to select portions of an in-memory array (possibly discontiguous) that an I/O operation will access. The technique is similar to the use of datatypes to access memory buffers in MPI. A dataspace can define a list of distinct points in an array or a logically contiguous section of a multidimensional array called a *hyperslab.*

As in the netCDF example, this program creates separate arrays to hold the coordinate values for each dimension of the temperature array. However, each of these arrays has its own dataspace. HDF5 does not use named dimensions in arrays as netCDF does.

In the multidimensional `tempseries` array, hdf5-write.c uses `time` as the first dimension, followed by `width` and `height`. NetCDF requires `time` to be the first dimension because it is unlimited. HDF5 does not impose such a restriction, but listing `time` first makes it the slowest-varying dimension in the logical ordering of the file, so when `h5dump` prints an array, all the values for one time step appear together instead of being interleaved. Any array that a program can extend along one or more dimensions must have chunking parameters defined for it. The three-dimensional temperature array has a natural chunk size equal to the size of a two-dimensional array of data for a single time step. (In the tiny example array here, a chunk size of eight-by-four is probably too small for efficient access and file control. A real program would likely use much larger arrays.) For the one-dimensional array that keeps track of the time values for each time step, the natural chunk size is not as obvious. You could extend the array by a single element for each time step. However, that choice would require HDF5 to use a chunk size of one, which is likely to be inefficient. Instead, hdf5-write.c uses an arbitrary chunk size of 100. Each time the array grows past a factor-of-100 boundary, the program extends the time array by another 100 elements. A real program might choose a larger chunk size, perhaps one that would match the file block size if it could determine what that size was.

Types for individual data elements are defined separately from the dataspaces that determine the dimensions of an array. HDF5 defines a number of standard datatypes for integer, floating-point, and character values. The types must be specified separately for the memory side and file side of a data transfer. For example, hdf5-write.c uses the type `H5T_NATIVE_FLOAT` to read C language `float` values from memory and `H5T_IEEE_F32BE` to write them in a file. The latter type specifies a floating-point number in standard IEEE format with 32 bits and big-endian byte ordering. HDF5 automatically converts between the memory and file data representations during data accesses. Whereas netCDF always converts data from native format to a standard format when writing a file, HDF5 programs can choose to store data in native format if the programmer expects to read the data back in the same format; this avoids conversion costs in both the read and the write operations. If later it turns out that the data must be read on a different architecture, an HDF5 program can perform the conversion between the two native formats when reading the data. A program can also convert the data to the native format of a different machine during the write operation, so that subsequent reads on the other machine require no conversion.

Programs can modify the standard types, as hdf5-write.c does when it defines a string type for attribute data. The standard type `H5T_C_S1` defines a C-style (null-terminated) string of length one. The program creates a modified version of this type for strings of length 256 (255 characters plus a terminating null) using a call to `H5Tset_size`.

Programs can set attributes on datasets, groups, or types. Like ordinary datasets, attributes have a dataspace and a datatype. However, the designers of HDF5 intend for attributes to hold relatively small amounts of data so the library can store and manage them efficiently. How much data is a "small amount" is not specified.

Finally, once a program has defined a file, a group, a dataspace, a datatype, a dataset, and attributes, it is ready to write data. Unlike netCDF, HDF5 does not have separate define and data modes; the program can write to a dataset as soon as it creates it. The function `H5Dwrite` takes a dataset (which implicitly determines a file, group, dataspace, and datatype), a type for the data in memory, a dataspace for the data in memory, a dataspace for data in the file (which may be a subset of the dataspace defined for the dataset), a set of transfer properties, and the address of a data buffer in memory. The use of datatypes and dataspaces has been described already. The transfer properties control buffering and other features to be described later. Passing `H5S_ALL` in the third and fourth arguments of `H5Dwrite` causes HDF5 to move an amount of data equal to the size of the dataspace from memory to the file. To move a smaller amount, or to specify discontiguous access to memory, the program must define a subspace, using `H5Sselect_hyperslab` or `H5Sselect_elements`, as shown in the do-loop. In this example, it might seem needless to query the dataset on each loop iteration to retrieve the dataspace to be modified. However, selecting a hyperslab or a set of elements is a permanent change to a dataspace. Therefore, reusing a dataspace on successive loop iterations would amount to selecting a subspace from the previous subspace instead of the original dataspace.

When hdf5-write.c writes time values, it stores only a single floating-point value at each loop iteration. Therefore, the call to `H5Sselect_elements` uses a two-dimensional array with only one element: a single index into the one-dimensional "array" that holds the current time value. Alternatively, the program could have created an array of time values in memory and stored them all at the end of the run. To do this, the program would either need to know in advance a fixed maximum number of time steps, or else it would have to increase the size of the time value array in memory as needed. Another alternative would be to collect time values from successive iterations in a fixed-size array in memory and write them out as a block when the array filled up.

Like netCDF, HDF5 has a standard text format for displaying the contents of a file and a tool, `h5dump`, to print files. For the file created by the example in Figure 6.11, `h5dump` prints the output shown in Figure 6.12.

The tool automatically displays datasets in alphabetical order, regardless of the order in which the program created them. For each dataset, the tool lists the datatype, dataspace, and data values (in row-major order). Although the example program created attributes, the version of `h5dump` used to generate this text does not recognize the 256-character string type that the attributes use. This is a limitation of `h5dump`, not HDF5 itself. Likewise, the version of `h5dump` used here does not display comments. The example program in the next section shows how to read the attributes and comments from this file.

6.3.4 Reading HDF5 Files

Reading an HDF5 file whose structure is already known involves a series of steps similar to writing the file, except that the program retrieves dataspaces and datatypes from the file as needed instead of creating them. The program must define matching file and memory spaces (with the same number of elements), just as for write operations. The steps to read a file are

1. Open the file.
2. Open the group, if one exists.
3. Open each of the datasets in the group.
4. Look up the dimensions.
5. Allocate space to hold the data.
6. Read the data.
7. Read any attributes.
8. Read any comments.
9. Close all objects.

The program hdf5-read.c in Figure 6.13 illustrates these steps. This program produces output identical to that of netcdf-read.c. Unlike `h5dump`, it reads the attributes and comments that hdf5-write.c stored in the file.

Although it is longer than the netCDF version, this program is relatively straightforward. Like hdf5-write.c, it opens a file, a group, a series of datasets, and a series of dataspaces, and then it accesses the data. The program does not need to distinguish between chunked and nonchunked datasets, except when it determines how many elements are in a dataset that was written in increments smaller than the chunk size.

```
HDF5 "tempseries.h5" {
GROUP "/" {
   GROUP "tempseries" {
      DATASET "height" {
         DATATYPE { "H5T_STD_I32BE" }
         DATASPACE { ARRAY ( 4 ) ( 4 ) }
         DATA {
            0, 50, 100, 150
         }
         ATTRIBUTE "units" {
            DATATYPE { "undefined string" }
            DATASPACE { ARRAY ( 0 ) ( 0 ) }
            DATA {
               Unable to print data.
            }
         }
      }
      DATASET "temperature" {
         DATATYPE { "H5T_IEEE_F32BE" }
         DATASPACE { ARRAY ( 3, 8, 4 ) ( H5S_UNLIMITED, 8, 4 ) }
         DATA {
            350, 327, 320.6, 318.5, 325, 319.2, 317.7, 317.8, 316.6,
            315.7, 316.4, 317.9, 312.5, 313.8, 315.9, 318.5, 310, 312.7,
            315.9, 319.4, 308.3, 312.1, 316.2, 320.5, 307.1, 311.8,
            316.7, 321.8, 306.2, 311.7, 317.4, 323.1, 325, 318.6, 316.5,
            316, 316.6, 315.1, 315.2, 316.1, 312.5, 313.2, 314.7, 316.7,
            310, 312.1, 314.7, 317.6, 308.3, 311.5, 315, 318.7, 307.1,
            311.2, 315.5, 320, 306.2, 311.1, 316.2, 321.3, 305.5, 311.2,
            316.9, 322.7, 316.6, 314.5, 314, 314.3, 312.5, 312.6, 313.5,
            314.9, 310, 311.5, 313.5, 315.8, 308.3, 310.9, 313.8, 316.9,
            307.1, 310.6, 314.3, 318.2, 306.2, 310.5, 315, 319.5, 305.5,
            310.6, 315.7, 320.9, 305, 310.7, 316.5, 322.4
         }
         ATTRIBUTE "units" {
            DATATYPE { "undefined string" }
            DATASPACE { ARRAY ( 0 ) ( 0 ) }
            DATA {
               Unable to print data.
```

Figure 6.12 Output of `h5dump` for the file created by hdf5-write.c in Figure 6.11.

```
          }
        }
      }
      DATASET "time" {
        DATATYPE { "H5T_IEEE_F32BE" }
        DATASPACE { ARRAY ( 100 ) ( H5S_UNLIMITED ) }
        DATA {
          0, 10, 20, 0, 0, 0, 0, 0, 0, 0, 0, 0, 0, 0, 0, 0, 0, 0, 0, 0,
          0, 0, 0, 0, 0, 0, 0, 0, 0, 0, 0, 0, 0, 0, 0, 0, 0, 0, 0, 0,
          0, 0, 0, 0, 0, 0, 0, 0, 0, 0, 0, 0, 0, 0, 0, 0, 0, 0, 0, 0,
          0, 0, 0, 0, 0, 0, 0, 0, 0, 0, 0, 0, 0, 0, 0, 0, 0, 0, 0, 0,
          0, 0, 0, 0, 0, 0, 0, 0, 0, 0, 0, 0, 0, 0, 0, 0, 0, 0, 0, 0
        }
        ATTRIBUTE "units" {
          DATATYPE { "undefined string" }
          DATASPACE { ARRAY ( 0 ) ( 0 ) }
          DATA {
            Unable to print data.
          }
        }
      }
      DATASET "width" {
        DATATYPE { "H5T_STD_I32BE" }
        DATASPACE { ARRAY ( 8 ) ( 8 ) }
        DATA {
          100, 200, 220, 230, 240, 250, 270, 370
        }
        ATTRIBUTE "units" {
          DATATYPE { "undefined string" }
          DATASPACE { ARRAY ( 0 ) ( 0 ) }
          DATA {
            Unable to print data.
          }
        }
      }
    }
  }
}
```

Figure 6.12 *(Continued)*

```
/* hdf5-read.c */

#include <hdf5.h>
#include <stdlib.h>
#include <string.h>

#define MAXCOMMENT 256

void main()
{
    float * temps;
    int * heightvals;
    int * widthvals;
    float * timevals;
    hid_t group;
    hid_t tempspace, timespace;
    hid_t heightspace, widthspace;
    hid_t tempset, timeset;
    hid_t heightset, widthset;
    hid_t memspace;
    hsize_t * dims;
    hsize_t arraysize, stringlen;
    hsize_t timedim, widthdim, heightdim;
    hssize_t zerooffset = 0;
    hid_t h5file;
    hid_t attrtype, attrmemtype;
    hid_t widthattr, heightattr;
    hid_t timeattr, tempattr;
    int rank, i;
    hsize_t t, w, h;
    char * tempunits, * timeunits;
    char * widthunits, * heightunits;
    char comment[MAXCOMMENT];

    /* Step 1: Open the file */
    h5file = H5Fopen("tempseries.h5", H5F_ACC_RDONLY, H5P_DEFAULT);
```

Figure 6.13 Reading a file with HDF5.

```
/* Step 2: Open the group */
group = H5Gopen(h5file, "tempseries");

/* Step 3: Open the datasets */
tempset = H5Dopen(group, "temperature");
timeset = H5Dopen(group, "time");
widthset = H5Dopen(group, "width");
heightset = H5Dopen(group, "height");

/* Steps 4, 5, and 6: Look up dimensions, allocate space,
 * read the data.
 */
/* For tempspace, assume we don't know the
 * number of dimensions, so look that up too.
 */
tempspace = H5Dget_space(tempset);
rank = H5Sget_simple_extent_ndims(tempspace);
dims = (hsize_t *)malloc(rank * sizeof(hsize_t));
H5Sget_simple_extent_dims(tempspace, dims, NULL);
arraysize = 1;
for(i = 0; i < rank; i++ ) {
    arraysize *= dims[i];
}
temps = (float *)malloc(arraysize * sizeof(float));
memspace = H5Screate_simple(1, &arraysize, NULL);
H5Dread(tempset, H5T_NATIVE_FLOAT, H5S_ALL,
   tempspace, H5P_DEFAULT, temps);
H5Sclose(memspace);

/* Assume we already know the remaining objects
 * are one-dimensional arrays.
 * The time array is extended in chunks, so it may
 * be larger than the actual number of valid entries
 * it contains.  To get a true count, we use the
 * time dimension of the temps dataset and select
 * an appropriate initial "hyperslab" in the filespace.
 * The width and height datasets are fixed size, so
 * they can be read as a whole.
 */
```

Figure 6.13 *(Continued)*

```
timedim = dims[0];
timespace = H5Dget_space(timeset);
H5Sselect_hyperslab(timespace, H5S_SELECT_SET,
    &zerooffset, NULL, &timedim, NULL);
timevals = (float *)malloc(timedim * sizeof(float));
H5Dread(timeset, H5T_NATIVE_FLOAT, H5S_ALL,
   timespace, H5P_DEFAULT, timevals);
free(dims);

widthspace = H5Dget_space(widthset);
H5Sget_simple_extent_dims(widthspace, &widthdim, NULL);
widthvals = (int *)malloc(widthdim * sizeof(int));
H5Dread(widthset, H5T_NATIVE_INT, H5S_ALL,
   widthspace, H5P_DEFAULT, widthvals);

heightspace = H5Dget_space(heightset);
H5Sget_simple_extent_dims(heightspace, &heightdim, NULL);
heightvals = (int *)malloc(heightdim * sizeof(int));
H5Dread(heightset, H5T_NATIVE_INT, H5S_ALL,
   heightspace, H5P_DEFAULT, heightvals);

/* Step 7: Read the attributes */
/* Assume we know they are strings */
tempattr = H5Aopen_name(tempset, "units");
attrtype = H5Aget_type(tempattr);
stringlen = H5Tget_size(attrtype);
tempunits = (char *)malloc(stringlen);
attrmemtype = H5Tcopy(H5T_C_S1);
H5Tset_size(attrmemtype, stringlen);
H5Aread(tempattr, attrmemtype, tempunits);
H5Aclose(tempattr);
H5Tclose(attrtype);

/* Omit the size queries for the other attributes */
timeattr = H5Aopen_name(timeset, "units");
```

Figure 6.13 *(Continued)*

```
timeunits = (char *)malloc(stringlen);
H5Aread(timeattr, attrmemtype, timeunits);
H5Aclose(timeattr);

widthattr = H5Aopen_name(widthset, "units");
widthunits = (char *)malloc(stringlen);
H5Aread(widthattr, attrmemtype, widthunits);
H5Aclose(widthattr);

heightattr = H5Aopen_name(heightset, "units");
heightunits = (char *)malloc(stringlen);
H5Aread(heightattr, attrmemtype, heightunits);
H5Aclose(heightattr);
H5Tclose(attrmemtype);

/* Step 8: Read the comment */
H5Gget_comment(group, "temperature", MAXCOMMENT, comment);
/* Ensure string termination for too-long comments */
comment[MAXCOMMENT-1] = '\0';

/* Step 9: Close all objects */
H5Sclose(timespace);
H5Sclose(tempspace);
H5Sclose(widthspace);
H5Sclose(heightspace);
H5Dclose(widthset);
H5Dclose(heightset);
H5Dclose(tempset);
H5Dclose(timeset);
H5Gclose(group);
H5Fclose(h5file);

printf("%s\n", comment);
printf("temperature values in %s\n", tempunits);
printf("width in %s, height in %s\n", widthunits, heightunits);
```

Figure 6.13 *(Continued)*

```
    for(t = 0; t < timedim; t++) {
        /* Print a header for each time step */
        printf("\ntime = %f %s\n\n",
            timevals[t], timeunits);
        printf("      ");
        for(w = 0; w < widthdim; w++) {
            printf("%6d", widthvals[w]);
        }
        printf("\n");

        for(h = 0; h < heightdim; h++) {
            printf("%5d:", heightvals[h]);
            for(w = 0; w < widthdim; w++) {
                printf("%6.1f",
                    temps[(t * heightdim + h)
                    * widthdim + w]);
            }
            printf("\n");
        }
    }

    free(temps);
    free(timevals);
    free(widthvals);
    free(heightvals);
    free(tempunits);
    free(timeunits);
    free(widthunits);
    free(heightunits);
}
```

Figure 6.13 *(Continued)*

Like netCDF programs, this HDF5 program must take some care when reading text from a file. The netCDF example netcdf-read.c explicitly stores a null character at the end of the text attributes it reads because netCDF does not observe the C convention for terminating strings. HDF5 does observe this convention if the string is read with an appropriate memory datatype (derived from `H5T_C_S1`); a call to read the string automatically places a terminating null at the end of the string in memory. However, when hdf5-read.c retrieves the comment from the file, it does not know in advance how long the comment will be. If it is longer than the allocated space, HDF5 will truncate the string but will not store a null character, so for safety hdf5-read.c stores a null in the last character of the string.

6.3.5 Querying HDF5 Files

The HDF5 mechanism for querying files is somewhat different from the netCDF method. Instead of giving programs a range of object identifiers to iterate over, HDF5 supplies a function that performs the iteration internally. For each object in a group, an HDF5 iterator calls a user-defined function to process it. By querying objects recursively, a program can traverse the tree-structured collection of objects in an HDF5 file. Like the netCDF example, the query program presented in this section is not a complete and fully general tool for discovering all the information about an HDF5 file. Its main purpose is to demonstrate how the recursive traversal method works. This example uses a depth-first search of the object hierarchy; that is, the program examines all the subordinate objects in a group before examining the next group at a given level of the hierarchy. This example shows the iteration technique for groups and objects. A similar function iterates over the attributes of an object.

The general steps in querying a file are

1. Open the file.
2. Call the iterator for the "root" object in the file.
3. For each subordinate object, determine whether that object is a dataset or a group.
4. If the object is a group, iterate over it recursively.
5. If the object is a dataset, examine its properties.
6. After completing the iteration over the root object, close the file.

The example program appears in Figure 6.14. The HDF5 iterator functions allow the calling program to pass information to the callback functions through an untyped (void) pointer. The hdf5-query.c program uses this feature to keep track of the parent group names so it can print a full path name for each object. Alternatively, a program could pass a pointer to a data structure that would store information about the objects as the iterator traversed them.

The output of hdf5-query.c when compiled and run on the file that hdf5-write.c creates is shown in Figure 6.15.

```
/* hdf5-query.c */
#include <hdf5.h>
#include <stdio.h>
#include <string.h>
#include <malloc.h>

herr_t query_file(hid_t id, const char * name, void * data);

void main()
{
    int h5file;

    /* Step 1: Open the file */
    h5file = H5Fopen("tempseries.h5", H5F_ACC_RDONLY, H5P_DEFAULT);

    /* Step 2: Iterate over the objects in the file */
    H5Giterate(h5file, "/", NULL, query_file, "");

    /* Steps 3, 4, and 5: See query_file function below */

    /* Step 6: Close the file */
    H5Fclose(h5file);
}

/* H5Giterate calls this function once for each object
 * in a group or file.  The id and name passed in are those
 * of the current object, which may be a group, a dataset,
 * or a symbolic link.
 */
herr_t query_file(hid_t id, const char * name, void * data)
{
    H5G_stat_t objinfo;
    hid_t dataset, dataspace;
    hsize_t * dims, * maxdims;
    int i, ndims;
    hsize_t nelements;
    char * prefix = data;
    char * fullname;
```

Figure 6.14 Querying a file with HDF5.

```
/* Step 3: Determine what kind of object this is */
H5Gget_objinfo(id, name, 0, &objinfo);

switch(objinfo.type) {
case H5G_GROUP:
    /* Step 4: If the object is a group, iterate */
    fullname = (char *)malloc(strlen(prefix) +
        strlen(name) + 2);
    sprintf(fullname, "%s/%s", prefix, name);
    H5Giterate(id, name, NULL, query_file, fullname);
    free(fullname);
    break;
case H5G_DATASET:
    /* Step 5: If it's a dataset, examine it */
    /* This example looks at the dimensions of the
     * object's dataspace.  It is also possible to
     * get information about the datatype and to
     * iterate over the object's attributes,
     * examining each one in turn.
     */
    dataset = H5Dopen(id, name);
    dataspace = H5Dget_space(dataset);
    ndims = H5Sget_simple_extent_ndims(dataspace);
    dims = (hsize_t *)malloc(ndims * sizeof(hsize_t));
    maxdims = (hsize_t *)malloc(ndims * sizeof(hsize_t));
    nelements = H5Sget_select_npoints(dataspace);
    H5Sget_simple_extent_dims(dataspace, dims, maxdims);
    printf("%s/%s has %d dimensions and %lld elements\n",
        prefix, name, ndims, (long long int)nelements);
    printf("Dimensions: %lld", dims[0]);
    for(i = 1; i < ndims; i++) {
        printf(" x %lld", dims[i]);
    }
    printf("\n");

    if(maxdims[0] == H5S_UNLIMITED) {
        printf("Max dimensions: UNLIMITED");
    } else {
        printf("Max dimensions: %lld", maxdims[0]);
```

Figure 6.14 *(Continued)*

```
        }
        for(i = 1; i < ndims; i++) {
            if(maxdims[i] == H5S_UNLIMITED) {
                printf(" x UNLIMITED");
            } else {
                printf(" x %lld", maxdims[i]);
            }
        }
        printf("\n");
        free(dims);
        free(maxdims);
        H5Sclose(dataspace);
        H5Dclose(dataset);
        break;
    case H5G_LINK:
        /* HDF5 also supports symbolic links, which
         * a program can follow to get to an object.
         */
    }

    return 0; /* zero means continue iterating */
}
```

Figure 6.14 *(Continued)*

```
/tempseries/height has 1 dimension and 4 elements
Dimensions: 4
Max dimensions: 4
/tempseries/temperature has 3 dimensions and 96 elements
Dimensions: 3 x 8 x 4
Max dimensions: UNLIMITED x 8 x 4
/tempseries/time has 1 dimension and 100 elements
Dimensions: 100
Max dimensions: UNLIMITED
/tempseries/width has 1 dimension and 8 elements
Dimensions: 8
Max dimensions: 8
```

Figure 6.15 Output produced by hdf5-query.c in Figure 6.14.

6.3.6 Parallel I/O in HDF5

HDF5 includes extensions to support parallel I/O. In the initial release of HDF5, these extensions can be enabled as an option when the library is compiled. The parallel extensions call MPI-IO to implement collective transfers, so applications that use parallel HDF5 must also have an MPI-IO implementation available.

Ordinarily, HDF5 accesses each file from a single process. With the parallel extensions enabled, however, programs can open files, create datasets, and access files collectively. The benefits of this collective access are the same as for low-level parallel I/O interfaces: the parallel I/O system can coordinate requests for multiple processes to transfer data more efficiently.

Although the parallel extensions are designed to work with MPI-IO, HDF5 does not define separate collective and independent versions of the file access interfaces as MPI-IO does. Instead, programs modify a list of properties passed to the standard HDF5 file creation, file open, and data access routines. These properties tell HDF5 to perform the operations collectively.

To create or open a file collectively, a program defines a property list that includes the MPI communicator and file info objects to be used when HDF5 opens the file. The program uses `H5Pset_mpi` to define this list as shown in Figure 6.16.

A similar technique works for opening existing files collectively. Using file properties that include MPI information turns the call to create a file into a collective operation. Creating a dataset in a file opened collectively is automatically a collective operation as well, though the function call does not use any special properties or parameters. (A future version of HDF5 may allow programs to create groups and datasets using independent calls in files opened for collective I/O.) Files and datasets opened collectively do not need to be read or written collectively. Programs can use both collective and independent data access operations, and HDF5 again uses a property list to distinguish between these alternatives.

```
hid_t fileprops;
hid_t h5file;

fileprops = H5Pcreate(H5P_FILE_ACCESS);
H5Pset_mpi(fileprops, MPI_COMM_WORLD, MPI_INFO_NULL);

h5file = H5Pcreate("tempseries.h5", H5F_ACCESS_TRUNC,
    H5P_DEFAULT, fileprops);

H5Pclose(fileprops);
```

Figure 6.16 Setting the file properties for collective I/O in HDF5.

Before accessing data collectively, however, a program must first define a set of interleaved file dataspaces on the processes that will access the file. These dataspaces work like the file views in MPI-IO to determine which part of a dataset each process will access. Processes define these dataspaces within the overall dataspace for the dataset using standard HDF5 functions such as `H5Sselect_hyperslab`. For example, consider a two-dimensional array partitioned cyclically by rows among the processes, as shown in Figure 6.17. Using this formulation, each process will define its own subspace that includes a different collection of interleaved rows in the larger dataspace.

The program can then define a dataset in the usual way using the full `filespace`. Once the dataset exists in a file opened for collective I/O, a program can access it collectively as shown in Figure 6.18.

```
#define NDIMS 2
hid_t filespace;
hsize_t dims[NDIMS] = {ROWS, COLUMNS};
hsize_t count[NDIMS], stride[NDIMS];
hssize_t start[NDIMS];
int rank, size;

/* Create the dataspace for the whole dataset */
filespace = H5Screate_simple(NDIMS, dims, NULL);

/* Subdivide the space for each MPI task */
MPI_Comm_rank(MPI_COMM_WORLD, &rank);
MPI_Comm_size(MPI_COMM_WORLD, &size);

count[0] = 1;
count[1] = COLUMNS;
start[0] = rank;
start[1] = 0;
stride[0] = size;
stride[1] = 1;

H5Sselect_hyperslab(filespace, H5S_SELECT_SET,
    start, stride, count, NULL);
/* close the filespace after using it */
```

Figure 6.17 Two-dimensional array partitioned cyclically by rows in HDF5.

```
hid_t accessprops;
hid_t dataset;
hid_t memspace, filespace;
hsize_t localdims[NDIMS] = {ROWS_PER_TASK, COLUMNS};
float data[ROWS_PER_TASK, COLUMNS];

/* ... Create file with collective access and define
 * filespace subsets as shown above; initialize data.
 */

accessprops = H5Pcreate(H5P_DATASET_XFER);
H5Pset_xfer(accessprops, H5D_XFER_COLLECTIVE);
memspace = H5Screate_simple(NDIMS, localdims, NULL);

H5Dwrite(dataset, H5T_NATIVE_FLOAT, H5S_ALL, filespace,
    accessprops, data);
H5Pclose(accessprops);
H5Sclose(memspace);
```

Figure 6.18 Writing a distributed array collectively with HDF5.

These simple examples assume that the number of tasks is at least as large as the array dimension that is distributed over the tasks, and that the number of tasks divides this dimension evenly.

The HDF5 developers have chosen a design for the parallel interface that changes the sequential interface only minimally. This is possible in part because the sequential interface already has the expressive power to describe the discontiguous access patterns that are common in parallel file accesses. However, this design does make the collective semantics of certain operations implicit: one cannot tell by looking at a particular read or write operation out of context whether it requires all tasks to participate. In MPI-IO, on the other hand, the `_all` suffix makes it easy to distinguish collective calls from noncollective ones.

6.3.7 Other HDF5 Features

Two other useful features of HDF5 are on-the-fly data filtering and low-level I/O drivers.

Data Filtering

HDF5 programs can manipulate chunks of data as they are read and written. These are the same chunks that HDF5 uses to split up multidimensional datasets for more efficient access (Section 6.3.2). The data manipulation operations work only on whole data chunks. The technique is similar to the data representation conversion facility in MPI-IO, but the HDF5 model is more flexible because it can operate on whole chunks of data instead of one data item at a time, and the number of basic data elements that a filter outputs need not equal the number of elements it receives. As a result, filters can perform run-length-encoding compression, checksum computations, and other operations that do not preserve the number of data elements.

As in MPI-IO, programs register a callback function with the I/O library, but in HDF5 the same function converts data for both input and output. HDF5 passes the callback function a flag to indicate which direction the data is moving. When a program registers a callback function, it assigns an identifying number to it. The program can then instruct HDF5 to apply this filter either on every access to a particular dataset or only during specified I/O operations. Filters associated with a dataset are called permanent filters; those used only in selected I/O operations on a dataset are called temporary filters. Programs can chain together a series of filters and specify the order in which HDF5 should apply them. The designers of HDF5 anticipated that users would create a variety of filters with useful and well-defined features, and these could be given specific, fixed identifying numbers (to be assigned by the HDF5 development team). Then a program could annotate a dataset in a file with a list of filters to be applied when another program read the data. Of course, if these filters were not available, it might be impossible to read the data correctly.

Low-Level I/O Drivers

For HDF5 to read and write data to disk, it must eventually call low-level data access functions. HDF5 allows programs to tailor the I/O library to the needs of the program by choosing which functions it should use. The parallel I/O interface is an example of the use of these low-level drivers. By opening a file with collective access enabled, a program instructs HDF5 to use the MPI-IO data access functions to read and write data. Other choices include the Unix `read` and `write` functions, which move data without buffering it in memory, and `fread` and `fwrite`, which do buffer data. As discussed in Section 3.4.3, unbuffered I/O works best when programs read or write large blocks of data without reusing them, while buffered I/O is better for programs that repeatedly access the same data in a file. Another driver lets programs read and write files to memory instead of disk. This capability is useful for short-lived temporary files. HDF5 also supports drivers that split logical HDF5 files into multiple physical files. An HDF5 "address space" (the collection of groups and datasets in a logical HDF5 file) can be stored either as a collection of fixed-size "member files" or as a pair of files, one containing data and the other containing metadata.

The method that programs use to select a driver is similar to the one shown in Figure 6.16 for enabling parallel I/O. First the program creates a property list object, and then it modifies the object to select an I/O driver.

6.4 Higher-Level Data Models

The development of scientific data libraries is moving toward higher levels of abstraction and very general data models that can represent many kinds of data. The reorganization of the HDF data models from a collection of special-purpose models to a single, more generic model (plus another model for collecting objects into groups) is an example of this trend. However, for some applications, even the HDF5 data model is not expressive enough.

Every data model can represent some kinds of data objects (e.g., scalar values, arrays, lists, etc.) directly and other objects indirectly. An indirect representation means that while a data model can store a particular kind of data, programs must observe certain conventions external to the model to interpret the data correctly. For example, the Unix byte sequence model represents bytes directly. Programs can also store floating-point numbers in this model, but to make sense of these numbers they must observe conventions about the number of bytes used for each value, the order of the bytes, and the interpretation of the bits as a sign, mantissa, and exponent. Such conventions are not part of the Unix byte sequence model, but they are part of some higher-level models defined by MPI-IO, netCDF, and HDF, and other I/O systems.

Similarly, the HDF5 array data model directly represents multidimensional, regular-grid arrays, but it does not directly support irregular grids. Programs that store irregular grid data in HDF5 must adopt external conventions about how to store these grids. The ultimate goal for high-level data models is to represent directly any kind of data object used in scientific computing. Such a model would permit a wide variety of programs to exchange data with each other. At this high level, it is important to distinguish the mathematical notion of a data model from the representation of data in a file or memory. As an analogy, consider the mathematical notion of a set. Sets have well-defined properties that transcend any particular representation of a set in a computer program. Likewise, a high-level data model defines the mathematical structure of data separately from its representation in a file. Of course, defining a common data representation is also valuable, but programs that share a high-level data model can agree on the *meaning* of data independent of its representation.

Since most programming languages do not directly support high-level data structures like irregular grids, programs must generally access data in a high-level model using lower-level data models, such as arrays or lists. An I/O library supporting a high-level model must define specifically the correspondence between the high-level view of the data and the lower-level data structures that programs use.

Some scientific simulation codes use specialized I/O libraries that represent specific high-level data structures. For example, an I/O library for fluid dynamics codes may support various computational meshes and certain kinds of data at the mesh points, such as temperature, pressure, and material type. Such a library could use a data model that was a specialization of a more general data model. The general data model would be able to represent directly the structures used by the specialized fluid dynamics model, but since the fluid dynamics model would use a subset of the functionality of the general model, the fluid dynamics I/O library could have a simpler programming interface with features tailored to that problem domain. The general model would capture all the mathematical structure of the data, however, so another program written to perform a different but related computation (for example, modeling chemical reactions) could read this data correctly without being restricted to use the data structures of the fluid dynamics simulation.

6.4.1 Fiber Bundles

One proposed general model for high-level scientific data uses *fiber bundles,* which Butler and Pendley [22] proposed in 1989. The U.S. Department of Energy's Accelerated Strategic Computing Initiative (ASCI) is leading an effort to define a common scientific data model that uses fiber bundles [3, 39]. A complete mathematical presentation of fiber bundles is beyond the scope of this discussion, but an intuitive description should suffice. First, consider a *base space,* which is essentially a computational mesh of arbitrary size and structure. Next, consider a *fiber,* which is a range of legal values for some quantity at a particular location in the base space. This range need not be continuous. A fiber bundle is the Cartesian product of the fibers and the base space; in other words, it is the collection of valid data ranges for all points in the base space. A fiber bundle represents all possible values of a data set in a base space. A *fiber bundle section* is one particular set of values for the points in the base space. Figure 6.19 shows a simple example of a fiber bundle with a two-dimensional base space.

The fiber bundle model has an obvious connection to the HDF5 data model: a base space is analogous to an HDF5 dataspace, a fiber is analogous to a datatype, and a dataset is a fiber bundle. The main difference between the HDF5 model and

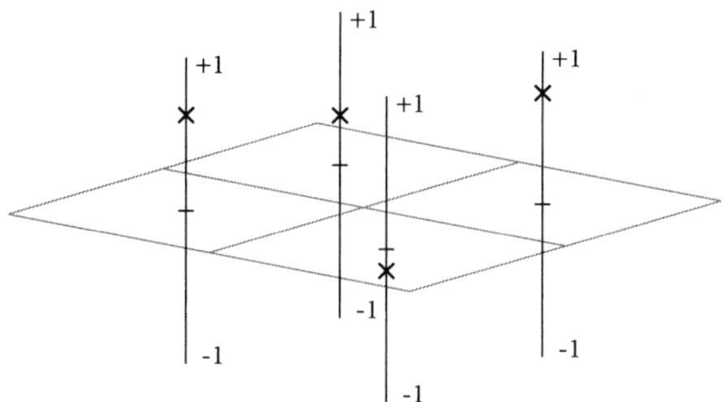

Figure 6.19 A simple fiber bundle. The *base space* (in gray) has four *zones.* Each zone has an associated *fiber,* which represents a valid range of values for some variable associated with that zone. The valid range here is -1 to $+1$. The base space and its fibers form a *fiber bundle.* The $\times$ marks on each fiber indicate specific values associated with the zones. The collection of these values for all the zones in the base space is a *fiber bundle section.*

fiber bundles is that HDF5 currently supports only regular grid dataspaces rather than arbitrary base spaces.

A visualization tool developed by IBM called Open Visualization Data Explorer uses an internal data model that is also similar to the fiber bundle model. This general model allows the tool to read data in a variety of file formats and interpret them in a uniform way; the various data models that the tool can understand are specializations of its more general internal data model.

6.4.2 A Layered I/O Infrastructure

The fiber bundle abstraction defines a very general model for scientific data. One use of this model is in a hierarchy of I/O systems that a variety of applications can use for storing and exchanging data. The ASCI Data Models and Formats (DMF) project is implementing a hierarchy of this kind. Applications at the top of this hierarchy (Figure 6.20) call specialized I/O libraries designed for a particular type of computation. These libraries describe the data to be moved in terms of the fiber bundle model to the Data Model Kernel (in which the fiber bundle model described above has been extended somewhat to handle a broader range of data structures). The Data Model Kernel stores the data to HDF5. HDF5 in turn makes MPI-IO calls, which move data in parallel to the native file system. Alternatively, if HDF5 is using sequential I/O, it interacts directly with the native file system. Applications can bypass some of these layers, but then they forego the data portability benefits that the higher layers offer.

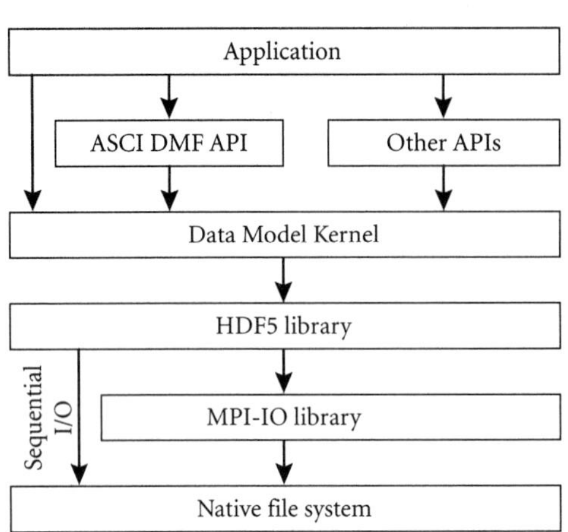

Figure 6.20 The Accelerated Strategic Computing Initiative (ASCI) I/O model includes several layers to implement a general data model, access data in an appropriate format, and transfer data in parallel. Applications can use a high-level, application-specific programming interface or call one of the lower layers directly. See the text for further description of the layers. (Adapted from ASCI documents [39].)

This design raises two obvious questions: are all these layers necessary, and do the multiple layers hurt performance?

To answer the first question, the DMF designers note that each layer serves a distinct purpose: The top-level I/O library interface presents a data abstraction that is easy for the program to use. The Data Model Kernel implements a general, high-level data model that allows various applications to share data. To this point, the layers have been concerned mainly with implementing the fiber bundle data model, independent of any particular data layout. The HDF5 layer manages the organization of data in files and performs any necessary translations between data representations. MPI-IO provides a standard parallel I/O interface for HDF5, and the native file system manages the low-level file I/O. Thus, the layers do not duplicate each other's functions. A system designed from scratch to carry out all the functions in this hierarchy of I/O systems would likely be designed with many of the same layers, though some of the portability interfaces could be omitted.

For the second question, the answer depends on the details of the implementation of the layers. Certainly, if each layer copied the data between two buffers and possibly transformed it, the I/O performance would be very poor. However, the DMF designers have avoided copying between the layers. Instead, each layer merely passes through the data and adds some annotations to describe its meaning and format. Transformations are necessary only to change the data representation (e.g., from big-endian to little-endian).

A more subtle potential problem with the multiple layers is the management of discontiguous and collective I/O. For regular grids that are distributed among processes in a simple pattern, the description of a collective data access to a parallel I/O system can be relatively compact. An algorithmic description of a transfer is often sufficient. However, for irregular grids or complex data distributions, initiating a collective operation may require a list-oriented description of the data transfer. The size of this list may be a significant fraction of the total amount of data to be moved. In MPI-IO, the list takes the form of a view based on an MPI datatype built with `MPI_Type_struct`. In HDF5, the dataspaces used on each process would be defined with `H5Sselect_elements`. Higher levels of the hierarchy might use other structures. For discontiguous transfers of small portions of data, the cost of translating the *description* of the operation as the request moves from level to level could be significant. Therefore, it seems sensible to perform any data aggregation (e.g., a shuffle operation in two-phase collective I/O) at the highest possible level, so that lower levels of the hierarchy can work with large blocks of data and simple, algorithmic descriptions of the transfer. However, a major purpose of the MPI-IO layer is to implement collective I/O as efficiently as possible for a given file system and hardware configuration. As Chapter 4 shows, the performance of collective I/O depends strongly on these configuration details, so a high-quality collective I/O implementation will likely be aware of system configuration information. Implementing collective I/O at the lowest level possible insulates higher levels from these details. Indeed, some collective techniques, such as server-directed I/O, require access to computing resources that are normally inaccessible to a high-level library. Obviously, these two performance considerations are in conflict, and this conflict is one argument in favor of a more monolithic approach to building a complex I/O system, since a unified design could avoid the cost of translating requests as they move between I/O layers.

6.5 Summary

This chapter has introduced two higher-level programming libraries for scientific applications, netCDF and HDF. Both libraries use more sophisticated data models than lower-level interfaces such as MPI-IO, POSIX, and LLAPI. These models allow application programmers to specify data access operations on complex data structures rather than blocks of bytes. So far, only HDF5 supports parallel I/O. In a parallel program, using sequential I/O in HDF and netCDF is likely to incur a large performance penalty compared to a parallel I/O.

Efforts are under way to design more general and expressive data models for scientific applications; these would provide a mathematical foundation for I/O libraries that would allow scientific applications to share data with each other easily and accurately. I/O libraries designed to use high-level data models face an important question: what is the right balance between a modular design that uses many separate layers for different I/O functions and a monolithic design that eliminates needless internal interfaces but is more difficult to port to different computing platforms?

6.6 Further Reading

Both netCDF [136] and HDF [66, 67] have extensive documentation online, and these manuals are the best source of information about the libraries. They include user guides, programming references, and sample code. A comparison of scientific data libraries appears in a 1993 article by the designers of four different systems (CDF, HDF, netCDF, and PDB) [21]. The ASCI Data Models and Formats Web site [39] describes their multilayered approach to managing I/O.

Chapter Seven
Special-Purpose I/O Techniques

This chapter looks at two special-purpose I/O techniques used in high performance computing: out-of-core data access and checkpointing. These are two of the three major categories of I/O noted in Chapter 4 (the third being required I/O), and both areas have been the subject of considerable research. The general-purpose I/O libraries described in Chapters 5 and 6 are certainly capable of performing the I/O needed for out-of-core computations and checkpointing, but the specialized techniques described here can make these operations more efficient or easier to program.

7.1 Out-of-Core Computations

An out-of-core computation is one whose data set is larger than the available primary storage. These computations require the program (or the operating system) to move portions of the data set from secondary to primary storage and back as the data is needed. Out-of-core techniques (also called *external memory* techniques) date to the early days of electronic computers, when programs often needed to stage both data and instructions into primary storage.

Virtual memory systems have moved most of the responsibility for data staging from the application developer to the operating system and the hardware. However, standard virtual memory algorithms that are adequate for general-purpose computing perform poorly in some very large computations: they do not prefetch data, and they may access data in inefficient patterns. Some users avoid the performance problems inherent in virtual memory by sizing their computations to fit in the primary storage of the computer they will be using. Indeed, some Cray supercomputers did not support virtual memory even after the technique had become common in general-purpose computers.

For users whose applications cannot fit into primary storage, a number of techniques and specialized I/O systems have been developed to improve performance. All these techniques are based on two familiar optimizations: hiding the disk access time and minimizing the number of accesses. Out-of-core techniques can also be categorized in other ways:

- *Compiler-based methods vs. library-based methods.* In compiler-based methods, the compiler examines the data access patterns in a program to determine when data must be staged in from secondary storage. The compiler then automatically inserts I/O calls into the program. These methods are often tied to a specific programming language, which may have new keywords to identify out-of-core variables. Library-based methods use explicit calls to stage data. The I/O library may be a general-purpose system like the ones described in previous chapters, or it may be specifically designed for out-of-core computations. Library-based systems give programmers greater flexibility to manage data staging, but they make the program more complex.
- *Global data view vs. local view.* Out-of-core techniques developed for distributed memory computers may view distributed data structures as a global whole or as separate pieces owned by each process. Systems that take a global view make it easy for any process to access any part of a shared data structure. They can also store a structure in a single file, which is useful if the file will be used after the parallel job terminates. However, these systems must manage the communication between processes as well as I/O. Indeed, two-phase collective I/O (Section 4.4.2) was developed specifically for out-of-core I/O. A local view of data greatly simplifies out-of-core implementations, and on computers with locally attached disks for each compute node, out-of-core I/O can proceed in parallel on each node without using the interconnection network. However, whenever any process needs data that another process owns, it must handle the interprocess communication explicitly.

Many specialized algorithms have been developed to improve the out-of-core performance of common operations, such as sorting, matrix multiplication, and performing Fourier transforms.

This section will first review the standard virtual memory model as a basis for comparison with other techniques. Then it will present several compiler-based and library-based techniques for managing out-of-core data. It will conclude with a brief look at algorithms for out-of-core computation.

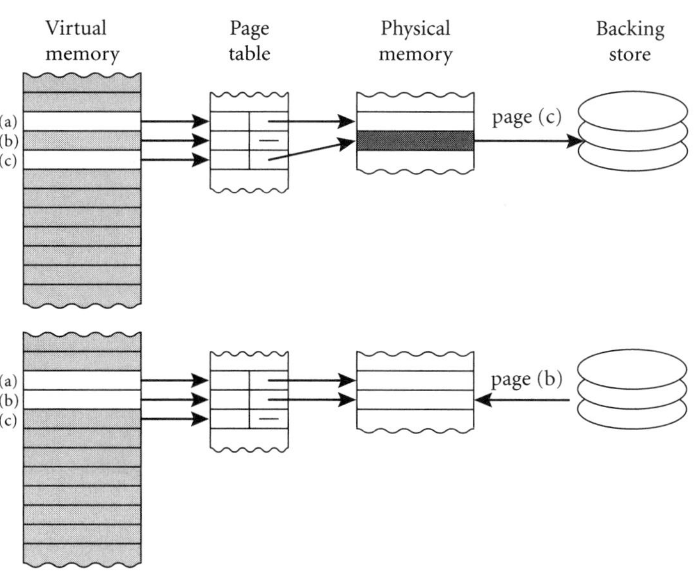

Figure 7.1 Handling a page fault in a virtual memory system. In the top diagram, pages (a) and (c) reside in physical memory, and the program has just tried to access page (b), which is swapped out. The virtual memory system chooses to evict page (c) and write it to backing store. In the bottom diagram, page (b) now resides in physical memory, and the page table has been updated accordingly.

7.1.1 Virtual Memory

Virtual memory allows applications to access data in a very large address space. This space represents a range of memory locations that is typically much larger than the amount of primary storage available, and it can even be larger than the available secondary storage. The virtual address space, primary storage, and secondary storage are divided into equal-size pages, which typically contain 8 KB of data. (File system block sizes are often chosen to match the page size.) The operating system, with assistance from the computer hardware, translates virtual addresses to physical addresses in primary storage with the help of a data structure called a *page table* (Figure 7.1). Since the virtual address space is larger than primary storage, not every virtual page can reside in primary storage at the same time. However, all pages containing valid data in the virtual address space do reside in secondary storage (also called *backing store*). When a program refers to a virtual address in a page that is not currently mapped to a physical address, a page fault occurs, and the operating system must arrange to move the page containing the data for the requested virtual address into primary storage. This process involves several steps:

1. The operating system evicts (or "swaps out") a page of data that currently resides in primary storage to make room for the page being brought in. If any data in this victim page has changed since the victim was last read from secondary storage (i.e., the page is "dirty"), then the victim page is written out; otherwise, it is simply erased.
2. The page corresponding to the requested address is read from secondary storage.
3. The page table is updated to reflect the new mapping from the virtual addresses in the new page to primary storage addresses.

Once these steps are complete, the program can access the data at the referenced virtual address. Because the operating system loads pages into primary storage as needed by the program, this technique is sometimes called *demand paging*. Obviously, a page fault is an expensive operation, since it incurs both disk access time and a significant amount of computation. However, demand paging works well on general-purpose, multiprogrammed systems because many programs can each have the illusion of a large address space while sharing the use of hardware. Moreover, when one program stalls waiting for I/O, other programs can be scheduled to run, so the CPU remains busy. Practical virtual memory systems include many optimizations and special cases, which are not discussed here.

An important consideration for the first step of the page fault sequence is deciding which page to evict from primary storage. Ideally, the victim page should be one that the program will not need for a while, so the system won't have to retrieve it from secondary storage shortly after evicting it. Since operating systems typically know very little about programs' future memory references, they cannot identify such pages directly. Instead, many systems use a policy called *least recently used*, or LRU. The operating system (possibly with hardware assistance) keeps track of the order in which physical memory pages are accessed by programs. When a page must be evicted, the one used least recently is chosen, based on the assumption that it is not likely to be needed again soon. In programs that use certain data repeatedly in a computation and then move on to other data, LRU works reasonably well. On the other hand, LRU works poorly for programs that cycle through very large data structures, touching each item only once per cycle. In these computations, a page of data may be read in, used once, and then kept unused in primary storage for a long time while the program works with other data. The page may finally be evicted only to be retrieved a short time later as the program cycles through the data again.

Some programs try to reduce the number of page faults they incur by organizing their loops so that each data item is used repeatedly over a short span of time rather than periodically over a longer span. This technique also improves cache performance. However, grouping references to the same memory location is precisely the wrong technique for vector-based computer architectures, which work best when given a long list of independent data items to operate on.

The out-of-core methods described in the remainder of this section aim to improve on the performance of standard virtual memory. Some are designed to work with little or no change to the original program, while others require substantial code modifications, perhaps including changes to the basic algorithms.

As noted above, out-of-core techniques improve on standard virtual memory by hiding disk access time and by reducing the number of separate I/O operations. Hiding access time relies on the standard asynchronous I/O methods described in previous chapters; the main question is what data to prefetch and when to issue the request.

Reducing the number of operations can be done in many ways. These include grouping requests for pages so that a few large transfers can take the place of many smaller ones; arranging the data layout in a file so that the order of access matches the order of use; and improving data access patterns or page replacement policies so that a given page of data is moved between primary and secondary storage as infrequently as possible.

7.1.2 Compiler and O/S Support

The simplest techniques from the user's point of view require minimal changes to the original program. Compiler-based out-of-core methods analyze the user's source code to determine the patterns of data access, then automatically generate appropriate I/O calls to stage the data, and in some cases, to store it in an order that will give good performance.

Automatic Prefetching

Mowry et al. [111] developed a compiler-based method that requires no changes in the user source code. It extends the basic virtual memory model by adding two steps. First it analyzes the memory access patterns at compile time, and then it issues directives to the operating system to load virtual memory pages before they are actually needed. The system also gives hints to the operating system that tell it when the program no longer needs certain pages, so the system does not have to rely only on the LRU strategy to select victim pages. Like standard virtual memory, automatic prefetching is not specifically a parallel I/O technique. Both are applied to individual tasks and work equally well in parallel and sequential programs. Indeed, many parallel file systems do not support the operations necessary to make them usable as backing store for a virtual memory system, so most parallel computers use a standard sequential file system for backing store. Automatic prefetching requires support from the operating system to implement prefetch and release requests. However, the changes required are relatively minor in systems that already support virtual memory.

The code analysis technique is an extension of an earlier design by Mowry [110] for improving cache performance in dense-matrix and sparse-matrix codes. The basic idea is to predict the pattern of access requests that a collection of loops will generate, to determine which of these references could produce page faults, and then to initiate page accesses that will complete before the program needs the data. The system groups requests whenever possible to minimize their total cost.

An important consideration in this technique is that the compiler's prefetch requests are advisory only; the operating system can ignore them or abort them as necessary. For example, if the system is already busy reading pages in response to actual page faults, it may not have time for prefetching. Also, if a program changes a memory location after it has prefetched a page containing that data but before data arrives, the system should use the updated value rather than the value in secondary storage. This situation can arise if the compiler is unable to recognize that two memory references in a program refer to the same virtual address. Allowing the run-time system to drop prefetch requests in this situation helps it preserve correct operation while giving the compiler the flexibility to schedule prefetches aggressively. This problem is analogous to what can happen in programs that issue explicit nonblocking I/O requests, where the programmer must ensure that a buffer being filled asynchronously is not accessed until the I/O operation is complete. The difference between the two cases is that in programmer-scheduled nonblocking requests, the programmer must understand the memory reference patterns and avoid conflicts, but in automatic prefetching, the system recognizes conflicts as they happen.

Automatic prefetching can hide the access time that some page faults would incur, but it must avoid prefetching data too aggressively. If the compiled program contains many prefetch requests for data that is already in memory, the overhead of the extra requests can wipe out any performance gains from prefetching, even if the operating system recognizes the request as being unnecessary and ignores it. For optimum performance, the program must filter out unnecessary requests before they reach the operating system. For this reason, Mowry's system uses a run-time filter that keeps track of the pages in memory. Any prefetch request for a page already in memory is dropped before the request is sent to the operating system. For many sample applications that Mowry's group examined, more than 95% of the prefetch requests that the compiler inserted were unnecessary, and if they had not been eliminated early, the system would have performed worse than ordinary virtual memory in many cases. However, with the filtering mechanism active, compiler-directed prefetching reduced the running time of a series of applications by factors ranging from about 10% to more than 70%.

A challenge for compiler-based prefetching is to determine how far in advance to issue a prefetch request. If the request comes too late, the program will refer to the missing data and incur a page fault before the prefetch operation is complete. But if the request comes too early, the page will occupy memory that might be used more productively by another page. The prefetched page could even be evicted before the program has a chance to use it. In the Mowry group's tests, although most prefetches succeeded in preventing a page fault, prefetches that came too late were more common than those that came too early. The problem of scheduling prefetches at the appropriate time is likely to become more difficult as computational speeds increase relative to disk access times.

Compiler-Directed File Layout

Automatic prefetching hides disk access time, but it does not directly attempt to minimize the number of I/O operations. In many cases, the performance gains available from such reductions are far greater than those available from prefetching. As noted in Section 6.3.2, the order in which a program accesses the dimensions of a multidimensional array in a file strongly affects the number of disk blocks read and therefore the I/O performance. Using chunking instead of a row-major or column-major data layout gives good overall performance, but if the dominant patterns of data access are known in advance, arrays can be stored with a layout that further improves performance.

Kandemir et al. [85] have developed compilation techniques that evaluate the order in which programs read data from out-of-core arrays and automatically store the data using a layout that minimizes the number of blocks to be read. Unlike automatic prefetching, which requires operating system support, these layout techniques are implemented separately from the virtual memory system.

Kandemir's layout technique assumes that a parallel program is coded in a data parallel model, with global arrays partitioned among several tasks. HPF-style languages implement this model. Each task owns specific portions of global arrays and is responsible for staging its own data in a local file. Therefore, a global array is not stored as a single unit in this model. However, the local files may be stored separately for each processing node or on a shared global file system, depending on the configuration of the parallel computer.

For each task, the file layout algorithm examines the use of multidimensional arrays in nested loops. In many cases, the order of the loops in a nest can be changed without altering the meaning of a program. For example, consider the loop nest

```
c This is pseudocode. stage_in and stage_out represent
c moving portions of an out-of-core array between
c secondary and primary storage.  In a real program,
c the loop bounds and indices would have to be adjusted
c to map from out-of-core to in-core indexing.
do i = 1, l
  do j = 1, m
    call stage_in(b(i,j,1:n))
    call stage_in(c(i,j,1:n))
    do k = 1, n
      a(i,j,k) = b(i,j,k) + c(i,j,k)
    end do
    call stage_out(a(i,j,1:n))
  end do
end do
```

Figure 7.2 Pseudocode showing how one dimension of a set of arrays might be staged in and out.

shown in Figure 7.2. This loop nest will produce the same results as the nest in Figure 7.3. However, in Figure 7.2, `k` is the fastest-changing dimension, and in Figure 7.3, `i` is the fastest-changing dimension. If the arrays are stored in the file such that all the `k` dimension values are contiguous for each `i` and `j`, then the first loop nest will perform better than the second one.

If the compiler had complete freedom to choose the file layout and the loop ordering, several arrangements of the loop nest could produce good performance.

```
do k = 1, n
  do j = 1, m
    call stage_in(b(1:l,j,k))
    call stage_in(c(1:l,j,k))
    do i = 1, l
      a(i,j,k) = b(i,j,k) + c(i,j,k)
    end do
    call stage_out(a(1:l,j,k))
  end do
end do
```

Figure 7.3 Pseudocode showing a different staging order for the loop nest in Figure 7.2.

However, some loop nests contain multiple array references with the same loop variable indexing different array dimensions. This situation limits the compiler's options. Kandemir's algorithm evaluates possible loop nest orders, taking into account constraints on the storage order of data in existing files. It tries to rearrange the loops in a program and issue staging commands to produce optimal I/O performance. The basic approach is to look at each possible permutation of loops that produces a correct sequence of array references. Permutations are evaluated according to the degree of locality in the resulting array references. The best of these is chosen as the new arrangement for the loop nest.

This algorithm considers only one loop nest at a time; a global optimization would have to consider the possibility of different access patterns for the same array. Kandemir et al. suggest that a compiler could estimate the I/O cost of each loop nest and preferentially optimize the most expensive ones.

Performance measurements for this algorithm were done with hand-coded (instead of compiler-generated) loop transformations. I/O calls used the Passion library, described later in this section. The optimizations significantly reduced the number of I/O calls and the amount of data read. Performance on the optimized loop nests improved over unoptimized nests by factors ranging from about 2 to more than 30, depending mainly on the ratio of the in-core data size to the out-of-core array size. The optimizations became more effective as the proportion of out-of-core data grew.

Another compiler-based system for improving out-of-core performance combines asynchronous access with restructuring of the data layout and a number of optimizations that reduce the I/O volume. Colvin and Cormen's ViC* compiler [31] uses a data parallel programming model based on the C* parallel language that was originally developed for Thinking Machines computers.

ViC* programs can declare global objects (distributed arrays) to be out-of-core. The compiler applies several optimizations to minimize the number of disk accesses required to use these out-of-core objects. Optimizations of this kind are widely used to improve cache performance, but they also work for out-of-core objects. First, the compiler merges adjacent loops that use the same global objects. This loop fusion operation allows the program to read in data and use it several times before writing it back out. Next, the compiler determines when it can recalculate data instead of retrieving it from storage. The cost of recomputation may be much less than accessing it on disk. Finally, if a data item does not need to be read back from disk (because it is recalculated later), it may not need to be stored in the first place, so both the write and the read operations can be eliminated.

In addition to these compile-time optimizations, ViC* applies a limited form of file layout optimization. Normally, C stores an array of data structures in memory as a sequence of whole structures; the fields of a given structure occupy contiguous memory locations ("struct-major layout"). ViC* stores these arrays in files with all the corresponding fields of each structure residing together ("field-major layout"). One purpose of this transposition is to improve performance for computations that access one field at a time in arrays of structures. This layout also allows ViC* to store data in homogeneous blocks (e.g., all doubles or all ints), which are easier for the system to manage.

ViC* compiles data staging operations into programs automatically, and it uses prefetching and write behind to hide latency. It writes data in parallel to multiple disks whenever possible.

7.1.3 Library-Based Out-of-Core Methods

The out-of-core techniques described so far require little effort from the application programmer, but they depend on support from the compiler or the operating system. Since this support is not yet widely available (except for virtual memory, of course), many application developers manage data staging explicitly in their programs using a sequential or parallel I/O library.

Programs can use general-purpose interfaces like MPI-IO, netCDF, HDF, or Unix to stage data. NetCDF and HDF in particular can easily access sections of large arrays, and they are convenient choices if the application will be using data that another program has already stored in one of those libraries' standard formats. However, as noted in Chapter 6, only HDF5 supports parallel I/O. A number of special-purpose libraries have appeared that are designed specifically for use in parallel, out-of-core problems. Two examples, ChemIO and Passion, use an array-based data model, and they have simpler programming interfaces than netCDF or HDF. In particular, since they are not designed to create portable or self-describing data files, they lack much of the metadata support that high-level scientific data libraries offer.

ChemIO

ChemIO was developed by Nieplocha et al. [117] for parallel computational chemistry problems, but its interface is general enough to use for many array-based out-of-core computations. The system supports three separate I/O models: disk resident arrays (DRAs), which store globally shared out-of-core arrays using collective I/O; exclusive access files (EAFs), which are used by individual processes; and shared files (SFs), which support global access but only noncollective I/O.

The DRA interface in ChemIO takes advantage of a distributed shared memory programming library called Global Arrays [118]. This library presents programs running on distributed memory computers with a view of global array data structures. Processes in a parallel program can move data between local memory and

```
c rc is an integer return code, ignored in this example
rc = dra_init(max_arrays, max_array_size,
    total_disk_space, max_memory)
rc = dra_create(MT_DBL, 2000, 4000, 'Big Array',
    'bigfile', DRA_W, -1, -1, d_a)
rc = dra_write_section(.false., g_a, 600, 1600,
    300, 2300, d_a, 750, 1750, 500, 2500, request)
rc = dra_wait(request)
rc = dra_close(d_a)
rc = dra_terminate()
```

Figure 7.4 Using the ChemIO programming interface to access array sections. (Adapted from Nieplocha, Harrison, and Littlefield [118].)

global arrays. The DRA interface adds another level to this hierarchy, so programs can move data between global arrays and disk resident arrays. However, they cannot move data directly between a disk resident array and the local memory of any process. The ChemIO designers believe that allowing transfers to skip the intermediate level of abstraction would lead to poor performance and problems with portability.

The example shown in Figure 7.4 illustrates the programming interface. This code fragment defines a 2000×4000 disk resident array of double-precision values called "Big Array" in a file called "bigfile," and it stores a handle to this object in `d_a`. Assuming a global array object called `g_a` has already been defined and initialized, the code stores a 1000×2000 rectangular region of this array into a rectangular region of the DRA. The operation is collective and nonblocking, but the example code immediately waits for the operation to complete before proceeding. The `.false.` boolean in the `dra_write_section` call indicates that the array should not be transposed when it is written, and the two -1 values passed to `dra_create` are empty hint values.

ChemIO can store a DRA in a single file (using either a parallel or a sequential file system), or it can stripe data over multiple files to improve the transfer rate.

The DRA interface supports only collective I/O. For programs that require noncollective access to shared files, the SF interface is more appropriate. Unlike the DRA interface, it uses a simple linear byte sequence data model. Processes in a parallel job open shared files collectively, but read and write operations are noncollective. Data accesses are nonblocking and use explicit file offsets rather than file pointers, and the application is responsible for concurrency control.

Finally, the EAF interface is used by individual processes for local files. The interface supports both blocking and nonblocking access, and programs specify file locations using explicit offsets.

The purpose of these three models is to support three kinds of out-of-core access. Disk resident arrays give programs efficient, coordinated access to shared data. Exclusive access files support local staging of data by individual tasks, and shared files allow tasks to share file data asynchronously.

Passion

The Passion project [161] is a large effort that has studied many aspects of parallel I/O. The Passion I/O library is a general-purpose parallel I/O system with an array-based data model. Some of the optimizations it includes were designed specifically to address problems that arise in out-of-core computations. Applications can call the Passion library directly, or a compiler can generate library calls automatically after analyzing the patterns of data access in a nest of loops, as described above.

Passion supports both local and global views of arrays. In the local view, each process in a program reads and writes array sections from its own file. In the global view, processes share access to global arrays in a common file. Applications can choose to store arrays in row-major or column-major order, and Passion supports nonblocking I/O.

Global array accesses can use collective I/O routines, which implement two-phase I/O and data sieving (Section 4.4.2); both optimizations were developed as part of the Passion project.

7.1.4 Out-of-Core Algorithms

When using explicit I/O calls to stage data, application developers must decide what data to move and when. Many algorithms have been developed for out-of-core computations that focus on minimizing the I/O rather than computation. The research literature on this subject includes both theoretical models of performance and practical algorithms. This subsection will present a simple and widely used model of performance for out-of-core algorithms and then outline some basic algorithms. See the references for more detailed information on this topic.

The Parallel Disk Model

Vitter and Shriver [170] proposed the parallel disk model (PDM) as a basis for predicting the performance of external memory (out-of-core) algorithms. The full model uses five parameters:

$$
\begin{aligned}
N &= \text{problem size (in data items)} \\
M &= \text{memory size (in data items)} \\
B &= \text{disk block size (in data items)} \\
D &= \text{number of independent disk drives} \\
P &= \text{number of processors}
\end{aligned}
$$

For an out-of-core problem, $N > M$. M includes the aggregate primary storage available on all the nodes to store the computation's data; it does not include memory used for program instructions, bookkeeping information, or other ancillary data. The model does not distinguish between shared memory and distributed memory computer architectures, nor does it account for interprocess communication time. Indeed, many estimates of running time that use this model focus only on the number of I/O operations and ignore the computation time entirely. As a result, these estimates don't use the P parameter.

D is the number of *independent* disks. This means that programs must be able to access blocks separately on each of the D disks. If the file system stripes data over a collection of disks and only moves data a full stripe at a time, then the collection of disks is considered a single disk in this model ($D = 1$) and B is taken to be the stripe factor times the block size on an individual disk.

In discussions of computer algorithms, it is common to use the so-called "big-oh" notation [9], which gives the rate of increase of the running time (or in this case, the number of I/O operations) as a function of the problem size or some other parameter. Informally, an algorithm's running time is "in $O(f(N))$" if its running time grows no faster than $kf(N)$, where N is the input size of the problem and k is some constant. More formally, $O(f(N))$ is a "complexity class" that includes all functions that grow no faster than $kf(N)$ for sufficiently large N. For example, the best in-core algorithms for sorting N values have running times in $O(N \log N)$. Several algorithms fall within this bound, but the expressions that give their exact running times have different values of k and additional lower-order terms, which the big-oh notation hides. Less commonly used is $\Omega(f(N))$, which denotes a lower bound on the growth rate rather than an upper bound. By definition, an algorithm's running time is in $\Theta(f(N))$ if the running time is in both $O(f(N))$ and $\Omega(f(N))$. In other words, the O notation indicates a worst-case upper bound, while Θ denotes a more exact bound.

Perhaps the simplest out-of-core operation is scanning a list of N items, which a program might do to find an item with a particular value. This requires $O(N/DB)$ I/O operations; so the number of accesses is a linear function of the number of values to be scanned. Likewise, scanning a list of in-core data items has running time that is linear in the number of items. Note also that in the expression $O(N/DB)$, D and B appear together as a product. This means that for a given number of disks, it doesn't matter whether they are independent or not. You could change the configuration so that $D' = 1$ and $B' = DB$ without changing the theoretical running time; this corresponds to striping the data over all D disks and accessing all the disks at once. This works as long as $DB \leq M/2$, and it assumes that the aggregate I/O bandwidth is the same for independent or striped access.

In many cases, algorithms that assume $D = 1$ are simpler to implement than more general algorithms. The reason is that many out-of-core algorithms work in stages, and at each stage the algorithm must have useful data available on all (or most) of the D disks to take advantage of the parallelism. Therefore, the preceding stages must distribute the data that they write so that most disks will have useful data for most stages. Some algorithms use analytical techniques to balance the load over the available disks; others randomize the storage locations. The parallel disk model assumes that all processors have equal access to all disks, whether they are accessed independently or striped. In distributed memory systems that give each node exclusive access to its own local disks, an analysis using the parallel disk model must treat each node as a separate system.

Scanning is one of the few basic operations for which the number of I/O accesses is comparable to the in-core running time and for which the performance with full striping ($D = 1$) is the same as for independent disk access. Out-of-core sorting, on the other hand, has been shown to require $\Theta((N/DB)\log_{M/B}(N/B))$ I/O accesses (see Vitter [171] and the references therein). In this expression, setting $D = 1$ and increasing B correspondingly will decrease not only the N/B term but also the base of the logarithm. The result (theoretically) is an increase in the number of I/O operations for typical values of the parameters. In other words, sorting is theoretically faster when the disks are independent. In practice, the added complexity of managing independent disk accesses may outweigh any theoretical gain.

The general technique in out-of-core algorithms is to divide the problem into large pieces that can each be accessed as a block and manipulated in-core, and then find an appropriate order in which to manipulate the pieces. For example, out-of-core matrix operations often divide the matrices into square blocks of $\sqrt{B} \times \sqrt{B}$ elements.

Sorting

To see how this divide-and-conquer strategy works in more detail, consider out-of-core sorting algorithms. Most are variations on well-known in-core algorithms such as bucket sort and merge sort.

The out-of-core merge sort algorithm (Figure 7.5) first creates N/M sequences of sorted data using an in-core sorting algorithm. Then the algorithm loads one

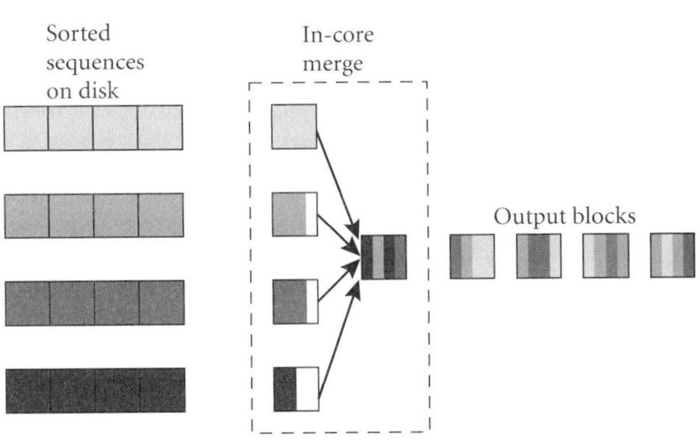

Figure 7.5 Out-of-core merge sort creates sorted sequences using in-core techniques and then stores them on disk. Blocks from these sequences are then brought into memory and merged to form a longer sequence of sorted output blocks. The process repeats until all sequences have been merged to a single output sequence.

block from each sequence (up to M/B sequences) and merges them by writing to a buffer the smallest (or largest) unwritten value from among the blocks. Since the blocks are already sorted, the algorithm need only examine one value per block in determining which value to write. When a buffer fills, it is written to secondary storage using asynchronous I/O, and when all the input values from a given block are consumed, the next block in the sequence is read in using prefetching. If the number of sequences is so large that there are too many blocks to fit in memory, then subsets of sequences can be sorted into longer sequences, and these can be merged on a subsequent pass.

Another out-of-core sorting algorithm, bucket sort, recursively divides the input data into progressively smaller partitions (buckets), such that each item in a given bucket is larger than all the items in the preceding partition and smaller than those in the following bucket. Each level of recursion subdivides the current buckets and sorts them.

Performance of Out-of-Core Methods

There are two important issues in considering the performance of out-of-core techniques: do performance models such as the parallel disk model accurately predict the observed performance of real codes, and do explicit out-of-core techniques perform significantly better than simple demand paging?

To help answer the first question, Cormen and Hirschl [35] implemented an out-of-core sorting algorithm (radix sort) and an out-of-core bit permutation technique called BMMC (bit-matrix-multiply/complement). The sorting algorithm uses disk striping, while BMMC requires independent disk I/O. Their tests varied the problem size, the number of disks, the block size, and the memory size. They found that the number of I/O operations for these two algorithms did vary with problem size and memory size, as the parallel disk model predicted. However, the block size parameter was less useful in predicting performance. Very small blocks produced worse performance than predicted, as might be expected if the block size falls below the file system block size. Also, large blocks failed to improve performance to the degree that the model predicted. Moreover, the number-of-disks parameter, D, failed to predict performance accurately, probably because the system's I/O bandwidth did not increase linearly with the number of disks.

A study by Cormen and Nicol [36] offers data on the performance of an out-of-core algorithm compared to virtual memory. Three in-core and one out-of-core fast Fourier transform algorithms were implemented. For problem sizes that fit into physical memory, the in-core methods' running time grew roughly in proportion to $N \log N$, as predicted theoretically. However, when the problem size exceeded physical memory and demand paging became necessary, the performance dropped abruptly. The out-of-core method was first tested with a single disk, to make a meaningful comparison with demand paging. With this configuration, the out-of-core algorithm was generally a few times slower than the in-core methods for small problems, but its running time grew smoothly with the problem size. With up to eight disks available, the out-of-core algorithm nearly matched the best in-core method for problems that fit in physical memory, and it performed many times better than the best in-core method with demand paging on problem sizes that didn't fit into memory.

7.2 Checkpointing

A checkpoint records the state of a computation partway through its execution. It contains enough information to restart the computation from that point. Restarting a computation from a checkpoint takes less time than restarting it from the beginning and running to the state recorded in the checkpoint. There are many techniques for checkpointing a program, and most store information in secondary storage. Checkpointing parallel programs, especially distributed memory programs, requires extra measures to ensure that the checkpoint records a self-consistent state of the computation.

Checkpointing serves two general purposes: fault tolerance and resource allocation. A program that runs for many hours or days can use checkpointing to protect itself from system failures. If the computer goes down in the middle of a computation, a checkpoint allows the program to resume execution at the state recorded in the checkpoint when the computer comes back up.

Programs may also need to be halted or redistributed due to planned events rather than system failures. Some computer centers give preference to short interactive jobs during working hours and to larger batch jobs at other times. A computation that runs over many nights can save and then recover its state each day as the computer changes between scheduling policies. Likewise, checkpointing gives a program running on a network of workstations a way to migrate gracefully off machines that are needed for interactive use.

7.2.1 Features of Checkpointing Techniques

No single checkpointing system handles every situation well. The techniques described in this section differ in the degree to which the application is involved in storing checkpoint data, the portability of the checkpointing system and data, the time required to store and retrieve a checkpoint, and the ability to checkpoint entire parallel jobs rather than single processes. As with other I/O techniques, there are two standard ways of improving performance: overlapping I/O with computation and reducing the amount of data stored.

Checkpoint Initiation

The first consideration in a checkpointing strategy is whether the system or the application program initiates the checkpoint. In system-initiated checkpointing, either the computer's run-time system or the machine operator determines when to take a checkpoint. The alternative is for the application program itself to initiate a checkpoint. System-initiated checkpoints are especially useful for resource management. If a computer center needs to checkpoint all the jobs on a system, either to make room for interactive jobs or in preparation for a system shutdown, it can initiate a systemwide checkpoint to save the state of all running jobs. These jobs can be restored later without the involvement of the users who own them. System-initiated checkpoints can also target individual jobs.

In program-initiated checkpoints, the application itself determines when to store its state. A *synchronous checkpoint* is one that the checkpointing system begins to store immediately in response to an explicit request. Programs can also request *asynchronous checkpoints,* which are initiated by events such as the periodic expiration of a timer. The difference between a system-initiated checkpoint and a program-initiated, asynchronous checkpoint is that the timing of the latter is controlled from within the program.

In most system-initiated checkpoint strategies, the system determines what data to store. However, in some designs, the system just signals each application when it's time to take a checkpoint, and the application is responsible for storing whatever data it will need to resume operation.

Blocking vs. Nonblocking Checkpoints

A simple strategy for checkpointing a job is to halt it and save the contents of its address space, along with some processor status data such as the program counter and other register contents. Restoring the system is the reverse operation. Since the data for a checkpoint cannot be saved instantaneously, this technique requires the process being checkpointed to stop executing until the data has been written. Otherwise, the program could change the contents of memory while the checkpoint is being stored, so the checkpoint would not represent a consistent program state.

Stopping a program to store the data is sometimes called *sequential checkpointing*. In this context, "sequential" does not refer to the program itself but rather to the fact that checkpoint I/O and program execution happen in sequence, not concurrently. In other words, a sequential checkpoint uses blocking I/O. To avoid confusion, this discussion will use the term "blocking" rather than "sequential." Also, note that whether a checkpoint is synchronous or asynchronous is independent of whether it blocks or not. "Synchronous" and "asynchronous" refer to how the checkpoint is initiated. An asynchronously initiated checkpoint may still block the program, and a synchronous checkpoint can perform nonblocking I/O.

Blocking checkpoints are appropriate for saving a program's state just before the program is halted or migrated to a different system. However, when checkpoints are used as a precaution against system failure, the delays they incur may be unacceptable. Nonblocking checkpointing techniques allow programs to continue running while their state is being saved.

Like other write-behind techniques, nonblocking checkpointing can defer output until I/O traffic is light; the major time constraint is that the checkpoint operation must complete before the next one is initiated. The key challenge for nonblocking checkpointing strategies is to store a single, consistent state of the program while the program continues to run. The Unix operating system's `fork` call neatly solves this problem. A `fork` call creates a new "child" process whose address space is an identical copy (with a few minor exceptions) of the parent process. The parent and child run concurrently after the `fork` executes: the parent runs the application, while the child stores the data in its address space, which is a snapshot of the parent's data at the moment of the `fork`. Once the child has finished writing the data, it terminates. An application or a user-level library can implement this kind of checkpoint with standard system calls; no changes to the operating system are required. Therefore, the checkpointing code is relatively portable, although the checkpoint data is not.

Duplicating the parent process's address space during the `fork` operation could be very expensive, since it involves copying all of the data in memory. However, many operating systems use an optimization called "copy on write" to avoid making a full copy. The parent and the child's address spaces use the same memory pages until one of them modifies a page. Then the operating system automatically creates a duplicate of that page, so the two processes use different versions of it. This strategy allows the operating system to duplicate only the pages that differ between the processes, and the copies are made as they are needed and not all at once when the `fork` call is issued.

To store an accurate checkpoint, the system must also record the state of the CPU and certain data that resides in the operating system, in addition to the contents of memory. However, since these steps require only minimal I/O, this section does not discuss them. See the references on the libckpt [128] and Condor [98] tools for further information.

Checkpoint Size and Content

Saving the full contents of memory can take a long time. Consider a parallel computer with 1 TB of primary storage and 1 GB per second of aggregate I/O bandwidth. Since the checkpoint includes essentially all the data in memory, the transfer can be contiguous and therefore very efficient. Writing every byte of memory at maximum transfer rates would take about 1000 seconds (16 minutes and 40 seconds). This may be an acceptable delay when a system is being brought down for maintenance or when a collection of batch jobs is being saved at the end of the night. However, if the system is saving checkpoints to avoid losing data in case of an unexpected crash, it is probably unreasonable to halt operation for this much time at frequent intervals (say, once an hour). Since memory capacity is growing faster than disk transfer rates, this problem will only become more acute.

Fortunately, there are many techniques to reduce the size of checkpoint files. One simple optimization is to store only program data and not the executable code. Since operating systems place code and data in different parts of virtual memory, checkpointing systems can easily distinguish them. In most cases, when the checkpointing system restores a program, it can read the program instructions from the original executable file. However, in systems that use dynamically linked libraries, it is possible that these libraries will change between the time a checkpoint is written and the time the program is restored. To avoid this problem, a checkpointing tool can store a complete image of the executable code at the first checkpoint or whenever a dynamically loaded library is invoked [74, 98].

In some programs, much of the data remains unchanged from one checkpoint to the next. An *incremental checkpoint* stores only data that has changed since the previous checkpoint. The challenge for incremental checkpointing systems is to identify the changed or "dirty" data. The operating system's memory protection features can help with this task. The standard `mprotect` call can be used to instruct the operating system to issue a signal whenever the program attempts to write to specified memory pages. The checkpointing code catches these signals, notes the page being written, and then allows the write to proceed. When the program needs to store a checkpoint, the checkpointing code has a list of all pages that have been written since the last checkpoint was taken, and it need only save those pages. After the checkpoint is recorded, the checkpointing system clears its list of dirty pages, so at the next checkpoint it will only record the pages that have changed in the interim.

Checkpointing systems that record the full contents of memory can restore a program using only the latest checkpoint file, but incremental checkpointing requires data from all the previous checkpoints to construct a complete record of the program's state. Therefore, the size of checkpoint data generated by an incremental checkpoint grows as the program runs. Some of this data will become obsolete, since pages may change many times over the course of a run. The checkpointing tool can alleviate this problem by using an auxiliary program to consolidate checkpoint data and eliminate obsolete pages from time to time.

The effectiveness of incremental checkpointing depends on the details of the application program. Some algorithms create data structures that remain unchanged throughout the execution of the program, while others rewrite much of the address space repeatedly. In the latter case, using the operating system to signal changes to memory pages can actually slow down execution because the overhead of handling the signals outweighs the minimal savings in the amount of data written. Also, in programs with fine-grained data structures such as linked lists, changes to data may be scattered over a large proportion of the memory pages even though the changes may amount to a small fraction of the total data.

Another technique for minimizing the amount of data in a checkpoint is to identify data in memory that may have changed between checkpoints but does not affect the state of a computation [128, 129]. Programs can mark this data explicitly through hints to the checkpointing system, or the system can try to find it automatically by identifying unused portions of the stack or the memory allocation pool. It may also be possible for compilers to mark this data automatically.

The timing of a checkpoint within the execution cycle of a program can also affect its size. If a checkpoint is taken in the middle of a calculation, it may include many intermediate or temporary data structures. Checkpoints taken at the end of a time step can be smaller in some applications because these intermediate structures are no longer an essential part of the program's state. Although they may have changed since the last checkpoint was taken, the data they contain is "dead," since it will not be read again. Checkpointing tools that rely on the operating system to identify dirty pages will not be able to identify this dead data to avoid checkpointing it, but programmers can often find this data and eliminate it from checkpoint files.

In general, managing both the timing and the contents of a checkpoint from within a program greatly simplifies the checkpointing system. Not only can the programmer take advantage of application-specific knowledge to reduce the size of the checkpoint, but writing a consistent checkpoint in a parallel program (see below) is easier because the programmer can often identify a quiescent state when no messages are in transit between processes. Finally, the programmer can choose an appropriate interval at which to checkpoint a job. (Section 7.2.4 looks at an analytical model for making this determination.)

Another potential optimization is for programs to combine checkpointing with data staging or required I/O. For example, many programs store intermediate results of a computation at each time step, and this data can be useful not only as the output of the computation but also as the basis for restarting the program after an interruption.

Combining Checkpointing with Paging

Since the virtual memory system already writes pages of memory to secondary storage, it is possible to combine demand paging with checkpointing. An early example of this technique appeared in the KeyKOS [92] operating system. KeyKOS defines two pools for pages in secondary storage. The *working area* holds the current set of swapped-out pages, and the *checkpoint area* holds the most recent checkpoint data. When the system takes a checkpoint, any dirty pages in memory that have not been saved to the working area are written out, and then the roles of the two areas are switched. As the system uses the former checkpoint area for backing store, data in the new checkpoint area is migrated to a permanent location.

Hsu and Chang [74] refined this strategy by eliminating the migration step. As in KeyKOS, the pages in backing store become part of the checkpoint file when a checkpoint is taken, and any dirty pages in memory are written out at the time of the checkpoint. However, instead of migrating the checkpoint file to another file, the system marks all the pages in the checkpoint file as read-only. Then it duplicates any pages that change after the checkpoint operation using a copy-on-write technique. The virtual memory system uses these duplicate pages as backing store until the next checkpoint is taken. At that time, the system replaces any outdated pages in the checkpoint file with the new copies that the virtual memory system was using simply by modifying the file's metadata to replace the disk blocks containing the old pages with the new ones that already reside on disk; no data needs to be copied.

Both systems store additional data at the time of a checkpoint to capture the state of the processor and other operating system data. Both systems require operating system support; they cannot be implemented in user-level code.

As with other checkpointing optimizations, the effectiveness of combined checkpointing and paging depends on the details of the program being checkpointed. However, an important advantage of this integrated technique is that it avoids extra paging when a checkpoint is taken. In other systems, if a user-level checkpointing system stores a data structure that is currently swapped out of primary storage, the system must read in the data from the backing store before the checkpointing system can write it out to a checkpoint file. In paging-based systems, the swapped-out data automatically becomes part of the checkpoint file, so it does not need to be brought back in.

Portability

There are two kinds of portability to consider in a checkpointing system: the portability of the checkpointing software and the portability of the checkpoint data.

System-supported checkpointing techniques often have system dependencies because they are closely tied to the operating system. Likewise, the stored checkpoint data is useful only on the system that generated it, not only because the data representation is unique to a particular vendor's hardware but also because system configurations vary between machines from the same vendor.

When the program defines what to store in a checkpoint file, the data can be more portable. Although some checkpointing systems treat data as sequences of untyped bytes, other methods use higher-level data models, so they can write portable checkpoint files. To store portable checkpoint data, the programmer can determine what structures to store and have the program write them out in a portable data format. In more automated checkpointing systems that store portable checkpoint files, the application may have to use a particular programming language or model of parallelism.

Concurrent Checkpointing

All checkpointing systems must restore the computation to a consistent state. This is straightforward in a sequential or shared memory computer because there is a single pool of memory whose contents can be recorded at a well-defined moment in time, using a blocking or nonblocking algorithm.

Recording a program's state is more difficult in distributed memory systems. In these machines, it may be impossible to initiate a checkpoint at the same instant on every node, and messages may be in transit between two nodes when the checkpoint is taken. If the sending node records its checkpoint after transmitting the data, and the receiving node records its checkpoint before the data arrives, then the message could be lost when the program resumes. There are several ways to solve this problem (Figure 7.6).

The simplest technique is to require the program to be in a quiescent state with no messages in transit when the processes record their checkpoints. This generally works best for synchronous checkpointing techniques, since an asynchronous method could wait a long time before detecting that no messages are in transit. The quiescent state may be preceded by a special checkpoint signal that is broadcast to

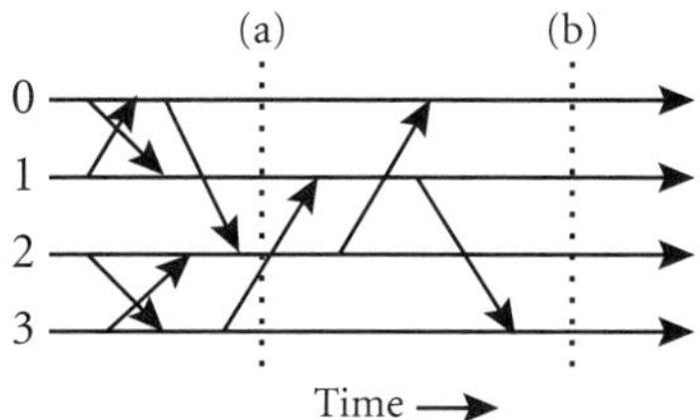

Figure 7.6 If all the tasks in a distributed memory program record their state at the same time, as in checkpoint (a), messages in transit between nodes (such as the message from task 3 to task 1) must be not be lost. A simple way to avoid the problem is to take checkpoints only when no messages are in transit, as in checkpoint (b). Figure 7.7 illustrates another solution.

all the processes. Even if the tasks do not all record their states at precisely the same moment, the timing variations won't affect the status of messages in transit.

Some parallel computers do have a mechanism to initiate checkpoints in all the processes simultaneously. This requires some form of globally synchronized clock. The processes will all be in a consistent state, but messages may still be in transit within the network at the moment of the checkpoint. To avoid losing these messages, the checkpointing system must wait for some time until all the messages arrive at their destination nodes. Then it captures and saves these messages and feeds them back to the application when the program resumes operation.

Chandy and Lamport [24] developed a technique for capturing a consistent global state in computers that do not have a globally synchronized clock (Figure 7.7). Their algorithm uses "marker" messages that are sent between pairs of processes at the time of a checkpoint. It works as follows: Suppose P_0 is a process that is

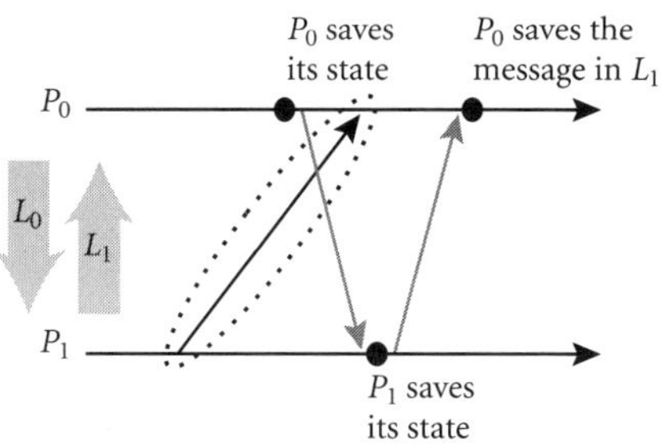

Figure 7.7 The Chandy-Lamport algorithm saves the state of a distributed program without requiring a globally synchronized clock.

initiating a checkpoint, and suppose P_1 is another process in the parallel job. The communication link from P_0 to P_1 is called L_0, and the link in the reverse direction is L_1. The process on the receiving end of each link is responsible for recording the state of that link. P_0 records its process state using a standard, single-process checkpointing technique. Then before it sends any more messages, it sends a marker along L_0 to P_1 (and to all the other processes with which it communicates). The marker is indicated by a light shaded arrow in the figure. P_1 receives the marker and immediately checkpoints its own process state. P_1 also records the state of L_0 as being empty; that is, there are no messages in transit along L_0. Then P_1 sends a marker to all the other processes that it communicates with, including P_0. Processes receiving a marker from P_1 will fall into two categories: those that have already checkpointed their states and those that have not. Processes in the latter category will respond to a marker just as P_1 did, by checkpointing their process and incoming link states and then forwarding the marker. Processes that *have* already checkpointed their state (such as P_0) do not repeat the operation. Instead, each records the state of the link on which the marker arrived (L_1 in the case of P_0) as containing all the messages that have arrived on that link since the process recorded its last checkpoint, and the process does not forward the marker. The message that P_0 records is circled in Figure 7.7. The result of the exchange between P_0 and P_1 is that process states are recorded for both processes, but at different times. Any messages that were in transit between these times are also recorded in the state of one of the connecting links. Since the markers are propagated to all communicating processes in the program along all links, every process and link is eventually recorded. Since a process does not propagate markers it receives if it has already taken a checkpoint, the algorithm eventually terminates (assuming each process eventually reads its messages and responds appropriately). The algorithm also assumes that each link delivers messages in the order that they are sent.

An interesting feature of the Chandy-Lamport algorithm is that it does not record the state of all processes at the same instant in time; it cannot do so because markers do not travel between processes instantaneously. However, it still records a *consistent* state of the program, in the sense that the collection of states recorded is one that the program *could* have legally reached. The subsequent execution of a program restarted from the checkpointed states is therefore guaranteed to be a valid execution of the program.

Many other techniques exist for determining a consistent global state of a parallel program. For example, some add marker information to existing messages instead of sending explicit markers. Elnozahy et al. [49] have surveyed these techniques.

File Checkpointing

Since open files can be left in an inconsistent state when a program is halted, it is important to save their state along with the rest of the program state. In general, this is a straightforward task: flush commands can force buffered data to secondary storage, and checkpointing software can record the values of file pointers along with other program information. Nonblocking access requests must be completed before the program halts.

Complications arise when a program needs to take a checkpoint in the middle of a collective I/O operation. For example, what happens when a program needs to take a checkpoint during a two-phase I/O operation? The simplest solution is to wait for the operation to complete before initiating the checkpoint. If this isn't possible (for example, because a system-initiated checkpointer doesn't recognize the multiple steps of two-phase I/O as forming a single operation), then another solution would be to treat the operation as a set of discrete steps, which the checkpointer can interrupt and later restart. In that case, messages that formed a shuffle exchange operation would be stored like any other messages, and the intermediate buffers on the various nodes would be saved like other memory. The states of the I/O nodes would need to be saved along with the other nodes, but this doesn't present any special challenges.

Most checkpointers don't replicate the contents of the files, since they assume that secondary storage is stable. However, if a program modifies a file after recording its last checkpoint, the restarted program could find incorrect data in the file. Systems can checkpoint the files themselves using copy-on-write techniques. Each time the system takes a checkpoint, it marks the blocks in a file as "clean." When a program later changes a clean block, the file system or other software duplicates the block. One version is updated and becomes part of the current version of the file. The unmodified block is saved for use with the corresponding checkpoint; if the program is restored to that checkpoint, the checkpointing software replaces any modified blocks with the "clean" versions. Files opened after a checkpoint is taken must be also have their blocks marked for copy-on-write if the system is to restore their contents correctly.

7.2.2 Single-Process Checkpointing Systems

Most parallel checkpointing techniques rely on single-process checkpointing software to save the state of individual processes. Two well-known single-process checkpointing systems are Condor and libckpt.

Condor Checkpointing Library

Condor [98] is a set of tools for running distributed programs on networks of Unix workstations. It was developed at the University of Wisconsin, and it includes a basic, portable checkpointing package for single-process programs. (The Condor group has also developed a multiprocess checkpointing tool called CoCheck [132].

One of its significant features is that it can use a separate server on the network to store checkpoint data.)

Since Condor uses checkpointing as a way to migrate processes between workstations, it does not need to support nonblocking checkpoints; when a program needs to move off a workstation, Condor halts its execution and saves its state immediately. Checkpoints are initiated by the system through the Unix signaling mechanism. The application program plays no role in determining the timing or content of a checkpoint. The application does need to be linked with the checkpointing library, but the code within the application is not modified.

Condor stores checkpoints using straightforward techniques: it locates and saves all the program data and any dynamically loaded libraries, but it does not store the program's executable code. It attempts to save the state of any open files by intercepting all of a program's Unix system calls that open or duplicate a file handle. It builds a list of these files, and at checkpoint time it queries and saves the state of the file pointers. Condor does not attempt to checkpoint the contents of the files themselves.

The Condor checkpointing code is relatively portable. It requires no changes to the operating system, and it uses standard system calls to locate and save program data. It does require a small amount of architecture-specific code to save the CPU status. The checkpoint data itself can be migrated to other systems of the same type but not to different architectures.

Libckpt

Plank et al. implemented nonblocking checkpointing and several size reduction techniques in a freely available checkpointing library called libckpt [128]. This is a user-level library that requires minimal changes to the user code. The programmer must change the program's entry point (`main` in C or the `PROGRAM` module in Fortran) to `ckpt_target` and link in the checkpointing library. When the program is executed, the checkpointing library initializes itself before passing control to the application.

Programs can initiate checkpoints synchronously using a `checkpoint_here` call or asynchronously by specifying a checkpoint interval in a start-up file that the libckpt reads. Libckpt supports blocking and nonblocking checkpoints, and on certain Unix implementations, nonblocking checkpoints use the copy-on-write optimization to reduce the cost of duplicating the program's address space.

The system can reduce the size of checkpoints using either incremental checkpointing or explicit memory exclusion calls. The incremental checkpointing algorithm identifies pages that change between checkpoints by write-protecting memory with `mprotect`, as described earlier. The memory exclusion method allows programs to specify ranges of memory to include or exclude from a checkpoint. Programs can also identify excluded ranges of memory as being read-only, so they will be saved once at the first checkpoint but not afterward. The developers of libckpt have observed that these calls must be used with considerable care to avoid excluding necessary data from a checkpoint. Libckpt also includes an instrumented version of the memory allocation library that automatically causes freed memory to be excluded from checkpoints.

Experiments with several applications using libckpt showed the effects of the checkpoint optimizations that it implements. First, Plank's group found that compared to blocking checkpoints, nonblocking checkpoints using copy-on-write reduced the overhead of taking a checkpoint by more than 70% for most codes. The effect of incremental checkpointing varied greatly between programs. For some applications, the checkpoint size was reduced by 80% or more; for others, there was little or no size reduction. In applications that benefited most from incremental checkpointing, the reduction in checkpoint size produced similar reductions in the checkpointing time. In other applications, the checkpointing time actually increased when incremental checkpointing was used because the added cost of handling write protection faults was not offset by any significant reduction in the volume of data stored. However, explicit memory exclusion did improve the performance of these applications. For a linear equation solver, memory exclusion reduced the checkpoint size by more than 90%. For a cellular automata code, checkpoints were reduced by 50%. Incremental checkpointing had failed to reduce the checkpoint size significantly in either of these codes, but the explicit techniques were more effective because they were able to identify dead data structures.

7.2.3 Parallel Checkpointing Systems

Different types of parallel computers require different checkpointing techniques. For shared memory computers, the techniques are similar to those used for single-processor computers [94]. One important difference is that nonblocking checkpointing tools can use one of the shared memory computer's processors to manage checkpoint storage.

Checkpointing systems for distributed memory computers must save the states of multiple nodes and ensure that they form a consistent view of a parallel job. The three checkpointing systems described later in this section demonstrate different solutions to this problem, from nonportable but nonintrusive methods to more portable and intrusive techniques.

Distributed shared memory computers create the appearance of a single global address space, but in reality the memory is distributed, and there is usually no global clock. Checkpointing tools for these computers generally implement a consistency protocol like the Chandy-Lamport algorithm or one of its variations; that is, they work much like the checkpointing tools for message passing computers [83, 146].

In general, there appears to be a necessary trade-off between the transparence of a checkpointing tool on the one hand and the portability and compactness of the data on the other hand. To produce portable and compact checkpoint data, the system must have application-specific information, and the need for this information forces the application to interact directly with the checkpointing tool.

NERSC T3E Checkpointing System

The National Energy Research Supercomputer Center (NERSC) at Lawrence Berkeley National Laboratory developed the first transparent, system-initiated checkpointing tool for a distributed memory parallel computer [116, 41]. It runs on a Cray T3E and was first demonstrated in 1997. The T3E computer has a globally synchronized clock, so the checkpointing system can initiate checkpoints for all processes at the same instant. When a checkpoint is initiated, each parallel job is frozen. The system tries to identify barrier points within the applications so that the message passing channels will be quiescent. However, if no barrier occurs within a short period of time, the checkpointing software simply halts the processes and waits for any messages in transit to arrive at their destination. These messages are recorded and then delivered to the program when it resumes.

Checkpoints are initiated only by the system and not from within the applications, but the system can checkpoint individual jobs without affecting others. The checkpointing system is run daily to save long-running jobs before the system is switched from batch mode to interactive mode. The saved jobs are then restored when the system changes back to batch mode at the end of the workday. The NERSC T3E has approximately 1.5 TB of physical memory, and a full checkpoint takes 8 to 12 minutes.

Since this tool requires system support for freezing the jobs, identifying barriers, and emptying the message queues, neither the checkpointing software nor the checkpoint data is portable to other architectures.

CLIP

CLIP (Checkpointing Library for the Intel Paragon) [28] is, as its name suggests, designed to work only on the Paragon. It is based on the libckpt single-process checkpointing tool, but unlike libckpt, it does not support asynchronous checkpointing.

As in libckpt, programs initiate checkpoints by calling `checkpoint_here`. The tool compensates for the lack of asynchronous checkpointing by allowing users to specify a minimum checkpoint interval. When a program calls `checkpoint_here`, the system initiates a checkpoint only if this minimum interval has elapsed since the last checkpoint was taken. The techniques that libckpt offers for reducing the amount of checkpoint data—incremental checkpointing and memory exclusion—are also available in CLIP. In CLIP, recording a checkpoint is a collective operation. It causes a barrier synchronization in the program, and as a result it flushes all messages in transit out of the interconnection network and into the node memory. Once the messages are in the nodes' memory, they can be saved along with the rest of the checkpoint data even if they have not yet been received by their destination process.

Since CLIP is designed to run on the Paragon, it takes advantage of the Intel Parallel File System in two ways. First, it attempts to write data in block-size units that match the file block size. It does this by gathering small pieces of data into buffers before sending them to disk. CLIP produces these small fragments not only as a result of memory exclusion but also because it needs to save bookkeeping information on where these fragments fit into the application. Second, it stores the data for a single checkpoint of all the processes in a single PFS file using `M_ASYNC` mode. Programs can also store checkpoints to the standard sequential Unix file system.

Dome

Checkpointing systems that store the contents of memory without interpreting it cannot easily produce portable checkpoint files because the layout of data in memory differs among computer architectures. Heterogeneous parallel computers that store checkpoints must either restore applications on collection machines that are compatible with the computers on which the program was checkpointed, or else they must save the data in a system-independent format. The Dome project at Carnegie-Mellon University developed a checkpointing tool using the latter technique [15].

Dome (Distributed Object Migration Environment) is a programming environment designed to support applications running on a network of heterogeneous workstations. Programs must be written in C++ using the Dome class library, which supports distributed data objects, communication, and other basic operations. Because all distributed data structures are known to the Dome system in advance, and because Dome performs all interprocess communication invisibly to the user, the system can control many aspects of the checkpointing process. Programs initiate checkpoints synchronously by calling `dome_checkpoint`. Since Dome performs all communication internally, it can ensure that no messages are in transit when the checkpoint is taken.

The data stored in the checkpoint is the set of "Dome variables," which the program declares as members of classes defined in Dome. Since these classes include checkpointing capabilities, Dome can create a list of all objects to be stored, along with their types. This allows Dome to store the data in a system-independent format.

The remaining difficulty for Dome is determining the state of the computation when the checkpoint is taken. Other checkpointing tools store the program stack and CPU registers, but this data is not portable between different computer architectures. Instead, Dome uses a program preprocessor that adds instrumentation to the source code. This instrumentation records events such as the entry and exit of functions. When the program is restarted, Dome uses this data and a series of `goto` statements that the preprocessor embeds in the source code to skip to the point in the program where the checkpoint was taken.

7.2.4 Checkpoint Intervals

When checkpointing is used for process migration, the question of when to take a checkpoint is a matter of policy outside the application's control. In the case of a systemwide checkpoint, data is stored when the system is about to be brought down or when the scheduling policy changes. In networks of workstations, a task running on a single machine might be checkpointed when a user begins an interactive session.

Checkpointing for fault tolerance is a more complicated issue. Users want to repeat as little as possible of a computation after a program resumes execution, which suggests that frequent checkpoints are desirable. On the other hand, most checkpointing techniques increase the overall running time of an application, and if the program runs to completion without incurring a system failure, the extra checkpointing time is wasted. Of course, the more frequently a system crashes, the more likely it is that a checkpoint will be needed. Several models have been developed to determine the optimum checkpoint interval based on these considerations. This interval would produce the minimum expected total running time for a given mean time between failures and checkpoint overhead. One simple model by Wong and Franklin [174] gives the optimum checkpoint rate, α_{opt}, as

$$\alpha_{\text{opt}} = \sqrt{0.5\phi\beta},$$

where ϕ is the mean rate of system failure and $1/\beta$ is the time needed to take a checkpoint. The factor of 0.5 represents the portion of work done during a checkpoint interval that would be lost if the system failed. On average, you expect failures to occur halfway through a checkpoint interval. As an example, suppose the mean time between failures in a system is 100 hours or 3.6×10^5 seconds, and each checkpoint adds 100 seconds to the running time. Then the optimum checkpoint rate according to this model would be

$$\alpha_{\text{opt}} = \sqrt{\frac{0.5}{3.6 \times 10^7 \text{sec}^2}}.$$

This works out to an optimum checkpoint interval of 8485 seconds, or about 2 hours and 22 minutes. This model assumes that the entire system is either completely functional or completely unusable; it doesn't account for the possibility of running on a reduced number of nodes. More complex models allow for reducing the number of tasks in a parallel job and other factors.

Further analysis with other models shows that the expected running time of a program using checkpoints is more sensitive to the added cost of frequent checkpoints than to the lost work that results from infrequent checkpoints. In other words, it is better to save too few checkpoints than too many.

7.3 Summary

This chapter has described two special types of I/O: data staging for out-of-core applications and checkpointing for saving and restoring program states. Standard I/O interfaces could be used for both purposes, but specialized libraries and algorithms offer important benefits. For out-of-core applications, staging libraries optimize common I/O requests, such as reading and writing sections of distributed arrays. Moreover, out-of-core algorithms that explicitly recognize the role of secondary storage can improve performance compared to using standard virtual memory to simulate a very large primary storage space.

Checkpointing techniques fall into two categories: those initiated within the application and those initiated by the system. The former are generally easier to implement because the application can initiate requests at times when it is in a consistent and easily recorded state. However, system-initiated checkpointing eliminates the need for users to include checkpointing requests explicitly in their code. Therefore, computer centers can use system-initiated checkpointing to save all programs on a machine just before bringing it down or changing its scheduling policies. All checkpointing software represents a trade-off between three competing goals: minimizing the application programmer's effort, minimizing the size of the checkpoint file, and making the checkpoint data portable.

7.4 Further Reading

There are numerous algorithms for various out-of-core computations. Abello and Vitter's book [1] covers many of these. The references for the tools discussed earlier describe how to write out-of-core programs, and they note areas where compilers can provide assistance.

In the area of checkpointing, Deconinck et al. [42] briefly survey checkpointing techniques for parallel systems. Elnozahy et al. [49] present a more detailed review that focuses on how to create consistent checkpoints in distributed memory computers. Also, the paper by Plank et al. [128] on libckpt is a good survey of optimizations for single-process checkpointing, while Litzkow et al. [98] describe the mechanics of saving and restoring the state of a running process.

Chapter Eight

Data Management and Analysis

Many applications have begun to deal with data sets measured in terabytes. These applications include scientific simulation codes, large-scale experiments, commercial databases, and digital libraries. Managing data at this scale is a major challenge. This chapter assumes that the user has collected a large quantity of data and now needs help to manage it. Most of the programming interfaces discussed so far in this book create discrete data files. These self-contained units are convenient for users to examine, move, and duplicate. As later sections will show, however, files are not always the most useful way to store data. Databases and files augmented with metadata offer many sophisticated search and analysis mechanisms. This chapter refers to files and databases collectively as "data sets." Techniques for managing these data sets focus on three main tasks:

- Determining what data exists and where it resides.
- Searching the data for answers to specific questions.
- Discovering interesting new data elements and patterns.

When data resides in a small collection of files, the file names alone may contain enough information to help a user with the first task. Large collections of files, distributed collections, and complex data sets require more sophisticated techniques. Data management techniques are also useful for files that reside in tertiary storage, since browsing these files interactively is not usually practical.

For the second task, finding specific information in a data set, users can exploit database storage and querying techniques. However, relational database management systems (RDBMSs) developed for commercial applications use a data model that is poorly suited to many kinds of scientific data. Also, standard database querying techniques are not expressive enough to answer many interesting scientific questions. For example, an astronomer might want to search a sky survey database for objects with a particular shape or with complex spatial relationships to each other. Standard database techniques must be augmented with pattern recognition capabilities and other application-specific analysis tools to meet these needs. A further problem with standard database technology is that while some commercial database management systems (DBMSs) can manage terabytes of data, they cannot necessarily do so *efficiently* for large scientific databases.

The last task presents the greatest challenge in data management: discovering previously unknown (and possibly unsuspected) information within a data set. This "knowledge discovery" may involve finding unexpected relationships or patterns in a set of data elements. A number of interesting techniques, some borrowed from commercial data mining, can be applied to this problem.

Previous chapters have described I/O methods for data generated and used by application programs. The techniques described in this chapter also apply to data generated by experimental observations (e.g., satellite or telescope images, seismic data, etc.) and to other large data collections such as digital libraries.

8.1 Finding Data

A user looking for a particular piece of data has several options. Scanning a list of file names is the obvious choice if the directory is small and the file names are descriptive. If not, the user can search for specific words or phases in text files using a tool like the Unix `grep` utility. Alternatively, the user can list files directly or view them using a visualization tool. However, when data is decomposed over many files or files are scattered among many directories or when the data resides in tertiary storage, direct searches like these are impractical because they require too much I/O. More efficient methods use additional information called *metadata* to reduce the amount of I/O that a search entails. Metadata can also describe or define the structure of the data, permitting more sophisticated searches.

8.1.1 Metadata

Two common definitions of metadata are "data about data" and "data needed to make other data useful." Previous chapters have already described several kinds of metadata. The inodes that file systems use to keep track of disk blocks are a form of metadata; so are the annotations that scientific data libraries can add to data structures in files. In the context of data management, metadata is information that helps a user or an analysis tool use the data. With a definition this broad, metadata can take many forms. Examples include

- Information maintained by the file system, such as the name, size, creation time, modification time, and owner of a file.
- A description of the format of data within a file, such as the numeric representation or layout.
- A description of the circumstances in which data was gathered. For computational simulations, this may include software version numbers, hardware information, input data, iteration numbers, and so on. For experimental data, metadata may include the time and location of measurements and descriptions of instrumentation.
- A computed summary of data, such as statistical properties (mean, standard deviation, minimum, maximum, etc.) or thumbnail views of large images.
- A text annotation made by a user, such as "Anomalous behavior begins at this time step."

Metadata can be stored together with the file it describes or separately. Storing metadata with a file makes the file a self-contained package, which is convenient for some analysis tools. Storing it separately allows tools to examine metadata efficiently when the underlying data is large or inaccessible. Separating the metadata can also be useful when the data and metadata are in different formats. For example, text metadata is easier for a human user to examine directly, without special tools, when it is not intermixed with binary numeric data that it describes.

Some metadata can be generated automatically, either when the data file is created or during a postprocessing step. Other metadata requires human input. The last few types of metadata in the list above tend to be application-specific; generating it (either automatically or with human assistance) requires knowledge of the meaning of the data within the file. This kind of metadata is sometimes called "high-level" or "content-oriented" metadata to distinguish it from metadata that the file system or I/O library generates automatically to describe aspects of the file that are independent of its contents.

As the use of application-specific metadata has grown, efforts have arisen to develop standard formats for it. These standards allow people working in the same discipline to share not only data and metadata but also the tools to browse and analyze the metadata. Much of the work in this area is focused on metadata for indexing Web-based resources so that search engines can produce more detailed and reliable information. For example, XML (extensible markup language) [19, 172] is emerging as a standard format for creating "structured" documents. Older text markup languages like html and LaTeX describe both the structure of a document (by labeling elements such as headings, sections, lists, figures, etc.) and its appearance (fonts, spacing between lines, placement of figures and text, etc.) XML, on the other hand, defines only the structure of a document without assigning any meaning to the structural elements. Users place XML tags (short text labels) into a document, but XML itself doesn't assign any meaning to those tags. Users are free to define their own tags and to specify their meaning separately. The meaning of the tags is specified through external programs or through style sheets. The XML syntax supports marking sections of a document as raw data and adding structured descriptive elements (i.e., metadata) to a document. Other programs can use this metadata to index XML documents. Although XML is used mainly for Web-based documents at present, some observers believe that it will eventually replace current standard data formats for scientific data, such as those used by netCDF and HDF.

8.1.2 Browsing Metadata

Once metadata is associated with a data set, there are many ways to search it. Several of these methods are already familiar to most computer users. The Unix `ls -l` command is a very simple metadata browser. It presents a list of files and some of the metadata that the file system maintains. More sophisticated versions of this tool are also common: the file browsers in most graphical windowing systems present a listing of all the files in a given directory, and the user can choose to sort the files in the view according to the file name, the creation or modification date, the file size, the file type (spreadsheet, word processing document, etc.), and other criteria.

A further extension of the simple file list presents graphical information about the contents of a file. Applications that create graphical files (e.g., drawing tools) often have file selection dialog boxes that show a small preview image of each file that the user highlights. This helps the user to determine whether the file contains the image being sought.

These tools are well known and widely used; the point of mentioning them here is to show that basic metadata browsing tools already exist. For large data sets and more sophisticated data, users can turn to specialized tools, such as SimTracker [99].

SimTracker

SimTracker was developed at the Lawrence Livermore National Laboratory to help computational scientists manage the output of large scientific simulation codes. The tool has two components: one that gathers and organizes data files and another that presents information to users.

Simulation codes typically produce output files each time the code completes a certain number of time steps. The data generation component of SimTracker catalogs these files and generates metadata from them. The metadata usually includes application-specific information such as an iteration number and a thumbnail view of the data for that file. SimTracker can be programmed to call a separate data visualization package or other postprocessing utility to help it generate this metadata. Since the generation component updates its catalog periodically while the simulation code is running, users can browse partial results of a run before it completes. Once the application has finished the simulation run, SimTracker can automatically move files to archival storage. SimTracker uses a Web browser interface to present the metadata. This browser component is based on common gateway interface (CGI) scripts, which are implemented in the Perl programming language. The generation component is also implemented in Perl. SimTracker first presents a high-level view of the data collection for various simulations (Figure 8.1). By clicking on thumbnail images in this view, the user can go to pages that describe individual collections of files for different time steps of a simulation (Figure 8.2). This midlevel view shows a series of thumbnail sketches along with more metadata

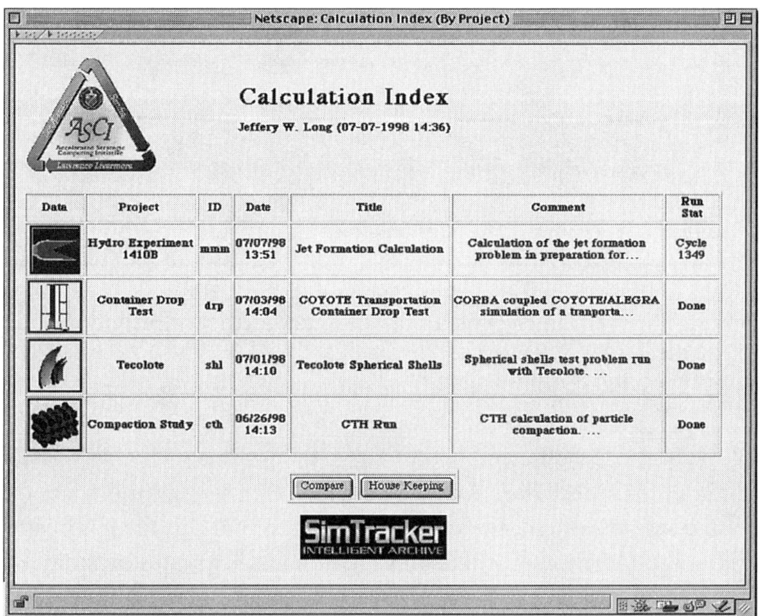

Figure 8.1 The high-level view in SimTracker shows a list of the user's simulation data. The user can click on an item to see more details on a particular run. The Hydro Experiment data shown here is from a simulation run that is still in progress, as indicated by the cycle number in the "Run Stat" column. (From Long, Spencer, and Springmeyer [99].)

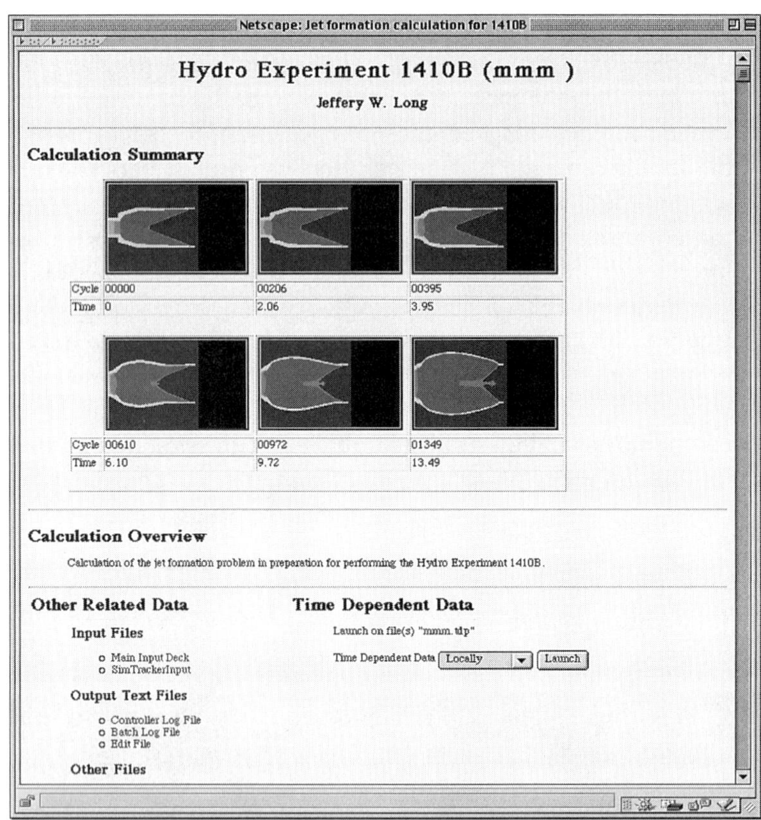

Figure 8.2 The midlevel SimTracker view shows data from different time steps in a simulation run. The user can click on an image to get further information about the corresponding file, and to retrieve that file from archival storage if necessary. (From Long, Spencer, and Springmeyer [99].)

about the simulation. A low-level view lets users see metadata from a specific time step and, if desired, the underlying data file. If this file has been moved to archival storage, SimTracker will retrieve it. SimTracker stores metadata separately from the data being cataloged. This separation is necessary to allow interactive browsing of files in archival storage.

Much of the data that SimTracker generates is application-specific. The user must program the system to call the appropriate postprocessing utilities to produce this data. Users can also enter metadata directly in the form of text annotations.

8.1.3 Metadata Databases

SimTracker and other browsing tools help users navigate collections of files, but they still require users to browse information manually. To automate this browsing, systems can store metadata in a metadata database. These systems can query the metadata to find data sets meeting specific criteria.

A simple example would be finding all the files produced by a particular simulation program within a certain range of dates. A standard database management system (given the appropriate metadata) could easily handle such a query, and it would be a simple matter to produce a list of matching files on a Web page with links to the actual data.

A more sophisticated query might involve an unexpected combination of criteria, such as "find all output files produced by Versions 3.1 through 3.4 of the Aero3D simulation code run on the MultiFlops computer in parallel jobs with more than 128 processes." Such requests are called *ad hoc queries.* A simple range-of-dates query could be anticipated in the design of the metadata database, so the database might be organized to respond to this kind of request quickly. An ad hoc request, on the other hand, is one that was not anticipated in the design of the application that is using the DBMS. Assuming all the necessary metadata was available, the DBMS managing the metadata could handle this kind of query correctly, but depending on the organization of the database, it might respond slowly.

The Storage Resource Broker (SRB) [12], developed at the San Diego Supercomputer Center, uses a metadata database for two purposes. First, the database (called MCAT, for "metadata catalog") stores application-specific information that programs can search to find data of interest. Second, it stores the metadata necessary to present directory-like views of collections of files. The SRB can present these views even when the data resides on different systems, such as Unix file systems, databases, and archival storage systems. Section 8.3.2 describes additional features of the SRB.

8.2 Hierarchical Data Models

The model in which data is stored influences the kind of queries that can be done and the efficiency of those queries. Section 8.3.1 describes how data models are used when a DBMS manages the data itself. Specialized data models can also support sophisticated metadata database techniques. Hierarchical data models are an important category of metadata models. Their main feature is that they summarize the underlying data.

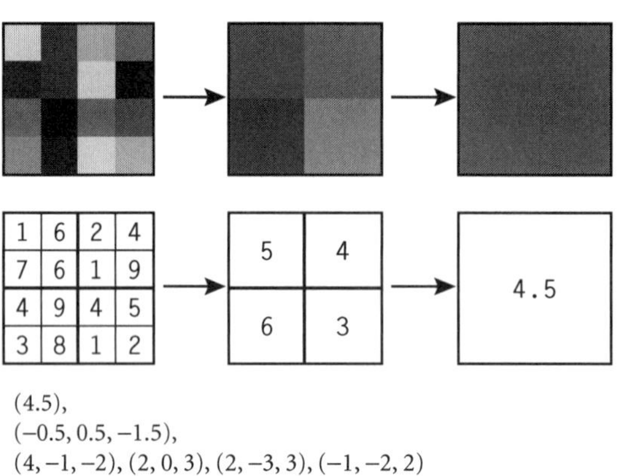

Figure 8.3 A simple hierarchical data model summarizes smaller regions in successively larger ones. See the text for details.

Hierarchical models are designed for data sets in which one or more parameters vary (more or less) continuously over a regular spatial grid. Examples include climate data, terrain maps, and some kinds of images. The model is not limited to any specific dimensionality, but it is easiest to understand in two dimensions.

Suppose that the data set is an $N \times N$ monochrome image (where N is the size of each dimension in pixels), and the parameter that varies over the two-dimensional space is a gray-scale level. (To simplify the arithmetic, this example makes the rather unrealistic assumption that gray-scale levels are stored as floating-point numbers.) You can divide this image into $N^2/4$ blocks of 2×2 adjacent pixels. For each block, the gray-scale level can be approximated as the average value of the four pixels. Figure 8.3 shows an example of a two-level hierarchy. The top set of squares shows how the image looks at successive levels, while the bottom set of squares shows the original data and the computed mean values. This technique produces an approximation of the original data set at each level that uses one-quarter as many values. This reduction can be continued by aggregating the new blocks into larger blocks at successively higher levels until (assuming that N is a whole power of two) the top level consists of a single mean gray-scale value for the whole image. Each level above the base data is metadata that describes the data below. Image processing programs can use this technique to generate a low-resolution thumbnail image of a larger data set.

A very useful property of this model is that you can reconstruct the finer detail of each underlying level for each group of four pixels using only the mean value and the differences between this mean and three of the four pixel values. Specifically, let $x_1 \cdots x_4$ be the values for the four pixels that make up a block. The mean of these values is $\bar{x}$. For the first three pixels, the difference values are $d_i = \bar{x} - x_i$. There is no need to compute or store d_4 because x_4 can be recovered from $\bar{x}$ and the other three difference terms:

$$x_4 = \bar{x} + d_1 + d_2 + d_3.$$

By storing one mean value at the top level and a series of difference values for each level below, a program can encode all the levels of the hierarchy in the same amount of space as the original, base-level data. Moreover, data can be arranged in the file so that the top of the hierarchy comes first, followed by difference terms needed to construct the second level, then the third level, and so on. For example, the numbers shown at the bottom of Figure 8.3 are the final mean (first line); the 3 values needed (along with the global mean) to reconstruct the intermediate representation (second line); and the 12 values needed to reconstruct the original image from the intermediate level (third line). The total number of values stored (16) is the same as the number of original values at the finest level of detail. This arrangement lets a browsing tool retrieve progressively more detail from a file, while reading the file in sequential order. At any point, the user may decide not to view the next finer level of detail, thus avoiding the need to read the whole file.

Hierarchical data models using this averaging technique are common in image processing applications, and they are especially useful for transmitting images over slow connections, since the user sees a whole image appear in increasing detail instead of seeing it drawn from top to bottom at full resolution. Of course, these models require extra computation both when the data is stored and when it is retrieved.

Higher-dimensional data can use the same technique. In three dimensions, the standard hierarchical model averages eight blocks instead of four to produce each higher-level block.

This basic model is similar to another hierarchical data model called a *quadtree.* In that model, different regions of a data set can be stored at different resolutions. The main difference between quadtrees and hierarchies lies in how they manage multiresolution data. In a quadtree, the resolution of data is fixed for a given region of space, but different regions can be represented at different resolutions. A hierarchical model, on the other hand, stores data at multiple resolutions for all regions of space [140].

Hierarchical models are poorly suited to data sets in which there are large variations in values between adjacent regions. For example, in a celestial image, many stars would be blurred away when the pixels representing them were averaged with adjacent dark pixels.

Another disadvantage of this simple hierarchical model is that it does not support sophisticated queries of the data. For example, in a data set containing temperature measurements, you might want to find all the points in the base data for which the temperature exceeded some threshold value. Examining mean values for a collection of points wouldn't work because the means would give no information about the underlying extremes. To produce correct results, the query algorithm would have to decode all the data and examine it directly.

An alternative model that supports range queries more efficiently was developed by Li et al. [96] and is called a *pyramid model*. Data at each level in this model is treated as a set of cells. A cell is defined as a region in space and a collection of values for specific parameters, such as temperature, pressure, and so on. The bottom level of the pyramid is the original data. Groups of cells at this level are mapped to one cell at the next level up, and groups of cells at that level are mapped to cells at a higher level, and so on up to the top of the pyramid. Unlike the basic hierarchical model, Li's pyramid structure maps a large number of cells (1000 or more) to each cell in the next level up. Also, the lower-level cells mapped to a single upper-level cell need not be contiguous with each other.

The other important difference between Li's model and the basic hierarchy is that instead of storing only the mean value for each parameter in the cells below, each upper-level cell represents the parameters in its lower-level cells using six pieces of information: the number of measurements, the mean, the standard deviation, the minimum, the maximum, and an approximate probability density function. This function describes the distribution of values in the lower-level cells, and the approximation is equivalent to a histogram of the values. The histogram data is replaced with the actual values from the lower-level cells if there are fewer than about 1000 values.

Using this data, a program can compute *estimated* results for range queries on the base data, such as how many cells contain values exceeding a certain threshold. The results are estimates because the histogram data only approximates the base data. Nevertheless, the form of this data and its compactness compared to the base data allow faster querying than techniques that must examine all the base data. Li's pyramid data model was developed specifically for earth science applications, but it could be applied to other disciplines as well.

8.3 Scientific Databases

A step beyond storing metadata in a database is to store an entire data set in a database. This allows users to examine their data in more sophisticated ways than is possible with a simple "flat" file. For example, a user can ask for a list of all the data points in a computational grid whose position is within a specified range and whose temperature exceeds a certain value. Unlike the metadata-based techniques described above, a scientific database can produce an exact response rather than an approximate one, and it can evaluate a query involving any combination of parameters.

Two important impediments to creating scientific databases are the enormous size of the data and the inability of database management software to handle sophisticated queries efficiently. Both topics are areas of active research. Before looking at the work being done in these areas, it is helpful to review some basic database technology.

8.3.1 Database Management Systems

A typical database management system is a software tool that stores data reliably, supports concurrent access by multiple users, and includes a mechanism to query the data. More broadly defined, a *database* is a collection of related data, and a *database management system* is a suite of programs that creates and maintains a database [48]. The latter definition encompasses many of the I/O systems described in this book.

Like other I/O systems, DBMSs support specific data models. The most common model is the *relational* model, and DBMSs that support this model are called *relational database management systems* (RDBMSs). RDBMSs have been available and widely used since the 1970s. In the late 1980s, some DBMSs began to include more sophisticated data models using constructs from object-oriented programming. These newer systems are called *object-oriented* and *object-relational DBMSs.* Stonebraker and Moore [153] categorized DBMSs in a two-by-two matrix (Figure 8.4), according to the data models they support and whether they include a specialized query language. The features of basic file systems have already been discussed in previous chapters. The next few pages describe the other three quadrants of the matrix.

	Simple data	Complex data
Query	Relational DBMS	Object-relational DBMS
No query	File system	Object-oriented DBMS

Figure 8.4 Database management systems categorized by data model and support for queries. (Adapted from Stonebraker and Moore [153].)

Long	Lat	Elev	Time	Temp	InstSN
132.21	38.67	103	1999-10-23 12:22	16	3122
132.32	38.40	97	1999-10-23 12:22	18	4067
...	...	...	...	...	...
132.32	38.40	97	1999-21-31 23:59	2	4067

Figure 8.5 A simple relation that records a series of temperature measurements.

Relational DBMSs

In the relational model, a database is viewed as a group of tables (Figure 8.5). A row in the table is a collection of information (called a *record*, a *tuple*, or an *entry*) that describes one entity. A column is a list of attribute values for the records. One example of a relational database is an address book, in which each row of a table represents a person, and each column represents an attribute such as the person's first name, last name, street address, city, and so on. An entire table is called a *relation*. The names of the relations and all their attributes is called a *schema*. Section 6.3 described a "vdata model" used in HDF4 for unstructured grids. This is an example of a relational model, but HDF does not support database-style queries on vdatas.

A *primary key* is a set of one or more attributes whose values uniquely identify each record in a relation. A relation may have more than one possible key, but only one of these is designated as the primary key. In the address book example, there may be several people with the same first name or last name, but if no two entries have *both* the same first and last name, then the combination of the first name and last name is a valid primary key for that relation. In practice, of course, you cannot depend on having no duplicate names in an address book, so the primary key is often a unique identifying number. Every relation must have a primary key, so every record is unique. Therefore, a relation can be viewed as a set (in the mathematical sense) of records. In a scientific database that represents a collection of atmospheric measurements at various locations over a period of time, a valid primary key might be the geographic location (longitude, latitude, elevation) at which the measurement was made together with the time of the measurement. In that case, you can think of the primary key as the domain or the independent variables of a function.

Applying the relational model to databases was first proposed by Codd in 1970 [30]. A major benefit of this model is that it defines a set of data structures and operations that are independent of how the data is stored in the computer. This separation allows database algorithms and applications to be developed that are not tied to a specific DBMS product. The standard relational database operations are called the *relational algebra.* RDBMS applications express these operations through a programming language called SQL (structured query language). Operations to update a relation include adding, modifying, and deleting entries. To extract information from a database, the most basic operation is `select`, which produces a set of entries from the relation that satisfy specified criteria. Finding all entries for which the temperature exceeds 30°C is an example of a `select` operation.[1] The resulting set of entries form a new relation with the same attributes as the original but a smaller set of entries (unless of course the `select` returns all the entries from the original relation). Whereas `select` retrieves a subset of the rows of a relation, the `project` operation retrieves a subset of the columns. That is, `project` creates a new relation whose attributes are a subset of the attributes in the original relation. Since `project` could eliminate attributes that form part of a relation's primary key, simply removing columns from a table might produce a relation that contained duplicate records, which would be invalid. Therefore, in theory, `project` is also defined to eliminate any duplicate records from the resulting relation. However, in practice, RDBMSs allow `project` operations that retain duplicate entries. The resulting tables are not valid relations, but they can be useful in certain tasks.

A single database may contain several relations. In an atmospheric database, one relation may include records describing a series of measurements. The attributes would include the location and time, the atmospheric data (temperature, wind direction and velocity, barometric pressure, etc.), and the serial number of each instrument that recorded the measurement. A second relation could store information about each instrument, such as the serial number, the model, the date of installation, the date it was last calibrated, and so on. In the first relation, the key would be the location and time of each measurement; in the second, the key would be the instrument serial number. When the schema for a relation includes a reference to a key in another relation, that reference is called a *foreign key;* it acts like a pointer from an entry in one relation to an entry in another relation. An RDBMS can combine data from two or more relations in several ways to form new relations. The most common example is a `join` operation. Creating a list of instruments used to collect a set of temperature measurements requires a `join` operation. `Join` creates a new relation whose attributes are all the attributes of both relations. Each entry in this relation is formed by concatenating a pair of entries from the two relations if and only if the two entries have equal values for

1 The `select` operation defined in the relational algebra is different from the `SELECT` statement in SQL; the latter is a general-purpose request that includes the functionality of the `select`, `project`, and `join` operations in relational algebra.

Long	Lat	Elev	Time	Temp	InstSN
132.21	38.67	103	1999-10-23 12:22	16	3122
132.32	38.40	97	1999-10-23 12:22	18	4067
...	...	...	...	...	...
132.32	38.40	97	1999-21-31 23:59	2	4067

SerialNo	Model	Installed	Calibrated
1019	Acme Temp-o-matic 2000	1994-06-02	1999-02-26
3122	Thermbuddy TB60	1989-09-15	1999-07-09
...	...	...	...
4067	HotSpot 5X	1998-08-03	1999-07-13

Long	...	InstSN	SerialNo	Model	...
132.21	...	3122	3122	Thermbuddy TB60	...
132.32	...	4067	4067	HotSpot 5X	...
...	...	...	...	...	...

Figure 8.6 An `equijoin` operation combines entries from two relations where values of specific attributes match.

a specified pair of attributes. More specifically, this is an example of an `equijoin`, because the condition for admitting an entry into the new relation is that two attribute values be equal. Figure 8.6 shows an example of an `equijoin`. The first two relations have been joined based on the `InstSN` and `SerialNo` attributes to form a list of the instruments used in the temperature measurements. (Instrument number 1019 was not used for any of the measurements, so it doesn't appear in the new relation.) As this example shows, the attributes used in the `join` need not have the same name. `Joins` can also be defined for other relationships between attributes in pairs of entries. The user may not be interested in all the attributes of the relation created by a `join`; in particular, an `equijoin` will create a relation with a pair of attributes whose values are equal for all entries. Therefore, a `join` is often followed by a `project`, which eliminates the unwanted attributes from the new relation.

SQL differs from languages like C, C++, and Fortran in that SQL programs specify tasks but not algorithms. In C, a program might select records (structs) from a relation by looping over an array or a linked list and explicitly examining the relevant fields. In SQL, the program simply directs the DBMS to retrieve the records matching certain criteria, and the DBMS figures out how to fulfill the request. This not only simplifies programming, it also gives the DBMS the flexibility to optimize its data access patterns. In the terminology of programming language design, SQL is a *declarative* language, and C, C++, and Fortran are *procedural* languages. Since SQL is designed specifically for database access and is not a general-purpose programming language, DBMSs provide ways to issue SQL queries from within programs written in other languages.

Mathematically, a relation is a set of records, not an ordered list, so a DBMS can store entries in whatever order it chooses. In particular, a DBMS can store the entries of a relation sorted by their primary key. Any database of significant size will occupy many disk blocks, and these blocks may not all fit in primary storage at once. To make searches more efficient, the DBMS can create a *clustered index*, which lists key values and their block numbers. Since the index usually occupies less space than the full relation, much (or all) of it can fit into primary storage, so the DBMS can search it for a particular key more efficiently than it can search the full relation. Since both the index and the entries on disk are sorted by the key values, not every key needs to appear in the index. Only the keys for entries at the beginning of a block are necessary; the DBMS can interpolate the block locations for other key values.

Users often want to find entries based on attributes other than the primary key. DBMSs can speed up these queries by creating a *secondary index*, which records the location of each entry for a corresponding set of attribute values. Unlike a clustered index, a secondary index cannot rely on interpolation to locate entries, so it must include every set of index values explicitly along with the exact location of the corresponding record. When the attribute values that form a secondary index are not unique for each record, various techniques are available to list all the entries that correspond to each index value.

Although an index could be implemented as a simple list of key values and record locations, DBMSs often use more sophisticated data structures, such as B-trees and their variants. These structures may occupy more space than a simple list, but they offer some important advantages over lists: B-trees and their variants reduce the number of disk accesses needed to find a particular key in an index, and they handle insertion and deletion of records more efficiently.

Most RDBMSs incorporate many features to ensure that data remains accurate and available. In particular, they implement a transactional model in which operations are guaranteed to be carried out atomically, so the actions of multiple concurrent users or the failure of hardware or software cannot corrupt the database. Since these DBMSs are often used in business applications where the loss or temporary unavailability of data would have a large monetary cost, I/O performance is usually secondary to integrity and availability in these systems. Scientific data may also have monetary value, but data integrity and availability tend to be less important than I/O performance in scientific applications. Also, scientific applications often write data once and then read it back many times, whereas business data is usually read and written repeatedly. For these reasons, a transactional model is often inappropriate for scientific data, and these differing design priorities are an important drawback to the use of standard RDBMSs for scientific data.

Object-Oriented DBMSs

For many emerging applications, such as very large scientific data sets and multimedia data, the relational data model is too limited. Object-oriented DBMSs (OODBMSs) use data models adapted from object-oriented programming to describe collections of data in sophisticated ways [8].

While RDBMSs use a query language to give users access to a database, applications using an OODBMS typically access data through extensions to an object-oriented programming language, such as C++ or Smalltalk. This gives users a great deal of flexibility in using objects, since they can manipulate data in any way that the programming language allows. You can think of an OODBMS as a system for creating persistent, out-of-core objects.

Attributes in the relational model have the standard numerical and character data types supported in most programming languages, as well as other predefined types, such as dates, times, and *blobs* (binary large objects). OODBMSs extend the standard data type system in several important ways.

First, records can be defined in terms of attributes whose types correspond more closely to objects in the real world. For example, a `TemperatureMeasurement` can be defined in terms of a `Position`, a `Time`, a `Temperature`, and a `Thermometer`. The `Position` can then be defined in terms of `Longitude`, `Latitude`, and `Elevation`, and the `Thermometer` can be defined in terms of a `SerialNumber`, a `Manufacturer`, and so on. Since several `TemperatureMeasurement` objects will use the same `Thermometer`, each measurement can use one of several `Thermometer` objects, just as in the relational database. At first, this hierarchical grouping of types may seem like a minor convenience at best, but in combination with other object-oriented features, it can be quite powerful.

A second important feature of the object-oriented model is that objects (i.e., records) can be "active"; that is, they can specify functionality as well as data. A trivial example would be for the `Temperature` object to be able to report its value in Celsius, Fahrenheit, or Kelvin units. A `Position` object could include functionality to compute its distance from another `Position`. Active objects like these open up many possibilities for sophisticated queries.

Thirdly, *inheritance* allows users to extend existing data models and to define families of record types (Figure 8.7). A *base type* defines a minimal set of attributes and functions that one or more *derived types* share and extend. For example, a database could have a `Measurement` type that included a `Position`, a `Time`, and an `Instrument`. From this base type, a collection of derived types could be defined, such

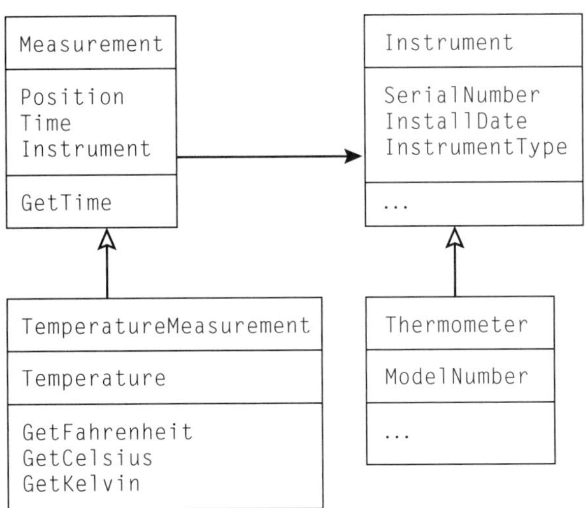

Figure 8.7 This partial collection of classes shows how data can be organized in an object-oriented schema. Each large box represents a class. The name of the class is at the top, followed by a list of attributes and then a list of *methods* (functions). Some methods have been omitted for brevity. The unfilled arrowheads indicate inheritance; the arrow with the solid head indicates a reference from one class to another.

as `TemperatureMeasurement`, `PressureMeasurement`, and `WindMeasurement`. Each would have all the attributes of a `Measurement` object plus additional attributes such as a `Temperature` or `BarometricPressure`. (Of course each of these measurements will use a different type of `Instrument`, so that type will also need to be extended to define the specific type of instrument used to collect the data.) The advantage of this arrangement is that objects can define some operations that apply to all objects with a common base type and others that apply only to specific derived types. For example, you could find all `Measurements` of any kind that were made at a particular elevation, or you could find all `TemperatureMeasurements` collected on a certain date.

These and other features of the object-oriented model help users define a database that more accurately reflects the organization of the world that the data is supposed to represent.

In the relational model, objects are identified by a primary key, as described above. For several reasons, the object-oriented model does not define primary keys. First, the complexity of the model can make it more difficult to identify a set of attributes whose values uniquely identify all objects. Second, since a primary key defines the identity of a record, if this key is modified, the record itself becomes a different object, and the DBMS may need to move it and update all the indices that refer to it. In an OODBMS, this would be very expensive, since objects can be quite large, and they may all have different sizes. Therefore, OODBMSs identify objects with unique *object identifiers* (OIDs), which do not change for the lifetime of the object (and in many systems are never reused for new objects). Users never need to see the value of an OID; they simply use them as references to the full object, much as C programs use pointers without ever displaying their value to the user. However, OIDs present their own set of challenges. OODBMSs are tightly coupled to the host programming language and must make the database appear as a seamless extension of primary storage. The OID plays the role of a pointer, but it is not literally a virtual memory location: it can never be reused and may reference an address space much larger than the operating system supports. To create the appearance of a large virtual store, the OODBMS must interact with the virtual memory system and cause it to treat the OID as a valid memory address.

The object-oriented model can often produce better I/O performance than an RDBMS for scientific applications. OODBMSs eliminate some transaction-oriented RDBMS operations, which are superfluous in scientific applications [113]. On the other hand, the lack of a specialized query language forces the programmer to specify how certain operations are implemented.

Object-Relational DBMSs

Despite their flexible data model, object-oriented databases have remained a minor part of the DBMS marketplace. Two reasons are their lack of standard interfaces and their focus on a persistent object model rather than a more traditional transaction processing model (although some OODBMSs do support transaction processing.) Some observers also believe that OODBMSs forego too many benefits of the relational model and fail to provide an easy transition path between the two models.

The object-relational DBMSs (ORDBMSs) [38] represent a compromise design. As the name suggests, these systems combine features of the other two data models, but current ORDBMSs have more in common with relational DBMSs than object-oriented DBMSs. They are less tightly coupled to procedural programming languages than OODBMSs, and they use relations as their basic data structure. Initial ORDBMS offerings from vendors support user-defined types in a more limited way than OODBMSs; in particular, many lack a rich inheritance mechanism. ORDBMSs differ from RDBMSs mainly in their extensibility. Users can insert code to perform specialized operations on data that is not stored in the database itself. For example, an ORDBMS can access a flat (i.e., nonrelational) file created by a scientific data library through *wrapper* functions supplied by the user. These functions let the DBMS view this external data in the relational model without incurring the cost of converting the flat file to a relational format and storing the data directly into the database. The resulting performance gains can be significant because even a sequential scientific data library often stores data at a higher rate than an RDBMS does. Also, the object-relational model gives the DBMS access to more complex data objects than the standard relational model. User-defined extensions allow the system to access and interact with sound and image data, for example. Plans for ORDBMSs, as laid out by various authors [38, 153], call for more sophisticated data models, similar to those supported by OODBMSs.

The object-relational data model is relatively new. A number of DBMS vendors support it, but its capabilities and limitations are not yet fully understood.

8.3.2 Scientific Data

Managing scientific data differs in important ways from managing business and other data. Pfaltz et al. [127] have pointed out three significant features of scientific data:

- The elements in a scientific data set are complex and highly interrelated. Neighboring points in a computational grid have much more in common with each other than, say, a group of names in an address book. The points in the grid are all really aspects of a larger physical phenomenon, while the names in an address book are usually independent of each other.
- Scientific databases are seldom transaction-oriented. Data is usually written once and then read repeatedly. Although parallel I/O libraries for scientific computing often support concurrent access by multiple tasks, managing this kind of concurrency is far simpler than, say, supporting thousands of users simultaneously updating an airline reservation database.
- Queries of scientific data often involve simultaneous selections over two or more separate ranges. An example of this type of query would be selecting temperature measurements taken between 1000 and 1500 meters whose value was between 25°C and 30°C on dates between 1 March and 30 June. (This type of query has also become common in business applications.)

These features, together with the very large size of many scientific databases, present unique requirements for DBMSs. The first point suggests that scientific databases can benefit from a flexible data model, such as the object-oriented model. The mismatch between common data structures used in scientific programs, most notably arrays, and the relational data model, has been cited as a major weakness of scientific databases [113]. A multidimensional array in Fortran or C naturally and implicitly records the fact that data items with sequential indices are adjacent to each other: array element `a(3,2,4)` is obviously "next to" element `a(4,2,4)`, and using the clustering techniques described in Chapter 6, an I/O system can store nearby array values in the same disk block. The relational model, on the other hand, cannot express adjacency in this way. Programs must store the array indices explicitly as attributes of a record, and to find neighboring entries, they must store explicit links to other records or search for records with array indices that differ from the current index by one along one dimension and by zero along all other dimensions. There is no guarantee that the DBMS will store these neighboring items together, so traversing an array can involve a significant amount of inefficient I/O.

On the positive side, the lack of transactions in scientific databases can eliminate the need for much of the database consistency checking and the locking protocols designed to keep multiple users from interfering with each other. Even if multiple users access a scientific database, they will usually all be reading it, so there is little danger that one user will find the data in an inconsistent state as a result of actions by another. Whether commercial RDBMSs can be made to operate more efficiently in light of these relaxed consistency requirements is an open question.

Finally, the frequent use of multidimensional range queries in both scientific and business databases calls for specialized query optimization techniques. DBMSs use these techniques to process requests more efficiently. Such techniques are akin to the out-of-core algorithms presented in Chapter 7. They focus on reducing the number of records that the DBMS must examine to complete the query and on minimizing the number of times that a particular block of records must be read from secondary storage.

Perhaps the greatest challenge for scientific database systems is to manage storage efficiently for very large data sets. Some data sets are too large to reside entirely in secondary storage, let alone primary storage. Therefore, a DBMS must account for the added cost of querying data on tertiary storage and carefully minimize the number of times each record is read. Many standard DBMSs try to optimize data access by controlling the reading and writing of disk blocks. These systems bypass the file system interfaces and the associated caching and buffering mechanisms, so the DBMS can access disk blocks directly. This allows the system to prefetch blocks intelligently and to ensure that critical data has reached nonvolatile (secondary or tertiary) storage when a transaction completes.

Parallel file systems and multilevel mass storage systems can mask low-level information that DBMSs need to manage storage efficiently and reliably. Designing efficient DBMSs for these storage systems has been a challenge. Brown et al. [20] proposed to improve the performance of database-style access to large, hierarchical storage systems by giving the DBMS more control over storage systems without exposing all their low-level details. They suggested an interface that presented a uniform view of different types of storage resources (Unix files, hierarchical storage systems, etc.) The interface also lets the application pass in information about future access patterns and recommended caching and buffering actions.

This system was never implemented, but Choudhary et al. [29] have designed a similar system. Their programming interface lets applications negotiate with hierarchical storage systems through a standard set of hints. These hints fall into two categories: layout directives and access pattern directives. Layout directives tell the storage system how and where to store data. For example, a program can request that data be migrated to tape or striped over a set of disks in a particular way. Access pattern directives work at a higher level. They tell the storage system what kinds of requests to expect in the future so the system can determine for itself how to optimize these requests. Layout requests instruct the system to take a particular action, and the system will comply if it is able to do so. Access pattern requests are advisory; the system is free to respond to them however it sees fit. One advantage of the higher-level requests is that the system can evaluate them in combination with access pattern directives from other applications and try to optimize performance globally.

The Storage Resource Broker (Section 8.1.3) takes a similar approach. It presents a uniform programming interface to a variety of storage systems, including Unix-like file systems, archival storage systems like HPSS, and DBMSs. Applications can connect to the SRB over a network and access data using either a Unix-like programming interface or an interface that supports `gets` and `puts` on individual objects.

Choudhary's interface and the SRB represent yet another kind of programming interface for accessing scientific data, with a different set of goals from the interfaces described in the last three chapters. Instead of focusing on how to manage parallel transfers or how to record scientific data conveniently, they present a simple view of a complex and heterogeneous set of storage resources. However, they include enough expressive power to help applications access data efficiently. Although they obviously allow applications to store data, these interfaces are more concerned with helping applications retrieve data.

8.3.3 Example Applications

Several projects are under way that use databases to store and manage very large scientific data sets. The examples presented here manage data from several disciplines, including astronomy, high energy physics, and medical imaging. Two of these examples use the object-oriented data model because it is more expressive than the relational model. The object-relational model is not widely used for scientific data, although this may change as the software matures. A third example uses custom software designed to optimize a specific class of queries.

In the object-oriented examples, the databases store very large numbers of relatively small records. Some researchers are considering scientific databases that will contain a small number of very large records, where a record might be a complete computational grid and the data that a simulation code generates on it. However, work on these databases has not progressed as far as the work using smaller records.

Sloan Digital Sky Survey

The Sloan Digital Sky Survey (SDSS) [156] is an effort to create an electronic catalog of celestial objects. Over five years, the project expects to collect more than 40 TB of data from a dedicated telescope. This data will represent more than 200 million objects, each with about 500 attributes.

A particular challenge will be supporting a wide range of multidimensional queries. The planned architecture has a three-level hierarchy consisting of a user interface, a query engine, and a data warehouse. Queries posed through the user interface are evaluated by the query engine and restructured into a query execution tree. This tree represents an expression consisting of subqueries and logical operators. Suboperations within this tree can be executed in parallel on the servers that compose the data warehouse. The system is built on a commercial object-oriented DBMS, but the designers expect to do considerable custom development.

The system will construct indices to execute common queries efficiently, and the system will also support complex queries involving geometric relationships. For example, a user might pose a query that involves finding two or more objects within a certain distance of each other. Finding such objects is more difficult than finding all points within a specified range because the latter type of query can be satisfied by examining the position along each dimension separately. For a standard DBMS, finding entries with attributes x and y that satisfy

$$(X_1 \leq x \leq X_2) \wedge (Y_1 \leq y \leq Y_2)$$

(where X_1, X_2, Y_1, and Y_2 are fixed values) is straightforward, but finding pairs of entries that satisfy

$$\sqrt{(x_1 - x_2)^2 + (y_1 - y_2)^2} \leq D$$

is not. A brute-force approach would require the system to examine every pair of objects in the database. Fortunately, the system can eliminate much of the work by grouping objects according to their location. It can place all objects from the same region of the sky in a single container, and the containers can be organized in a hierarchical data structure. Then finding objects within a specified distance involves searching only those objects in a particular set of containers.

Even with these optimizations, some queries will need to scan all the data. The designers of the SDSS database propose two techniques for handling these queries. First, a scan machine will continuously scan the entire database, evaluating all pending user queries as it goes. The designers estimate that by the time the database is complete in 2004, a relatively inexpensive system built from commodity hardware available then could complete a scan in about 12 seconds. Second, for more complex queries, a hash machine will gather data with related attributes (geometric or otherwise) into "buckets" and then continue the query evaluation in parallel on each bucket. The idea is that each bucket will contain all the relevant objects for its portion of the query, so little communication between buckets will be necessary. Some objects may be distributed to multiple buckets.

In all cases, the queries will have to be implemented so that different portions of a request can be pipelined: each phase of a data evaluation algorithm must begin before the preceding phase is complete. Not only does this improve parallelism, it avoids the need to store and retrieve large intermediate data sets.

CERN/SLAC Database

Two high energy physics laboratories—the European Laboratory for Particle Physics (known by its French acronym, CERN) and the Stanford Linear Accelerator Center (SLAC)—are collaborating on a database project to store results from collider experiments [46, 64]. At SLAC, a long-term project called BaBar, begun in 1999, is expected to generate 2 PB of data over 10 years. CERN is building a new Large Hadron Collider (LHC) that is expected to enter service in 2005. It will generate 100 PB of data over 20 years.

The collaboration has chosen initially to store data using a commercial object-oriented DBMS called Objectivity/DB. The system has been specially modified by its vendor and SLAC to work with the HPSS archival storage system, since it was deemed impractical to store the expected volume of data only in secondary storage.

Objectivity/DB uses a client-server model. Much of the DBMS's computation and data manipulation takes place on the client. To read data, it issues simple requests for blocks of data to one or more servers. In the initial implementation, the server retrieved data directly from HPSS. However, this design performed poorly because while the DBMS tends to access data in blocks of no more than 64 KB, HPSS performs optimally only for much larger transfer sizes, about 1 MB or more. Part of the reason for the bias toward large transfers is the third-party transfer mechanism that HPSS uses. Although it permits very high transfer rates once a connection has been established between a data source and destination, setting up this connection incurs a long latency that cannot easily be amortized over short transfers.

To alleviate this performance mismatch, the CERN/SLAC group added a layer of secondary storage between the DBMS and HPSS. This layer acts as a very large data cache. When the DBMS requests data from the server that is not resident in the secondary storage layer, the software automatically stages the data from HPSS.

A large portion of data is moved during each staging operation so that HPSS can perform well. Once the data is in the secondary storage layer, the DBMS can access it in smaller blocks more efficiently.

The client-server model helps Objectivity/DB scale up its performance as the I/O load increases because the system can use multiple servers. Although HPSS keeps a master copy of the data, several secondary storage servers can cache copies of data that is in high demand. If one server becomes heavily loaded, another copy of the data can be staged to a different server, which can then take on some of the load. This is possible because once data has been stored in the database, it is very rarely changed. Consequently, nearly all accesses are read-only, so the system does not need an elaborate and potentially costly coherence protocol.

The largest database tested so far with this system is 1 TB. Data rates up to 150 MB/sec have been observed, and the system has supported about 200 users concurrently reading data.

An important challenge for this project is keeping the technology current over its anticipated lifetime. The CERN LHC won't come online until nearly 10 years after the project was begun, and its DBMS must continue operating for another 20 years after that. Since it is impossible to anticipate the evolution of database systems over that period of time, the designers of the CERN/SLAC database have tried to keep their options open as much as possible. Indeed, their choice of the DBMS on which their system is based is only provisional; they expect to reevaluate it in 2001. They are also preparing for the possibility of having to develop a DBMS themselves if no commercial system meets their needs. These potential technological changes, more than mammoth data sizes and high transfer rates, present the greatest challenges to the project.

Active Data Repository

The Active Data Repository (ADR) [90] is a project at the University of Maryland that is developing software to manage multidimensional scientific data. Example applications include medical imaging, satellite observations, and scientific simulations. The common feature of the data sets is that each comprises a collection of values over a region of space. The basic problem that the ADR addresses is this: given an input data set with a specified range of locations and an aggregation function, compute an output data set. The aggregation function carries out some user-specified computation on collections of input data points, and a mapping function assigns input data points to regions of the output data set. It may assign many input locations to a single output location or one input to many outputs. In general, the output data set is smaller than the input, but both are too large to fit in main memory.

Input data is partitioned into "chunks," which contain one or more input data records. The system tries to assign records for nearby regions of space to the same chunk. As part of the data preprocessing step, the system computes an index of the chunks so that it can rapidly find records meeting specified range criteria. The chunks are stored on disks connected to the nodes of a parallel computer. To compute an output data set, the system divides the expected output region into contiguous "tiles" that are small enough to fit into memory. For each tile, the system reads input chunks and carries out the aggregation operation to compute the output for that tile, then it writes the tile to disk and proceeds to work on another tile. The input chunks needed to compute a tile do not necessarily reside on a disk that is attached to the node where the tile is being computed. Therefore, one of the challenges for the ADR is to determine a method for assigning work to the processors that balances memory usage with interprocess communication. One option is to reserve memory for each active tile on all the processors. Each processor reads its local input chunks to generate partial tile data, and then the partial tiles are combined in a global merge step. This approach minimizes interprocess communication at the outset of the computation for each tile, but it can waste memory, and it requires communication to combine the partial tiles. A variation on this method reserves space for tiles only on the nodes where input chunks for those tiles reside. An alternative approach is to assign each tile only to the node where it will be stored on disk. The system must then determine what input chunks will be needed on each node, read them, and forward them as appropriate. This approach conserves memory but requires more processing before each tile is generated. Experiments with various types of data found that no strategy always worked best, although the first and second were frequently better and never much worse than the third.

The ADR uses nonblocking techniques to overlap the aggregation computation with communication and I/O. It tightly integrates I/O with computation in order to avoid copying data between I/O buffers and computation buffers.

8.4 KDD and Data Mining

Standard database-style queries work best when the user is looking for something specific and can describe the request precisely. In a catalog of celestial images, "find all objects of color *C*" is a simple, specific query. "Find all objects that look like galaxies" is a query that is beyond the abilities of a standard database. Even more challenging is "find unusually shaped objects that warrant further study."

The terms *knowledge discovery in databases* (KDD) and *data mining* are often used interchangeably, but a more precise definition holds that KDD "is the nontrivial process of identifying valid, novel, potentially useful, and ultimately understandable patterns in data," while data mining "is a step in the KDD process consisting of applying computational techniques that . . . produce a particular enumeration of patterns (or models) over the data" [50]. In other words, KDD is an interactive and iterative process that involves both human skill and computation, and data mining is a set of computational techniques used in KDD.

Data mining techniques are used in many kinds of applications, such as analyzing consumer purchases, detecting credit card fraud, and recognizing speech. They are also used in a variety of scientific disciplines. The problems that data mining techniques address fall into three categories: classification, association rule discovery, and clustering. Algorithms in all these areas have been studied widely and tuned for specific applications. The next sections introduce techniques used in each of these three areas.

Initial versions of the algorithms were designed for in-core processing on sequential computers. As scientific users have brought these techniques to bear on their enormous data sets, it has been necessary to adapt some algorithms to work with out-of-core data and on parallel computers.

8.4.1 Classification

Classification consists of placing records into a predefined set of categories based on the data they contain. (Clustering, described in Section 8.4.3, is similar but does not use predefined categories.) The basic approach is this: given a set of records containing certain predictor attributes, determine the value of a dependent attribute (i.e., a classification). If the dependent attribute is a numeric value, the problem is called *regression;* otherwise, the problem is called *classification.*

Examples of classification problems abound in scientific data analysis: finding quasars in sky surveys, tracking vortices in fluid dynamics data, identifying tumors in medical images, and so on. In some cases, the user wants to categorize each record into one of a fixed set of bins. In others, a program might search a large collection of "uninteresting" data to find a specific unusual pattern. In both cases, the computer can do a significant amount of preprocessing and then present to the user a manageable collection of data records for further analysis.

Classification techniques generally use a training set of data. The user inputs a collection of records, each of which contains values for predictor attributes and a corresponding dependent attribute. The classification algorithm must then determine how to derive dependent attribute values from the predictor attributes based on these examples. This analysis can be done in many ways. A common technique is to construct a decision tree, in which each interior node evaluates one of the

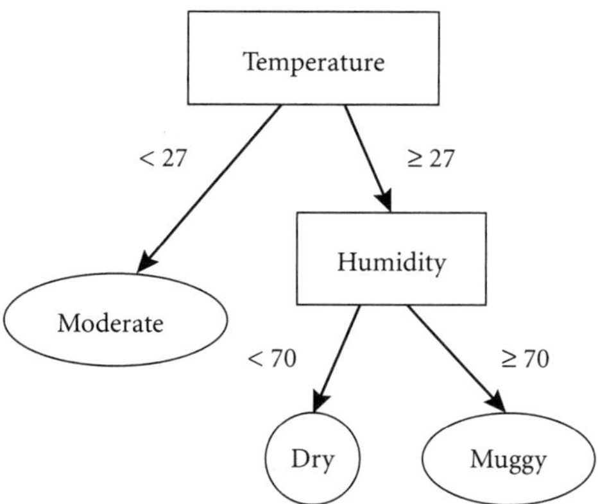

Temperature (°C)	Humidity (%)	Description
28	85	muggy
15	90	moderate
20	40	moderate
27	30	dry
30	70	muggy

Figure 8.8 This simple decision tree classifies temperature and humidity data (the predictor attributes) as a verbal description (the dependent attribute). The table below the decision tree is the training set on which the tree was based. (This tree was constructed by hand, not by a computer algorithm.)

attributes and each edge represents the outcome of an evaluation. The leaf nodes represent the possible dependent attribute values (Figure 8.8).

Of course, the main challenge is constructing the decision tree. Once the tree is built, new records can be classified easily. The general technique for building a decision tree is to select one of the predictor attributes and a *splitting criterion.* A splitting criterion is a logical predicate that partitions the records into two groups. Applying this criterion removes one of the predictor attributes from consideration. In each group, another predictor attribute and splitting criterion are chosen, and this process continues until a tree has been built that contains a unique path to one leaf node for any possible set of predictor attribute values [55].

Now the question is how to choose an attribute and splitting criterion at each step of the algorithm. Many techniques have been proposed; their goal is to make a choice that maximizes distinctions between the two resulting groups.

Preparing data for use in a decision tree requires a preprocessing step known as *feature extraction.* This is the process of decomposing complex records into a set of basic components. Choosing a good set of components can be quite difficult, and it requires human expertise. The problem amounts to answering questions like "What features distinguish a human face from a dog's face?" A feature set should be small, and the features are often, though not always, orthogonal. In some cases, the most useful attributes for constructing a decision tree (the ones that best predict the dependent attribute) do not appear in the original data. Instead, they may be computed from a combination of existing attributes, such as the ratio of two distances.

Exactly what constitutes a feature depends on the data being classified. If the records are a set of images, the features might include a straight line at a certain location, a dark blob of a particular shape, and so on. Once a feature set has been defined, each record to be classified can be decomposed into a *feature vector,* a list of coefficients indicating the strength of each feature in the data. This feature vector becomes the set of predictor attributes for the classification algorithm.

For some applications, it may be difficult to determine the "ground truth" classifications. A human expert might not be certain whether an image represents a particular object. Two human experts given the same data to classify might reach different conclusions. In this situation, a classification algorithm cannot be expected to do better than one of the experts.

8.4.2 Association Rule Discovery

It is often useful to find combinations of attribute values that occur together in a database. If the user knows in advance the attributes in question, it's a simple matter to query the database for records that contain a given combination. The more difficult problem is to find *unknown* combinations of attribute values, which can represent interesting and novel correlations.

Retail stores use this technique to study customers' buying patterns. They want to discover what combinations of items customers often buy together. (The classic, possibly apocryphal, example is that people often buy diapers and beer at the same time.) Observations about the frequent occurrence of items together in a data set are called *association rules.*

A simple formulation of the problem of finding association rules is this: Consider a set of items, $\mathcal{I}$, (e.g., all products sold in a store) and a collection of transactions, $\mathcal{T}$, each of which includes a subset of the items in $\mathcal{I}$. The task is to find itemsets, $\mathcal{X}$, (where $\mathcal{X} \subset \mathcal{I}$) among the transactions such that the proportion of transactions that include $\mathcal{X}$ is at least some threshold value. This proportion, s, is called the *support* of $\mathcal{X}$ in $\mathcal{T}$.

A naïve approach to this problem would be to find all possible itemsets in $\mathcal{I}$ and count the occurrences of each one in $\mathcal{T}$. This would be extremely expensive, since the number of possible itemsets is $2^{|\mathcal{I}|} - 1$. Fortunately, there are better solutions.

The standard technique for finding association rules is the Apriori algorithm [2]. It relies on the observation that an itemset $\mathcal{X} = \{x_1, x_2, \ldots, x_n\}$ cannot have support greater than s unless each of its components x_i also has support greater than s. Therefore, to find all two-element itemsets with a given level of support, you begin by finding all single-item itemsets with that level of support. The algorithm need only consider combinations of these single-item sets. When all two-item itemsets with the required support have been found, the algorithm can consider three-item itemsets that consist of combinations of one-item and two-item itemsets with the specified support.

In principle, the number of sets considered using this technique is not necessarily less than the $2^{|\mathcal{I}|} - 1$ sets considered by the brute-force method. It is possible that every combination of items has the required support, in which case Apriori will consider all these combinations. Of course in practice, this would rarely happen. Few customers go to a store and buy one of everything! However, if the requested level of support is set too low, many more combinations of items will be considered than for higher thresholds. Not only will setting the minimum level of support too low cause the algorithm to run longer, it is likely to produce a great deal of useless information, since it will capture many rare and probably meaningless associations.

The Apriori algorithm has the disadvantage that it requires many passes over the data. Each time the size of the candidate itemset is increased by one, the algorithm must scan all transactions to see if the new candidates are present in each transaction. However, the Apriori algorithm can be parallelized relatively easily. Transactions can be partitioned among the processes, and each process can evaluate the same candidate itemsets on its local data. The processes can then exchange information on the local levels of support for these candidates to determine which ones meet the requirement globally.

A more general version of this technique finds association rules of the form "Given that an itemset contains a set of items $\mathcal{X}$, the probability is c that it also contains an additional item y." This rule can be written more compactly as $\mathcal{X} \Rightarrow y \mid c$. For example, a store might want to know how often a transaction that includes beer and diapers also includes milk. Again, the support s indicates the frequency of the association in $\mathcal{T}$. The basic association problem discussed above is a special case of this general version. If y is an item in an itemset $\mathcal{Y}$ for a simple association, and $\mathcal{X} = \mathcal{Y} - y$, then saying that $\mathcal{Y}$ has support s in $\mathcal{T}$ is equivalent to saying that $\mathcal{X} \Rightarrow y \mid 1$ with support s in $\mathcal{T}$. General-form associations can easily be found given a collection of simple associations: dividing the support of $\mathcal{Y}$ by the support of $\mathcal{X}$ yields c for $\mathcal{X} \Rightarrow y \mid c$ and $\mathcal{X} = \mathcal{Y} - y$.

Association rules have potential applications well beyond retail databases. Discovering previously unsuspected associations is a very powerful tool in nearly all areas of science. A data management system that could automatically find an association between certain genetic patterns and a predisposition for an illness would be enormously valuable. Likewise, a system managing climate data could find associations like the El Niño effect, in which elevated ocean temperatures in one part of the world are correlated with specific unusual weather patterns elsewhere. The difficulty in such applications is that the scientific data in which such associations could be discovered is often incomplete and not in a form that is easily mined. To discover the genetic associations automatically, the database would have to contain a considerable amount of genetic information on many people, along with their medical histories. In the El Niño example, the association spans a period of time; the unusual weather patterns appear several months after the elevated ocean temperatures are observed, so the causal relationship is less apparent.

8.4.3 Clustering

The goal in *clustering* is to partition a collection of records into groups of "similar" records. The criterion for similarity depends of course on the nature of the data. Examples include searching a database for customers with similar shopping habits or forming images of celestial objects from individual points of light in a telescope image. The number of clusters may or may not be specified in advance. Clustering is similar to classification in that both techniques assign individual records to one of several categories, which may have sharp or fuzzy boundaries. The difference between the two is that in clustering, the dependent attribute values are unspecified. It is up to the algorithm to define them.

Most clustering techniques use some kind of distance metric that represents the difference between pairs of records. For image data, the distance may correspond to the planar distance between two pixels. For other types of data, you can define a feature vector and compute the Cartesian distance between two records based on the coefficients in the vectors.

Clustering algorithms work in one of two directions: some start with all the records in the same cluster and then proceed to subdivide them, while others initially place each record in its own cluster and then merge them. In both cases, it is impractical to consider every possible assignment of records to clusters. Instead, the algorithms use some kind of heuristic to produce a candidate assignment and then assess its quality using an objective criterion, such as minimizing the mean square distance between each record and the "centroid" of the cluster to which it belongs. Optimization methods that solve this kind of problem are widely studied. They include genetic algorithms, simulated annealing, and hill climbing. Fortunately, most of these methods are quite amenable to parallelization.

One problem with using the mean distances to the cluster centroids as an objective measure is that it favors compact, centralized clusters. This may be appropriate for many applications, but some interesting clusters have more complicated shapes.

Therefore, some clustering algorithms use alternative metrics, such as the distance between neighboring records in a cluster rather than the distance to the centroid. This approach avoids penalizing candidate clusters that have significant extent. More sophisticated techniques balance a number of distance metrics to identify unpredicted and complex shapes in data [86].

8.4.4 Interactive Knowledge Discovery

As noted earlier, KDD is supposed to be an iterative, interactive activity. A user cannot expect to gain complete insight into a data set with a single, well-chosen run of a data mining algorithm. Knowledge discovery can be seen as a sequence of four steps: data collection, data preparation, data analysis, and data interpretation. (Some experts specify these steps differently, but the basic process is the same.) The data collection phase consists of either gathering data empirically or computing it in a simulation. Data preparation includes several application-specific operations, such as "cleaning" data (removing obviously incorrect data, filtering out artifacts due to the sampling or computation method, etc.) and converting data into a form that subsequent analysis and interpretation steps can use (e.g., locating objects within an image, feature extraction). Data analysis uses the data mining techniques described above. These operations are at the heart of computer-aided knowledge discovery, but they can only find *candidate* information of interest. The final step, data interpretation, requires the expertise of a human specialist to determine the meaning and significance of the data.

Many data analysis operations require long running times for large data sets. A user may wait hours for a result, only to find that the question was ill-posed (for example, a minimum support threshold was set too low in an association rule algorithm).

Several projects have investigated the use of statistical and random sampling techniques to estimate results quickly for what would otherwise be lengthy computations. For example, the Control project [68], which includes both academic and industrial researchers, is developing data mining tools and algorithms that allow users to work more interactively. This will let them cut off unproductive analysis runs before they finish and focus computing resources on the most promising areas. The project team notes that they are not necessarily reducing the time to completion for the analysis techniques; instead they are developing ways to provide partial results sooner.

The techniques that the Control project is developing range from simple user interface improvements to new versions of data mining algorithms.

On the user interface side, the group is developing various display methods that show partial results of analyses as they run. They are also creating spreadsheet-style tools that let users browse through portions of a database. A standard spreadsheet would not have the capacity or processing power to manage a very large data set, but a spreadsheet interface to a DBMS can show the user only a portion of the data and update that visible portion first in response to user requests. Other processing on the remainder of the data set can continue in the background while the user examines the data in the window.

In the area of algorithms, the group has developed a new technique for finding association rules. This technique presents ongoing information on the support for various itemsets, complete with confidence bounds. The user can also change the requested support threshold during the initial phase of the algorithm.

The key idea behind the association rule algorithm and other techniques developed by the Control project is random sampling of data. Their data mining tools progressively retrieve and process records, so they can initially produce a rough estimate of the final result and then refine it as new records are evaluated. The group also applies this technique to standard database query operations (`select`, `join`, etc.) so that tools can display partial results. Users can direct the analysis process to focus first on records of greatest interest. For example, in a `select` operation, the user can ask to see records meeting certain additional criteria first (e.g., data visible in the current window of a spreadsheet or records with a particular attribute value).

These interactive techniques are still under development, but as data sizes continue to grow, it seems likely such methods will be necessary to make interactive knowledge discovery practical.

8.5 Summary

This section has looked briefly at a variety of techniques for organizing and understanding large data sets. When applications generate thousands of individual files, users often need help sorting through them and finding the information they need. This help can be as simple as a directory browsing tool or as complex as a metadata database, which stores descriptive or summary information about the contents of each file in a collection.

A step beyond these techniques is to store the data itself in a database management system, which then allows users to pose queries directly on the data. Although commercial software packages are available that can handle very large databases, scientific data presents some unique challenges, including the complexity of the relationships between data items and the complexity of the queries over the data.

The greatest challenge in data management is using computers to help automate the process of discovering interesting information within a large data set. This is an area of active research for scientific applications and for commercial and other uses.

8.6 Further Reading

Metadata and data indexing is such a broad topic that it is difficult to point out just a few references that cover the field. Books and articles on database technology are a good starting point. There is also a conference series, the IEEE Meta-Data Conference, whose proceedings present a range of projects that produce and use metadata. A survey article by Samet [140] describes some hierarchical data models.

Database technology, especially the relational model, is covered well in many textbooks. Elmasri and Navathe's book [48] was helpful in preparing this chapter, and there are many other good choices. OODBMSs and ORDBMSs are usually covered less thoroughly than RDBMSs in basic textbooks. A good definition of the OODBMS model appears in a paper by Atkinson et al. [8], "The Object-Oriented Database System Manifesto." This 1989 paper helped initiate a debate in the database community about the proper evolutionary direction for DBMSs. A response presenting a more conservative point of view appeared in the "Third Generation Database Management System Manifesto" [32], by a group called the Committee for Advanced DBMS Function (which included a number of prominent DBMS researchers). Then Darwen and Date [38] published "The Third Manifesto," which aimed for a middle ground. It proposed evolutionary changes to the relational model, but rejected SQL. Stonebraker, one of the "Third Generation" authors, argues for the object-relational model in a subsequent book [153], and Date and Darwen [40] have also published a book on ORDBMSs. It is not clear which model will prevail. Which model is best for large scientific databases is a separate question; Musick and Critchlow [113] describe some of the considerations.

Several survey papers discuss data mining techniques from different perspectives. Ganti et al. [55] describe the basic techniques mentioned here, mainly using examples from commercial databases and noting the scaling issues that arise for very large databases. The paper appears in a special issue of *Computer* devoted to data mining. Fayyad [50] covers many of the same techniques in the context of scientific data. Another version of that paper [51] appears in a special issue of *Communications of the ACM* on data mining; the latter includes several case studies. Finally, a book chapter by Kamath and Musick [84] discusses parallelization issues for data mining algorithms.

Glossary

Boldfaced terms in definitions are also defined in this glossary.

Access control list (ACL) A list of users and their access privileges that a **file system** assigns to files and directories.

Access time In a storage device, the time to move the first unit of data after a read or write request is issued. For disk drives, access time includes **latency** and **seek time.**

Address space A range of (usually numeric) names of storage locations in memory or a file.

Ad hoc query In a database management system (**DBMS**), a request to search for data based on a combination of parameters that was not anticipated in the design of the application. Such requests are usually inefficient.

AFS (1) Andrew File System. A research **distributed file system.** (2) A commercial distributed file system based on the Andrew File System—this definition is not an acronym but uses the initials "AFS" only.

Areal density The theoretical number of **bits** per unit area on a storage medium, equal to **track density** times **linear density.**

Association rule discovery In **data mining,** the automated process of finding items that frequently appear together in a set of transactions or **records.**

Asynchronous checkpoint A **checkpoint** operation initiated by a timer or other asynchronous event.

Asynchronous I/O I/O that proceeds concurrently with the computation that uses it.

Attribute In an **RDBMS,** one of the fields in a **relation,** such as a surname or a telephone number in an address book.

Backing store In **virtual memory,** the **secondary storage** space that holds the data.

Bandwidth In networking and storage devices, a synonym for **transfer rate.**

Base space In a **fiber bundle,** the mesh of data points on which the **fibers** are defined.

Bit Binary digit, equal to 0 or 1.

Blobs Binary large objects. In a traditional **database,** these can be difficult to store and index efficiently.

Block The basic unit of storage for a file. Blocks consist of one or more disk **sectors.** Typical block sizes range from 512 **bytes** to 64 KB.

Block distribution A **data decomposition** pattern in which one dimension of a multidimensional array is split into approximately equal, contiguous segments.

Buffering A collection of techniques used in networking and I/O. Data is temporarily saved in an intermediate location before it is moved to its final destination. Buffering can improve performance in various ways, most notably by gathering small pieces of data into large ones.

Bus A data transmission medium that is shared among two or more components in a computer.

BXFM A research file system for **cluster computers.**

Byte A unit of data. In modern computers, equal to eight **bits.**

Cache A region of memory (sometimes high performance memory) that stores frequently used data or data that is expected to be used soon. Caches replicate a portion of an **address space** whose contents are stored in a slower storage medium, such as main memory or secondary storage.

Cache coherence Maintaining identical copies of data in separate **caches** or in a cache and the **address space** it replicates.

Cache coherence unit The smallest unit of data managed by a **cache coherence** protocol. A change to any value within this unit is viewed as a change to the entire unit.

Callback function A function defined by an application that lower-level software calls to carry out some user-defined portion of an operation.

Capacity The amount of data that a storage device can hold.

CFS Concurrent File System. A **parallel file system** developed by Intel for its parallel computers; replaced by **PFS.**

Checkpoint A snapshot of the state of a **process** that is sufficient to allow the process to resume execution from the point the checkpoint was recorded.

Chunked array A multidimensional array that is divided into rectangular chunks such that all the data from each chunk is stored together in a file. In contrast to **row-major** or **column-major** storage, chunked arrays can be accessed reasonably efficiently along any dimension.

Classification In **data mining,** the automated process of assigning **records** to one of several predefined categories based on their contents.

Client-based collective I/O **Collective I/O** techniques in which the **compute nodes** rearrange data among themselves to form more efficient access requests.

Client buffering In a **parallel** or **distributed file system, buffering** data on a **compute node.**

Cluster computer A parallel computer built from separate, stand-alone computers.

Clustered index In a **DBMS,** an index that maps **keys** to the **blocks** in which the corresponding **records** are stored. (Compare to a **secondary index,** which stores the location of a record within a block.)

Clustering In **data mining,** the automatic partitioning of **records** into groups with similar characteristics. Unlike **classification** algorithms, clustering algorithms are not given a fixed set of groups in advance.

Coarse-grained access Access to large, contiguous chunks of data.

Cold swapping Replacing a failed hardware component (such as a disk drive in a **RAID** system) when the system is powered off.

Collective buffering A **client-based collective I/O** technique.

Collective I/O A class of I/O optimization techniques that merge read or write requests from multiple **processes** in a parallel program to form requests that can be carried out more efficiently.

Column-major order A data layout pattern for multidimensional arrays in which array elements with the same rightmost index are stored together.

Compute node In a **distributed memory** parallel computer, a **node** that runs application code.

Concurrency control Ensuring that concurrent accesses by multiple tasks to the same file produce correct results.

Consistent checkpoint **Checkpoint** from multiple **processes** in a parallel **job** that represents a valid state of the whole computation.

Copper In networking, any transmission medium that carries electrical signals over metallic wires.

CPU Central Processing Unit. The main computational engine in a computer.

Crossbar A switch that creates direct, exclusive paths between pairs of communicating devices.

CXFS Cluster XFS. A parallel file system based on SGI's **XFS.**

Cyclic distribution A **data decomposition** pattern in which data along one dimension of a multidimensional array are decomposed in **round-robin** order.

Cylinder In a disk drive, a group of **tracks** on different disk surfaces that are at equal radial distance from the center of the disks.

Database A collection of related data, usually organized in a form that allows searching and manipulation of individual data **records.**

Data decomposition Separation of a data structure into parts for assignment to **tasks** in a parallel program or stripes in a file.

Data mining A collection of computational techniques that help automate knowledge discovery in databases (**KDD**).

Data model The definition of the data types and data structures that an I/O programming interface manipulates directly.

Data sieving An optimization technique for **discontiguous accesses.** For read accesses, a contiguous unit of data is read, and the requested items are extracted from it. For writes, a **read-modify-write** sequence is used.

DBMS Database management system. Software that creates and maintains a **database.**

Declustering In a file system, the separation of a file into pieces that are stored separately, allowing parallel access.

Delayed write An optimization technique in which a file system **buffers** data from write requests and then sends it to **external memory** at a later time. This can smooth out bursty request patterns.

Demand paging The standard technique for implementing **virtual memory.** When a program requests data from a **page** that is not in **primary storage,** the page is read from **secondary storage.**

DFS Distributed File System. A commercial **distributed file system.**

Differential See **double-ended.**

Discontiguous access Access to data that resides in nonadjacent portions of an **address space.**

Disk-directed I/O (DDIO) A type of **server-based collective I/O.**

Distributed file system A type of **file system** that makes a collection of files available to multiple computers or **compute nodes.** It does not necessarily support efficient concurrent access to the same file by different processes.

Distributed memory computer A type of parallel computer in which multiple **compute nodes** each have a separate memory **address space.**

Distributed shared memory (DSM) computer A parallel computer with multiple compute nodes that presents a single shared **address space** to applications.

DMA Direct Memory Access. Hardware that moves data between components in a computer with minimal intervention by the **CPU.**

Domain In a disk drive, a single region on a disk surface that is magnetized with one of two polarities. **Bits** of data are encoded in the transitions between these magnetized regions.

Double buffering An **asynchronous I/O** technique in which two memory buffers are used: one holds data being read or written by a computation in progress, while the other is used as the source or destination of an I/O operation. When the computation and I/O operation are complete, the buffers exchange roles.

Double-ended A type of electrical connection in a network that uses a separate pair of wires for each signal line. It uses more wires than **single-ended** systems but is less susceptible to electrical noise and therefore supports longer **extents.**

Exa Prefix meaning 10^{18} or 2^{60}.

Extent In a network, the maximum distance that the communication medium can carry a signal between two directly connected devices.

External memory **Secondary** and **tertiary storage.**

False sharing In **cache coherence** protocols, an undesirable effect that occurs when different **tasks** repeatedly access separate data items in the same **cache coherence unit.** This causes needless communication or serialization because the coherence protocol fails to recognize that the accesses don't interfere with each other.

Feature extraction In **classification** algorithms, the decomposition of complex **records** into a set of basic features that allow the records to be identified as similar to or different from each other.

Fiber (1) In networking, a strand of transparent material that carries pulses of light representing data. (2) In a **fiber bundle,** the range of legal values for a specific point in the **base space.**

Fiber bundle A **data model** for representing complex scientific data.

Fiber bundle section In a **fiber bundle,** a set of values consisting of one legal value for each fiber in a **base space.**

Fibre Channel A collection of standards defining a network often used in **SANs.** The standard describes a variety of communication media (both **copper** and **fiber**) and communication protocols.

File allocation table (FAT) A data structure used in Microsoft's MS-DOS **file system** to keep track of disk **blocks.**

File descriptor A value (usually an integer) assigned by a **file system** to refer to an open file. Programs use this value in calls to read, write, or otherwise interact with the file.

File offset The numeric address of a location in a file.

File pointer A variable maintained by a **file system** that contains the **file offset** of the next location to be accessed in an open file.

File system Software that manages a collection of files. (This term is sometimes used to refer to a specific collection of files.)

Fine-grained access Accessing a file with many requests for small amounts of data.

FLOP Floating-point operation; for example, addition or multiplication of two floating-point numbers.

Foreign key In an **RDBMS,** an **attribute** in a **relation** that can be used as a **key** for another relation in the **database.**

Format The organization of the recorded area of a disk or tape into **tracks, sectors,** and so on; also, the data stored by a **file system** on a disk that helps it organize these lower-level structures into files and directories.

GFS Global File System. A research file system for **cluster computers.**

Giga Prefix meaning 10^9 or 2^{30}.

GPFS General Parallel File System. Developed by IBM for its parallel computers; based on **Tiger Shark** and a successor to **PIOFS.**

GSN Global Scalable Network. A major revision of the **HIPPI** standard that improves performance and permits multiple **tasks** to use a network link concurrently.

HDF Hierarchical Data Format. An I/O library with a sophisticated **data model,** designed for storing and managing scientific data.

HDF5 Version 5 of the **HDF** library.

Head In a magnetic disk or tape drive, the device that transforms magnetic impulses to electric impulses, or vice versa.

Helical scan A type of tape recording system in which the tape moves across a rotating drum that carries the **heads.** This allows high **transfer rates** with low tape speeds.

Hidden Markov model (HMM) A technique for predicting the future behavior of a system based on past behavior.

Hierarchical data model A **data model** that stores descriptions or approximations of a larger underlying data set. It may also store the underlying data set itself.

Hint Information that an application passes to an I/O library. This information helps the library adjust its configuration to give good performance for the application's anticipated data access patterns.

HIPPI High Performance Parallel Interconnect. A network technology widely used for **SANs.**

HIPPI-6400 See **GSN.**

Holographic storage An experimental storage technology that records data using laser interference patterns and photosensitive material.

Hot spare A hardware component (such as a disk drive in a **RAID** system) that is kept idle but powered on. It is automatically brought online if another component fails.

Hot swapping Replacing a failed hardware component (such as a disk drive in a **RAID** system) while the system that uses it continues to operate.

HPF High Performance Fortran. A parallel programming language based on Fortran.

HPSS High Performance Storage System. A software system that controls disk and tape drives to manage large data archives.

Hyperslab An array of data (possibly multidimensional) that consists of a rectangular subset of another array.

Idempotent An operation that has the same effect whether it is carried out once or multiple times.

Incremental checkpointing A **checkpointing** technique that stores only the parts of a program's state that have changed since the last checkpoint was taken.

InfiniBand A proposed standard architecture for communicating data between processors, memory, and peripheral devices.

Inode Index node. A **block** of data in a **file system** that lists the other blocks that compose a single file.

I/O node In a **distributed memory computer,** a **node** that acts as an intermediary between **compute nodes** and storage devices or networks.

JBOD Just a Bunch Of Disks. The use of multiple disk drives to store a collection of files without any special redundancy techniques.

Job A collection of **tasks** executing a parallel program.

Join An operation in the **relational algebra.** It produces a new **relation** by logically examining all possible pairs of **records** from two existing relations. A pair is admitted to the new relation if and only if its **attribute** values satisfy a specified condition.

Journaled file system A type of **file system** that records a log of planned changes to files and bookkeeping data before carrying out those changes. This data allows the file system to quickly restore a collection of files to a consistent state in case a crash corrupts data structures on a disk.

KDD Knowledge Discovery in Databases. The interactive process of finding useful information in a database with the help of computers.

Key In a **relation,** an **attribute** or a combination of attributes for which each **record** has a unique value or set of values. A relation may have multiple keys.

Kilo Prefix meaning 1000 or 1024.

LAN Local Area Network.

Land In an optical disk, an area of the reflective material that has not been etched; analogous to a polarized **domain** in a magnetic disk.

Latency In a disk drive, the time needed for a requested **sector** to rotate into position under the **head.** More generally, the time that elapses from the moment a request to move data is issued until the data begins to move.

Linear density In storage devices, the number of **bits** encoded per unit length of a **track.**

Linear scan A type of tape recording system in which the tape moves straight over the **heads,** and all the data is accessed in a single pass over the tape. (Compare with **helical scan** and **serpentine scan.**)

LLAPI Low-Level Application Programming Interface. A programming interface for parallel I/O, designed by **SIO** as a proposed extension to **POSIX.**

Local file pointer A **file pointer** in a parallel program that is used and updated only by a single **process.**

Local-to-global mapping A description of how a portion of a computational grid (usually assigned to a single **task**) fits into a global data structure.

Magneto-optical disk A rewritable storage medium that uses a laser to heat **domains** selectively on the recording surface under the influence of a magnetic field. The resulting change in the magnetic polarity of the selected domains causes them to reflect light differently from the unheated domains, and these differences can be detected when the disk is later read.

Magnetoresistive head A type of read **head** in a disk drive that modulates its resistance to electric current in response to the varying magnetization of **domains** on the disk. The high sensitivity of this type of head has allowed greatly improved **areal density** in hard disks.

Main memory **Primary storage,** usually excluding high speed **cache** memory.

Mega Prefix meaning 10^6 or 2^{20}.

Metadata Data that describes the organization or contents of other data. The term is used in many contexts, from **file systems** to large-scale data management.

Mirroring A **RAID** technique that writes complete copies of data on two or more separate disks.

MPI Message Passing Interface. A standard library of functions for passing data between **processes** in a **parallel program.**

MPI-IO A programming interface for parallel I/O that was defined in **MPI-2.**

MPI-2 A set of extensions to **MPI.**

MPP Message Passing Processor or Massively Parallel Processor. Usually synonymous with **distributed memory computer.**

Multiple block disk-directed I/O (MB-DDIO) A variation on **disk-directed I/O,** similar to **packet-based disk-directed I/O,** but **records** from multiple **blocks** are sent in a single message.

NASD Network-Attached Storage Device (or Secure Disk).

NetCDF Network Common Data Form. An I/O library for scientific data.

NFS Network File System. A commercial **distributed file system.**

Node (1) In a network, a sender or receiver of data. (2) In a parallel computer, a stand-alone computing element with its own memory and one or more **CPUs.**

Nonblocking I/O A form of **asynchronous I/O** in which an application issues a request to read or write data and then proceeds with other work while the data transfer happens concurrently.

NUMA Nonuniform Memory Access. A **shared memory computer** design in which accesses to different **main memory** locations from the same processor take different amounts of time.

Object identifier (OID) In a **DBMS** (usually an **OODBMS**), a value assigned by the DBMS software that uniquely identifies an object.

OODBMS Object-Oriented Database Management System. A **DBMS** that allows programs to view a database as an extended **address space,** which applications can manipulate using object-oriented programming techniques.

ORDBMS Object-Relational Database Management System. A **DBMS** that combines the flexible data structures of an **OODBMS** with the standard tabular model of an **RDBMS.**

O/S bypass See **scheduled transfer.**

Out-of-core A type of computation that **stages** data between primary and secondary storage because the input or output data set is too large to fit into **main memory.**

Packet-based disk-directed I/O (PB-DDIO) A variation on **disk-directed I/O** in which all the **records** in an incoming disk **block** that are destined for a particular **compute node** are sent from the **I/O node** in a single message.

Page A unit of storage in **virtual memory.** Data is moved between **primary storage** and **secondary storage** in page-size units.

Page fault In **virtual memory** systems, a failure to find a requested virtual address in **main memory;** typically, a page fault forces the system to read or write **secondary storage.**

Page table In **virtual memory** systems, a data structure that specifies the location in **main memory** or **secondary storage** for each address in the virtual **address space.**

Panda A research parallel I/O library.

Parallel Disk Model (PDM) A mathematical model for estimating the performance of **out-of-core** algorithms.

Parallel file system A **file system** that supports efficient concurrent access to files by multiple **tasks.**

Parallel I/O Reading and writing data on multiple storage devices at the same time from a **parallel program.**

Parallel program A program in which multiple **tasks** work concurrently on a single problem.

Parity In error detection and correction algorithms, a logical operation on two or more **bits.** Parity is "even" or 0 if the number of bits equal to one is even and "odd" or 1 if the number of ones is odd.

Peta Prefix meaning 10^{15} or 2^{50}.

PFS Parallel File System. A **parallel file system** developed by Intel for its parallel computers; successor to **CFS.**

PIOFS Parallel I/O File System. A **parallel file system** developed by IBM for its parallel computers; based on the **Vesta** research parallel file system.

PIOUS A research **file system** for **cluster computers.**

Pit In an optical disk, an etched area of the reflective material that holds the data; analogous to a polarized **domain** in a magnetic disk.

Platter The rotating disk in a disk drive.

Point-to-point network A network that creates direct, exclusive links between **nodes.**

POSIX Portable Operating System Interface. A set of operating system interface standards based on Unix.

PPFS Portable Parallel File System. A research **parallel file system.**

Prefetching Initiating a request to retrieve data **asynchronously** before it is needed, so the program will not have to wait for it to arrive. Prefetching can be done explicitly by a program or automatically by the I/O system.

Primary key A designated **key** in an **RDBMS.**

Primary storage Storage in electronic memory.

Process One or more program **threads** executing in a single memory **address space.**

Project In the **relational algebra,** an operation that creates a new **relation** by eliminating specified **attributes** from an existing relation.

PVFS A research **file system** for **cluster computers.**

Pyramid model A data structure that represents a larger data set using statistical descriptions of subsets of the data.

Quadtree A data structure used in image processing and data management that represents a range of data at different spatial resolutions in different areas.

Query A request to extract data meeting specified criteria from a **database.**

RAID Redundant Array of Inexpensive (or Independent) Disks. A type of storage system that uses multiple disk drives to improve performance and capacity. It also uses some form of data replication to ensure that the loss of one disk won't corrupt stored data.

RAID level The configuration of a **RAID** system. Different levels optimize performance for different kinds of workloads.

Random access The ability of a storage device or memory system to retrieve data at any location in equal time.

RDBMS Relational Database Management System. The classic type of **database** system, it views data as a collection of **records** organized in tabular form.

Read ahead See **prefetching.**

Read-modify-write The sequence of operations required when only a portion of a disk **sector** or other basic unit of data storage is changed. The entire sector is read into memory, a portion of the data is altered, and then the sector is written back.

Record In an **RDBMS,** a single row of data in a relation table. More generally, a record is a collection of one or more data values that are usually accessed together.

Regression A form of **classification** in which the assigned categories correspond to numerical values.

Relation In the **relational algebra,** a table in which the rows are **records** and each column contains values for some **attribute.**

Relational algebra The set of operations defined on **relations,** such as **select, project,** and **join.**

Required I/O I/O done by an application to read input data or store results; compare to **checkpointing** and **staging.**

River A research **parallel file system** based on a dataflow model of parallelism.

Round-robin An ordering in which each one of a set of items numbered 1 to *N* is chosen in sequence; after item *N* has been chosen, item 1 is chosen again, and the pattern continues repeatedly.

Row-major order A data layout pattern for multidimensional arrays in which array elements with the same leftmost index are stored together.

SAN System Area Network. A network that connects computers with nearby peripheral devices, such as disk and tape drives.

Scheduled transfer A data transfer protocol in which the sender arranges with the receiver to transmit a specified amount of data to a specified memory location. Once the arrangement has been made, the receiver can move data directly from the network to its final destination without making intermediate copies.

Schema In an **RDBMS,** the names of the **relations** and their **attributes.** Under some definitions, a schema also includes information about how the data is indexed and stored.

SCSI Small Computer System Interface. A network technology widely used for connecting computers to storage devices and other peripherals.

Secondary index In a **DBMS,** an index that maps **key** values to the corresponding **records'** exact storage locations within **blocks.** (Compare to a **clustered index,** which stores only the block location.)

Secondary storage Storage on hard disk and some types of optical disk.

Sector In a disk drive, a sequence of a fixed number of **domains** on a single **track.** A sector is the smallest unit of data that a disk drive can access.

Seek time The time needed for a disk drive to move its **head** to a requested **track.**

Select (1) In the **relational algebra,** an operation that creates a new **relation** that is a subset of an existing relation. The **records** for the new relation are chosen based on the values of one or more of their **attributes.** (2) In **SQL,** a general-purpose operation that retrieves information from a **database.**

Sequential access A characteristic of a storage device that causes its **access time** for a given storage location to depend on the location of the last data accessed. Tape drives are sequential access devices.

Sequential checkpoint A **checkpoint** operation that halts the application whose state is being saved until the entire checkpoint is recorded.

Sequential consistency The property of a set of concurrent operations (for example, on a file) that the net effect of the operations is the same as if they had been carried out in some sequential (but unspecified) order.

Serpentine scan A type of tape recording system in which the tape moves straight over the **head.** Separate **tracks** must be read in different passes. (Compare with **helical scan** and **linear scan.**)

Server-based collective I/O **Collective I/O** techniques in which the **I/O nodes** collect data from multiple **compute nodes** to form large, contiguous access requests.

Server buffering In a **parallel** or **distributed file system, buffering** data on the **I/O nodes** or on the computer that manages the disks that hold the files.

Server-directed I/O A type of **server-based collective I/O.**

Shared access network A type of network in which more than two **nodes** can be connected to a single communication medium.

Shared file pointer In a **parallel file system,** a **file pointer** that is used and updated by multiple **processes.**

Shared memory computer A parallel computer in which multiple **CPUs** can directly access a single memory **address space.**

Shuffle operation In **client-based collective I/O,** the rearrangement of data between **compute nodes** to create (or disperse) larger blocks of data.

Signaling rate In an interconnection network, the maximum rate at which bits can travel over a single wire or fiber in a link.

Simulated annealing An optimization technique based on the physical process of annealing in materials. Candidate solutions to a problem are constructed from random combinations of partial solutions. Based on the quality of the solution, as evaluated by an objective function, the candidates are broken apart and recombined. The range of possible recombinations is gradually restricted to force the system to converge on a final solution.

Single-ended A type of electrical connection in a network that uses a single return wire for multiple signal wires. It uses relatively few wires but is more susceptible to interference than **double-ended** systems.

SIO Scalable I/O Initiative. A research collaboration formed by several universities, computer vendors, and research laboratories to study various parallel I/O issues.

SMP Shared Memory Processor or Symmetric Multiprocessor.

Spindle The rotating shaft on which the **platters** in a disk drive are mounted.

SQL Structured Query Language. A standard programming language for **RDBMSs.**

SRB Storage Resource Broker. A research system for cataloging and managing large data sets.

Staging Moving data between levels of storage (**primary, secondary,** and **tertiary**) for the purpose of managing available space.

Strided access A read or write operation that accesses fixed-size units of data at units intervals in memory or a file.

Stripe depth The unit of data assigned to each disk or **I/O node** in a striped **declustering** pattern.

Stripe factor The number of disks or **I/O nodes** to which units of data are assigned in a striped **declustering** pattern.

Striping A form of **declustering** in which fixed-size pieces of a file are assigned cyclically to a collection of disks or **I/O nodes.**

Synchronous checkpoint A **checkpoint** that begins to store data immediately in response to an explicit request. The application may or may not continue its work while the checkpoint data is being recorded.

Task As used in this book, a **process** or **thread** in a **parallel program.**

Tera Prefix meaning 10^{12} or 2^{40}.

Tertiary storage Tape or removable-media storage, used for archiving data.

Third-party transfer A transfer of data between two points (such as a storage device and a computer) that is initiated by a **task** running on another device.

Thread A single executing sequence of steps in a program.

Tiger Shark A research **parallel file system** developed by IBM; **GPFS** is based on it.

Token A short electronic message or piece of data used in certain algorithms to coordinate distributed activities in a computer. Holding a token typically gives a **task** the right to perform some action; passing the token transfers the right to another task.

Topology In an interconnection network, the logical layout of links and **nodes.**

Track In a disk drive, a ring of **domains** on one side of a **platter.** On a tape, a line of domains.

Track buffer Memory in a disk drive that stores the contents of an entire **track** for rapid access.

Track density (1) In a disk drive, the number of **tracks** per unit radius of the disk. (2) In a tape drive, the number of tracks per unit width of the tape.

Transfer rate The rate at which a network or storage device moves data.

Two-phase I/O (2PIO) A form of **client-based collective I/O.**

UMA Uniform Memory Access. A **shared memory computer** design in which accesses from one processor to all locations in **main memory** take essentially the same amount of time.

Vesta A research **parallel file system** developed by IBM; **PIOFS** is based on it.

Virtual memory A technique for expanding the apparent size of **main memory** by storing pages of data in **secondary storage** and moving them into and out of **main memory** as needed.

WAN Wide Area Network.

Warm swapping Replacing a failed hardware component (such as a disk drive in a **RAID** system) while the system is powered on but offline. (Compare with **hot swapping** and **cold swapping.**)

Write behind See **delayed write.**

XDR External Data Representation. A standard binary representation for various types of numeric data.

xFS A research **file system** for **cluster computers.**

XFS A **file system** developed by SGI for its computers.

Zoning In a disk drive, grouping **tracks** on a **platter** such that all the tracks in a zone have the same number of **sectors,** but zones farther from the center of the platter have more sectors per track than the inner zones. This technique allows drives to store data more efficiently on the surface of a platter.

Bibliography

[1] Abello, James M., and Jeffrey Scott Vitter, editors. *External Memory Algorithms*, volume 50 of *DIMACS: Series in Discrete Mathematics and Theoretical Computer Science.* DIMACS, American Mathematical Society, Providence, Rhode Island, 1999.

[2] Agrawal, Rakesh, Tomasz Imielinski, and Arun N. Swami. Mining association rules between sets of items in large databases. In *Proceedings of the 1993 ACM SIGMOD International Conference on Management of Data*, pages 207–216, May 1993. Introduces the problem of finding association rules and examines several potential algorithms.

[3] Ambrosiano, John, David M. Butler, Celeste Matarazzo, Mark Miller, and Larry Schoof. Development of a common data model for scientific simulations. Unpublished paper describing fiber bundles, cell complexes, sheaves, and other mathematical constructs in a common data model for the Accelerated Strategic Computing Initiative, 1999.

[4] Anderson, Thomas E., David E. Culler, and David A. Patterson. A case for NOW (Networks of Workstations). *IEEE Micro*, 15(1):54–64, February 1995.

[5] Anderson, Thomas E., Michael D. Dahlin, Jeanna M. Neefe, David A. Patterson, Drew S. Roselli, and Randolph Y. Wang. Serverless network file systems. *ACM Transactions on Computer Systems*, 14(1):41–79, February 1996. Describes Berkeley's xFS file system for NOW.

[6] Arpaci-Dusseau, Remzi H., Eric Anderson, Noah Treuhaft, David E. Culler, Joseph M. Hellerstein, David Patterson, and Kathy Yellick. Cluster I/O with River: Making the fast case common. In *Proceedings of IOPADS '99*, May 1999.

[7] Ashar, Kanu G., *Magnetic Disk Drive Technology: Heads, Media, Channel, Interfaces, and Integration.* IEEE Press, New York, 1997. Technical description of magnetic disk drive technology. The chapters on disk integration and future trends are accessible to the nonspecialist.

[8] Atkinson, Malcolm, François Bancilhon, David De Witt, Klaus Dittrich, David Maier, and Stanley Zdonik. The object-oriented database system manifesto. In *Proceedings of the First International Conference on Deductive and Object-Oriented Databases*, pages 223–240, December 1989.

[9] Baase, Sara. *Computer Algorithms: Introduction to Design and Analysis.* Addison-Wesley Publishing Company, Reading, Massachusetts, second edition, 1988. An undergraduate textbook on algorithms, with a definition of big-oh notation and discussion of sorting algorithms.

[10] Bach, Maurice J. *The Design of the UNIX Operating System.* Prentice Hall, Inc., Englewood Cliffs, New Jersey, 1986. A standard textbook on Unix, with thorough coverage of the file system.

[11] Barkes, Jason, Marcelo R. Barrios, Francis Cougard, Paul G. Crumley, Didac Marin, Hari Reddy, and Theeraphong Thitayanun. *GPFS: A Parallel File System.* IBM International Technical Support Organization, April 1998. Thorough documentation on GPFS for users and system administrators. Available at *www.redbooks.ibm.com.*

[12] Baru, Chaitanya, Reagan Moore, Arcot Rajasekar, and Michael Wan. The SDSC storage resource broker. In *Proceedings of COMPCON '98*, November–December 1998.

[13] Baylor, Sandra Johnson, Caroline Benveniste, and Yarsun Hsu. Performance evaluation of a massively parallel I/O subsystem. In Jain et al. [81], chapter 13, pages 293–311. A study of the appropriate ratio of compute nodes to I/O nodes in a distributed memory computer.

[14] Becker, Donald J., Thomas Sterling, Daniel Savarese, John E. Dorband, Udaya A. Ranawake, and Charles V. Packer. Beowulf: A parallel workstation for scientific computation. In *Proceedings of the 1995 International Conference on Parallel Processing*, pages 11–14, August 1995.

[15] Beguelin, Adam, Erik Seligman, and Peter Stephan. Application level fault tolerance in heterogeneous networks of workstations. *Journal of Parallel and Distributed Computing*, 43(2):147–155, June 1997. Describes a portable checkpointing strategy that works on heterogeneous systems, based on the Dome system.

[16] Bergeron, Robert J. Measurement of a scientific workload using the IBM hardware performance monitor. In *Proceedings of SC98*, November 1998. Reports on long-term measurements of various hardware performance parameters for a large parallel system at NASA.

[17] Bordawekar, Rajesh. Implementation of collective I/O in the Intel Paragon parallel file system: Initial experiences. In *Conference Proceedings of the 1997 International Conference on Supercomputing*, pages 20–27, July 1997.

[18] Bordawekar, Rajesh, Juan Miguel del Rosario, and Alok Choudhary. Design and evaluation of primitives for parallel I/O. In *Proceedings of Supercomputing '93*, pages 452–461, November 1993. An early paper on two-phase I/O that shows encouraging results for collective reads on an Intel machine.

[19] Bosak, Jon. Media-independent publishing: Four myths about XML. *Computer*, 31(10):120–122, October 1998. Presents a basic introduction to XML partly by saying what it is not.

[20] Brown, Paul, Richard Troy, Dave Fisher, Steve Louis, James R. McGraw, and Ron Musick. Metadata for balanced performance. In *Proceedings of the First IEEE Metadata Conference*, 1996. Proposes giving database systems more control over hierarchical storage systems through a uniform interface to improve performance.

[21] Brown, Stewart A., Mike Folk, Gregory Goucher, and Russ Rew. Software for portable scientific data management. *Computers in Physics*, 7(3):304–308, May–June 1993. Compares netCDF and HDF with two other scientific data libraries, CDF and PDB.

[22] Butler, D. M., and M. H. Pendley. A visualization model based on the mathematics of fiber bundles. *Computers in Physics*, 3(5):45–51, September–October 1989.

[23] Cettei, Matthew M., Walter B. Ligon III, and Robert B. Ross. Support for parallel out-of-core applications on Beowulf workstations. In *Proceedings of the 1998 IEEE Aerospace Conference*, volume 4, pages 355–365, March 1998.

[24] Chandy, K. Mani, and Leslie Lamport. Distributed snapshots: Determining global states of distributed systems. *ACM Transactions on Computer Systems*, 3(1):63–75, February 1985. Introduces an algorithm for saving a consistent state of a distributed program without using a globally synchronized clock.

[25] Chen, Y., Y. Cho, S. Kuo, K. E. Seamons, M. Subramanian, and M. Winslett. Server-directed input and output in Panda: A commodity-parts approach to high-performance I/O. Submitted for journal publication and available at *drl.cs.uiuc.edu/panda/publications.html*, 1997. Describes a version of server-based I/O adapted from disk-directed I/O. Argues for layerable I/O libraries and presents performance data for different buffer sizes.

[26] Chen, Y., M. Winslett, Y. Cho, and S. Kuo. Automatic parallel I/O performance optimization in Panda. In *Proceedings of the 10th Annual ACM Symposium* *on Parallel Algorithms and Architectures*, pages 108–118, June 1998. Panda uses rule-based methods and optimizations based on simulated annealing to find the best settings for various I/O parameters.

[27] Chen, Y., M. Winslett, K. E. Seamons, S. Kuo, Y. Cho, and M. Subramanian. Scalable message passing in Panda. In *Proceedings of the Fourth Workshop on Input/Output in Parallel and Distributed Systems*, pages 109–121, May 1996. Proposes a modified communication strategy for server-directed I/O in Panda that reduces the amount of message traffic.

[28] Chen, Yuqun, James S. Plank, and Kai Li. CLIP: A checkpointing tool for message-passing parallel programs. In *Proceedings of Supercomputing '97*, November 1997. CLIP extends the libckpt checkpointing library to work on parallel computers. It supports only user-initiated checkpointing.

[29] Choudhary, A., M. Kandemir, H. Nagesh, J. No, X. Shen, V. Taylor, S. More, and R. Thakur. Data management for large-scale scientific computations in high performance distributed systems. In *Proceedings of the 8th IEEE Symposium on High Performance Distributed Systems*, August 1999. Describes a standardized interface through which programs can access a variety of storage resources and pass in hints about data layout and future accesses.

[30] Codd, E. F. A relational model of data for large shared data banks. *Communications of the ACM*, 13(6):377–387, June 1970. The seminal paper on relational databases. Argues for an implementation-independent data model and outlines the relational model and relational algebra.

[31] Colvin, Alex, and Thomas H. Cormen. ViC*: A compiler for virtual-memory C*. In *Proceedings of the Third International Workshop on High-Level Parallel Programming Models and Supportive Environments*, pages 23–33, March 1998. Compiler-based out-of-core programming model that applies a number of optimizations to reduce data movement. Also available as Dartmouth College Technical Report PCS-TR97-323.

[32] Committee for Advanced DBMS Function. Third generation database management system manifesto. *SIGMOD Record*, 19(3):31–44, September 1990. Argues for evolutionary changes to the relational data model, including the addition of complex types and inheritance.

[33] Corbett, Peter F., and Dror G. Feitelson. The Vesta parallel file system. *ACM Transactions on Computer Systems*, 14(3):225–264, August 1996. Vesta is the research project that led to IBM's PIOFS file system.

[34] Corbett, Peter F., Jean-Pierre Prost, Chris Demetriou, Garth Gibson, Erik Riedel, Jim Zelenka, Yuqun Chen, Ed Felten, Kai Li, John Hartman, Larry Peterson,

Brian Bershad, Alec Wolman, and Ruth Aydt. Proposal for a common parallel file system programming interface version 1.0. *www.pdl.cs.cmu.edu/SIO/SIO.html*, 1996. The official SIO Low-Level API standard.

[35] Cormen, Thomas H., and Melissa Hirschl. Early experiences in evaluating the parallel disk model with the ViC* implementation. *Parallel Computing*, 23(4–5):571–600, June 1997. Compares the performance of two out-of-core algorithms with predictions made by the parallel disk model.

[36] Cormen, Thomas H., and David M. Nicol. Performing out-of-core FFTs on parallel disk systems. *Parallel Computing*, 24(1):5–20, January 1998. Compares the performance of an out-of-core fast Fourier transform with in-core methods using virtual memory.

[37] Cortesi, David, Arthur Evans, Wendy Ferguson, Jed Hartman, and Susan Thomas. *Topics in IRIX Programming*. Silicon Graphics, Inc., 1998. Contains information on high performance I/O programming for SGI systems. Available at *techpubs.sgi.com*.

[38] Darwen, Hugh, and C. J. Date. The third manifesto. *SIGMOD Record*, 24(1), March 1995. Proposes an object-relational model as an alternative to a pure object-oriented model for databases.

[39] Data models and formats. *www.ca.sandia.gov/asci-sdm/*. The Accelerated Strategic Computing Initiative's (ASCI) Data Models and Formats project is defining a high-level data model for scientific computation. Their presentations and whitepapers are linked from this Web page.

[40] Date, C. J., and Hugh Darwen. *Foundation for Object/Relational Databases: The Third Manifesto*. Addison-Wesley, Reading, Massachusetts, 1998. Presents an object-relational database model in detail.

[41] Declerck, Michael. Private communication, 1999.

[42] Deconinck, G., J. Vounckx, R. Lauwereins, and J. Peperstraete. Survey of backward error recovery techniques for multicomputers based on checkpointing and rollback. *International Journal of Modelling and Simulation*, 18(1):66–71, 1998. A brief survey of checkpointing techniques for parallel computers.

[43] Dedek, Jan. *Basics of SCSI*. ANCOT Corporation, Menlo Park, California, second edition, 1994.

[44] Dedek, Jan, and Gary Stephens. *What Is Fibre Channel?* ANCOT Corporation, Menlo Park, California, 1994.

[45] Devarakonda, Murthy, Ajay Mohindra, Jill Simoneaux, and William H. Tetzlaff. Evaluation of design alternatives for a cluster file system. In *Proceedings* *of the 1995 Usenix Technical Conference*, pages 35–46, January 1995. Describes an experimental system called PJFS, but useful mainly for its discussion of cluster file system architectures.

[46] Düllmann, Dirk, and Jamie Shiers. Object databases and petabyte storage—dreams or reality? In *Proceedings of the 13th European Conference on Object-Oriented Programming*, June 1999. Describes the SLAC/CERN collaboration on a very large database for collider experiments, with an emphasis on how various design options were evaluated.

[47] Ellis, Susan, and Steven Levine. *IRIX Admin: Disks and Filesystems.* Silicon Graphics, Inc., 1998. SGI documentation for XFS and XLV, aimed at system administrators. Available at *techpubs.sgi.com.*

[48] Elmasri, Ramez, and Shamkant B. Navathe. *Fundamentals of Database Systems.* Addison-Wesley Publishing Company, Menlo Park, California, second edition, 1994.

[49] Elnozahy, E. N., D. B. Johnson, and Y. M. Wang. A survey of rollback-recovery protocols in message-passing systems. Technical Report CMU-CS-96-181, School of Computer Science, Carnegie-Mellon University, October 1996. An extensive review of parallel checkpointing techniques and implementations.

[50] Fayyad, Usama. Data mining and knowledge discovery in databases: Implications for scientific databases. In *Proceedings of the Ninth International Conference on Scientific and Statistical Database Management*, pages 2–11, August 1997.

[51] Fayyad, Usama, David Haussler, and Paul Stolorz. Mining science data. *Communications of the ACM*, 39(11), November 1996. Describes data mining algorithms in the context of scientific applications; similar to an extended abstract published elsewhere [50], but includes more case studies.

[52] Feitelson, Dror G., Peter F. Corbett, Sandra Johnson Baylor, and Yarsun Hsu. Parallel I/O subsystems in massively parallel supercomputers. *IEEE Parallel and Distributed Technology*, 3(3):33–47, Fall 1995.

[53] Fogg, Chad. DVD technical notes. *www.mpeg.org/MPEG/DVD/*, July 1996.

[54] Foster, Ian, and Carl Kesselman. The Globus project: A status report. In *Proceedings of the Seventh Heterogeneous Computing Workshop*, pages 4–18, March 1998.

[55] Ganti, Venkatesh, Johannes Gehrke, and Raghu Ramakrishnan. Mining very large databases. *Computer*, 32(8):38–45, August 1999.

[56] García, F., J. Carretero, F. Pérez, and P. de Miguel. Evaluating the ParFiSys cache coherence protocol on the IBM SP2. Technical Report FIM/104.1/DATSI/98, Dep.

de Arquitectura y Tecnología de Sistemas Informáticos, Universidad Politécnica de Madrid, Madrid, Spain, January 1998. Discusses client buffering and a protocol to implement cache coherence.

[57] Gibson, Garth A., David F. Nagle, Khalil Amiri, Jeff Butler, Fay W. Chang, Howard Gobioff, Charles Hardin, Erik Riedel, David Rochberg, and Jim Zelenka. A cost-effective, high-bandwidth storage architecture. In *Proceedings of the 8th Conference on Architectural Support for Programming Languages and Operating Systems*, 1998. One of many NASD papers; this one gives some performance data for prototype NASD disks.

[58] Gibson, Garth A., David F. Nagle, Khalil Amiri, Fay W. Chang, Eugene Feinberg, Howard Gobioff, Chen Lee, Berend Ozceri, Erik Riedel, and David Rochberg. A case for network-attached secure disks. Technical Report CMU-CS-96-142, School of Computer Science, Carnegie-Mellon University, Pittsburgh, Pennsylvania, September 1996.

[59] Gould, E., and M. Xinu. The network file system implemented on 4.3 BSD. In *USENIX Association Summer Conference Proceedings*, pages 294–298, June 1986.

[60] Greenberg, David S., Ron Brightwell, Lee Ann Fisk, Arthur B. Maccabe, and Rolf Riesen. A system software architecture for high-end computing. In *Proceedings of SC '97*, November 1997. Describes the Cplant architecture, including plans for a parallel file system.

[61] Grimshaw, Andrew S., Michael J. Lewis, Adam J. Ferrari, and John F. Karpovich. Architectural support for extensibility and autonomy in wide-area distributed object systems. Technical Report CS-98-12, Department of Computer Science, University of Virginia, Charlottesville, Virginia, June 1998. Overview of the Legion run-time architecture.

[62] Grochowski, Ed. IBM leadership in disk storage technology. *www.storage.ibm.com/technolo/grochows/grocho01.htm,* November 1999. An informative set of Web pages describing trends in disk technology.

[63] Gropp, William, Steven Huss-Lederman, Andrew Lumsdaine, Ewing Lusk, Bill Nitzberg, William Saphir, and Marc Snir. *MPI: The Complete Reference*, volume 2—The MPI-2 Extensions. The MIT Press, Cambridge, Massachusetts, 1998. The official MPI-2 standard, also available in a different form at *www.mpi-forum.org*.

[64] Hanushevsky, Andrew, and Marcin Nowak. Pursuit of a scalable high performance multi-petabyte database. In *Proceedings of the 16th IEEE Symposium on Mass Storage Systems*, March 1999. Presents some architectural details of the CERN/SLAC database for collider experiments.

[65] Haskin, R. L. Tiger Shark—A scalable file system for multimedia. *IBM Journal of Research and Development*, 42(2):185–197, March 1998. Tiger Shark is the research project that led to IBM's GPFS file system.

[66] HDF4 Documentation. Online documentation for HDF4 and earlier at *hdf.ncsa.uiuc.edu/doc.html*. This page has links to a variety of HDF documentation.

[67] HDF5—A New Generation of HDF. Online HDF5 documentation at *hdf.ncsa.uiuc.edu/HDF5/*. This page has links to an HDF5 user guide, a reference manual, and several design documents.

[68] Hellerstein, Joseph M., Ron Avnur, Andy Chou, Christian Hidber, Chris Olston, Vijayshankar Raman, Tali Roth, and Peter J. Haas. Interactive data analysis: The Control project. *Computer*, 32(8):51–59, August 1999. Proposes interactive analysis techniques for data mining.

[69] High Performance Fortran. *Scientific Programming*, 2(1–2):1–170, Spring–Summer 1993. The official HPF-1 standard. An updated version is available at *www.crpc.rice.edu/HPFF/versions/hpf1/index.html*.

[70] High Performance Fortran Forum. High Performance Fortran language specification version 2.0. *www.crpc.rice.edu/HPFF/versions/hpf2/index.html*, 1997.

[71] Hoffman, James. HIPPI-6400 technology dissemination. In *Proceedings of SPIE—The International Society for Optical Engineering: Broadband Access Systems*, volume 2917, pages 422–430, November 1996.

[72] Howard, J. H. An overview of the Andrew File System. In *Proceedings of the USENIX Association Winter Conference*, pages 213–216, February 1988.

[73] HPSS Tutorial. *www.sdsc.edu/hpss*. This Web site has a description of the operation and features of HPSS, and there are links to a number of other papers.

[74] Hsu, Shang-Te, and Ruei-Chuan Chang. Continuous checkpointing: Joining the checkpointing with virtual memory paging. *Software—Practice and Experience*, 27(9):1103–1120, September 1997. Describes a technique for creating checkpoint files from virtual memory pages on disk.

[75] Huber, James V., Jr., Christopher L. Elford, Daniel A. Reed, Andrew A. Chien, and David S. Blumenthal. PPFS: A high performance portable parallel file system. In *Conference Proceedings of the 1995 International Conference on Supercomputing*, pages 385–394, July 1995. An early version of PPFS that uses hints to control caching, prefetching, and other file system policies.

[76] IBM Corporation. *IBM AIX Parallel I/O File System: Installation, Administration, and Use*, 1995.

[77] InfiniBand Trade Association. *www.infinibandta.org,* February 2000. Brief technical description of the proposed InfiniBand architecture.

[78] Institute of Electrical and Electronics Engineers, New York. *IEEE Standard for Information Technology: Portable Operating System Interface (POSIX)—Part 1: System Application Program Interface (API)*, 1996. The POSIX standard defines a Unix-like programming interface for operating systems.

[79] Intel Corporation. *Paragon System User's Guide*, April 1996. Includes a chapter on using PFS but has little information on its underlying design.

[80] Jain, Raj. *FDDI Handbook: High-Speed Networking Using Fiber and Other Media.* Addison-Wesley Publishing Company, Reading, Massachusetts, 1994.

[81] Jain, Ravi, John Werth, and James C. Browne, editors. *Input/Output in Parallel and Distributed Computer Systems.* Kluwer Academic Publishers, Norwell, Massachusetts, 1996. The first part of this book is a series of tutorial articles on parallel I/O. The last two parts are reprints of selected papers from the 1994 and 1995 Workshops on I/O for Parallel and Distributed Systems.

[82] Johnson, Lori. *CXFS Software Installation and Administration Guide.* Silicon Graphics, Inc., 1999. SGI documentation for CXFS, written for system administrators. Available at *techpubs.sgi.com.*

[83] Kalaiselvi, S., and V. Rajaraman. A checkpointing algorithm for an SCI-based distributed shared memory system. *Microprocessors and Microsystems*, 22(9):515–522, 29 March 1999. Distributed shared memory checkpointing system that uses an algorithm similar to distributed memory techniques.

[84] Kamath, Chandrika, and Ron Musick. Scalable data mining through fine-grained parallelism: The present and future. In H. Kargupta and P. Chan, editors, *Advances in Distributed Data Mining.* AAAI Press, 2000 (to appear). Reviews a number of data mining algorithms and techniques for parallelizing them.

[85] Kandemir, M., A. Choudhary, J. Ramanujam, and R. Bordawekar. Compilation techniques for out-of-core parallel computations. *Parallel Computing*, 24(3–4):597–628, May 1998. Compiler-based techniques for optimizing the layout of out-of-core arrays in files. Assumes an HPF-style programming model.

[86] Karypis, George, Eui-Hong Han, and Vipin Kumar. Chameleon: Hierarchical clustering using dynamic modeling. *Computer*, 32(8):68–75, August 1999. Describes an algorithm for identifying complex, unpredicted shapes in a collection of points.

[87] Kazar, Michael L., Bruce W. Leverett, Owen T. Anderson, Vasilis Apostolides, Beth A. Bottos, Sailesh Chutani, Craig F. Everhart, W. Anthony Mason, Shu-Tsui Tu, and Edward R. Zayas. DEcorum File System architectural overview. In *Proceedings of the Summer 1990 USENIX Conference*, pages 151–163, June 1990. Introduces the file system that became DCE's DFS.

[88] Koelbel, Charles H., David B. Loveman, Robert S. Schreiber, Guy L. Steele Jr., and Mary E. Zosel. *The High Performance Fortran Handbook*. The MIT Press, Cambridge, Massachusetts, 1994.

[89] Kotz, David. Disk-directed I/O for MIMD multicomputers. *ACM Transactions on Computer Systems*, 15(1):41–74, February 1997. Introduces disk-directed I/O and compares its performance with two-phase I/O and an ordinary parallel file system through a series of simulations.

[90] Kurc, Tashin, Chialin Chang, Renato Ferreira, Alan Sussman, and Joel Saltz. Querying very large multi-dimensional datasets in ADR. In *Proceedings of SC99*, November 1999. Describes data placement and I/O techniques for computations using out-of-core spatial data.

[91] Kuskin, J., D. Ofelt, M. Heinrich, J. Heinlein, R. Simoni, K. Gharachorloo, J. Chapin, D. Nakahira, J. Baxter, M. Horowitz, A. Gupta, M. Rosenblum, and J. Hennessy. The Stanford FLASH multiprocessor. In *Proceedings of the 21st International Symposium on Computer Architecture*, pages 302–313, April 1994. An early example of a ccNUMA architecture.

[92] Landau, Charles R. The checkpoint mechanism in KeyKOS. In *Proceedings of the Second International Workshop on Object Orientation in Operating Systems*, pages 86–91, September 1992. KeyKOS combines checkpointing with virtual memory paging.

[93] Laudon, James, and Daniel Lenoski. The SGI Origin: A ccNUMA highly scalable server. In *Proceedings of the 24th Annual International Symposium on Computer Architecture (ISCA '97)*, pages 241–251, May 1997. Describes the architecture of the Origin series of computers, with some information on the I/O subsystem. This paper is also available at the SGI Web site.

[94] Li, Kai, Jeffrey F. Naughton, and James S. Plank. Low-latency, concurrent checkpointing for parallel programs. *IEEE Transactions on Parallel and Distributed Systems*, 5(8):874–879, August 1994. Compares the performance of several checkpointing algorithms on shared memory computers. These algorithms are similar to single-process techniques.

[95] Li, Qun, Jie Jing, and Li Xie. BFXM: A parallel file system model based on the mechanism of distributed shared memory. *Operating Systems Review*, 31(4):30–40, October 1997. A research file system for workstation clusters; it uses caching extensively.

[96] Li, Zuotao, X. Sean Wang, Menas Kafotos, and Ruixin Yang. A pyramid data model for supporting content-based browsing and knowledge discovery. In *Proceedings of the 10th International Conference on Scientific and Statistical Database Management*, pages 170–179, July 1998. The pyramid model uses a multiresolution technique and statistical summaries of the underlying data to support sophisticated queries.

[97] Ligon, W. B., III, and R. B. Ross. Implementation and performance of a parallel file system for high performance distributed applications. In *Proceedings for the 5th IEEE International Symposium on High Performance Distributed Computing*, pages 471–480, August 1996.

[98] Litzkow, Michael, Todd Tannenbaum, Jim Basney, and Miron Livny. Checkpoint and migration of UNIX processes in the Condor distributed processing system. Technical Report 1346, Computer Sciences Department, University of Wisconsin, Madison, Wisconsin, April 1997. Describes the basic techniques for saving and restoring single-process checkpoints on Unix systems.

[99] Long, Jeffrey, Paul Spencer, and Rebecca Springmeyer. SimTracker—using the Web to track computer simulation results. In *Proceedings of the 1999 International Conference on Web-Based Modeling and Simulation*, January 1999.

[100] Madhyastha, Tara M., Garth A. Gibson, and Christos Faloutsos. Informed prefetching of collective input/output requests. In *Proceedings of SC99*, November 1999. Compares prefetching to disk-directed reads for small files and block-size transfers.

[101] Madhyastha, Tara M., and Daniel A. Reed. Exploiting global input/output access pattern classification. In *Proceedings of Supercomputing '97*, November 1997. Automatic detection of access patterns for selecting PFS modes.

[102] Massiglia, Paul, editor. *The RAIDbook: A Source Book for Disk Array Technology*. The RAID Advisory Board, St. Peter, Minnesota, fourth edition, 1994. A good, technical discussion of RAID technology, useful to both specialists and nonspecialists.

[103] May, John, and Linda Stanberry. Testmpio and testrep. *www.llnl.gov/sccd/lc/piop/testmpio.tar.Z*. These programs test many features of the MPI-IO interface, and testrep includes a nearly complete example of a user-defined data conversion function.

[104] Mee, C. Denis, and Eric D. Daniel, editors. *Magnetic Storage Handbook*. McGraw-Hill, New York, second edition, 1996. Technical discussions of magnetic disk and tape technology.

[105] Miller, Ethan L., and Randy H. Katz. Input/output behavior of supercomputing applications. In *Proceedings of Supercomputing '91*, pages 567–576, November 1991. Examines the I/O characteristics of seven applications on a Cray Y-MP.

[106] Miller, Ethan L., and Randy H. Katz. RAMA: An easy-to-use, high-performance parallel file system. *Parallel Computing*, 23(4–5):419–446, June 1997. RAMA uses a unique striping technique and supports migration of data to tertiary storage.

[107] Mohindra, Ajay, and Murthy Devarakonda. Distributed token management in Calypso file system. In *Proceedings of the Sixth IEEE Symposium on Parallel and Distributed Processing*, pages 290–297, October 1994. Compares token management in Calypso with other file systems, especially DFS.

[108] Moody, D. The Intel iPSC/2 concurrent file system. In R. H. Perrott, editor, *Software for Parallel Computers*, chapter 15, pages 229–241. Chapman & Hall, London, 1992. High-level description of CFS, the predecessor of Intel's PFS.

[109] Moore, Jason A., and Michael J. Quinn. Enhancing disk-directed I/O for fine-grained redistribution of file data. *Parallel Computing*, 23(4):477–499, June 1997. Proposes several enhancements to DDIO and presents analytic models of their performance.

[110] Mowry, Todd C. *Tolerating Latency Through Software-Controlled Data Prefetching*. Ph.D. thesis, Stanford University, 1994. Presents a technique for predicting memory access patterns to improve cache utilization; used as the basis for a compiler-based virtual memory prefetching method.

[111] Mowry, Todd C., Angela K. Demke, and Orran Krieger. Automatic compiler-inserted I/O prefetching for out-of-core applications. In *Second Symposium on Operating Systems Design and Implementations*, pages 3–17, October 1996. Out-of-core technique in which the compiler determines memory access patterns and issues prefetch requests to avoid page faults.

[112] Moyer, Steven A., and V. S. Sunderam. Scalable concurrency control for parallel file systems. In Jain et al. [81], chapter 10, pages 225–243. Describes PIOUS, a parallel file system that uses a database-like mechanism for concurrency control.

[113] Musick, Ron, and Terence Critchlow. Practical lessons in supporting large-scale computational science. *SIGMOD Record*, 28(4):49–57, December 1999. Evaluates types of databases for managing scientific data.

[114] Nadler, Jeffrey N., and Robert J. Wiesenberg. CD-ROM hardware. In Chris Sherman, editor, *The CD-ROM Handbook*. Intertext Publications, McGraw-Hill, New York, second edition, 1994. Focuses on applications of CD-ROM technology, with a relatively brief discussion of the hardware technology.

[115] NCR Corporation. *SCSI: Understanding the Small Computer System Interface.* Prentice Hall, Englewood Cliffs, New Jersey, 1990.

[116] NERSC first to reach decade-long goal of seamless shutdown, restart on massively parallel processing system. NERSC news release. *www.nersc.gov/news/checkpoint10-21-97.html,* October 1997. Nontechnical description of the NERSC parallel checkpointer for the Cray T3E.

[117] Nieplocha, Jarek, Ian Foster, and Rick A. Kendall. ChemIO: High performance parallel I/O for computational chemistry applications. *The International Journal of High Performance Computing Applications,* 12(3):345–363, Fall 1998. ChemIO supports out-of-core computations on large parallel arrays.

[118] Nieplocha, Jaroslaw, Robert J. Harrison, and Richard J. Littlefield. Global arrays: A non-uniform-memory-access programming model for high-performance computers. *The Journal of Supercomputing,* 10(2):169–189, 1996. Describes a distributed shared memory programming tool kit.

[119] Nieuwejaar, Nils, and David Kotz. The Galley parallel file system. *Parallel Computing,* 23(4–5):447–476, June 1997. Galley is a research system that offers discontiguous file access but not collective I/O. This paper shows very good performance for interleaved accesses.

[120] Nieuwejaar, Nils, David Kotz, Apratim Purakayastha, Carla Schlatter Ellis, and Michael L. Best. File-access characteristics of parallel scientific workloads. *IEEE Transactions on Parallel and Distributed Systems,* 7(10):1075–1088, October 1996. Measures I/O characteristics of applications running on an Intel iPSC and a Thinking Machines CM-5.

[121] Nitzberg, Bill, and Virginia Lo. Collective buffering: Improving parallel I/O performance. In *Proceedings of the Sixth IEEE International Symposium on High Performance Distributed Computing,* pages 148–157, August 1997. Compares the performance of several collective I/O strategies on an Intel Paragon and an IBM SP2.

[122] Open Software Foundation. *Introduction to OSF DCE.* Prentice Hall, Englewood Cliffs, New Jersey, 1992. Brief description of all of DCE, including a chapter on DFS.

[123] Ousterhout, John K., Hervé Da Costa, David Harrison, John A. Kunze, Mike Kupfer, and James G. Thompson. A trace-driven analysis of the UNIX 4.2 BSD file system. In *Proceedings of the Tenth ACM Symposium on Operating System Principles,* volume 19 of *Operating Systems Review,* pages 15–24, December 1985. A widely cited study of Unix file system access patterns.

[124] Pasquale, Barbara K., and George C. Polyzos. Dynamic I/O characterization of I/O-intensive scientific applications. In *Proceedings of Supercomputing '94*, pages 660–669, November 1994. A study of two I/O-intensive applications on a Cray C90.

[125] Patterson, David A., Garth A. Gibson, and Randy H. Katz. A case for redundant arrays of inexpensive disks (RAID). In *Proceedings of the 1988 ACM SIGMOD Conference on Management of Data*, pages 109–116, June 1988.

[126] Patterson, R. Hugo, Garth A. Gibson, Eka Ginting, Daniel Stodolsky, and Jim Zelenka. Informed prefetching and caching. In *Proceedings of the 15th ACM Symposium on Operating System Principles*, pages 79–95, December 1995. Presents an algorithm for file prefetching that attempts to optimize the allocation of buffer space among competing I/O requests.

[127] Pfaltz, John L., Russell F. Haddleton, and James C. French. Scalable, parallel, scientific databases. In *Proceedings of the 10th International Conference on Scientific and Statistical Database Management*, pages 4–11, July 1998. Describes some unique features of scientific databases and presents an object-oriented DBMS for scientific data.

[128] Plank, James S., Micah Beck, Gerry Kingsley, and Kai Li. Libckpt: Transparent checkpointing under Unix. In *USENIX Winter 1995 Technical Conference*, pages 213–223, January 1995. Describes a variety of checkpointing optimizations for single processes as implemented in a checkpointing library.

[129] Plank, James S., Yuqun Chen, Kai Li, Micah Beck, and Gerry Kingsley. Memory exclusion: Optimizing the performance of checkpointing systems. *Software—Practice and Experience*, 29(2):125–142, February 1999. Reviews several techniques for minimizing the size of checkpoint data.

[130] Poole, James C. T. Scalable I/O initiative. *www.cacr.caltech.edu/SIO/*, 1999. Describes SIO and has links to their collaborators and some technical reports.

[131] Preslan, Kenneth W., Andrew P. Barry, Jonathan E. Brassow, Grant M. Erickson, Erling Nygaard, Christopher J. Sabol, Steven R. Soltis, David C. Teigland, and Matthew T. O'Keefe. A 64-bit, shared disk file system for Linux. In *Proceedings of the Sixteenth IEEE Mass Storage System Symposium*, March 1999. Describes GFS, a distributed file system for clusters. Supports striping and read caching, but not yet write caching.

[132] Pruyne, Jim, and Miron Livny. Managing checkpoints for parallel programs. In *Job Scheduling Strategies for Parallel Processing, International Parallel Processing Symposium 1996*, pages 140–154, April 1996. Describes the CoCheck parallel checkpointer, which can store data on a specialized checkpoint server. Part of the Condor project.

[133] Psatis, Demetri, and Geoffrey W. Burr. Holographic data storage. *Computer*, 31(2):52–60, February 1998.

[134] Ranade, Sanjay. *Mass Storage Technologies*. Meckler Publishing, Westport, Connecticut, 1991. Good general coverage of disk and tape technology, though now somewhat dated.

[135] Rew, R., and G. Davis. NetCDF: An interface for scientific data access. *IEEE Computer Graphics and Applications*, 10(4):76–82, July 1990.

[136] Rew, Russ, Glenn Davis, Steve Emmerson, and Harvey Davies. *NetCDF User's Guide for C: An Access Interface for Self-Describing, Portable Data, Version 3*. Unidata Program Center, June 1997. NetCDF documentation; a similar manual covers the Fortran interface. Available at *unidata.ucar.edu/packages/netcdf/docs.html*.

[137] Rosch, Winn L. *Winn L. Rosch Hardware Bible*. Sams Publishing, Indianapolis, Indiana, premier edition, 1997. Comprehensive review of desktop computer technology, with much information applicable to larger systems.

[138] Rostky, George. Disk drives take an eventful spin. *Electronic Engineering Times*, (1016):22, 13 July 1998. A history of the development of the magnetic disk drive.

[139] Ruemmler, Chris, and John Wilkes. An introduction to disk drive modeling. *Computer*, 27(3):17–28, March 1994. The focus is on modeling disk performance, but it begins with a good discussion of disk technology.

[140] Samet, Hanan. The quadtree and related hierarchical data structures. *ACM Computing Surveys*, 16(2):187–260, June 1984. Reviews a variety of data structures, including pyramids and quadtrees.

[141] Saulsbury, A., T. Wilkinson, J. Carter, and A. Landin. An argument for simple COMA. In *First IEEE Symposium on High Performance Computer Architecture*, January 1995.

[142] Schaller, Robert R. Moore's law: past, present, and future. *IEEE Spectrum*, 14(6):52–59, June 1997.

[143] Seamons, K. E., Y. Chen, P. Jones, J. Jozwiak, and M. Winslett. Server-directed collective I/O in Panda. In *Proceedings of the 1995 ACM/IEEE Supercomputing Conference*, December 1995. Reports the performance of Panda on an IBM SP2.

[144] Sheldon, Tom. *LAN TIMES Encyclopedia of Networking*. Osborne McGraw-Hill, Berkeley, California, 1994.

[145] Silberschatz, Abraham, and Peter B. Galvin. *Operating System Concepts.* Addison-Wesley Publishing Company, Reading, Massachusetts, fourth edition, 1994.

[146] Silva, Luis M., and João Gabriel Silva. Checkpointing distributed shared memory. *The Journal of Supercomputing*, 11(2):137–158, 1997. Checkpointing tool for software-based distributed shared memory system; uses an algorithm similar to distributed memory techniques.

[147] Simitci, Huseyin, Daniel A. Reed, Ryan Fox, Mario Medina, James Oly, Nancy Tran, and Guoyi Wang. A framework for adaptive storage input/output on computational grids. In *Proceedings of the Third Workshop on Runtime Systems for Parallel Programming*, April 1999. Describes the architecture of PPFS II and examines some techniques for predicting file access patterns.

[148] Smirni, Evgenia, Ruth A. Aydt, Andrew A. Chien, and Daniel A. Reed. I/O requirements of scientific applications: An evolutionary view. In *Proceedings of the Fifth IEEE International Symposium on High Performance Distributed Computing*, pages 49–59, August 1996. Describes I/O optimization efforts on two codes running on an Intel Paragon.

[149] Smirni, Evgenia, and Daniel A. Reed. Workload characterization of input/output intensive parallel applications. In *Proceedings of the Conference on Modeling Techniques and Tools for Computer Performance Evaluation*, volume 1245 of *Springer-Verlag Lecture Notes in Computer Science*, pages 169–180, June 1997. Studies I/O characteristics of five applications on an Intel Paragon.

[150] Snir, Marc, Steve W. Otto, Steven Huss-Lederman, David W. Walker, and Jack Dongarra. *MPI: The Complete Reference.* The MIT Press, Cambridge, Massachusetts, 1996. The official MPI-1 standard, also available at *www.mpi-forum.org.*

[151] Steenkiste, Peter A. A systematic approach to host interface design for high-speed networks. *Computer*, 27(3):47–57, March 1994.

[152] Stephens, Gary R., and Jan V. Dedek. *Fibre Channel Volume 1: The Basics.* ANCOT Corporation, Menlo Park, California, 1995. A detailed description of Fibre Channel, but it doesn't cover all of the current standard.

[153] Stonebraker, Michael, and Dorothy Moore. *Object-Relational DBMSs: The Next Great Wave.* Morgan Kaufmann Publishers, San Francisco, California, 1996.

[154] Sun Microsystems, Inc. The NFS distributed file service. Online whitepaper available at *www.sun.com/software/white-papers/wp-nfs/,* March 1995. Describes Version 3 of NFS.

[155] Sweeney, Adam, Doug Doucette, Wei Hu, Curtis Anderson, Mike Nishimoto, and Geoff Peck. Scalability in the XFS file system. In *Proceedings of the 1996 Usenix*

Technical Conference, pages 1–14, January 1996. Describes the architecture of SGI's XFS file system, with some initial performance data.

[156] Szalay, Alexander S., Peter Kunszt, Ani Thakar, and Jim Gray. Designing and mining multi-terabyte astronomy archives: The Sloan Digital Sky Survey. Technical Report MS-TR-99-30, Microsoft Corporation, Redmond, Washington, June 1999. Describes the proposed design of a database for a large astronomical data set.

[157] Taylor, Jim. DVD demystified: DVD frequently asked questions. *www.dvddemystified.com/dvdfaq.html,* March 2000. Describes DVD technology at various levels, including low-level recording information.

[158] Tera Computer Company. Major system characteristics of the Tera MTA. Online whitepaper available at *www.tera.com/www/library/system.html,* 1999.

[159] Thakur, Rajeev. Private communication, 1999.

[160] Thakur, Rajeev, and Alok Choudhary. An extended two-phase method for accessing sections of out-of-core arrays. *Scientific Programming*, 5(4), Winter 1996. Improvements to two-phase I/O that reduce the number of I/O operations.

[161] Thakur, Rajeev, Alok Choudhary, Sachin More, and Sivaramakrishna Kuditipudi. Passion: Optimized I/O for parallel applications. *Computer*, 29(6), June 1996.

[162] Thakur, Rajeev, William Gropp, and Ewing Lusk. A case for using MPI's derived datatypes to improve I/O performance. In *Proceedings of SC98*, November 1998. Reports the performance of the ROMIO implementation of MPI-IO on several computers for various file access patterns and optimization techniques.

[163] Thakur, Rajeev, Ewing Lusk, and William Gropp. Users guide for ROMIO: A high-performance, portable MPI-IO implementation. Technical Report ANL/MCS-TM-234, Mathematics and Computer Science Division, Argonne National Laboratory, Argonne, Illinois, October 1997.

[164] Thor, Anders J. IEC standardizes prefixes for binary multiples—Amendment 2 to IEC 60027-2. *TC Newsletter*, (6):4, February 1999. A brief note in an International Electrotechnical Commission newsletter announcing the standardization of prefix names for binary quantities. Available at *www.iec.ch/tclet6.pdf.*

[165] Többicke, Rainer. Distributed file systems: Focus on Andrew File System/Distributed File System (AFS/DFS). In *Proceedings of the Thirteenth IEEE Symposium on Mass Storage Systems*, pages 23–26, June 1994. A brief but useful comparison of AFS, DFS, NFS, and some other distributed file systems. Has no references.

[166] Toigo, Jon William. *The Holy Grail of Data Storage Management.* Prentice Hall, Upper Saddle River, New Jersey, 2000. Describes large storage systems and networks; it is written for information technology professionals.

[167] Tolmie, Don, and Don Flanagan. HIPPI: It's not just for supercomputers anymore. *Data Communications*, May 8, 1995. A basic description of HIPPI by two of its originators.

[168] Top 500 supercomputer sites. *www.top500.org*, November 1999. The University of Mannheim and the University of Tennessee maintain a list of the reported peak and maximum observed performance for supercomputers around the world.

[169] Van Praag, Arie. Introduction to the HIPPI specifications. *www.cern.ch/HSI/hippi/spec/introduc.htm*, September 1994.

[170] Vitter, J. S., and E. A. M. Shriver. Algorithms for parallel memory I: Two-level memories. *Algorithmica*, 12(2–3):110–147, 1994. Presents the parallel disk model for evaluating out-of-core algorithms.

[171] Vitter, Jeffrey Scott. External memory algorithms and data structures. In Abello and Vitter [1]. Surveys out-of-core alogorithms, with an emphasis on performance modeling. Also available electronically from *www.cs.duke.edu/ jsv/.*

[172] Walsh, Norman. A technical introduction to XML. *nwalsh.com/docs/articles/xml/*, February 1998.

[173] Watson, Richard W., and Robert A. Coyne. The parallel I/O architecture of the High Performance Storage System (HPSS). In *Proceedings of the Fourteenth IEEE Symposium on Mass Storage Systems*, pages 27–44, September 1995.

[174] Wong, Kenneth F., and Mark Franklin. Checkpointing on distributed computing systems. *Journal of Parallel and Distributed Computing*, 35(1):67–75, May 1996. Develops a model for estimating the optimum checkpointing interval in distributed programs.

Index

G

M

O

P

S

T

U